"Rosemary — thats' for
remembrance.

Muriel

November 14. 1965.

THE NEW
YEAR OF GRACE

THE NEW
YEAR OF GRACE

AN ANTHOLOGY
FOR YOUTH AND AGE
compiled and edited
with personal commentaries

by

VICTOR GOLLANCZ

LONDON
FOURTEEN HENRIETTA STREET
COVENT GARDEN

FOR
ANDREW · BENJAMIN · BUTTERCUP
CLARISSA · COLWITH · FELICITY
JAMES · JEREMY · JONATHON
JULIA · KATY · MANESTY
MARK · MARIA · NICOLAS
ROBERT · SOPHIE

We bless thee for our creation.

THE BOOK OF COMMON PRAYER

FOREWORD

THIS is a book intended for people of any age (including, I dare to hope, my own) from fifteen or sixteen upwards.

A Year of Grace, I have come to feel, has two conspicuous defects. First, it is ill adapted for readers of, say, under eighteen. Secondly, I planned it very carefully as a continuous whole, a closely knit statement of my own way of looking at the "God and man" of its subtitle: but as it consists solely of extracts from other people's writings, the idea behind it has failed, in practice, to prove capable of any but the sketchiest realization.

The New Year of Grace seeks to avoid these defects. My own introductions to particular sections and subsections, as well as my incidental commentaries, aim at clarifying the whole conception, while binding the book together from first page to last. (I call them "personal" on the title-page because I would not claim that they are in any way authoritative.) In writing them, I have tried to make them easily intelligible to young people of fifteen or sixteen, but at the same time to avoid irritating older readers, whatever their age. I cannot know whether I have succeeded.

In my general planning of the book I have pursued a similar twofold aim; for while I greatly desire to attract the kind of public that has welcomed *A Year of Grace* with such generosity, I am equally anxious to interest the younger generation in ideas I consider important, particularly at the present time. In other words, I have been concerned to produce, for "youth and age", an ordered account of one man's religious and human philosophy, expressed, to a minor degree, in his own language, and, to a major one, in other people's: the man being very much, in both senses of the word, an amateur. All this will explain why I have made no use of certain passages that I chose, a decade ago, for *A Year of Grace*: have shortened, lengthened or paraphrased, in varying degree, certain others: and have included some new material (drawn from my *From Darkness to Light*), amounting to about a quarter of the final whole. In the hope that people even younger than the ones I have mentioned may find some extracts to interest them, I have added, in an unobtrusive appendix, an explanation of a few words or phrases they might otherwise find difficult.

*   *   *

One star in front of an author's name means that the passage above it, whether in the original or in the particular translation, has been slightly shortened or paraphrased or both: two stars mean that it has been considerably, sometimes very considerably, shortened or paraphrased or both. A numeral in the same position indicates that an explanation of some word or words in the extract will be found on that page of the appendix.

I have tried to be very scrupulous in paraphrasing: but no word in a starred passage must be assumed to be the author's or translator's own. A few dots within a passage indicate an omission: where I have used dots I have dispensed with stars.

In the case of the following, I have usually modernised the spelling, the capitalisation, and once or twice the punctuation: Blake, Boehme, Sir Thomas Browne, Traherne, Whichcote and Thomas Vaughan. I have sometimes modified the translations I have used for Hasidic passages, and Jowett's translation of Plato.

My own introductions and commentaries have been placed in square brackets.

V. G.

CONTENTS

(I have included, in italics, my own principal pieces)

TO BEGIN

HEAR, O ISRAEL

Hear, O Israel: the Lord our God, the Lord is One.

And thou shalt love the Lord thy God with all thine heart, and with all thy soul, and with all thy might. And these words, which I command thee this day, shall be upon thine heart: and thou shalt teach them diligently unto thy children, and shalt talk of them when thou sittest in thine house, and when thou walkest by the way, and when thou liest down, and when thou risest up. And thou shalt bind them for a sign upon thine hand, and they shall be for frontlets between thine eyes. And thou shalt write them upon the door posts of thy house, and upon thy gates.

DEUTERONOMY

[The first sentence of this passage, which was written nearly 3,000 years ago, is like a trumpet suddenly ringing out in a great orchestra—the orchestra of the whole human race. And what the sentence proclaimed and proclaims is that basic or central belief at which the Hebrew people had at this time arrived or were in process of arriving: namely that there are not many gods (their own and a number of others) but only one God. I call the belief "basic" or "central" because on it depends everything else in fully developed Judaism and in the Christianity that came out of Judaism.

This one God, they felt, had created everything, including what appeared to be bad: "Shall there be evil in the city, and I the Lord not have created it?" says one of the Hebrew writers, speaking in God's name. And the Creator of everything was also the King of everything: King not only of the Israelites (who found it difficult, however, to get rid of the notion that He was still rather special to them) but also of the Egyptians and the Amalekites and the rest of Israel's enemies, however little these enemies might be aware of the fact.

Meanwhile, the Hebrew leaders and prophets were gradually developing their idea of this one God's character. As god of a mere tribe or two, he had been bloodthirsty, tyrannical,

15

jealous, revengeful, and guilty of outrageous favouritism to "his own" people: as God of the whole earth He was becoming the God of impartial love—a sort of universal Father, recalling a human father at his best, only more so. And because He was lovable, because He was the God of love, He was worthy of His children's love in return: immediately after that great affirmation of Unity comes the passionate demand or appeal, "And thou shalt love the Lord thy God with all thine heart, and with all thy soul, and with all thy might"

Moreover, as the passage goes on to declare, we have to keep constantly in our hearts, amid all the temptations to hatred and disunity that surround us every day of our lives, an awareness of the divine unity and the divine love. At one period the great majority of Israelites obeyed the whole series of injunctions contained in this passage, sometimes as a mere matter of formal observance—"in the letter" as the New Testament puts it— and sometimes for their real purpose—"in the spirit". My father, for instance, always fastened to his hand, for morning prayers, a little box enclosing the very passage in question, and bound on his forehead a similar box—the "frontlet" of the verses above. I myself (who am, I suppose, more of a Christian than a Jew— in what I endeavour to do rather than in what I actually manage to do) have on the lintel of my front door what is called a *mezuzah*: a thing similar to my father's box, but revealing, through a hole in the silver, the first letter of the name of God. "And thou shalt write them on the door posts of thy house, and upon thy gates"

*   *   *

Now what, for us in the twentieth century, does all this amount to? It amounts to something like the following, when the rough outline has been filled in with a detail or two:

(i) Everything that exists, has existed, or will ever exist is bound together, is linked up, with everything else that exists, has existed, or will ever exist—linked up as but one particle of a many-particled Whole: every man, woman and child, every animal, every plant, every stone. "We are members one of another": what happens to each happens to all, for all are affected by what happens to each. Everything we think or feel or say or do brings a change, immediately or eventually, to the entire earth on which we live.

(ii) This Whole, however, is not a *mechanical* whole: it is not like an engine that runs perfectly because all its components fit perfectly together. It does *not* run perfectly, as we very well know in this age of the hydrogen bomb and the cold war: its components do *not* fit perfectly together: and it isn't *dead* in the sense in which a machine is dead, but is at least partly made up, on the contrary, of living, developing, jostling creatures, each one of whom has something free, something spontaneous about it, but no one of whom is independent of the rest. This freedom or spontaneity or unpredictability or power to will things and plan things, or however you may care to describe it, is what we imply by the word "spiritual" in contradistinction to the word "mechanical": and the Whole of which we are speaking is, in its main characteristics, a spiritual rather than a mechanical whole. Further, it isn't *finished*, in the way a machine is finished: nothing can ever be finished so long as there's anything free or spontaneous about it. It isn't a thing, so to speak, you can say "once and for all" about.

(iii) There is a conscious Will or Purpose behind all this, the nature of which we can dimly imagine by thinking of our own will or purpose (by thinking, that is to say, of what we spontaneously feel, of what we freely decide we must do) in our own best moments: and almost everyone recognizes what his own best moments are. They are the moments inspired by love—love of people, love of work (particularly creative work, such as carving statues or writing poetry or composing music) and love of the world.

(iv) We call that Will or Purpose (not our own will or purpose, but somehow including it) God: and in the familiar old expression we say that God—the source of everything, the very basis of the wholeness of things—"is love". For God cannot be "less",

He must be infinitely "more", than the best thing He is the source of, which is love: and when we use the word "love" of Him, we do so only to give the roughest possible idea of His character. God's love, for instance, unlike that of all but a very few men in the world's history, must be all-inclusive, must extend to everything and everybody. We may also say that God—free, creative, spontaneous—is the very essence, as He is the source, of Spirit, of the spiritual: He *is* Spirit: but as He is also the source of matter, of the material—of "dead" stones and suchlike—the material must somehow be all mixed up with the spiritual, the "lower" somehow involved with the "higher". Have you ever looked at a stone glistening in the sun after a shower, and wondered whether, after all, it was "dead"?

(v) Among the purposes of the supreme Purpose is, not indeed to "finish" the Whole—for, as has already been said, nothing with any freedom or spontaneity about it can ever be completely "finished"—but to make it more and more an expression of love and delight: more and more a rejoicing, harmonious Whole, and less, as it is so largely at present, a Whole torn by internal hatreds and strife. To bring this about, God relies very largely on us, on human beings, as his "fellow-workers" (the expression is St. Paul's). Why should that be necessary? Why shouldn't the thing have been perfect, so to speak, "from the beginning"? Because it could then only have been a perfect machine: and a machine, however perfect, lacks those "highest", most delightful things of all—spontaneity (doing a thing because you feel you must do it and at the same time feel happy in doing it), creativity (achieving "off your own bat" something new, something that has never been done, or even thought of, in quite the same way before) and love.

You can't *impose* spontaneity, creativity and love on people— even God, the supreme Will or Purpose behind everything, can't do that. To say you *compelled* a man to be spontaneous, creative and loving would be a ludicrous self-contradiction: for it is of the very essence of spontaneity, creativity and love to be free and un-compelled. So God "created man in His own image", created creatures, that is to say, who were capable of His own creativity, spontaneity and love: and it is only through the use they may make of these qualities that the Whole can become a fuller expression of harmony and delight.

What then must men do? What does God rely on them to do? The answer is simple, though the doing is difficult. They must wish well to more and more of their fellows: they must give themselves more and more, in good will, to the service of others: they must get nearer and nearer to the point at which everyone —"enemies" and people they think "bad" not excluded—is an object of their benevolence. That is another way of saying that they must learn to love God: it is also another way of saying that they must learn to love their neighbours as themselves. The two are, as near as makes no matter, indistinguishable: or, at any rate, one is impossible without the other.

I said, a little earlier, that everything we think or feel or say or do brings a change, immediately or eventually, to the whole earth on which we live. The more we think or feel or express, in word or act, a warm good will towards others, the more good will there will be in the world, the more joy, the more harmony: not merely by just so much, but by far more than so much. For the most beautiful thing about love or good will is that, in most cases, it *evokes* love and good will: it draws them from where they lie hidden in others, as a magnet draws iron. So hatred, in most cases, evokes hatred. If you show a man love he tends to love you in return, and not only you, but other people also: and a similar thing is true about hatred.

How then do we learn to love more? Mainly by the example of people we have read or heard about, or have come into some sort of contact with at some period of our lives. Most of us have the capacity to love, but some, it would seem, have a greater capacity than others: they are nearer, as it were, to the Source of loving. So when we observe, in quite ordinary people like ourselves, some passing act of love, and particularly of loving self-sacrifice, we notice its rightness and beauty, and feel like imitating it. But there are also men, far from ordinary, whose whole lives have been radiant examples of love and self-sacrifice; and these, in greater or lesser degree, have transformed the world. This is where Jesus of Nazareth comes into our argument.

*   *   *

I must make it clear that a great deal of the above would be rejected as nonsense by a large number of people, some of them with brains a lot better than mine. But I have written what *I* believe: and it is I, after all, who am compiling this anthology.]

FROM THE SERMON ON THE MOUNT

1. And seeing the multitudes, he [Jesus] went up into a mountain: and when he was set, his disciples came unto him:

2. And he opened his mouth, and taught them, saying,

3. Blessed are the merciful: for they shall obtain mercy.

4. Blessed are the peace-makers: for they shall be called the children of God.

5. Ye have heard that it was said by them of old time, Thou shalt not kill; and whosoever shall kill shall be in danger of the judgment:

6. But I say unto you, That whosoever is angry with his brother shall be in danger of the judgment . . .

7. Therefore if thou bring thy gift to the altar, and there rememberest that thy brother hath ought against thee;

8. Leave there thy gift before the altar, and go thy way; first be reconciled to thy brother, and then come and offer thy gift.

9. Ye have heard that it hath been said, An eye for an eye, and a tooth for a tooth:

10. But I say unto you, That ye resist not evil: but whosoever shall smite thee on thy right cheek, turn to him the other also.

11. And if any man will sue thee at the law, and take away thy coat, let him have thy cloke also.

12. And whosoever shall compel thee to go a mile, go with him twain.

20

13. Give to him that asketh thee, and from him that would borrow of thee turn not thou away.

14. Ye have heard that it hath been said, Thou shalt love thy neighbour, and hate thine enemy.

15. But I say unto you, Love your enemies, bless them that curse you, do good to them that hate you, and pray for them which despitefully use you, and persecute you;

16. That ye may be the children of your Father which is in heaven: for he maketh his sun to rise on the evil and on the good, and sendeth rain on the just and on the unjust.

17. Be ye therefore perfect, even as your Father which is in heaven is perfect.

18. No man can serve two masters: for either he will hate the one, and love the other; or else he will hold to the one, and despise the other. Ye cannot serve God and mammon.

19. Judge not, that ye be not judged.

20. For with what judgment ye judge, ye shall be judged: and with what measure ye mete, it shall be measured to you again.

21. And why beholdest thou the mote that is in thy brother's eye, but considerest not the beam that is in thine own eye?

22. Or how wilt thou say to thy brother, Let me pull out the mote out of thine eye; and behold, a beam is in thine own eye?

23. Thou hypocrite, first cast out the beam out of thine own eye; and then shalt thou see clearly to cast out the mote out of thy brother's eye.

24. Therefore all things whatsoever ye would that men should do to you, do ye even so to them: for this is the law and the prophets.

[About 800 years after the writing of *Hear, O Israel*, and at the beginning of our era, Jesus of Nazareth was born into a Hebrew carpenter's household. Some believe he was God Incarnate: a Being, that is to say, not merely endowed with the spiritual as all men, in some degree or another, are endowed with it, but very Spirit itself—very Source of the spiritual—in a human body. There is something about this in the section entitled *The Imitation of Christ* that begins on page 45. But, whatever we may believe in

21

this matter, one thing to me at least seems quite certain, though some would deny it: by his teaching, by the way he lived and by his crucifixion—for he willed to die in agony and shame, rather than be false to the duty he felt imposed on him by his love of God and man—he did more than anyone else, so far at least as the West is concerned, by way of showing us how to bring nearer a world of harmony, love and delight.

The Sermon on the Mount (which may not have been an actual sermon, but a collection of his sayings as his disciples remembered them) is the most powerful and enduring expression of his teaching. In it he carries a stage further that whole development of ideas about God and man that had long been proceeding in Israel. But what a stage further! Go on heating water, and it becomes, at a certain point, not water but steam: go on making it colder, and it becomes, at a certain point, not water but ice. So when Jesus was no longer content that we should love our neighbour, but insisted that we should love our enemy, something new entered the world: something which, if we would but heed him, could bring the ultimate Purpose, of which I spoke earlier, far nearer fulfilment.

It is often said that what Jesus demands of us is impossible. This is untrue: Jesus himself and many others have achieved it. People also allege that the verse about loving our enemies is "sentimental" and "unrealistic". Don't believe it for a moment: that we should love our enemies is plain common sense and the hardest sort of realism. For now at least, in the middle of the twentieth century, we ought to realise that unless we can indeed love our enemies—can wish them utterly well, can enter into their hearts, can see things, so far as we are able, as they see them, and so eventually, we must hope, can compose our differences—we shall surely rend our whole world asunder.

*   *   *

A note or two on points of detail. (My reference is to the verse-numbers printed above, not to those in the Bible: as I have omitted many verses, the two are not identical.)

Verses 5 and 6. The law judges and condemns a man who has committed murder, but not a man who has been angry with another: yet in God's sight, says Jesus, if murder is worthy of "the judgment" so is anger, for anger is a murderous impulse in the heart. (The Authorized Version reads as follows: "Whosoever is angry with his brother *without a cause* shall be in danger of the judgment". I have omitted the italicized words, which are completely opposed to the whole spirit of Christ's teaching: if we must love our enemies, it is nonsense to suggest that we may be angry with a man if the cause be sufficient. Perhaps a monk who was copying a very early manuscript of the Gospel inserted εἰκῇ, "without a cause", as a marginal note, because he couldn't "take" such unusual teaching in all its purity—being rather, in this respect, like ourselves: then another copyist, imagining that his predecessor's comment was part of the original, may have transferred it from margin to text, where it was found by our translators.)[1]

Verses 7 and 8. Gifts were placed on God's altar in the temple as a token of gratitude for benefits received from Him, or to appease Him for personal or national sins. Thus a fruit might be given as a thank-offering, or animals slaughtered or burned as a sin-offering. One must remember, in this connection, that the old Hebrew Law stands midway between the barbarous ritual (including even human sacrifice) of many neighbouring tribes, and the fully developed ethic of the prophets and Jesus.

That God can want His creatures to give him presents—ordinary, material presents—is of course a primitive and simple-minded idea. Jesus, who loved the simple-minded, does not directly attack it: but he tells his listeners that what God really asks for is love and harmony among His creatures, and that to offer Him a minor present and withhold the all-important one is humbug.

Verse 9. Among some peoples in a very early stage of human development unlimited vengeance was practised: if a man put

[1] The words in question are omitted in *The New English Bible*, just published as I am correcting these proofs.

out another man's eye, not only might his own be put out by way of balancing things up, but he might lose his very life, and his whole family might be slaughtered; and so might his tribe down to the last baby, if the man he had outraged had belonged to some other tribe. The Mosaic law, the so-called *lex talionis*, was a great improvement on this: the man must lose his own eye, it enjoined, and that must be the end. Then came the Pharisees, who substituted compensation for the damage inflicted. And finally came Jesus, who taught a higher sort of justice, based on the brotherhood of man: namely unlimited love. This would mean dealing with all sorts of violence neither by violence nor by vengeance, but by returning good for evil in every possible circumstance.

Verse 18. There appears to be no evidence for regarding Mammon as a rebellious angel—"the least erected spirit that fell from Heaven", as Milton says in *Paradise Lost.* It is an Aramaic word, meaning simply "wealth".

Verse 21. The full force of this sentence is obscured unless their exact meaning is given to "mote" and "beam". A mote (literally a speck of dust) is a trifling blemish in the eye that slightly interferes with its ability to see: a beam (literally a lump of wood) is a far greater blemish that almost prevents any seeing at all.

Verse 24. "The law and the prophets" together make up the Old Testament. That whole book, Christ is saying, can be summarised in a single brief sentence.]

SACRED AND PROFANE

The Hebrew form of thought rebels against the very idea of a distinction between the secular and the religious aspects of life.

JOHN MACMURRAY

Jesus is not an idealist—for the same reason that he is not a

materialist—because the distinction between the ideal and the
material does not arise for him.

JOHN MACMURRAY

One should hallow all that one does in one's natural life. No
renunciation is commanded.

MARTIN BUBER

[There is nothing of greater importance in this whole anthology than these three passages.

Many people, perhaps most people, draw a more or less rigid
distinction between "religion" and "everyday life". They keep
the two in watertight compartments: one, they feel, has nothing
to do with the other. Religion is thought of, at best, as concerned
with the worship of God: ordinary everyday life—the secular, as
it is called—doesn't begin to come into the matter. (I say religion
"at best": because a lot of religion, so called, is a mere routine
matter of traditional observances, which once had real spiritual
significance but are now fossilised and dead.) And so you get
people genuinely devoted to religion, as they themselves understand it, who nevertheless in their secular lives, or "in the world",
behave as if God, as if that Will or conscious Purpose of which
love is the essence, just didn't exist. And they behave like this,
not out of weakness, as any of us might behave, but simply
because they can see no connection between the one thing and the
other. A common example may suffice: that of an honestly
professing Christian who, in his capacity as politician or statesman, puts the power or material "interests" of his own country
before the good of the world. The Hebrew prophets and the early
Christians were always protesting against such an attitude.

The idea of a distinction between the religious and the secular,
the sacred and the profane, is not only nonsense, but dangerous
nonsense. If the universe is "all of a piece"; if everything is

linked with, if everything affects and is affected by, everything else: then you cannot divide things up into categories and vary your conduct accordingly. The fact is that, as the universe is God's universe, everything is sacred and nothing profane: true religion consists in co-operating with God for the purpose of perfecting the Whole: and this means, in hard practice, behaving lovingly or "religiously" to our fellow human beings in everyday life. It is through this that we show our devotion to God and His creation: it is through this that we worship Him.

*   *   *

But there is another way of worshipping God, as Buber, in the third of the above passages, has reminded us: namely with our bodies and with all the enjoyments that are normal and natural to us. Nothing could be more opposed to the spirit of true religion than a gloomy asceticism: than a renunciation, that is—a renunciation because allegedly God wants it—, of "the good things of life". A god that did want it, a god that gave us pleasurable instincts and then required us to suppress them, would be a brutal and jealous tyrant and not at all the God of love, the God who is for ever striving, with the co-operation of His creatures, for more and more harmony and delight.

We worship God with our bodies and enjoyments by not merely enjoying them but rejoicing in them: by experiencing not merely pleasure but joy. Joy is to feel the wonder of being alive: pleasure is like an agreeable sort of tickling—though there's nothing much wrong with that either. So we glorify God the Creator when we eat with joy, drink (water as well as wine, wine as well as water) with joy, love our wives or our husbands with joy, walk with joy, run with joy, dance with joy. Joy is the touchstone: joy, which is essentially spiritual, hallows everything, makes everything holy.

There is in fact nothing in itself unholy, except anything that damages other people or the best in ourselves. Gluttony is unholy, because it satiates us, ruins our palate, and deprives us of joy in the savour of food. Drunkenness is unholy, for a similar reason. Lying and rape are unholy, because, besides damaging

26

ourselves, they interfere with the rights of other people—to know the truth (in the case of lying) and to choose a partner (in that of rape): not to mention the violence involved. All excesses are unholy, for they ruin our freshness, and make us harmful, and even murderous, to others. But, apart from things like that, nothing is unholy as such: and everything is hallowed, made positively holy, by joy.

For people of a certain temperament, however, there can be holiness in asceticism, in giving up "the good things of life"— provided it produces in the ascetic, not the sourness of unnatural frustration, but that utter peace, that feeling of blessedness, that sense of quiet communion with the Whole, which may well be oy at its highest.[1] People of this temperament are rare, but they exist: "the world"—everyday living as most of us live it— would distract them from that constant endeavour to be at one with the Source of all living which their nature demands: and they, also, glorify God in their own special way, for the communion they achieve with the Whole is itself a contribution towards unity. Then there are beloved ascetics like Saint Francis, for whom all other joys are as nothing beside the joy of devoting themselves utterly to the service of their suffering fellows. And finally there is value for almost everyone in *occasional* asceticism: there are times when it is good for us to "get away from it all", away even from the most joyful activities, and to renew ourselves by lying fallow . . .

And now let us get on to the anthology proper—which is all, really, a development of this introductory section.]

[1] See the quotation from Wordsworth, and the paraphrase of it, on page 81.

FIRST PART

I. GOD'S MERCY AND LOVE

God loves all existing things.

ST. THOMAS AQUINAS

Every man is born for heaven.

SWEDENBORG

Every living thing shall ripen and be saved.

MILAREPA

§ 2

THE FLOOD

And God remembered Noah, and every living thing, and all the cattle that was with him in the ark: and God made a wind to pass over the earth, and the waters asswaged;

The fountains also of the deep and the windows of heaven were stopped, and the rain from heaven was restrained;

And the waters returned from off the earth continually: and after the end of the hundred and fifty days the waters were abated.

And the ark rested in the seventh month, on the seventeenth day of the month, upon the mountains of Ararat.

And the waters decreased continually until the tenth month: in the tenth month, on the first day of the month, were the tops of the mountains seen.

And it came to pass at the end of forty days, that Noah opened the window of the ark which he had made:

And he sent forth a raven, which went forth to and fro, until the waters were dried up from off the earth.

Also he sent forth a dove from him, to see if the waters were abated from off the face of the ground;

But the dove found no rest for the sole of her foot, and she returned unto him into the ark, for the waters were on the face of the whole earth: then he put forth his hand, and took her, and pulled her in unto him into the ark.

And he stayed yet other seven days; and again he sent forth the dove out of the ark;

And the dove came in to him in the evening; and, lo, in her mouth was an olive leaf pluckt off: so Noah knew that the waters were abated from off the earth.

471 GENESIS

SODOM

[God tells Abraham that He is about to destroy Sodom because of its great wickedness.]

And Abraham drew near, and said, Wilt thou also destroy the righteous with the wicked?

Peradventure there be fifty righteous within the city: wilt thou also destroy and not spare the place for the fifty righteous that are therein?

That be far from thee to do after this manner, to slay the righteous with the wicked: and that the righteous should be as the wicked, that be far from thee: Shall not the Judge of all the earth do right?

And the Lord said, If I find in Sodom fifty righteous within the city, then I will spare all the place for their sakes.

And Abraham answered and said, Behold now, I have taken upon me to speak unto the Lord, which am but dust and ashes:

Peradventure there shall lack five of the fifty righteous: wilt thou destroy all the city for lack of five? And he said, If I find there forty and five, I will not destroy it.

And he spake unto him yet again; and said; Peradventure there shall be forty found there. And he said, I will not do it for forty's sake.

And he said unto him, Oh let not the Lord be angry, and I will speak: Peradventure there shall thirty be found there. And he said, I will not do it, if I find thirty there.

And he said, Behold now, I have taken upon me to speak unto the Lord: Peradventure there shall be twenty found there. And he said, I will not destroy it for twenty's sake.

And he said, Oh let not the Lord be angry, and I will speak yet but this once: Peradventure ten shall be found there. And he said, I will not destroy it for ten's sake.

And the Lord went his way as soon as he had left communing with Abraham: and Abraham returned unto his place.

471 GENESIS

NINEVEH

[In the story of Sodom a man pleads with God to be merciful: in the story of Nineveh—which comes later, when the way people think about God has greatly developed—a man is taught mercy by God. The prophet Jonah, as God's mouthpiece, "preaches unto" Nineveh, and "cries and says" that God will destroy it for its wickedness within forty days. The men of Nineveh repent.]

And God saw their works, that they turned from their evil way; and God repented of the evil, that he had said that he would do unto them; and he did it not.

But it displeased Jonah exceedingly, and he was very angry . . . Then said the Lord, Doest thou well to be angry?

So Jonah went out of the city, and sat on the east side of the city, and there made him a booth, and sat under it in the shadow, till he might see what would become of the city.

And the Lord God prepared a gourd, and made it to come up over Jonah, that it might be a shadow over his head, to deliver him from his grief. So Jonah was exceeding glad of the gourd.

But God prepared a worm when the morning rose the next day, and it smote the gourd that it withered.

And it came to pass, when the sun did arise, that God prepared a vehement east wind; and the sun beat upon the head of Jonah, that he fainted, and wished in himself to die, and said, It is better for me to die than to live.

And God said to Jonah, Doest thou well to be angry for the gourd? And he said, I do well to be angry, even unto death.

Then said the Lord, Thou hast had pity on the gourd, for the which thou hast not laboured, neither madest it grow; which came up in a night, and perished in a night:

And should not I spare Nineveh, that great city, wherein are more than sixscore thousand persons that cannot discern between their right hand and their left hand; and also much cattle?

471 JONAH

[Christ would have been familiar with the Book of Jonah, which is still read in all synagogues on the Day of Atonement: and the words "that cannot discern between their right hand and their left hand" (or, as we might say, "who can hardly put two and two together") may have passed through his mind when, in agony on the Cross, he prayed for his crucifiers with the most beautiful of all human prayers, "Father, forgive them, for they know not what they do".]

THE EXODUS FROM EGYPT

And it was told the king of Egypt that the people [of Israel] fled: and the heart of Pharaoh and of his servants was turned against the people, and they said, Why have we done this, that we have let Israel go from serving us?

And he made ready his chariot, and took his people with him:

And he took six hundred chosen chariots, and all the chariots of Egypt, and captains over every one of them.

And when Pharaoh drew nigh, the children of Israel lifted up their eyes, and, behold, the Egyptians marched after them; and they were sore afraid: and the children of Israel cried out unto the Lord.

And Moses said unto the people, Fear ye not, stand still, and see the salvation of the Lord, which he will shew to you today: for the Egyptians whom ye have seen today, ye shall see them again no more for ever.

The Lord shall fight for you, and ye shall hold your peace.

And the Lord said unto Moses, Wherefore criest thou unto me? speak unto the children of Israel, that they go forward:

But lift thou up thy rod, and stretch out thine hand over the sea, and divide it: and the children of Israel shall go on dry ground through the midst of the sea.

And Moses stretched out his hand over the sea; and the Lord caused the sea to go back by a strong east wind all that night, and made the sea dry land, and the waters were divided.

And the children of Israel went into the midst of the sea upon the dry ground: and the waters were a wall unto them on their right hand, and on their left.

And the Egyptians pursued, and went in after them to the midst of the sea, even all Pharaoh's horses, his chariots, and his horsemen.

And the Lord said unto Moses, Stretch out thine hand over the sea, that the waters may come again upon the Egyptians, upon their chariots, and upon their horsemen.

And Moses stretched forth his hand over the sea, and the sea returned to his strength when the morning appeared; and the Egyptians fled against it; and the Lord overthrew the Egyptians in the midst of the sea.

And the waters returned, and covered the chariots, and the horsemen, and all the host of Pharaoh that came into the sea after them; there remained not so much as one of them.

But the children of Israel walked upon dry land in the midst of the sea; and the waters were a wall unto them on their right hand, and on their left.

Thus the Lord saved Israel that day out of the hand of the Egyptians; and Israel saw the Egyptians dead upon the sea shore.

And Israel saw that great work which the Lord did upon the Egyptians: and the people feared the Lord, and believed the Lord, and his servant Moses.

Then sang Moses and the children of Israel this song unto the Lord, and spake, saying, I will sing unto the Lord, for he hath triumphed gloriously: the horse and his rider hath he thrown into the sea.

The Lord is my strength and song, and he is become my

salvation: he is my God, and I will prepare him an habitation: my father's God, and I will exalt him . . .

And Miriam the prophetess, the sister of Aaron, took a timbrel in her hand; and all the women went out after her with timbrels and with dances.

And Miriam answered them, Sing ye to the Lord, for he hath triumphed gloriously; the horse and his rider hath he thrown into the sea.

[That is how the story is told in the Old Testament. But centuries later a writer in the Talmud, a sort of supplement to the Old Testament, adds the following:]

And when the song of Miriam rose unto heaven, the angels, who stand around God's throne and minister unto Him, began to sing with her;

But God said, "My children lie drowned in the sea, and you would sing?"

EXODUS AND RABBI JOHANAN

§ 3

For to be greatly strong is thine at all times; and the might of thine arm who shall withstand? because the whole world before thee is as a grain in a balance, and as a drop of dew that at the morning cometh down upon the earth. But thou hast mercy on all men, because thou hast power to do all things, and thou overlookest the sins of men to the end that they may repent. For thou lovest all things that are, and abhorrest none of the things which thou didst make; for never wouldest thou have formed anything if thou didst hate it. And how would anything have endured, except thou hadst willed it? Or that which was not called by thee, how would it have been preserved? But thou sparest all things, because they are thine, O Sovereign Lord, thou lover of men's lives;

For thine incorruptible spirit is in all things.

THE WISDOM OF SOLOMON

I never give God thanks for loving me, because He cannot help it; whether He wished to or not it is His nature to.

★ MEISTER ECKHART

It longeth to the proper goodness of our Lord God courteously to excuse man.

471 JULIANA OF NORWICH

With Thee 'tis one to behold and to pity. Accordingly, Thy mercy followeth every man so long as he liveth, whithersoever he goeth, even as Thy glance never quitteth any.

NICHOLAS OF CUSA

A fire once broke out in Drokeret, but the neighbourhood of Rabbi Huna was spared. The people thought that this was due to the merit of Rabbi Huna, but they were told in a dream that Rabbi Huna's merits were too great, and the sparing of his neighbourhood from fire too small, a matter to attribute the marvel to him, and that it was due to the merits of a certain woman who used to heat her oven, and place it at the disposal of her neighbours.

THE TALMUD

Once a poor villager came to the town to earn money for the Passover. After nightfall on his return to the village, laden with purchases, his horse and wagon fell into a pit made swampy by the spring rains. A rich man, passing by, heard his cries, and helped his own driver to extricate the villager. He roped the latter's wagon to his carriage, and accompanied the poor man to his hut. On beholding the abject poverty in which the villager and his family lived, the magnate gave him several hundred thalers.

When the wealthy man died and was brought before the Heavenly Tribunal, it seemed as if his demerits because of certain business dealings would result in his sentence to Purgatory. Suddenly an Angel of Mercy appeared, and asked that the Heavenly Scales be used to determine whether the worth of his good deeds outweighed his sins. When consent was given, the Angel placed on the Scale of Good Deeds the poor villager and his family whom the rich man had saved from misery. But this did not suffice. The horse and the wagon were added, but they did not aid. Then the Angel placed on the Scale the mud and mire out of which the rich man had helped rescue the villager, and lo, the Scale of Good Deeds dipped with its weight, and the magnate was saved from Purgatory.

RABBI ISRAEL OF RIZHYN

[This is the first of the many Hasidic stories, sayings and parables that will be found in this anthology. Hasid is a Hebrew word meaning "pious" or "devout". There was a sect of Hasidism in Biblical time: but the word Hasid and its derivatives are used in this book with exclusive reference to the remarkable Jewish movement which originated in Podolia just before the middle of the eighteenth century, and which soon had millions of adherents, particularly in Eastern Europe. Martin Buber is its greatest contemporary interpreter. Louis I. Newman has well described the movement as follows: "Its chief emphasis has been upon a sense of mystical ecstasy in the communion of God and man; upon the joyful affirmation of life; upon compassion, charity and love; upon democracy and brotherhood between rich and poor; and upon the moral values of the religious system." Very few Hasidim survive: the sect was practically exterminated by Hitler.

The Hasidim loved, in particular, fairy-tale parables about what happened to a man after death. The idea was that he first went to Heaven, where he was tried for his conduct on earth by a Heavenly Court or Tribunal. There were advocates for the prosecution and defence: and the question was whether the man's good deeds had outweighed his bad ones, or vice versa. If the former he stayed in Heaven: if the latter, he went for a period to Purgatory (or occasionally even, for the time being, to a mild sort of Hell). God presided.

The leader of the Hasidic movement was the Baalshem, one of the world's greatest religious geniuses, who lived from A.D. 1700 to 1760. The word Baalshem stood for Rabbi Israel ben Eliezer Baal Shem Tov ("Rabbi Israel, son of Eliezer, Master of the Good Name"). He was called "Master of the Good Name" because he could pronounce the Ineffable Name of God (see p. 240).]

The goodness of God breaking forth into a desire to communicate good was the cause and the beginning of the creation. Hence it follows that to all eternity God can have no thought or intent towards the creature but to communicate good; because He made the creature for this sole end, to receive good. The first motive towards the creature is unchangeable; it takes its rise from God's desire to communicate good, and it is an eternal impossibility that anything can ever come from God as His will and purpose towards the creature but that same love and goodness which first created it; He must always will that to it which He willed at the creation of it. This is the amiable nature of God. He is the Good, the unchangeable, overflowing fountain of good that sends forth nothing but good to all eternity. He is the Love itself, the unmixed, unmeasurable Love, doing nothing but from love, giving nothing but gifts of love to everything that He has made; requiring nothing of all His creatures but the spirit and fruits of that love which brought them into being. Oh, how sweet is this contemplation of the height and depth of the riches of Divine Love! With what attraction must it draw every thoughtful man to return love for love to this overflowing fountain of boundless goodness!

471   WILLIAM LAW

Let me tell you then why the creator made this world of ours. He was good, and the good can never have any jealousy of anything. And being free from jealousy, he desired that all things should be as like himself as they could be. This is in the truest sense the origin of creation and of the world, as we shall do well in believing on the testimony of wise men: God desired that all things should be good and nothing bad, so far as this was attainable.

PLATO

ON ANOTHER'S SORROW

Can I see another's woe,
And not be in sorrow too?
Can I see another's grief,
And not seek for kind relief?

Can I see a falling tear,
And not feel my sorrow's share?
Can a father see his child
Weep, nor be with sorrow filled?

Can a mother sit and hear
An infant groan, an infant fear?
No, no! never can it be!
Never, never can it be!

And can He who smiles on all
Hear the wren with sorrows small,
Hear the small bird's grief and care,
Hear the woes that infants bear—

And not sit beside the nest,
Pouring pity in their breast,
And not sit the cradle near,
Weeping tear on infant's tear?

And not sit both night and day,
Wiping all our tears away?
Oh no! never can it be!
Never, never can it be!

He doth give His joy to all:
He becomes an infant small,
He becomes a man of woe,
He doth feel the sorrow too.

Think not thou canst sigh a sigh,
And thy Maker is not by:
Think not thou canst weep a tear,
And thy Maker is not near.

Oh, He gives to us His joy,
That our grief He may destroy:
Till our grief is fled and gone
He doth sit by us and moan.

BLAKE

FIRST PART

II. THE IMITATION OF CHRIST

[This short section, *The Imitation of Christ*, pleases me, the compiler, more than any other in the anthology: and I am most anxious not to intrude into it, once it has been started. But I am also anxious that the first four passages, which are all of the most moving beauty, should not be dismissed as mere poetic fantasies, however charming: so a few preliminary words may be desirable in an age like this, when a great many people regard the doctrine of God's Incarnation in Christ as irrational rubbish, and "The Father, the Son and the Holy Ghost" as a kind of outlandish abracadabra, without meaning for the educated. So let me have my say and be done with it.

There is nothing in the least irrational about the Incarnation, provided one accepts, as a starting-point, the general view I have endeavoured to outline in the section "To Begin". For the Incarnation means simply this: that at one particular moment of history God, as we call the Will or Purpose behind everything, revealed What He Was, showed us His true character as a God of love and compassion, by being born a human baby, living a human life, and dying a human death. Or, to put it a little differently: He taught us the right way to live by living, as if He were one of us, the right way Himself. His reason for this may be interpreted as follows. We may be able to *see* in something small and limited, especially in something like ourselves, a quality we may not be able to see in the vast everything: it's easier to know how a single battle's going, particularly if you're fighting in it yourself, than how a whole war's going of which that single battle is part. Seeing, that's the point. If you told a blind man, a man blind from birth, that the sunrise was beautiful, he could understand what you meant by the word "beautiful" at best imperfectly, by a supreme imaginative effort, and probably not at all: but cure his blindness, show him the sunrise, let him *see* it, and he'll understand perfectly. Or think about it like this: if we were told in a vague sort of way that there's something very good indeed about a man sacrificing his life for a friend (or, better still, for an enemy) we'd no doubt agree, and that would be that: but if we read about a real case in full detail, or, above all, if we

45

actually saw the thing happening before our very eyes, that wouldn't just be that—our whole life might be powerfully affected, in the sense that we might learn to think less of ourselves and more of others, and that, if the occasion were to arise, we should be rather more likely to do the same thing ourselves.

Whether I personally "believe in" the Incarnation is of no interest or importance: I have merely been concerned to remove the impression that no one of any intelligence could take it seriously. Many people, as a matter of fact, and among them some of the wisest, have experienced the Incarnation as literal truth—or so they have believed—in their own daily lives.

It would be dishonest, however, if I stopped there. That Christ's utterances, at what I dare to think of as their best, are a unique revelation of goodness, an ultimate expression of the wholesome and sane: that his passionate honesty, his blazing hatred of spiritual and intellectual falsehood, uncover the secret of honour: that many episodes in his few public years ("Father, forgive them"; "Neither do I condemn thee: Go, and sin no more") surpass, by reason of their sorrow and warmth, even the example of Socrates: that his life, as a whole, revealed the meaning of courageous self-sacrifice more compulsively than any other's: and that in these cases He (and for once I cannot resist the capital letter) was indeed the Way and the Life—all this, I am persuaded, is beyond question. And yet—every time I read the Gospels I ask myself, in fear and trembling, was he perfect: as perfect, I mean, as one can imagine that pure Divinity incarnate —with the necessary limitations, albeit, of finite existence— might conceivably be? I can only say that there are passages that trouble me, so that I find myself wondering "Are they authentic? Have I correctly interpreted them?" And then, a verse later, the splendour floods in again overwhelmingly, and doubts, for the time being, are forgotten.

May it perhaps be that the Jesus of history was not Christ absolute, but—to borrow Samuel Alexander's word about God —Christ emergent? If so, this must also be said: the prerequisite for Christ absolute is the Jesus of history. He alone, as the supreme standard, is our criterion for daring to question, even while we adore him, whether he was indeed Christ absolute. And there I may leave my own fumblings.

*   *   *

God as incarnate, or embodied, in Jesus Christ is sometimes called God the Son, and God as embodying Himself is, in that case, called God the Father. They are of course one and the same, the only, God. The Son is said to be "begotten" by the Father just as an ordinary human father begets his child.

*   *   *

For all that I have written above, I must repeat that, in the thought and hearts of many, there is nothing "metaphorical" about the Incarnation. So when Crashaw wrote, in the poem quoted below, that, on a unique occasion, all Eternity was shut up in a momentary span of time, and that the birth of Christ brought heaven down to earth, he meant precisely what he said. As to Milton's incomparable lines, they are probably the greatest of all statements about the Incarnation. They might be paraphrased as follows: "Jesus Christ, God's likeness, in whose glorious face we see God shining with no cloud to mar His radiance—the God whom otherwise no human being could see at all."]

> . . . the source of life
> Descends to be a weeping babe . . .

BLAKE

> Wellcome, all Wonders in one sight!
> Æternity shut in a span.
> Sommer in Winter. Day in Night.
> Heaven in earth, and God in Man.
> Great little one! whose all-embracing birth
> Lifts earth to heaven, stoopes heav'n to earth.

RICHARD CRASHAW

47

Begotten Son, Divine Similitude,
In whose conspicuous countenance, without cloud
Made visible, the Almighty Father shines,
Whom else no creature can behold. . . .

MILTON

The Divine Vision still was seen,
Still was the Human Form Divine.
    Weeping in weak & mortal clay,
O Jesus, still the Form was thine.

And thine the Human Face, & thine
The Human Hands & Feet & Breath,
    Entering thro' the Gates of Birth
And passing thro' the Gates of Death.

BLAKE

Then I see the Saviour over me,
Spreading his beams of love, and dictating the words of this
    mild song . . .
I am not a God afar off, I am a brother and friend;
Within your bosoms I reside, and you reside in me;
Lo! we are One; forgiving all evil; not seeking recompense. . . .

BLAKE

I saw myself, in dream, a youth, almost a boy, in a low-pitched wooden church. The slim wax candles gleamed, spots of red, before the old pictures of the saints.

A ring of coloured light encircled each tiny flame. Dark and dim it was in the church. . . . But there stood before me many people. All fair-haired, peasant heads. From time to time they began swaying, falling, rising again, like the ripe ears of wheat, when the wind of summer passes in slow undulation over them.

All at once some man came up from behind and stood beside me.

48

I did not turn towards him; but at once I felt that this man was Christ.

Emotion, curiosity, awe overmastered me suddenly. I made an effort . . . and looked at my neighbour.

A face like every one's, a face like all men's faces. The eyes looked a little upwards, quietly and intently. The lips closed, but not compressed; the upper lip, as it were, resting on the lower; a small beard parted in two. The hands folded and still. And the clothes on him like every one's.

"What sort of Christ is this?" I thought. "Such an ordinary, ordinary man! It can't be!"

I turned away. But I had hardly turned my eyes away from this ordinary man when I felt again that it really was none other than Christ standing beside me.

Again I made an effort over myself. . . . And again the same face, like all men's faces, the same everyday though unknown features.

And suddenly my heart sank, and I came to myself. Only then I realised that just such a face—a face like all men's faces—is the face of Christ.

TURGENEV

§ 2

To have salvation from Christ is nothing else but to be made like unto Him; it is to have His humility and meekness, His mortification and self-denial, His renunciation of the spirit, wisdom, and honours of this world, His love of God, His desire of doing God's will and seeking only His honour. To have these tempers formed and begotten in thy heart is to have salvation from Christ. But if thou willest not to have these tempers brought forth in thee, if thy faith and desire does not seek and cry to Christ for them in the same reality as the lame asked to walk and the blind to see, then thou must be said to be unwilling to have Christ to be thy Saviour.

WILLIAM LAW

I think, therefore, that the purpose and cause of the incarnation was that He might illuminate the world by His wisdom and excite it to the love of Himself.

PETER ABÉLARD

The death of Christ justifies us [i.e. makes us "just" or good], inasmuch as through it love is excited in our hearts.

PETER THE LOMBARD

The contemplation of Christ's life and death gives other men the power, as nothing else has done, to overcome temptation and to lead lives of love like His.

HASTINGS RASHDALL

If we can say that in humanity generally there is *some* revelation of God—a growing, developing, progressive revelation, and a higher degree of such revelation in the heroes, the saints, the prophets, the founders and reformers of great religions, then it becomes possible to think of Him as making a supreme, culminating, unique revelation of Himself in one human character and life.

Now if we believe that Christ's whole life was one of love for his fellows, that his death came to him as the direct and necessary consequence of this love, and that in him who so loved and died the love of God was uniquely and supremely manifested, then the love towards Christ that is awakened in us by our contemplation of him will also be love towards the Father whom in a supreme and unique way Christ reveals. And that love will express itself in repentance and a bettering of our lives.

It is only through human love at its highest that we can understand the divine love. Gratitude for ordinary human love—love pushed to the point of self-sacrifice—is the strongest power that exists in this world for attracting to that goodness, of which love is the supreme element, the soul that lacks it, and for producing repentance for that lack of love in which sin essentially consists. In proportion as it is felt that human love reveals the love of God, the answering love which the self-sacrifice awakens will be love towards God as well as love towards man. The love shown by Christ will have this regenerating effect in a supreme degree in proportion as it is felt that the love of Christ supremely reveals the character of God.

Christ's whole life was a sacrifice which takes away sin in the only way in which sin can really be taken away, and that is by making the sinner actually better.

And here I would particularly insist upon the importance in this connexion of our Lord's teaching—that is to say, of the moral ideal which it represents and the corresponding belief as to the character of the God whose nature is revealed by that moral ideal. For many of the early Christians, it is not too much to say, it was primarily by his teaching that Christ became the Saviour of the world. It was upon the appeal which this teaching made to the reason, the heart, the conscience of mankind that they based their conviction that in him God was supremely revealed: it was precisely in and through his teaching that his "Divinity" was manifested.

Unless Christ's teaching about God and human life does present itself to us as containing the very heart of the moral ideal, and a true representation of the essential character of God, the idea of Christ's divinity can have no meaning for us; and it is only in the light of his teaching about the love of God and the supreme place of love in the ethical ideal for man that the cross can be given its true meaning as the symbol of self-sacrifice— not of mere negative self-renunciation or self-denial for self-denial's sake, but of self-sacrifice inspired and directed by love of that moral ideal which is fully realised in God, and by love of the men who are made in the image of God.

More and more, I believe, the great spiritual dividing line between men will be the line between those who really accept

Christ's ideal of life—even if they refuse to follow with the great army of his professed disciples or to call themselves by his name —and those who do not.

★★ HASTINGS RASHDALL

He said to Judas, when he betrayed him: "Friend, wherefore art thou come?" as if he would say: "Thou hatest me and art my enemy; so do I love thee, and am thy friend." . . . Just as though God in human nature were saying: "I am pure, simple Goodness, and therefore I cannot will, or desire, or hope, or do or give anything but goodness. If I am to reward thee for thy evil and wickedness, I must do it with goodness, for I am and have nothing else."

THEOLOGIA GERMANICA

God became man that you also may learn from a man how a man becomes a God.

CLEMENT OF ALEXANDRIA

Our Lord says to every living soul, "I became man for you. If you do not become God for me, you do me wrong."

MEISTER ECKHART

Every Christian must be Christ himself.

ANGELUS SILESIUS

Each natural compassion that a man hath on his fellow Christians with charity, it is Christ in him.

JULIANA OF NORWICH

On account of Him there have come to be many Christs in the world, even all who, like Him, loved righteousness and hated iniquity.

ORIGEN

Is it unnatural to do what Jesus Christ hath done?

TRAHERNE

Christ does not really teach one anything, but by being brought into his presence one becomes something. And everybody is predestined to his presence. Once at least in his life each man walks with Christ to Emmaus.

OSCAR WILDE

[After Christ's death and burial, and the disappearance of his body from the sepulchre, two of his disciples went to a village called Emmaus near Jerusalem. They were joined on their way there by Jesus himself, risen from the dead, and they talked with him, and told him of the empty tomb; but they knew not who he was. When they came to Emmaus "he went in to tarry with them. And it came to pass, as he sat at meat with them, he took bread, and blessed it, and brake, and gave to them. And their eyes were opened, and they knew him; and he vanished out of their sight." This is recorded in the Gospel according to St. Luke.]

Truth nailed upon the cross compels nobody, oppresses no one; it must be accepted and confessed freely; its appeal is addressed to free spirits. . . . A divine Truth panoplied in power, triumphant over the world and conquering men's souls, would not be consonant with the freedom of man's spirit, and so the mystery of Golgotha is the mystery of liberty. . . . Every time in history that man has tried to turn crucified Truth into coercive truth he has betrayed the fundamental principle of Christ.

BERDYAEV

It is impossible not to love Christ. If we saw Him now, we should not be able to take our eyes off Him, we should "listen to Him in rapture"; we should flock around Him as did the multitudes in the Gospels. All that is required of us is not to resist. We must yield to Him, to the contemplation of His image—in the Gospels, in the saints, in the Church—and He will capture our hearts.

FATHER YELCHANINOV

§ 3

[I should like to round off this section with a brief word about the Trinity: three Persons—the Father and Son, and the Holy Spirit, the love that unites them—but nevertheless one God.

I understand the Trinity as follows. In all theistic religions, the Christian included, ultimate Reality is conceived of, not as a force, like electricity, nor as an inanimate regulator, like the Tao of the Chinese, but as something personal—something whose nature we can get a hint of, however obscure, by observing human persons. But the Christian doctrine implies more than that. A "one" can be simple or complex: a letter of the alphabet, as compared with a word, is a simple "one", and a word, as compared with a letter, is a complex "one". Ultimate Reality, says Trinitarianism, is a complex "One", like a word: a unity rich with the mutualities of inner love.

Returning to Christ, I end with a poem by Alice Meynell.]

CHRIST IN THE UNIVERSE

With this ambiguous earth
His dealings have been told us. These abide:
The signal to a maid, the human birth,
The lesson, and the young Man crucified.

But not a star of all
The innumerable host of stars has heard
How He administered this terrestrial ball.
Our race have kept their Lord's entrusted Word.

54

Of His earth-visiting feet
None knows the secret, cherished, perilous,
The terrible, shamefast, frightened, whispered, sweet,
Heart-shattering secret of His way with us.

No planet knows that this
Our wayside planet, carrying land and wave,
Love and life multiplied, and pain and bliss,
Bears, as chief treasure, one forsaken grave.

Nor, in our little day,
May His devices with the heavens be guessed,
His pilgrimage to thread the Milky Way,
Or His bestowals there be manifest.

But in the eternities,
Doubtless we shall compare together, hear
A million alien Gospels, in what guise
He trod the Pleiades, the Lyre, the Bear.

O be prepared, my soul!
To read the inconceivable, to scan
The million forms of God those stars unroll
When, in our turn, we show to them a Man.

ALICE MEYNELL

FIRST PART

III. JOY AND PRAISE

Arise, you little glancing wings, and sing your infant joy!
Arise, and drink your bliss, for every thing that lives is holy!

BLAKE

The Angel who presided at my birth
Said,—"Little Creature, formed for joy and mirth,
Go love, without the help of anything on earth."

BLAKE

Nothing is voiceless in the world: God hears always
In all created things His echo and His praise.

ANGELUS SILESIUS

It is good if man can bring about that God sings within him.

RABBI ELIMELEKH OF LIZHENSK

See, this kingdom of God is now found within us. The grace
of the Holy Spirit shines forth and warms us, and, overflowing
with many and varied scents into the air around us, regales our
senses with heavenly delight, as it fills our hearts with joy
inexpressible.

ST. SERAPHIM OF SAROV

All joys hail from paradise.

RABBI PINHAS OF KORETZ

From Delight all these beings are born, by Delight they exist
and grow, to Delight they return.

TAITTIRIYA UPANISHAD

There are halls in the heavens above that open only to the voice of song.

THE ZOHAR

Serve the Lord with gladness: come before his presence with singing.

FROM PSALM 100

I will praise thee; for I am fearfully and wonderfully made: marvellous are thy works; and that my soul knoweth right well.

FROM PSALM 139

Bless the Lord, O my soul. O Lord my God, thou art very great; thou art clothed with honour and majesty.

Who coverest thyself with light as with a garment: who stretchest out the heavens like a curtain:

Who layeth the beams of his chambers in the waters: who maketh the clouds his chariot: who walketh upon the wings of the wind:

Who maketh his angels spirits; his ministers a flaming fire. . . .

He sendeth the springs into the valleys, which run among the hills.

They give drink to every beast of the field: the wild asses quench their thirst.

By them shall the fowls of the heaven have their habitation, which sing among the branches.

He watereth the hills from his chambers: the earth is satisfied with the fruit of thy works.

He causeth the grass to grow for the cattle, and herb for the service of man: that he may bring forth food out of the earth;

And wine that maketh glad the heart of man, and oil to make

60

his face to shine, and bread which strengtheneth man's heart.

The trees of the Lord are full of sap; the cedars of Lebanon, which he hath planted;

Where the birds make their nests: as for the stork, the fir trees are her house.

The high hills are a refuge for the wild goats; and the rocks for the conies.

He appointed the moon for seasons: the sun knoweth his going down.

Thou makest darkness, and it is night: wherein all the beasts of the forest do creep forth. . . .

Man goeth forth unto his work and to his labour until the evening.

O Lord, how manifold are thy works! in wisdom hast thou made them all: the earth is full of thy riches.

So is this great and wide sea, wherein are things creeping innumerable, both small and great beasts.

There go the ships: there is that leviathan, whom thou hast made to play therein.

These wait all upon thee; that thou mayest give them their meat in due season.

That [which] thou givest them they gather: thou openest thine hand, they are filled with good. . . .

Thou sendest forth thy spirit, they are created: and thou renewest the face of the earth.

The glory of the Lord shall endure for ever: the Lord shall rejoice in his works. . . .

471 FROM PSALM 104

Though our mouths were full of song as the sea, and our tongues of exultation as the multitude of its waves, and our lips of praise as the wide-extended firmament; though our eyes shone with light like the sun and the moon, and our hands were spread forth like the eagles of heaven, and our feet were swift as hinds, we should still be unable to thank thee and to bless thy name, O Lord our God and God of our fathers, for one thousandth or one ten thousandth part of the bounties which thou hast bestowed upon our fathers and upon us.

THE HEBREW MORNING SERVICE

A man should utter daily a hundred Benedictions.

RABBI MEIR

BENEDICTIONS FOR VARIOUS OCCASIONS FROM THE HEBREW PRAYER BOOK

Blessed art thou, O Lord our God, King of the universe, who openest the eyes of the blind.

Blessed art thou, O Lord our God, King of the universe, who clothest the naked.

Blessed art thou, O Lord our God, King of the universe, who loosest them that are bound.

Blessed art thou, O Lord our God, King of the universe, who raisest up them that are bowed down.

Blessed art thou, O Lord our God, King of the universe, who givest strength to the weary.

[It may be objected that God does not appear, as a general rule, to act in this beneficent manner: many of the naked remain naked, and many of the bound remain bound. The answer is that God does all these things through us, if we want them sufficiently. See the section "Man, Fellow-worker with God".]

On drinking wine:

Blessed art thou, O Lord our God, King of the universe, who createst the fruit of the vine.

On eating Food, other than Bread, prepared from Grain:

Blessed art thou, O Lord our God, King of the universe, who createst various kinds of food.

On eating Fruit which grows on Trees:

Blessed art thou, O Lord our God, King of the universe, who createst the fruit of the tree.

On eating Fruit which grows on the Ground:

Blessed art thou, O Lord our God, King of the universe, who createst the fruit of the earth.

On eating Flesh, Fish, Eggs, Cheese, etc., or drinking anything except Wine:

Blessed art thou, O Lord our God, King of the universe, by whose word all things exist.

On smelling Fragrant Woods or Barks:

Blessed art thou, O Lord our God, King of the universe, who createst fragrant woods.

On smelling Fragrant Plants:

Blessed art thou, O Lord our God, King of the universe, who createst fragrant plants.

On smelling Fragrant Fruits:

Blessed art thou, O Lord our God, King of the universe, who givest a goodly scent to fruits.

On smelling Fragrant Spices:

Blessed art thou, O Lord our God, King of the universe, who createst divers kinds of spices.

On smelling Fragrant Oils:

Blessed art thou, O Lord our God, King of the universe, who createst fragrant oil.

On seeing Lightning, Falling Stars, Mountains, or Great Deserts:

Blessed art thou, O Lord our God, King of the universe, who hast made the creation.

At the sight of the Sea:

Blessed art thou, O Lord our God, King of the universe, who hast made the great sea.

On seeing Beautiful Trees or Animals:

Blessed art thou, O Lord our God, King of the universe, who hast such as these in thy world.

On seeing Trees blossoming the first time in the Year:

Blessed art thou, O Lord our God, King of the universe, who hast made thy world lacking in nought, but hast produced therein goodly creatures and goodly trees wherewith to give delight unto the children of men.

On seeing a beautiful Dawn:

Blessed art thou, O Lord our God, King of the universe, who createst thy world every morning afresh. [This is not in the Hebrew prayer book: it is a later addition.]

On seeing Wise Men:

Blessed art thou, O Lord our God, King of the universe, who hast given of thy wisdom to flesh and blood.

On seeing strangely formed Persons, such as Giants or Dwarfs:

Blessed art thou, O Lord our God, King of the universe, who variest the forms of thy creatures.

On tasting Fruit for the first time in the season; on entering into possession of a new House or Land; or on using new Raiment for the first time:

Blessed art thou, O Lord our God, King of the universe, who hast kept us in life, and hast preserved us, and hast enabled us to reach this season.

Blessed art thou, O Lord our God, King of the universe, who art good, and dispensest good.

Persons who have been in peril of their lives, during journeys by sea or land, in captivity or sickness, upon their deliverance or recovery say the following:

Blessed art thou, O Lord our God, King of the universe, who vouchsafest benefits unto the undeserving, who hast also vouchsafed all good unto me.

At the Wedding Service:

Blessed art thou, O Lord our God, King of the universe, who hath created all things to thy glory.

Blessed art thou, O Lord our God, King of the universe, Creator of man.

Blessed art thou, O Lord our God, King of the universe, who hast made man in thine image, after thy likeness, and hast prepared unto him, out of his very self, a perpetual fabric. Blessed art thou, O Lord, Creator of man.

O make these loved companions greatly to rejoice, even as of old thou didst gladden thy creature in the garden of Eden. Blessed art thou, O Lord, who makest bridegroom and bride to rejoice.

Blessed art thou, O Lord our God, King of the universe, who hast created joy and gladness, bridegroom and bride, mirth and exultation, pleasure and delight, love, brotherhood, peace and fellowship. Soon may there be heard in the cities of Judah, and in the streets of Jerusalem, the voice of joy and gladness, the voice of the bridegroom and the voice of the bride, the jubilant voice of bridegrooms from their canopies, and of youths from their feasts of song. Blessed art thou, O Lord, who makest the bridegroom to rejoice with the bride.

At a Circumcision:

Blessed be he that cometh.

O give thanks unto the Lord; for he is good; for his

loving-kindness endureth for ever. This little child, may he
become great. Even as he has entered into the covenant, so may
he enter into . . . the nuptial canopy and into good deeds.

At the Moment before Death:

Blessed be His name, whose glorious kingdom is for ever
and ever.

SAINT FRANCIS' PRAISE OF CREATED THINGS

Most High, Omnipotent, Good Lord,
Thine be the praise, the glory, the honour, and all benediction.
To Thee alone, Most High, they are due,
   and no man is worthy to mention Thee.

Be Thou praised, my Lord, with all Thy creatures,
   above all Brother Sun,
   who gives the day and lightens us therewith.

And he is beautiful and radiant with great splendour,
   of Thee, Most High, he bears similitude.

Be Thou praised, my Lord, of Sister Moon and the stars,
   in the heaven hast Thou formed them, clear and precious
      and comely.

Be Thou praised, my Lord, of Brother Wind,
   and of the air, and the cloud, and of fair and of all weather,
   by the which Thou givest to Thy creatures sustenance.

Be Thou praised, my Lord, of Sister Water,
   which is much useful and humble and precious and pure.

Be Thou praised, my Lord, of Brother Fire,
   by which Thou hast lightened the night,
   and he is beautiful and joyful and robust and strong.

Be Thou praised, my Lord, of our Sister Mother Earth,
   which sustains and hath us in rule,
   and produces divers fruits with coloured flowers and herbs. . . .

Praise ye and bless my Lord, and give Him thanks,
and serve Him with great humility.

471 THE MIRROR OF PERFECTION

§ 2

The Evil One is pleased with sadness and melancholy.

ST. FRANCIS DE SALES

Give not over thy soul to sorrow; and afflict not thyself in
thine own counsel. Gladness of heart is the life of a man; and
the joyfulnes of a man is length of days. Love thine own soul,
and comfort thy heart: and remove sorrow far from thee; for
sorrow hath destroyed many, and there is no profit therein.
Envy and wrath shorten a man's days; and care bringeth old
age before the time. A cheerful and good heart will have a care
of his meat and diet.

ECCLESIASTICUS

Man will hereafter be called to account for depriving himself
of the good things which the world lawfully allows.

ABBA ARIKA ("RAB")

For every creature of God is good, and nothing to be refused,
if it be received with thanksgiving . . .

I TIMOTHY

[The New English Bible reads "For everything that God
created is good": this makes the meaning clearer.]

When the Baalshem was still seeking the proper way to serve
the Lord, he found that the observance of the Sabbath according to the injunctions of the later Rabbis practically prohibited

any movement, and filled a man with anxiety lest he should transgress some strict regulation. He believed that this contradicted the command of Isaiah to "call the Sabbath a delight". He pondered on this for a long time, and in the night he had a dream:

An Angel took him up to Heaven and showed him two vacant chairs in the highest place in Paradise, brilliantly illumined, as if with vari-coloured gems. "For whom are these intended?" he asked. "For thee," was the answer, "if thou makest use of thy intelligence; and also for a man whose name and residence I am writing down for thee."

He was next taken to Hell at its deepest spot, and shown two vacant seats, burning with a terrible flame. "For whom are these intended?" he asked. "For thee," was the answer, "if thou makest no use of thy intelligence; and also for a man whose name and residence I am writing down for thee."

In his dream the Baalshem visited the man who was to be his companion in Paradise. He found him living among non-Jews, ignorant of Judaism, except that on the Sabbath he gave a banquet for his non-Jewish friends, wherein he greatly rejoiced.

"Why do you hold this banquet?" asked the Baalshem. "I know not," replied the man, "but I recall that in my youth my parents prepared admirable meals on Saturday, and sang many songs; hence I do the same." The Baalshem wished to instruct him in Judaism, inasmuch as he had been born a Jew. But the power of speech left him for the moment, since he realised that the man's joy in the Sabbath would be marred if he knew all his shortcomings in the performance of religious duties.

The Baalshem then departed, in his dream, to the place where his companion in Hell dwelt. He found the man to be a strict observer of Judaism, always in anxiety lest his conduct was not correct, and passing the entire Sabbath day as if he were sitting on hot coals. The Baalshem wished to rebuke him, but once more the power of speech was taken away from him, since he realised that the man would never understand that he was doing wrong.

Thereupon the Baalshem meditated on the whole matter, and evolved his new system of observance, whereby God is served in joy which comes from the heart.

HASIDIC LEGEND

[See page 38.]

God Himself dressed Eve's hair, that the first woman might better please the first man.

JEWISH LEGEND

The voice of my beloved! behold, he cometh leaping upon the mountains, skipping upon the hills.

My beloved is like a roe or a young hart: behold, he standeth behind our wall, he looketh forth at the windows, shewing himself through the lattice.

My beloved spake, and said unto me, Rise up, my love, my fair one, and come away.

For, lo, the winter is past, the rain is over and gone;

The flowers appear on the earth; the time of the singing of birds is come, and the voice of the turtle is heard in our land;

The fig tree putteth forth her green figs, and the vines with the tender grape give a good smell. Arise, my love, my fair one, and come away . . .

How beautiful are thy feet with shoes, O prince's daughter! the joints of thy thighs are like jewels, the work of the hands of a cunning workman.

Thy navel is like a round goblet, which wanteth not liquor: thy belly is like an heap of wheat set about with lilies.

Thy two breasts are like two young roes that are twins.

Thy neck is as a tower of ivory; thine eyes like the fishpools in Heshbon, by the gate of Bath-rabbim; thy nose is as the tower of Lebanon which looketh toward Damascus.

Thine head upon thee is like Carmel, and the hair of thine head like purple . . .

How fair and how pleasant art thou, O love, for delights!

This thy stature is like to a palm tree, and thy breasts to clusters of grapes.

I said, I will go up to the palm tree, I will take hold of the boughs thereof: now also thy breasts shall be as clusters of the vine, and the smell of thy nose like apples;

And the roof of thy mouth like the best wine for my beloved, that goeth down sweetly, causing the lips of those that are asleep to speak.

I am my beloved's, and his desire is toward me.

Come, my beloved, let us go forth into the field; let us lodge in the villages.

Let us get up early to the vineyards; let us see if the vine flourish, whether the tender grape appear, and the pomegranates bud forth; there will I give thee my loves.

The mandrakes give a smell, and at our gates are all manner of pleasant fruits, new and old, which I have laid up for thee, O my beloved. . . .

Set me as a seal upon thine heart, as a seal upon thine arm: for love is strong as death; jealousy is cruel as the grave: the coals thereof are coals of fire, which hath a most vehement flame.

Many waters cannot quench love, neither can the floods drown it: if a man would give all the substance of his house for love, it would utterly be contemned. . . .

471   FROM THE SONG OF SOLOMON

§ 3

I place before my inward eyes myself with all that I am— my body, soul, and all my powers—and I gather round me all the creatures which God ever created in heaven, on earth, and in all the elements, each one severally with its name, whether birds of the air, beasts of the forest, fishes of the water, leaves and grass of the earth, or the innumerable sand of the sea, and to these I add all the little specks of dust which glance in the sunbeams, with all the little drops of water which ever fell or are falling from dew, snow, or rain, and I wish that each of these had a sweetly sounding stringed instrument, fashioned from my heart's inmost blood, striking on which they might each send up to our dear and gentle God a new and lofty strain of praise for ever and ever. And then the loving arms of my soul stretch out and extend themselves towards the innumerable multitude of all creatures, and my intention is, just as a free and blithesome leader of a choir stirs up the singers of his company, even so to turn them all to good account by inciting them to sing joyously, and to offer up their hearts to God.

HENRY SUSO

FROM "THE SALUTATION"

[Traherne imagines himself a new-born babe, seeing the wonders of the world for the first time. He was one of those happy beings who, throughout their lives, retain the power, as he says in *Dumnesse* below, to feel the excellence of things "with a steady and immediate sense"—to feel it in a direct sort of way, with no need for anybody else to prompt or teach them: and to feel it always, not by fits and starts.]

I that so long
     Was nothing from Eternity,
Did little think such joys as ear or tongue
          To celebrate or see:
Such sounds to hear, such hands to feel, such feet,
Beneath the skies, on such a ground to meet.

          From dust I rise,
          And out of Nothing now awake;
These brighter regions which salute mine eyes,
          A gift from GOD I take.
The earth, the seas, the light, the day, the skies,
The sun and stars are mine, if those I prize.

Long time before
I in my mother's womb was born,
A GOD preparing did this glorious store,
The world, for me adorn.
Into this Eden so divine and fair,
So wide and bright, I come his son and heir.

A stranger here
Strange things doth meet, strange glories see;
Strange treasures lodg'd in this fair world appear,
Strange all, and new to me.
But that they mine should be, who nothing was,
That strangest is of all, yet brought to pass.

TRAHERNE

FROM "DUMNESSE"

No business serious seemd but one; no work
But one was found; and that did in me lurk.
D'ye ask me What? It was with clearer eyes
To see all creatures full of Deities;
Especially oneself: and to admire
The satisfaction of all true desire:
Twas to be pleased with all that God hath done;
Twas to enjoy *even All* beneath the sun:
Twas with a steady and immediate sense
To feel and measure all the excellence
Of things: twas to inherit endless treasure,
And to be filled with everlasting pleasure . . .

TRAHERNE

FROM "CENTURIES OF MEDITATION"

Those pure and virgin apprehensions I had in my infancy, and that divine light wherewith I was born, are the best unto this day wherein I can see the universe. By the gift of God they attended me into the world, and by His special favour I remember them till now. Verily they form the greatest gift His wisdom could bestow, for without them all other gifts had been dead and vain. They are unattainable by books, and therefore I will teach them by experience. Pray for them earnestly, for they will make you angelical and wholly celestial. Certainly Adam in Paradise had not more sweet and curious apprehensions of the world than I when I was a child.

All appeared new and strange at first, inexpressibly rare and delightful and beautiful. I was a little stranger which at my entrance into the world was saluted and surrounded with innumerable joys. My knowledge was divine; I knew by intuition those things which since my apostacy I collected again by the highest reason. My very ignorance was advantageous. I seemed as one brought into the estate of innocence. All things were spotless and pure and glorious; yea, and infinitely mine and joyful and precious. I knew not that there were any sins, or complaints or laws. I dreamed not of poverties, contentions, or vices. All tears and quarrels were hidden from mine eyes. Everything was at rest, free and immortal. I knew nothing of sickness or death or exaction. In the absence of these I was entertained like an angel with the works of God in their splendour and glory; I saw all in the peace of Eden; heaven and earth did sing my Creator's praises, and could not make more melody to Adam than to me. All time was eternity, and a perpetual Sabbath. Is it not strange that an infant should be heir of the whole world, and see those mysteries which the books of the learned never unfold?

The corn was orient and immortal wheat which never should be reaped nor was ever sown. I thought it had stood from everlasting to everlasting. The dust and stones of the street were as precious as gold: the gates were at first the end of the world. The green trees when I saw them first through one of the gates transported and ravished me; their sweetness and unusual beauty made my heart to leap, and almost mad with ecstasy,

73

they were such strange and wonderful things. The men! O what venerable and reverend creatures did the aged seem! Immortal Cherubims! And young men glittering and sparkling angels, and maids strange seraphic pieces of life and beauty! Boys and girls tumbling in the street were moving jewels: I knew not that they were born or should die. But all things abided eternally as they were in their proper places. Eternity was manifest in the light of the day, and something infinite behind everything appeared, which talked with my expectation and moved my desire. The city seemed to stand in Eden or to be built in Heaven. The streets were mine, the temple was mine, the people were mine, their clothes and gold and silver were mine, as much as their sparkling eyes, fair skins, and ruddy faces. The skies were mine, and so were the sun and moon and stars, and all the world was mine; and I the only spectator and enjoyer of it.

471 TRAHERNE

TILL EVERY MORNING YOU AWAKE IN HEAVEN

Your enjoyment of the world is never right, till every morning you awake in Heaven; see yourself in your Father's palace; and look upon the skies, the earth, and the air as celestial joys: having such a reverend esteem of all, as if you were among the Angels. The bride of a monarch, in her husband's chamber, hath no such causes of delight as you. . . .

You never enjoy the world aright, till the sea itself floweth in your veins, till you are clothed with the heavens, and crowned with the stars: and perceive yourself to be the sole heir of the whole world, and more than so, because men are in it who are every one sole heirs as well as you. Till you can sing and rejoice and delight in God, as misers do in gold, and kings in sceptres, you never enjoy the world. . . .

All things were made to be yours, and you were made to prize them according to their value: which is your office and duty, the end for which you were created, and the means whereby you enjoy. The end for which you were created, is that by prizing all that God hath done, you may enjoy yourself and Him in Blessedness.

TRAHERNE

If we had never before looked upon the earth, but suddenly came to it man or woman grown, set down in the midst of a summer mead, would it not seem to us a radiant vision? The hues, the shapes, the song and life of birds, above all the sunlight, the breath of heaven, resting on it; the mind would be filled with its glory, unable to grasp it, hardly believing that such things could be mere matter and no more. Like a dream of some spirit-land it would appear, scarce fit to be touched lest it should fall to pieces, too beautiful to be long watched lest it should fade away. So it seemed to me as a boy, sweet and new like this each morning; and even now, after the years that have passed, and the lines they have worn in the forehead, the summer mead shines as bright and fresh as when my foot first touched the grass.

RICHARD JEFFERIES

Remember the dreams of thy youth, if thou would'st learn to be a man.

SCHILLER

THOU HEAREST THE NIGHTINGALE

Thou hearest the nightingale begin the song of spring:
The lark, sitting upon his earthy bed, just as the morn
Appears, listens silent; then, springing from the waving corn-
    field, loud
He leads the choir of day—trill! trill! trill! trill!
Mounting upon the wings of light into the great expanse,
Re-echoing against the lovely blue and shining heavenly shell:

His little throat labours with inspiration; every feather
On throat and breast and wings vibrates with the effluence divine:
All nature listens silent to him, and the awful sun
Stands still upon the mountain, looking on this little bird
With eyes of soft humility and wonder, love and awe.
Then loud from their green covert all the birds begin their song:
The thrush, the linnet, and the goldfinch, robin, and the wren
Awake the sun from his sweet reverie upon the mountain:
The nightingale again assays his song, and thro' the day
And thro' the night warbles luxuriant, every bird of song
Attending his loud harmony with admiration and love . . .

Thou perceivest the flowers put forth their precious odours . . .
First, ere the morning breaks, joy opens in the flowery bosoms,
Joy even to tears, which the sun rising dries: first the wild thyme
And meadow-sweet, downy and soft, waving among the reeds,
Light springing on the air, lead the sweet dance; they wake
The honeysuckle sleeping on the oak; the flaunting beauty
Revels along upon the wind; the white-thorn, lovely may,
Opens her many lovely eyes; listening, the rose still sleeps—
None dare to wake her: soon she bursts her crimson-curtain'd bed
And comes forth in the majesty of beauty. Every flower,
The pink, the jessamine, the wallflower, the carnation,
The jonquil, the mild lily, opes her heavens; every tree
And flower and herb soon fill the air with an innumerable dance,
Yet all in order sweet and lovely. Men are sick with love!

BLAKE

THE SONG OF THE SINLESS SOUL

Rise up, O sun, most glorious minister & light of day.
Flow on, ye gentle airs, & bear the voice of my rejoicing.
Wave freshly, clear waters flowing around the tender grass;
And thou, sweet-smelling ground, put forth thy life in fruit &
  flowers.

Follow me, O my flocks, & hear me sing my rapturous song.
I will cause my voice to be heard on the clouds that glitter in the
    sun.
I will call; and who shall answer me? I will sing; who shall reply?
For from my pleasant hills behold the living, living springs,
Running among my green pastures, delighting among my trees.
I am not here alone: my flocks, you are my brethren;
And you birds that sing & adorn the sky, you are my sisters.
I sing, & you reply to my song; I rejoice, & you are glad.
Follow me, O my flocks; we will now descend into the valley.
O how delicious are the grapes, flourishing in the sun!
How clear the spring of the rock, running among the golden sand!
How cool the breezes of the valley, & the arms of the branching
    trees!
Cover us from the sun; come & let us sit in the shade . . .
Here will I build myself a house, & here I'll call on his name,
Here I'll return when I am weary & take my pleasant rest.

BLAKE

               . . . Magnificent
The morning rose, in memorable pomp,
Glorious as e'er I had beheld—in front,
The sea lay laughing at a distance; near,
The solid mountains shone, bright as the clouds,
Grain-tinctured, drenched in empyrean light;
And in the meadows and the lower grounds
Was all the sweetness of a common dawn—
Dews, vapours, and the melody of birds,
And labourers going forth to till the fields.

471   WORDSWORTH

Long-idling Spring may come
With such sweet suddenness
It's past the wit of man
    His joy to express.

77

To see in the cold clods
Green weed 'twixt stone and stone!
The violet nod in flower
  Its frail stalk on;

To watch the wintry sky
Shed pallor from its blue:
And beams of purest light
  And heat pierce through!

To share, to live, to be
Merely a reflex of
Earth's old divine delight,
  And peace, and love!

WALTER DE LA MARE

[Walter de la Mare was of the company of Traherne, though his range of experience was far wider: he could rejoice, throughout a long life, in being "merely a reflex of Earth's old divine delight"—in sharing it, as a reflection in a mirror shares what it reflects.]

He said the pleasantest manner of spending a hot July day was lying from morning till evening on a bank of heath in the middle of the moors, with the bees humming dreamily about among the bloom, and the larks singing high up over head, and the blue sky and bright sun shining steadily and cloudlessly. That was his most perfect idea of heaven's happiness: mine was rocking in a rustling green tree, with a west wind blowing, and bright white clouds flitti rapidly above; and not only larks, but throstles, and blackbirds, and linnets, and cuckoos pouring out music on every side, and the moors seen at a distance, broken into cool dusky dells; but close by great swells of long grass undulating in waves to the breeze; and woods and sounding water, and the whole world awake and wild with joy.

EMILY BRONTË (from Wuthering Heights)

The double door of the house stood open to an effect of hazy autumn sunshine, a wonderful windless waiting golden hour . . .

HENRY JAMES

I tremble with pleasure when I think that on the very day of my leaving prison both the laburnum and the lilac will be blooming in the gardens.

OSCAR WILDE

There are days now and again when the summer broods in Trafalgar Square; the flood of light from a cloudless sky gathers and grows, thickening the air; the houses enclose the beams as water is enclosed in a cup. . . . Either the light subdues the sound, or perhaps rather it renders the senses slumberous and less sensitive, but the great sunlit square is silent—silent, that is, for the largest city on earth. A slumberous silence of abundant light, of the full summer day, of the high flood of summer hours whose tide can rise no higher. A time to linger and dream under the beautiful breast of heaven, heaven brooding and descending in pure light upon man's handiwork.

RICHARD JEFFERIES

. . . and I think of lank and coaly steamships heaving on the grey rollers of the English Channel and darkling streets wet with rain, I recall as if I were back there the busy exit from Charing Cross, the cross and the money-changers' offices, the splendid grime of giant London and the crowds going perpetually to and fro, the lights by night and the urgency and eventfulness of that great rain-swept heart of the modern world.

H. G. WELLS (from The New Machiavelli)

I do not think there is anyone who takes quite such a fierce pleasure in things being themselves as I do. The startling wetness of water excites and intoxicates me: the fieriness of fire, the steeliness of steel, the unutterable muddiness of mud.

G. K. CHESTERTON

MIRACLES

Why, who makes much of a miracle?
As to me I know of nothing else but miracles,
Whether I walk the streets of Manhattan,
Or dart my sight over the roofs of houses toward the sky,
Or wade with naked feet along the beach just in the edge of the
    water,
Or stand under trees in the woods,
Or talk by day with any one I love, or sleep in the bed at night
    with any one I love,
Or sit at table at dinner with the rest,
Or look at strangers opposite me riding in the car,
Or watch honey-bees busy around the hive of a summer fore-
    noon,
Or animals feeding in the fields,
Or birds, or the wonderfulness of insects in the air,
Or the wonderfulness of the sundown, or of stars shining so
    quiet and bright,
Or the exquisite delicate thin curve of the new moon in
    spring;
These with the rest, one and all, are to me miracles . . .

To me every hour of the light and dark is a miracle,
Every cubic inch of space is a miracle,
Every square yard of the surface of the earth is spread with
    the same,
Every foot of the interior swarms with the same.

To me the sea is a continual miracle,
The fishes that swim—the rocks—the motion of the waves—
    the ships with men in them,
What stranger miracles are there?

WALT WHITMAN

When I go from hence let this be my parting word, that
what I have seen is unsurpassable.

*　　　*　　　*

The same stream of life that runs through my veins night
and day runs through the world and dances in rhythmic measures.

It is the same life that shoots in joy through the dust of the
earth in numberless blades of grass and breaks into tumultuous
waves of leaves and flowers.

*　　　*　　　*

And joy is everywhere; it is in the earth's green covering of
grass; in the blue serenity of the sky; in the reckless exuberance
of spring; in the severe abstinence of grey winter; in the living
flesh that animates our bodily frame; in the perfect poise of the
human figure, noble and upright; in living; in the exercise of
all our powers; in the acquisition of knowledge; in fighting evils;
in dying for gains we never can share . . . Joy is the realisation of
the truth of oneness, the oneness of our soul with the world and
of the world-soul with the supreme lover.

RABINDRANATH TAGORE

In such access of mind, in such high hour
Of visitation from the living God,
Thought was not: in enjoyment it expired.
No thanks he breathed, he proffered no request.
Rapt into still communion that transcends
The imperfect offices of prayer and praise,

His mind was a thanksgiving to the power
That made him; it was blessedness and love.

WORDSWORTH (from *The Excursion*)

[A paraphrase might read somewhat as follows:
"Suddenly he was 'out of himself', was pure heart and spirit. In that moment, in which God seemed to be visiting him, he did not *think* about things: thought was swallowed up in unreflecting joy. He gave no thanks, and he asked for nothing. He was no longer separate or distinct: hushed and at peace, he was merged into everything, into the Whole, into God: and this was a sort of worship far more complete than any ordinary worship with prayers and hymn-singing. It would be wrong to say that he was *giving* thanks, that he *knew* himself blessed, that he *felt* himself loving or loved: he, himself, his whole being, *was* thanks, *was* blessedness, *was* love."

This experience is the greatest that life can hold, and is by no means uncommon, though few, after experiencing it, could explain, or even understand, what had happened to them as Wordsworth understood and explained it. "The Beatific Vision' is a phrase often to be found in religious literature: this is what it means. We may judge it to be particularly common in childhood (see, for instance, Traherne on page 72): and happy are they who, in middle and old age, are still granted this blessedness.

How it has come to me personally may be of interest to those, if any, by whom the still ecstasy of communion is still unknown. It came to me as a boy when I was sitting one Sunday on a balcony over a deserted London street, its pavements ablaze with the noonday sun and a footstep or horse's hoof, I forget which, suddenly ringing out in the silence: and it came to me only a few weeks ago, in the Festival Hall on South Bank, just as the slow variation in the last movement of the Eroica symphony was beginning its solemn and inevitable course. To have lived in moments or eternities such as these is to be assured, with the Lady Julian, that "all shall be well, and all shall be well, and all manner of things shall be well".]

Hush! Hush! Hath not the world now become perfect? What hath happened unto me?

NIETZSCHE (from Thus Spake Zarathustra)

But do you know, dear Helmuth, what was the most important thing to me?—the fact that I perceived once again that most people take hold of things in order to do something stupid with them (as, for example, to tickle each other with peacocks' feathers), instead of looking at each thing properly and asking it about the beauty it possesses. Thus it comes about that most people simply don't know how beautiful the world is and how much splendour is revealed in the smallest things, in a common flower, in a stone, in the bark of a tree or the leaf of a birch. Grown-up people, who have occupations and cares and who worry themselves about mere trifles, gradually lose the eye for these riches, which children, if they are observant and good, quickly notice and love with their whole heart.

RAINER MARIA RILKE

> . . . for me
> Life's morning radiance hath not left the hills,
> Her dew is on the flowers.

WORDSWORTH

To breathe is a beatitude.

AMIEL

SECOND PART

I. GOOD AND EVIL

I believed in God and in Nature, and in the triumph of good over evil.

GOETHE

Whatever is, is in God, and nothing can exist or be conceived without God.

SPINOZA

All that happens is divine.

LÉON BLOY

§ 2

The depraved sinner, though bereft of the Good by his brutish desires . . . still hath a share in the Good in so far as there is in him a distorted reflection of true Love and Communion. And anger hath a share in the Good, in so far as it is a movement which seeks to remedy apparent evils, converting them to that which appears to be fair. And even he that desires the basest life, yet in so far as he feels desire at all and feels desire for life, and intends what he thinks the best kind of life, so far participates in the Good.

．　．　．　．　．　．　．　．

The Good must be the beginning and the end even of all evil things. For the Good is the final Purpose of all things, good and bad alike. For even when we act amiss we do so from a longing for the Good; for no one makes evil his definite object when performing any action. Hence evil hath no substantial being, but only a shadow thereof: since the Good, and not itself, is the ultimate object for which it comes into existence.

．　．　．　．　．　．　．　．

And if no thing in the world is without a share in the Good, and evil is the deficiency of Good and no thing in the world is

87

utterly destitute of Good, then the Divine Providence is in all things, and nothing that exists can be without it.

DIONYSIUS THE AREOPAGITE

I am often struck by the word Jesus used for sin. It comes from archery practice; to sin (in the thought of Jesus) means to miss the mark: miss the target. To miss the target at least implies that you are aiming at something. However wide of the mark the shots are going, a sinner is aiming at something. Take the lecherous man, the sex addict. What's he aiming at? A real experience of love surely—mad though his efforts be ever so to find it. Take the gambler: what is *he* aiming at? Surely making a big thing out of life: taking real risks to get it; real risks and terrifying. Isn't he playing (however upside down) with that precious gift called faith? He risks all on an Act. And our drunkards . . . what are they aiming at? Most solemnly I say it, they want to be filled: filled with life, filled with spirit. They want to recover hope. Faith, hope and love—that's their real target, all of them—Life! They want to be filled with it: they take appalling risks for it: they are determined to live; determined to love. I am not excusing it. Poor souls, they don't excuse it themselves. They are missing their mark; and don't they know it? But at least they go on demanding Life. Dare we say this is why Jesus loved them? I am sure the sinners crowded round Him (in the market-place and pub) because they knew He understood. He didn't just love sinners; He liked them. He saw their possibility. He loved sinners—not as the Pharisees did, because it was their duty to save; He loved them for wanting something badly: for wanting Life at all costs.

G. F. MACLEOD

With everything wrong right is always somehow involved . . . We seek base metal because we think it gold. Our delight in pursuing the bad comes from our belief that it is the good.

JALALU D-DIN RUMI

88

Evil is not wholly evil: it is misplaced good.

SAMUEL ALEXANDER

There is no not-holy, there is only that which has not yet been hallowed, which has not yet been redeemed to its holiness.

MARTIN BUBER

There is some soul of goodness in things evil,
Would men observingly distil it out . . .
Thus may we gather honey from the weed,
And make a moral of the devil himself.

SHAKESPEARE

There is nothing on earth though never so simple so vile and abject in the sight of man, but it beares the witness of God.

THOMAS VAUGHAN

God is . . . even in the depths of Hell.

BLAKE

The stuff of which evil is made is one with the stuff of which good is made. No tendency or desire could be pointed out in the worst of lives or of actions which is incapable of being, with addition or readjustment, incorporated in a good self.

BOSANQUET

Vice is still human, being mixed with something contrary to itself.

PLOTINUS

There was never sin of thine
But within its heart did dwell
A beauty that could whisper thee
Of the high heaven from which it fell.

A. E.

Man is a twofold being, one part capable of evil and the other capable of good; that which is capable of good is not also capable of evil, but that which is capable of evil is also capable of good.

BLAKE

The wise man . . . beholds all men as things made for holy uses.

TAO TÊ CHING

If you see something bad in a man, you must not overlook the fact that in this man too God is manifest. Praised be God, for no place is without Him.

THE BAALSHEM

When Christ wished to teach us what God is like He pointed to the God-like in men. Even in the worst sinner He could discover the hidden good and appeal to it, knowing that the good and not the evil is the essential man.

G. H. C. MACGREGOR

I have come to the stage of realisation in which I see that God is walking in every human form and manifesting himself alike in the sage and in the sinner.

SRI RAMAKRISHNA

There are people within whom everything that was good in Cain's soul has gone to dwell, and these people are very great.

RABBI URI OF STRELISK

[Even in the first murderer, the Rabbi is saying, there was something very precious, mixed up with the evil. And indeed one of the chief arguments against capital punishment is that by killing (or, as we call it, executing) a murderer we rule out the possibility —in this life at any rate—of the good in him conquering the evil, and so of his eventually evening things up a bit. About forty years ago a young American committed a murder notorious for its infamy, but escaped execution. He has recently left prison, where he saved many lives at the risk of his own as a volunteer for medical experiments: and is now devoting himself, in other ways, to the service of mankind.]

Men are free beings, living as such, and they learn from inner experience the nothingness of evil, how it defeats and destroys itself while it is being experienced; and when they have purged themselves of it they reach the light.

BERDYAEV

THE PORTRAIT OF MOSES

The whole world was shaken and enthralled by the miracle of the Exodus. The name of Moses was on everyone's lips. Tidings of the great miracle reached also the wise king of Arabistan. The king summoned to him his best painter and bade him go to Moses, to paint his portrait and bring it back to him. When the painter returned the king gathered together all his sages, skilled in judging a man from his features, and asked them to define by the portrait the character of Moses, his qualities, inclinations, habits and the source of his miraculous power.

"King," answered the sages, "this is the portrait of a man cruel, haughty, greedy of gain, possessed by desire for power and by all the vices which exist in the world."

These words roused the king's indignation.

"How can it be possible," he exclaimed, "that a man whose marvellous deeds ring through the whole world should be of such a kind?"

A dispute began between the painter and the sages. The painter affirmed that the portrait of Moses had been painted by him quite accurately, while the sages maintained that Moses' character had been unerringly determined by them according to the portrait.

The wise king of Arabistan decided to verify which of the disputing parties was right, and he himself set off for the camp of Israel.

At the first glance the king became convinced that the face of Moses had been faultlessly portrayed by the painter. On entering the tent of the man of God he knelt down, bowed to the ground and told Moses of the dispute between the artist and the sages.

"At first, until I saw thy face," said the king, "I thought it must be that the artist had painted thy image badly, for my sages are men very much experienced in interpreting a man's character from his portrait. Now I am convinced that they are quite worthless men and that their wisdom is vain."

"No," answered Moses, 'it is not so; both the painter and your sages are men highly skilled, and both parties are right. Be it known to thee that all the vices of which the sages spoke have indeed been assigned to me by nature and perhaps to an even higher degree than was found by them from my portrait. But I struggled with my vices by long and intense efforts of the will and gradually overcame and suppressed them in myself until all opposed to them became my second nature. And in this lies my greatest pride."

TALMUDIC LEGEND

All qualities are not only good, but infinitely perfect, as they are in God; and it is absolutely impossible that they should have any evil or defect in them, as they are in the one God, who is the great and universal All. But the same qualities, thus infinitely good and perfect in God, may become imperfect and evil in the human creature; because, in the creature, they may be divided and separated from one another by the creature itself.

God could not possibly create a creature to be an infinite All, like Himself, but only creatures that are finite and limited. Yet neither could He bring any creature into existence, save by imparting to it His own qualities and the freedom of His own nature, and so giving it the capability of dividing and separating these qualities from one another.

Thus strength and fire in the divine nature are nothing else but the strength and flame of love, and never can be anything else; but in the creature strength and fire may be separated from love, and then they are become an evil, they are wrath and darkness and all mischief: and thus that same strength and quality, which in creatures making a *right* use of their own will or freedom becomes their goodness and perfection, doth in creatures making a *wrong* use of their will or freedom become their evil and mischievous nature: and it is a truth that deserves well to be considered that there is no goodness in any creature, from the highest to the lowest, but in its continuing to be such a union of qualities and powers as God has brought together in its creation.

There is no evil, no guilt, no deformity in any creature, but in its dividing and separating itself from something which God had given to be in union with it. This, and this alone, is the whole nature of all good and all evil in the creature, both in spiritual and material things. For instance, dark, fiery wrath in the soul is not only very like, but it is the very self-same thing in the soul which a wrathful poison is in the flesh. Now, the qualities of poison are in themselves all of them good qualities and necessary to every life; but they are become a poisonous evil, because they are separated from some other qualities. Thus also the qualities of fire and strength that constitute an evil wrath in the soul, are in themselves very good qualities and necessary to every good life; but they are become an evil wrath because separated from some other qualities with which they should be united.

That which in a devil is an evil selfishness, a wrathful fire, a stinging motion, is in a holy angel the everlasting kindling of a divine life, the strong birth of a heavenly love, it is a real cause of an ever-springing, ever-triumphing joyfulness, an ever-increasing sensibility of bliss.

★ WILLIAM LAW

Good is that which makes for unity: Evil is that which makes for separateness.

ALDOUS HUXLEY

Freud [regards] love and hate as wholly independent of each other in their origin . . . I do not take this view, but regard hate as the *frustration aspect of love*, as "tails" is the obverse of "heads" in the same penny.

IAN SUTTIE

[People are born with an impulse, a natural eagerness, to love; but if this impulse cannot express itself freely because their parents or the world in general fail to welcome it and answer it with love, then it turns into what looks like its opposite, namely hate. But there are not two impulses, only one, to begin with.

The idea in the next quotation is very similar.]

It would seem that the amount of destructiveness to be found in individuals is proportionate to the amount to which expansiveness of life is curtailed. . . . Life has an inner dynamism of its own; it tends to grow, to be expressed, to be lived. It seems that if this tendency is thwarted the energy directed towards life undergoes a process of decomposition and changes into energies directed towards destruction. . . . The more the drive towards life is thwarted, the stronger is the drive towards destruction; the more life is realised, the less is the strength of destructiveness. *Destructiveness is the outcome of unlived life.*

ERICH FROMM

There is in man an upwelling spring of life, energy, love, whatever you like to call it. If a course is not cut for it, it turns the ground round it into a swamp.

MARK RUTHERFORD

§ 4

[God is speaking to Moses.]

Moab is come forth from lust; but Ruth shall come forth from Moab, and David from Ruth, and from David the Messiah.

EDMOND FLEG (from a Midrashic source)

[It is told in the Book of Genesis that, before the destruction of Sodom (see page 32), Lot, one of its inhabitants, was sent away to a place called Zoar: for he was a good man, and God had no wish to destroy him. From Zoar, which he thought unsafe, Lot presently fled to a mountain, and lived there with his two daughters, who were unmarried, but wanted children. As the only man in the mountain was their father they made him drunk, so that he should not know what he was doing, and then "went in unto him", as the Bible puts it. "And the firstborn bare a son, and called his name Moab: the same is the father of the Moabites unto this day."

Centuries later a Moabite woman called Ruth (whose name has come to mean, for all who have read her story in the Bible, the essence of loving fidelity) married an Israelite called Boaz. Their great-grandson was King David: and the old Hebrews believed that "from David would come the Messiah"—namely, that one of David's descendants would be a man specially chosen by God to purge the world of its evil. This Messiah, Christians think, has already come, in the person of Jesus Christ: and, according to the Gospel of St. Matthew, "Joseph the husband of Mary, of whom was born Jesus, who is called Christ" was one of David's descendants.

Now for a woman to "come in unto" her father—to have sexual intercourse with him—was regarded among the Hebrews as a particularly horrifying form of unnatural lust: and indeed most people instinctively feel, to this day, that there is something pretty vile about it. But out of this great evil there will come (said the Hebrews), there has already come (say Christians), a far greater good, a supreme good, the world's salvation.]

The roaring of lions, the howling of wolves, the raging of the stormy sea, and the destructive sword, are portions of eternity too great for the eye of man.

BLAKE

[But believe though we may that "the destructive sword", or its modern equivalent, is incidental to God's loving purpose, or (however inexplicably to our limited vision) even necessary for it, this does not absolve us from opposing the use of such villainies with all our heart and with all our powers. Only, perhaps, in the struggle against evil at its vilest can we develop such a passion for goodness as will fit us to be, in the fullest sense, "fellow-workers" with God.]

For whether they looked upward they saw the Divine Vision
Or whether they looked downward still they saw the Divine
    Vision,
Surrounding them on all sides beyond sin and death and hell.

BLAKE (from *Vala*)

SECOND PART

II. SIN AND REPENTANCE

I believe in the forgiveness of sins.

THE APOSTLES' CREED

For thou desirest not sacrifice; else would I give it: thou delightest not in burnt offering.

The sacrifices of God are a broken spirit: a broken and a contrite heart, O God, thou wilt not despise.

FROM PSALM 51

[See the note on verse 7 from the Sermon on the Mount, p. 20.]

God likes forgiving big sins more than small ones. The bigger they are the gladder he is and the quicker to forgive them.

MEISTER ECKHART

I say unto you, that likewise joy shall be in heaven over one sinner that repenteth, more than over ninety and nine just persons, which need no repentance.

ST. LUKE

Where is the foolish person who would think it in his power to commit more than God could forgive? and who will dare to measure, by the greatness of his crimes, the immensity of that infinite mercy which casts them all into the depths of the sea of oblivion, when we repent of them with love?

ST. FRANCIS DE SALES

Though a man be soiled
With the sins of a lifetime,
Let him but love me,
Rightly resolved,

99

In utter devotion:
I see no sinner,
That man is holy.

THE BHAGAVAD-GITA

Before God created the world, he created Penitence and said to him: "I am going to create a man in the world, on condition that every time he turns to you you are ready to forgive him his sins." And, indeed, whenever man does turn to him, Penitence entreats God to forgive all his sins.

THE ZOHAR

Failure to repent is much worse than sin. A man may have sinned for but a moment, but he may fail to repent of it moments without number.

RABBI BUNAM OF PZHYSHA

We are told by the Pslamist first to leave evil and then to do good. I will add that if you find it difficult to follow this advice, you may first do good, and the evil will automatically depart from you.

RABBI YITZHAK MEIR OF GER

When thou attackest the roots of sin, fix thy thought more upon the God whom thou desirest than upon the sin which thou abhorrest.

WALTER HYLTON

Man must be lenient with his soul in her weaknesses and imperfections and suffer her failings as he suffers those of others, but he must not become idle, and must encourage himself to better things.

ST. SERAPHIM OF SAROV

We should be in charity with ourselves as with our neighbours.

FÉNELON

[Charity, throughout this book, is used in the sense of *caritas*: love of our fellow-men.]

How shall we expect charity towards others, when we are uncharitable to our selves?

SIR THOMAS BROWNE

How could man live at all if he did not grant forgiveness every night to himself and all his brothers?

GOETHE

The superstitious, who know better how to condemn vice than to teach virtue, and who do not endeavour to lead men by reason, but to so inspire them with fear that they avoid evil rather than love virtue, have no other intention than to make the rest as miserable as themselves; and therefore it is not wonderful that for the most part they are a nuisance and hateful to men.

★ SPINOZA

Noble natures, and such as are capable of goodness, are railed into vice, that might as easily be persuaded into virtue.

SIR THOMAS BROWNE

I can hardly think there was ever any scared into heaven.

SIR THOMAS BROWNE

Detestable sinners have proved exemplary converts on earth, and may be glorious in the Apartment of Mary Magdalen in heaven. Men are not the same through all divisions of their ages. Time, experience, self-reflexions, and God's mercies, make in some well-temper'd minds a kind of translation before death, and men do differ from themselves as well as from other persons.

SIR THOMAS BROWNE

["By faith Enoch was translated that he should not see death; and he was not found, because God had translated him: for before his translation he had this testimony, that he pleased God."—Hebrews]

The sinner of to-day is the saint of to-morrow. Wherefore, unmindful of the sins and shortcomings of our neighbours, let us look to our own imperfections, surely forgetting what God has forgotten: sins truly repented, which God has forgotten, 'tis no business of ours to remember.

MEISTER ECKHART

Thou canst begin a new life! See but things afresh as thou usedst to see them; for in this consists the new life.

MARCUS AURELIUS

Do not feel qualms or despondency or discomfiture if thou dost not invariably succeed in acting from right principles; but when thou art foiled, come back again to them, and rejoice if on the whole thy conduct is worthy of a man, and love the course to which thou returnest.

MARCUS AURELIUS

If any one has committed a serious sin, let him beware thinking of it. For where our thoughts are, there we also are with our soul. Let not your soul sink into the mire of sin; it may not be able to extricate itself and repent.

And even if a man has committed a minor offence, why should he think of it? Why should he place his soul in the mire? Turn mire hither and thither, and it remains mire. What good can come to Heaven from disturbing your sin in your mind? During the time thus consumed you may perform a good deed which will truly be like presenting God with a pearl.

Turn away from evil; hold it not in remembrance; do good. If you have sinned much, balance it by doing much good. Resolve to-day, from the depth of your heart and in a joyful mood, to abstain from sin and to do good.

RABBI YITZHAK MEIR OF GER

Too much self-examination is as bad as too little; believe me, by God's help we shall advance more by contemplating the Divinity than by keeping our eyes fixed on ourselves.

★ ST. TERESA

When thou fallest into a fault, in what matter soever it be, do not trouble nor afflict thyself for it. . . . The Devil will make thee believe, as soon as thou fallest into any fault, that thou walkest in error, and therefore art out of God and his favour, and herewith would he make thee distrust of the divine Grace, telling thee of thy misery, and making a giant of it; and putting it into thy head that every day thy soul grows worse instead of better, whilst it so often repeats these failings. O blessed Soul, open thine eyes; and shut the gate against these diabolical suggestions, knowing thy misery, and trusting in the mercy divine. Would not he be a mere fool who, running a tournament with others, and falling when at full gallop, should lie weeping on the ground and afflicting himself with discourses upon his fall? Man (they would tell him), lose no time, get up and take the course again, for he that rises again quickly and continues his race is as if he had never fallen. If thou seest thyself fallen once and a thousand times, thou oughtest to make use of the remedy which I have given thee, that is, a loving confidence in the divine mercy. These are the weapons with which thou must fight and conquer cowardice and vain thoughts. This is the means thou oughtest to use—not to lose time, not to disturb thyself, and reap no good.

★ MOLINOS

[Grace is defined in the Oxford Dictionary as "the divine influence which operates in men to regenerate and sanctify, and to impart strength to endure trial and resist temptation". The definition is as good as any: but no one who has not experienced Grace can really understand it. Most people do experience it sooner or later.]

The wretch who constantly says "I am bound, I am bound" only succeeds in being bound. He who says day and night "I am a sinner, I am a sinner" verily becomes a sinner.

One must have such burning faith in God that one can say: "What? I have repeated God's name and can sin still cling to me? How can I be a sinner any more? How can I be in bondage any more?"

If a man repeats God's name, his body, mind, and everything becomes pure. Why should one talk only about sin and hell and such things? Say but once, "O Lord, I have undoubtedly done wicked things, but I won't repeat them". And have faith in His name.

SRI RAMAKRISHNA

["What? I have repeated God's name and can sin still cling to me?" If I may mention my own experience, I have occasionally had nightmare visions of existence as indescribably evil, myself being part of it, and have forced myself into wakefulness— but only for the terror to persist. I have learned, on these occasions, to make the sign of the Cross: not because I am an orthodox

104

Christian, but because I have wanted, in the face of apparently certain evil, to affirm certain and perfect goodness. And the goodness has banished the evil, and I have gone to sleep again, peaceful and happy.

A friend is "very doubtful about" the above, on the ground that it "smacks of abracadabra". But while certain ritual practices may smack in high measure of routine and superstition, that is not to prove them, essentially and in all cases, absurd or valueless.]

When I was a youth, newly married, I lived with my father-in-law, a watchmaker. I desired greatly to visit a famous Rabbi, but had no money for the journey. I said to my father-in-law: "If you will give me a few gulden, I will repair the little watch with which you have had no patience to bother." He agreed, and I took apart the watch to discover the cause of the difficulty. I soon saw that nothing was lacking, but that a tiny hairspring was twisted. This I soon made straight, placed everything together and the watch began to keep time once more. Does this not teach that a slight twist of the heart often halts the normal moral feeling? A little adjustment and the heart beats properly again.

RABBI YERAHMIEL OF PZHYSHA

> What is sin but a little
> Error and fault that is soon forgiven? but mercy is not a sin,
> Nor pity nor love nor kind forgiveness. O! if I have sinned,
> Forgive and pity me! O unfold thy veil in mercy and love!

BLAKE

> Injury the Lord heals, but Vengeance cannot be healed . . .
> [For] Vengeance is the destroyer of Grace and Repentance in the bosom
> Of the Injurer, in which the Divine Lamb is cruelly slain.

BLAKE

[The Divine Lamb is Christ, who is in every soul, prompting it to repent of its sins. Vengeance on a man for doing injury may destroy the Christ in him, for, by hardening his heart, it may prevent him from repenting.]

Man must and will have some religion; if he has not the religion of Jesus, he will have the religion of Satan, and will erect the synagogue of Satan, . . . destroying all who do not worship Satan under the name of God. Will any one say: Where are those who worship Satan under the name of God? Where are they? Listen! Every religion that preaches vengeance for sin is the religion of the Enemy and Avenger, and not of the Forgiver of Sin, and their God is Satan, named by the Divine Name. . . .

BLAKE

Love bade me welcome: yet my soul drew back
    Guiltie of dust and sinne.
But quick-ey'd Love, observing me grow slack
    From my first entrance in,
Drew nearer to me, sweetly questioning,
    If I lack'd any thing.

'A guest,' I answer'd, 'worthy to be here':
    Love said, 'You shall be he.'
'I the unkinde, ungratefull? Ah my deare,
    I cannot look on thee.'
Love took my hand, and smiling did reply,
    'Who made the eyes but I?'

'Truth Lord, but I have marr'd them: let my shame
    Go where it doth deserve.'
'And know you not,' sayes Love, 'who bore the blame?'
    'My deare, then I will serve.'
'You must sit down,' sayes Love, 'and taste my meat':
    So I did sit and eat.
                                    471 GEORGE HERBERT

[By Love is meant God or Christ. The words "Who bore the blame?" refer to the doctrine that Jesus took the burden of men's sins on His own shoulders. This doctrine is meaningful only in the sense that readiness to be punished unjustly for another's sin, as a means of relieving that other of punishment, is a mark of perfect love: and that the other, through the example of such sacrifice, becomes more loving himself and so is freed from the burden of sin.

In the last three lines the soul says that it will *serve* at the meal: but Love insists on its being His guest.]

Bad I am, but yet thy child.
Father, be thou reconciled,
Spare thou me, since I see
With thy might that thou art mild.
I have life before me still
And thy purpose to fulfil;
Yea a debt to pay thee yet:
Help me, sir, and so I will.

GERARD MANLEY HOPKINS
(from an unfinished prayer)

§ 2

THE PRODIGAL SON

Then drew near unto him all the publicans and sinners for to hear him.

And the Pharisees and scribes murmured, saying, This man receiveth sinners, and eateth with them.

And he spake this parable unto them, saying,

What man of you, having an hundred sheep, if he lose one of them, doth not leave the ninety and nine in the wilderness, and go after that which is lost, until he find it?

And when he hath found it, he layeth it on his shoulders, rejoicing.

And when he cometh home, he calleth together his friends and neighbours, saying unto them, Rejoice with me; for I have found my sheep which was lost.

I say unto you, that likewise joy shall be in heaven over one sinner that repenteth, more than over ninety and nine just persons, which need no repentance.

Either what woman having ten pieces of silver, if she lose one piece, doth not light a candle, and sweep the house, and seek diligently till she find it?

And when she hath found it, she calleth her friends and her neighbours together, saying, Rejoice with me; for I have found the piece which I had lost.

Likewise, I say unto you, there is joy in the angels of God over one sinner that repenteth.

And he said, A certain man had two sons:

And the younger of them said to his father, Father, give me the portion of goods that falleth to me. And he divided unto them his living.

And not many days after the younger son gathered all together, and took his journey into a far country, and there wasted his substance with riotous living.

And when he had spent all, there arose a mighty famine in that land; and he began to be in want.

And he went and joined himself to a citizen of that country; and he sent him into his fields to feed swine

And he would fain have filled his belly with the husks that the swine did eat: and no man gave unto him.

And when he came to himself, he said, How many hired servants of my father's have bread enough and to spare, and I perish with hunger!

I will arise and go to my father, and will say unto him, Father, I have sinned against heaven, and before thee,

And am no more worthy to be called thy son: make me as one of thy hired servants.

And he arose, and came to his father. But when he was yet a great way off, his father saw him, and had compassion, and ran, and fell on his neck, and kissed him.

And the son said unto him, Father, I have sinned against heaven, and in thy sight, and am no more worthy to be called thy son.

But the father said to his servants, Bring forth the best robe, and put it on him; and put a ring on his hand, and shoes on his feet:

And bring hither the fatted calf, and kill it; and let us eat, and be merry:

For this my son was dead, and is alive again; he was lost, and is found. And they began to be merry.

Now his elder son was in the field: and as he came and drew nigh to the house, he heard musick and dancing.

And he called one of the servants, and asked what these things meant.

And he said unto him, Thy brother is come; and thy father hath killed the fatted calf, because he hath received him safe and sound.

And he was angry, and would not go in: therefore came his father out, and intreated him.

And he answering said to his father, Lo, these many years do I serve thee, neither transgressed I at any time thy commandment: and yet thou never gavest me a kid, that I might make merry with my friends:

But as soon as this thy son was come, which hath devoured thy living with harlots, thou hast killed for him the fatted calf.

And he said unto him, Son, thou art ever with me, and all that I have is thine.

It was meet that we should make merry, and be glad: for this thy brother was dead, and is alive again; and was lost, and is found.

ST. LUKE

GO, AND SIN NO MORE

[Jesus, like Socrates, was an uncomfortable sort of person for worldly, respectable citizens to have about them, for he loved turning the old ideas upside down in the interest of truth, and this disturbed things and made people restless. So they tried, time after time, to "tempt" or provoke him into attacking the Mosaic commandments: for then they could prove him a bad Jew out of his own mouth, and might be able to get rid of him. But Jesus was that rarest of creatures, a supremely good man who was also a brilliant politician: and he usually managed to say what he meant without giving his enemies the means to destroy him.]

Jesus went unto the mount of Olives.

And early in the morning he came again into the temple, and all the people came unto him; and he sat down, and taught them.

And the scribes and Pharisees brought |unto him a woman taken in adultery; and when they had set her in the midst,

They say unto him, Master, this woman was taken in adultery, in the very act.

Now Moses in the law commanded us, that such should be stoned: but what sayest thou ?

This they said, tempting him, that they might have to accuse him. But Jesus stooped down, and with his finger wrote on the ground, as though he heard them not.

So when they continued asking him, he lifted up himself, and said unto them, He that is without sin among you, let him first cast a stone at her.

And again he stooped down, and wrote on the ground.

And they which heard it, being convicted by their own conscience, went out one by one, beginning at the eldest, even unto the last: and Jesus was left alone, and the woman standing in the midst.

When Jesus had lifted up himself, and saw none but the woman, he said unto her, Woman, where are those thine accusers ? hath no man condemned thee ?

She said, No man, Lord. And Jesus said unto her, Neither do I condemn thee: go, and sin no more.

ST. JOHN

SECOND PART

III. MAN, FELLOW-WORKER WITH GOD

God can no more do without us than we can do without him.

MEISTER ECKHART

God indeed preserves the ship, but the mariner conducts it into harbour.

ERASMUS

The husbandman gets in the increase, but it was God that gave it.

ERASMUS

If God works a miracle, he does it through Man.

PARACELSUS

Why stand we here trembling around
Calling on God for help, and not ourselves, in whom God dwells,
Stretching a hand to save the falling Man?

BLAKE

When Moses threw the wand into the Red Sea, the sea, quite contrary to the expected miracle, did not divide itself to leave a dry passage for the Jews. Not until the first man had jumped into the sea did the promised miracle happen and the waves recede.

JEWISH LEGEND

[See "The Exodus from Egypt", p. 34]

§ 2

There have always been men and women who have seemed

closer to the divine Will or Purpose than others, and specially able to understand and interpret it. These, if they use their gift, become prophets or poets or artists or musicians: and as the true leaders of mankind, who teach us how life should be lived and uncover for us the beauty and wonder of existence, they may be called, in a superlative sense, "fellow-workers" with God.

Anybody who *can* be this rare or special kind of fellow-worker, in however tiny a way, *should* be: everybody called by God ought to answer "Here am I". And the most unlikely of people have been called: Moses, God's mouthpiece, was a stammerer and Beethoven, God's singer, was deaf. It is as if God were saying "Those who appear to be the poorest may really be the richest, and the most unworthy the most worthy".]

And Moses said unto the Lord, O my Lord, I am not eloquent, neither heretofore, nor since thou hast spoken unto thy servant but I am slow of speech, and of a slow tongue.

And the Lord said unto him, Who hath made man's mouth? or who maketh the dumb, or deaf, or the seeing, or the blind? have not I the Lord?

Now therefore go, and I will be with thy mouth, and teach thee what thou shalt say.

EXODUS

Then answered Amos, and said to Amaziah, I was no prophet, neither was I a prophet's son; but I was an herdman, and a gatherer of sycomore fruit:

And the Lord took me as I followed the flock, and the Lord said unto me, Go, prophesy unto my people Israel.

AMOS

In the year that king Uzziah died I saw also the Lord sitting upon a throne, high and lifted up, and his train filled the temple.

Above it stood the seraphims: each one had six wings; with twain he covered his face, and with twain he covered his feet, and with twain he did fly.

And one cried unto another, and said, Holy, holy, holy, is the Lord of hosts: the whole earth is full of his glory.

And the posts of the door moved at the voice of him that cried, and the house was filled with smoke.

Then said I, Woe is me! for I am undone; because I am a man of unclean lips, and I dwell in the midst of a people of unclean lips: for mine eyes have seen the King, the Lord of hosts.

Then flew one of the seraphims unto me, having a live coal in his hand, which he had taken with the tongs from off the altar:

And he laid it upon my mouth, and said, Lo, this hath touched thy lips; and thine iniquity is taken away, and thy sin purged.

Also I heard the voice of the Lord, saying, Whom shall I send, and who will go for us? Then said I, Here am I; send me.

ISAIAH

[But the trouble with prophets etcetera is that they tend to get puffed up, and, like selfish actors, to "steal the show": they tell people, not what God seems to want, but what *they* want. When this happens they lose their value and become intolerable nuisances.

Christ, in the passage that follows, is warning his disciples against this tendency. He is telling them how to defend themselves if they are "brought before governors and kings" to face trial for preaching his gospel: and what, in these circumstances, he is telling them is what, in all circumstances, he might be telling everyone. "If you are anxious to do God's will," we can imagine him saying, "you mustn't try to think up, all by yourself, some grand way of doing it: you must listen—quietly, humbly, attentively—to the promptings of the voice that is in you, and remember that this voice is no more (and also no less) than a little bit—the bit that happens to have been given to *you*—of a far bigger, a universal Voice. The great thing is to keep yourself ready for God. That is the real way of 'working with Him'. "]

But when they deliver you up, take no thought how or what ye shall speak: for it shall be given you in that same hour what ye shall speak.
For it is not ye that speak, but the Spirit of your Father which speaketh in you.

ST. MATTHEW

The very best and utmost of attainment in this life is to remain still and let God act and speak in thee.

MEISTER ECKHART

So God when He wishes to perform in us, through us, and with us some act of great charity, first proposes it to us by His inspiration, secondly we favour it, thirdly we consent to it.

ST. FRANCIS DE SALES

The compassion that you see in the kindhearted is God's compassion: He has given it to them to protect the helpless.

SRI RAMAKRISHNA

§ 3

God himself awaits man's help and contribution towards Creation.

BERDYAEV

God expects from me a free creative act. My freedom and my creative activity are my obedience to the secret will of God, Who expects from man something much more than what is usually meant when we speak of His will.

BERDYAEV

Without man and without human freedom God cannot and will not establish His Kingdom, which is of necessity human as well as divine in character.

BERDYAEV

God suffers and bleeds when He fails to find in man an answer to His love, when human freedom does not play its part in His work, and when man does not place his creative forces at His disposal.

LÉON BLOY

It is ours to offer what we can, His to supply what we cannot.

ST. JEROME

"The Heavens are the Heavens of the Lord; but the earth hath He given to the children of men". This means: "The Heavens are already heavenly, but the earth hath the Lord given unto men that they may make of it the Heavens."

RABBI HANOKH OF ALEXANDER

And Isaac asked the Eternal: "King of the World! When Thou didst make the light, Thou didst say in Thy Book that the light was good; when Thou didst make the extent of the firmament and the extent of the earth, Thou didst say in Thy Book that they were good; and every herb Thou hast made, and

117

every beast, Thou hast said that they were good; but when Thou hadst made man in Thine image, Thou didst not say in Thy Book that man was good. Wherefore, Lord?" And God answered him: "Because man I have not yet perfected; man is to perfect himself and the world."

EDMOND FLEG (from a Midrashic source)

[See Genesis, Chapter I.]

When man is at one, God is One.

THE ZOHAR

[The ancient Hebrews proclaimed the unity of God in the passage from Deuteronomy, "Hear, O Israel: the Lord our God, the Lord is One", with which this anthology opens: see the verses at the top of page 15 and the comment that follows. But in the Zohar, or Book of Splendour, written much later (probably towards the end of the thirteenth century A.D.), God is said to be One *only* when man is at one: God's unity must itself be bound up with the unity of His creatures, for He embraces everyone and everything. The Zohar, if written in our own century, might have put it as follows: by our hydrogen bombs, and similar iniquities, we mar the perfection of God's unity, and only by renouncing them utterly can we restore it. God Himself, as it were, is in our hands.]

§ 4

[There is a moving example of divine-human co-operation, of God and man working together, in what is perhaps the greatest of all artistic achievements, Beethoven's opera *Fidelio*. I have failed to find an adequate description of it, so must attempt one myself.

Florestan, "a brave fighter for what is true and right", has long been rotting away in the deepest dungeon of a mediaeval fortress near Seville. This awful place is a sort of concentration camp for political prisoners, and Florestan has been flung into it by its governor, Don Pizarro, who hates him for his goodness. People believe that Florestan has suddenly died on a journey, but Leonora, his wife, suspects the truth.

Leonora, disguised as a boy and calling herself Fidelio ("the faithful one"), takes service with the jailer of the fortress, Master Rocco. Shortly afterwards Pizarro gets notice that Don Fernando, the Minister of State (a member of the Government) and a friend of Florestan's, will soon be visiting the fortress on a tour of inspection; and Pizarro, fearing that Florestan will be discovered, resolves to destroy all trace of him. After arranging for a trumpeter to post himself on a neighbouring rampart and to blow a call on his trumpet directly Fernando's carriage is sighted, Pizarro, with a bag of money in his hand, bids Rocco kill Florestan. When Rocco refuses, Pizarro screams, in a terrible rage, that he will do it himself, but that Rocco must first dig a grave in Florestan's cell by clearing away the rubble from an old cistern there. Leonora, who has overheard everything but the prisoner's name, gets permission to go down with Rocco and help him.

And now we are in Florestan's dungeon. The prisoner, chained to a post and half dead of starvation, imagines, in that awful silence and dark, that he sees a bright angel, come to help him: "an angel," he sings with growing rapture, "an angel, Leonora, my wife." But strength fails him: he sinks exhausted to the ground and covers his face with his hands. The real Leonora, still in disguise, enters with Rocco, but cannot see the prisoner's features or know whether they are indeed her husband's. They start to dig the grave: Florestan raises his head and looks towards Leonora: she almost faints as she recognises him. Florestan asks Rocco the governor's name: Rocco tells him: and Florestan, now certain of his fate, begs that Leonora may be sought for in Seville and brought to him. Rocco tells him that this is impossible. Leonora, longing to reveal who she is but unable to do so for fear of ruining her plan, gives Florestan a little bread and wine: "Who is he?", Florestan asks Rocco, and is told "My assistant".

The grave is now finished, and Rocco gives a loud whistle, so that Pizarro may know that all is ready. "Is that the signal for my death?" cries Florestan, and "Oh, my Leonora, shall I never see you again?" Leonora, struggling with her emotions, begs him to be calm: "Never forget, whatever you may hear or see, that there is a Providence over all. Yes, yes, there *is* a Providence!"

Pizarro enters, and tells Rocco to get rid of Fidelio: she, however, only moves to the back of the cell, and then gradually approaches Florestan in the darkness. Pizarro draws a dagger and tries to stab Florestan: Leonora springs between them, protects Florestan with her body, and cries "Kill first his wife!" In that moment of wonder Pizarro hesitates: then, as he rushes forward again with his dagger raised to strike, Leonora draws a small pistol from her bosom and threatens him with it. At that second—but at that very second—a trumpet rings out in the distance, to signify that Don Fernando, the Minister of State, is approaching. As you listen with an emotion I shall make no attempt to describe, you have the feeling, in a perfectly timed performance, that the movement of Leonora's arm has itself actually *produced* the trumpet-call—as indeed, in a manner of speaking, it has.

There are a few seconds of confusion: the trumpet sounds nearer: and Pizarro rushes away, leaving Florestan to ask Leonora "Oh my Leonora, what have you done for me?", and Leonora to reply "Nothing, nothing, my Florestan".

So Florestan is saved: saved, one might dare to say, by God and Leonora. God's trumpet-call could have done nothing without Leonora's pistol: Leonora's pistol could have done nothing without God's trumpet-call. Divine grace and human free-will have co-operated: man has worked in fellowship with God.]

THIRD PART

THE RELATION OF MAN TO MAN

I

We cannot know whether we love God, although there may be strong reasons for thinking so, but there can be no doubt about whether we love our neighbour or no. Be sure that in proportion as you advance in fraternal charity, you are increasing in your love of God, for His Majesty bears so tender an affection for us, that I cannot doubt He will repay our love for others by augmenting, in a thousand different ways, that which we bear for Him.

ST. TERESA

Abou Ben Adhem (may his tribe increase!)
Awoke one night from a deep dream of peace,
And saw, within the moonlight in his room,
Making it rich, and like a lily in bloom,
An angel writing in a book of gold:—
Exceeding peace had made Ben Adhem bold,
And to the presence in the room he said,
    'What writest thou?'—The vision rais'd its head,
And with a look made of all sweet accord,
Answer'd, 'The names of those who love the Lord.'
    'And is mine one?' said Abou. 'Nay, not so,'
Replied the angel. Abou spoke more low,
But cheerly still; and said, 'I pray thee, then,
Write me as one that loves his fellow men.'
    The angel wrote, and vanish'd. The next night
It came again with a great wakening light,
And show'd the names whom love of God had blest,
And lo! Ben Adhem's name led all the rest.

471 LEIGH HUNT

"Thou shalt love thy neighbour as thyself". Why? Because

every human being has a root in the Unity, and to reject the minutest particle of the Unity is to reject it all.

THE BAALSHEM

The man will love his greatest enemy who knows that that very enemy is God Himself.

VIVEKANANDA

Compassion is the chief law of human existence.

DOSTOEVSKY

If I can stop one heart from breaking,
I shall not live in vain;
If I can ease one life the aching,
Or cool one pain,
Or help one fainting robin
Unto his nest again,
I shall not live in vain.

EMILY DICKINSON

At some time in the day or the night think upon and call to mind all who are sick and sorrowful, who suffer affliction and poverty, the pain which prisoners endure who lie heavily fettered with iron.

ANONYMOUS (from the *Ancren Riwle*)

From every human being whose body has been racked by pain; from every human being who has suffered from accident or disease; from every human being drowned, burned, or slain by negligence, there goes up a continually increasing cry louder than the thunder. An awe-inspiring cry dread to listen to, which no one dares listen to, against which ears are stopped by the wax of superstition and the wax of criminal selfishness. . . . These miseries are your doing, because you have mind and thought, and could have prevented them. You can prevent them in the future. You do not even try.

RICHARD JEFFERIES

Our attitude to all men would be Christian if we regarded them as though they were dying, and determined our relation to them in the light of death, both of their death and of our own. A person who is dying calls forth a special kind of feeling. Our attitude to him is at once softened and lifted on to a higher plane. We then can feel compassion for people whom we did not love. But every man is dying, I too am dying and must never forget about death.

BERDYAEV

When I see a hunchback, my back aches for him.

ROMAIN ROLLAND (from *Jean-Christophe*)

How shall we comfort those who weep? By weeping with them.

FATHER YELCHANINOV

II

He who would do good to another, must do it in minute particulars.

General good is the plea of the scoundrel, hypocrite, and flatterer.

BLAKE

[We often come across people who in a large, general sort of way
want to benefit their fellow-men, but are far less ready to assist
a particular man in a particular case. For instance people may give
largely to charity, but pass a beggar in the street—usually
without a thought, which is bad, but occasionally with a mean
sort of thought, which is worse. ("He may have thousands put
away" or "It's probably his own fault" or "Who knows if he's
really blind?"). Or a man may disapprove of the colour-bar, and
yet refuse to let lodgings to a Negro, for fear of "ruining his
property" or "having a lot of unpleasantness with the neighbours" and so on.

This peculiar behaviour, which Blake denounces in the passage
above, is not confined to "other people": we often notice it,
alas, in ourselves.

Now the early Israelites were by no means content with the
simple generality "Thou shalt love thy neighbour as thyself":
their lawgivers proceeded to crystallize it, harden it into a number
of concrete particulars.

Some of the passages that follow merely advise people how to
behave: others regulate the national life by establishing institutions—such as the jubilee—that have the sanction of law.]

When thou cuttest down thine harvest in thy field, and hast
forgot a sheaf in the field, thou shalt not go again to fetch it:
it shall be for the stranger, for the fatherless, and for the widow:
that the Lord thy God may bless thee in all the work of thine
hands.

When thou beatest thine olive tree, thou shalt not go over the boughs again: it shall be for the stranger, for the fatherless, and for the widow.

When thou gatherest the grapes of thy vineyard, thou shalt not glean it afterward: it shall be for the stranger, for the fatherless, and for the widow.

And thou shalt remember that thou wast a bondman in the land of Egypt: therefore I command thee to do this thing.

DEUTERONOMY

And six years thou shalt sow thy land, and shalt gather in the fruits thereof:

But the seventh year thou shalt let it rest and lie still; that the poor of thy people may eat: and what they leave the beasts of the field shall eat. In like manner thou shalt deal with thy vineyard, and with thy oliveyard.

EXODUS

At the end of every seven years thou shalt make a release.

And this is the manner of the release; Every creditor that lendeth ought unto his neighbour shall release it: he shall not exact it of his neighbour, or of his brother; because it is called the Lord's release.

DEUTERONOMY

And ye shall hallow the fiftieth year, and proclaim liberty throughout all the land unto all the inhabitants thereof: it shall be a jubile unto you; and ye shall return every man unto his possession, and ye shall return every man unto his family. . . .

Ye shall not therefore oppress one another; but thou shalt fear thy God: for I am the Lord your God.

LEVITICUS

If there be among you a poor man of one of thy brethren within any of thy gates in thy land which the Lord thy God giveth thee, thou shalt not harden thine heart, nor shut thine hand from thy poor brother:

But thou shalt open thine hand wide unto him, and shalt surely lend him sufficient for his need, in that which he wanteth. . .

Thou shalt surely give him, and thine heart shall not be grieved when thou givest unto him: because that for this thing the Lord thy God shall bless thee in all thy works, and in all that thou puttest thine hand unto.

For the poor shall never cease out of the land: therefore I command thee, saying, Thou shalt open thine hand wide unto thy brother, to thy poor, and to thy needy, in thy land.

And if thy brother, an Hebrew man, or an Hebrew woman, be sold unto thee, and serve thee six years; then in the seventh year thou shalt let him go free from thee.

And when thou sendest him out free from thee, thou shalt not let him go away empty:

Thou shalt furnish him liberally out of thy flock, and out of thy [threshing] floor, and out of thy winepress: of that where-with the Lord thy God hath blessed thee thou shalt give unto him.

And thou shalt remember that thou wast a bondman in the land of Egypt, and the Lord thy God redeemed thee: therefore I command thee this thing to day.

DEUTERONOMY

No man shall take the nether or the upper millstone to pledge: for he taketh a man's life to pledge.

DEUTERONOMY

[A man cannot grind his corn, and therefore cannot live, without both his millstones. So you hold his very life in pawn if you take his millstones as security for a loan: and this you may not do.]

When thou dost lend thy brother any thing, thou shalt not go into his house to fetch his pledge.

Thou shalt stand abroad, and the man to whom thou dost lend shall bring out the pledge abroad unto thee.

DEUTERONOMY

[This is a matter of courtesy or respect, which are often indistinguishable from good morals.]

If thou at all take thy neighbour's raiment to pledge, thou shalt deliver it unto him by that the sun goeth down:

For that is his covering only, it is his raiment for his skin: wherein shall he sleep? and it shall come to pass, when he crieth unto me, that I will hear; for I am gracious.

EXODUS

Thou shalt not lend upon usury to thy brother; usury of money, usury of victuals, usury of any thing that is lent upon usury.

DEUTERONOMY

Thou shalt not see thy brother's ox or his sheep go astray, and hide thyself from them: thou shalt in any case bring them again unto thy brother.

And if thy brother be not nigh unto thee, or if thou know him not, then thou shalt bring it unto thine own house, and it shall be with thee until thy brother seek after it, and thou shalt restore it to him again.

In like manner shalt thou do with his ass; and so shalt thou do with his raiment; and with all lost thing of thy brother's, which he hath lost, and thou hast found, shalt thou do likewise: thou mayest not hide thyself.

DEUTERONOMY

If thou meet thine enemy's ox or his ass going astray, thou shalt surely bring it back to him again.

If thou see the ass of him that hateth thee lying under his burden, and wouldest forbear to help him, thou shalt surely help with him.

EXODUS

Thou shalt not deliver unto his master the servant which is escaped from his master unto thee:

He shall dwell with thee, even among you, in that place which he shall choose in one of thy gates, where it liketh him best: thou shalt not oppress him.

DEUTERONOMY

Thou shalt not oppress an hired servant that is poor and needy, whether he be of thy brethren, or of thy strangers that are in thy land within thy gates:

At his day thou shalt give him his hire, neither shall the sun go down upon it; for he is poor, and setteth his heart upon it: lest he cry against thee unto the Lord, and it be sin unto thee.

DEUTERONOMY

Ye shall not afflict any widow, or fatherless child.

If thou afflict them in any wise, and they cry at all unto me, I will surely hear their cry....

EXODUS

Thou shalt not avenge, nor bear any grudge against the children of thy people, but thou shalt love thy neighbour as thyself: I am the Lord.

LEVITICUS

But the stranger that dwelleth with you shall be unto you as one born among you, and thou shalt love him as thyself; for ye were strangers in the land of Egypt: I am the Lord your God.

LEVITICUS

III

FROM OLD TESTAMENT TO NEW

[The following are key passages in the transition from Old Testament morality of the earlier type to that of Jesus. The Israelites had been commanded, in the old days, to "afflict themselves" by fasting on various occasions, as a token of repentance for their sins or of obedience to the God of Israel as they then understood him. But now, many centuries before Christ, God is already becoming known in men's hearts as a God of universal love: and Isaiah tells them in His name that the "fast", the token of obedience, that He wants from them is not "the affliction of their souls" (especially as, by the very way they fast, they show their selfish rivalry with one another), but a loving compassion for their fellow human beings.

Similarly, says Micah, what God requires of us is not offerings or sacrifices on His altar, but righteousness, mercy and love.

There is a reference in the passage from Micah to "The Redemption of the First-born". In very primitive times the first-born, a man's first baby, was sacrificed to the tribal god: later the practice was to redeem it with a small coin.]

Behold, ye fast for strife and debate, and to smite with the fist of wickedness: ye shall not fast as ye do this day, to make your voice to be heard on high.

Is it such a fast that I have chosen? a day for a man to afflict his soul? is it to bow down his head as a bulrush, and to spread sackcloth and ashes under him? wilt thou call this a fast, and an acceptable day to the Lord?

Is not this the fast that I have chosen? to loose the bands of wickedness, to undo the heavy burdens, and to let the oppressed go free, and that ye break every yoke?

Is it not to deal thy bread to the hungry, and that thou bring the poor that are cast out to thy house? when thou seest the naked, that thou cover him; and that thou hide not thyself from thine own flesh?

Then shall thy light break forth as the morning, and thine health shall spring forth speedily: and thy righteousness shall go before thee; the glory of the Lord shall be thy reward.

Then shalt thou call, and the Lord shall answer; thou shalt cry, and he shall say, Here I am. If thou take away from the midst of thee the yoke, the putting forth of the finger, and speaking vanity;

And if thou draw out thy soul to the hungry, and satisfy the afflicted soul; then shall thy light rise in obscurity, and thy darkness be as the noon day:

And the Lord shall guide thee continually, and satisfy thy soul in drought, and make fat thy bones: and thou shalt be like a watered garden, and like a spring of water, whose waters fail not.

471   ISAIAH

Wherewith shall I come before the Lord, and bow myself before the high God? shall I come before him with burnt offerings, with calves of a year old?

Will the Lord be pleased with thousands of rams, or with ten thousands of rivers of oil? shall I give my firstborn for my transgression, the fruit of my body for the sin of my soul?

He hath shewed thee, O man, what is good; and what doth the Lord require of thee, but to do justly, and to love mercy and to walk humbly with thy God?

MICAH

IV

THE NEW TESTAMENT

Then one of them, which was a lawyer, asked him a question, tempting him, and saying,

Master, which is the great commandment in the law?

Jesus said unto him, Thou shalt love the Lord thy God with all thy heart, and with all thy soul, and with all thy mind.

This is the first and great commandment.

And the second is like unto it, Thou shalt love thy neighbour as thyself.

On these two commandments hang all the law and the prophets.

ST. MATTHEW

Then came Peter to him, and said, Lord, how oft shall my brother sin against me, and I forgive him? till seven times?

Jesus saith unto him, I say not unto thee, Until seven times: but, Until seventy times seven.

ST. MATTHEW

And, behold, a certain lawyer stood up, and tempted him, saying, Master, what shall I do to inherit eternal life?

He said unto him, What is written in the law? how readest thou?

And he answering said, Thou shalt love the Lord thy God with all thy heart, and with all thy soul, and with all thy strength, and with all thy mind; and thy neighbour as thyself.

And he said unto him, Thou hast answered right: this do, and thou shalt live.

But he, willing to justify himself, said unto Jesus, And who is my neighbour?

And Jesus answering said, A certain man went down from

Jerusalem to Jericho, and fell among thieves, which stripped him of his raiment, and wounded him, and departed, leaving him half dead.

And by chance there came down a certain priest that way: and when he saw him, he passed by on the other side.

And likewise a Levite, when he was at the place, came and looked on him, and passed by on the other side.

But a certain Samaritan, as he journeyed, came where he was: and when he saw him, he had compassion on him,

And went to him, and bound up his wounds, pouring in oil and wine, and set him on his own beast, and brought him to an inn, and took care of him.

And on the morrow when he departed, he took out two pence, and gave them to the host, and said unto him, Take care of him; and whatsoever thou spendest more, when I come again, I will repay thee.

Which now of these three, thinkest thou, was neighbour unto him that fell among the thieves?

And he said, He that shewed mercy on him. Then said Jesus unto him, Go, and do thou likewise.

ST. LUKE

[The Levites were what nowadays might be called assistant priests. The Samaritans were a religious sect with headquarters in and around Samaria, a city in Palestine. They claimed to be more Jewish than the Jews, towards whom they felt hostility and contempt: and the Jews felt the same towards them. The man who fell among thieves was of course a Jew.]

And one of the Pharisees desired him that he would eat with him. And he went into the Pharisee's house, and sat down to meat.

And, behold, a woman in the city, which was a sinner, when she knew that Jesus sat at meat in the Pharisee's house, brought an alabaster box of ointment.

And stood at his feet behind him weeping, and began to wash his feet with tears, and did wipe them with the hairs of her head, and kissed his feet, and anointed them with the ointment.

Now when the Pharisee which had bidden him saw it, he spake within himself, saying, This man, if he were a prophet, would have known who and what manner of woman this is that toucheth him: for she is a sinner.

And Jesus answering said unto him, Simon, I have somewhat to say unto thee. And he saith, Master, say on.

There was a certain creditor which had two debtors: the one owed five hundred pence, and the other fifty.

And when they had nothing to pay, he frankly forgave them both. Tell me therefore, which of them will love him most?

Simon answered and said, I suppose that he, to whom he forgave most. And he said unto him, Thou hast rightly judged.

And he turned to the woman, and said unto Simon, Seest thou this woman? I entered into thine house, thou gavest me no water for my feet: but she hath washed my feet with tears, and wiped them with the hairs of her head.

Thou gavest me no kiss: but this woman since the time I came in hath not ceased to kiss my feet.

My head with oil thou didst not anoint: but this woman hath anointed my feet with ointment.

Wherefore I say unto thee, Her sins, which are many, are forgiven; for she loved much: but to whom little is forgiven, the same loveth little.

And he said unto her, Thy sins are forgiven.

ST. LUKE

[Christ is speaking in the following passage of the Last Judgment. The King is Christ himself. See 301.]

Then shall the King say unto them on his right hand, Come, ye blessed of my Father, inherit the kingdom prepared for you from the foundation of the world:

For I was an hungred, and ye gave me meat: I was thirsty and ye gave me drink: I was a stranger, and ye took me in:

Naked, and ye clothed me: I was sick, and ye visited me: I was in prison, and ye came unto me.

Then shall the righteous answer him, saying, Lord, when saw we thee an hungred, and fed thee? or thirsty, and gave thee drink?

When saw we thee a stranger, and took thee in? or naked, and clothed thee?

Or when saw we thee sick, or in prison, and came unto thee?

And the King shall answer and say unto them, Verily I say unto you, Inasmuch as ye have done it unto one of the least of these my brethren, ye have done it unto me.

ST. MATTHEW

He riseth from supper, and laid aside his garments; and took a towel, and girded himself.

After that he poureth water into a bason, and began to wash the disciples' feet, and to wipe them with the towel wherewith he was girded . . .

Peter saith unto him, Thou shalt never wash my feet. Jesus answered him, If I wash thee not, thou hast no part with me.

Simon Peter saith unto him, Lord, not my feet only, but also my hands and my head . . .

So after he had washed their feet, and had taken his garments, and was set down again, he said unto them, Know ye what I have done to you?

Ye call me Master and Lord: and ye say well; for so I am.

If I then, your Lord and Master, have washed your feet; ye also ought to wash one another's feet.

ST. JOHN

And when they were come to the place, which is called Calvary, there they crucified him, and the malefactors, one on the right hand, and the other on the left.

137

Then said Jesus, Father, forgive them; for they know not what they do. And they parted his raiment, and cast lots.

ST. LUKE

Though I speak with the tongues of men and of angels, and have not charity, I am become as sounding brass, or a tinkling cymbal.

And though I have the gift of prophecy, and understand all mysteries, and all knowledge; and though I have all faith, so that I could remove mountains, and have not charity, I am nothing.

And though I bestow all my goods to feed the poor, and though I give my body to be burned, and have not charity, it profiteth me nothing.

Charity suffereth long, and is kind; charity envieth not; charity vaunteth not itself, is not puffed up,

Doth not behave itself unseemly, seeketh not her own, is not easily provoked, thinketh no evil;

Rejoiceth not in iniquity, but rejoiceth in the truth;

Beareth all things, believeth all things, hopeth all things, endureth all things . . .

And now abideth faith, hope, charity, these three; but the greatest of these is charity.

I CORINTHIANS

Recompense to no man evil for evil. Provide things honest in the sight of all men.

If it be possible, as much as lieth in you, live peaceably with all men.

Dearly beloved, avenge not yourselves, but rather give place unto wrath: for it is written, Vengeance is mine; I will repay, saith the Lord.

Therefore if thine enemy hunger, feed him; if he thirst, give him drink: for in so doing thou shalt heap coals of fire on his head.

Be not overcome of evil, but overcome evil with good.

471   ROMANS

Owe no man any thing, but to love one another: for he that loveth another hath fulfilled the law.

For this, Thou shalt not commit adultery, Thou shalt not kill, Thou shalt not steal, Thou shalt not bear false witness, Thou shalt not covet; and if there be any other commandment, it is briefly comprehended in this saying, namely, Thou shalt love thy neighbour as thyself.

Love worketh no ill to his neighbour: therefore love is the fulfilling of the law.

ROMANS

[The aim of "the law" (the Ten Commandments etcetera) is to prevent a man *negatively* or from the outside—by what he's forbidden to do—from injuring his neighbour. But if you love your neighbour as yourself, you cannot *want*, by the very fact of your love, to do him any injury: so everything the law requires of you is achieved *positively*, or from the inside, by this one thing, love.]

Where there is neither Greek nor Jew, circumcision nor uncircumcision, Barbarian, Scythian, bond nor free: but Christ is all, and in all.

Put on therefore, as the elect of God, holy and beloved, bowels of mercies, kindness, humbleness of mind, meekness, longsuffering;

Forbearing one another, and forgiving one another, if any man have a quarrel against any: even as Christ forgave you, so also do ye.

And above all these things put on charity, which is the bond of perfectness.

471   COLOSSIANS

Whosoever hateth his brother is a murderer: and ye know that no murderer hath eternal life abiding in him.

I JOHN

If a man say, I love God, and hateth his brother, he is a liar: for he that loveth not his brother whom he hath seen, how can he love God whom he hath not seen?

I JOHN

And we have known and believed the love that God hath in us. God is love; and he that dwelleth in love dwelleth in God, and God in him....

There is no fear in love; but perfect love casteth out fear ...

I JOHN

[All fear, when honestly examined, turns out to be fear for ourselves. When we fear, for example, that a loved one may have to suffer or die, any fear that may torture us—fear, not sympathy or sorrow, which is something far different—is fear that we may have to suffer with the other's suffering or may be left lonely. But if we really love someone we cannot fear for ourselves: we think only of the welfare of the man or woman or child whom we love.

And if we lose ourselves in the Whole, and believe that God is love, we cannot fear either for ourselves or for the Whole: there is no "we" now to do the fearing, and love cannot fear for itself, being nothing but love. And though we must struggle unremittingly (for instance) against the destruction of our world by human folly, we shall no longer fear it: to fear it, as a matter of fact, would be to hamper our struggle.

All this, of course, is a counsel of perfection: no one of us, and I, so it happens, least of all, can be sure of controlling, in all circumstances, our animal instincts. But we can try to control them as far as possible.]

For every kind of beasts, and of birds, and of serpents, and of things in the sea, is tamed, and hath been tamed of mankind:

But the tongue can no man tame; it is an unruly evil, full of deadly poison.

Therewith bless we God, even the Father; and therewith curse we men, which are made after the similitude of God.

Out of the same mouth proceedeth blessing and cursing. My brethren, these things ought not so to be.

Doth a fountain send forth at the same place sweet water and bitter?

Can the fig tree, my brethren, bear olive berries? either a vine, figs? so can no fountain both yield salt water and fresh.

Who is a wise man and endued with knowledge among you? let him shew out of a good conversation his works with meekness of wisdom.

But if ye have bitter envying and strife in your hearts, glory not, and lie not against the truth.

This wisdom descendeth not from above, but is earthly, sensual, devilish.

For where envying and strife is, there is confusion and every evil work.

But the wisdom that is from above is first pure, then peaceable, gentle, and easy to be intreated, full of mercy and good fruits, without partiality, and without hypocrisy.

And the fruit of righteousness is sown in peace of them that make peace.

471 JAMES

Brethren, if a man be overtaken in a fault, ye, which are spiritual, restore such an one in the spirit of meekness; considering thyself, lest thou also be tempted.

Bear ye one another's burdens, and so fulfil the law of Christ.

GALATIANS

[It has taken a long time for the idea in the first of the above verses to win general acceptance among the thoughtful: namely that a great deal of wrong-doing is a kind of illness which people fall victim to, and which others should help to cure, if they can, in a spirit of humility.]

For I mean not that other men be eased, and ye burdened: But by an equality, that now at this time your abundance may be a supply for their want, that their abundance also may be a supply for your want: that there may be equality ...

II CORINTHIANS

Look not every man on his own things, but every man also on the things of others.

PHILIPPIANS

Pure religion and undefiled before God and the Father is this, To visit the fatherless and widows in their affliction, and to keep himself unspotted from the world.

JAMES

V

This only is charity, to do all, all that we can.

JOHN DONNE

Charity can have no excess till . . . it is more than that which would lay down its life even for an enemy, till it exceeds that which the first Christians practised, when they had all things [in] common; till it exceeds that of St. John, who requires him that has two coats to give to him that has none, and him that has meat to do likewise; till it is loving our poor brethren more than Christ has loved us; till it goes beyond the command of loving our neighbour as we love ourselves . . .

WILLIAM LAW

He who withholds but a pennyworth of worldly goods from his neighbour, knowing him to be in need of it, is a robber in the sight of God. . . . Further I declare, who spares a penny for himself to put it by against a rainy day, thinking, I may need that for to-morrow, is a murderer before God.

MEISTER ECKHART

Moreover, brethren, though highwaymen robbers should with a two-handed saw carve you in pieces limb by limb, yet if the mind of any one of you should be offended thereat, such an one is no follower of my gospel.

THE BUDDHA

[Many saints have put into practice the teaching of Christ and the Buddha, even in the extreme form demanded by Meister Eckhart, and the Buddha himself, just above: they have returned good for evil, they have renounced the use of force, they have trusted and loved everyone. Some of them, as historical figures,

143

are recognized as among the immortal possessions of mankind: like St. Francis of Assisi, whose love of God's creation was so unconditional that he could talk of Brother Death and even of Brother Sin. But at the time, by and large, men "of the world" or "in the street" have found such people crazy and dangerous. What then, asks William James in the following passage, is the truth of the matter?]

No simple answer is possible. . . .

The saint may simply give the universe into the hands of the enemy by his trustfulness. He may by non-resistance prevent his own survival. Herbert Spencer tells us that the perfect man's conduct will appear perfect only when the environment is perfect: to no inferior environment is it suitably adapted. We may paraphrase this by cordially admitting that saintly conduct would be the most perfect conduct conceivable in an environment where all were saints already; but by adding that in an environment where few are saints, and many the exact reverse of saints, it must be ill adapted. We must frankly confess, then, . . . that in the world that actually is, the virtues of sympathy, charity, and non-resistance may be, and often have been, manifested in excess. The powers of darkness have systematically taken advantage of them. . . .

You will agree to this in general, for, in spite of the Gospel, in spite of Quakerism, in spite of Tolstoi, you believe in fighting fire with fire, in shooting down usurpers, locking up thieves, and freezing out vagabonds and swindlers.

And yet you are sure, as I am sure, that were the world confined to these hard-headed, hard-hearted, and hard-fisted methods exclusively, were there no one prompt to help a brother first, and find out afterwards whether he were worthy; no one willing to drown his private wrongs in pity for the wronger's person; no one ready to be duped many a time rather than live always on suspicion; no one glad to treat individuals passionately and impulsively rather than by general rules of prudence; the world would be an infinitely worse place than it is now to live in. The tender grace, not of a day that is dead, but of a day yet to be born somehow, with the golden rule grown natural, would be cut out from the perspective of our imaginations.

The saints, existing in this way, may, with their extravagances of human tenderness, be prophetic. Nay, innumerable times they have proved themselves prophetic. Treating those whom they met, in spite of the past, in spite of all appearances, as worthy, they have stimulated them to *be* worthy, miraculously transformed them by their radiant example. . . .

From this point of view we may admit the human charity which we find in all saints, and the great excess of it which we find in some saints, to be a genuinely creative social force, tending to make real a degree of virtue which it alone is ready to assume as possible. The saints are . . . increasers of goodness. The potentialities of development in human souls are unfathomable. So many who seemed irretrievably hardened have in point of fact been softened, converted, regenerated . . . that we never can be sure in advance of any man that his salvation by the way of love is hopeless. . . Since Christ died for us all without exception, St. Paul said, we must despair of no one. This belief in the essential sacredness of every one expresses itself to-day in all sorts of humane customs and reformatory institutions, and in a growing aversion to the death penalty and to brutality in punishment. The saints, with their extravagance of human tenderness, are the great torch-bearers of this belief. . . . Like the single drops which sparkle in the sun as they are flung far ahead of the advancing edge of a wave-crest or of a flood, they show the way and are forerunners. The world is not yet with them, so they often seem in the midst of the world's affairs to be preposterous. Yet they are impregnators of the world, vivifiers and animators of potentialities of goodness which but for them would lie forever dormant. It is not possible to be quite as mean as we naturally are, when they have passed before us. One fire kindles another; and without that over-trust in human worth which they show, the rest of us would lie in spiritual stagnancy.

Momentarily considered, then, the saint may waste his tenderness and be the dupe and victim of his charitable fever, but the general function of his charity in social evolution is vital and essential. If things are ever to move upward, some one must be ready to take the first step, and assume the risk of it. No one who is not willing to try charity, to try non-resistance as the saint is always willing, can tell whether these methods will or will not succeed. When they do succeed, they are far more powerfully successful than force or worldly prudence. Force destroys enemies; and the best that can be said of prudence is that it keeps what we already have in safety. But non-resistance, when successful, turns enemies into friends; and charity regenerates its objects. These saintly methods are, as I said, creative energies; and genuine saints find in the elevated excitement with which their faith endows them an authority and impressiveness which makes them irresistible in situations where men of shallower nature cannot get on at all without the use of worldly prudence. This practical proof that worldly wisdom can be safely transcended is the saint's magic gift to mankind. Not only does his vision of a better world console us for the generally prevailing prose and barrenness; but even when on the whole we have to confess him ill adapted, he makes some converts, and the environment gets better for his ministry. He is an effective ferment of goodness, a slow transmuter of the earthly into a more heavenly order.

WILLIAM JAMES

VI

A man may love evil by willing evil to his neighbours in three ways: For first, he may hope to be prosperous through his neighbour's degradation, and may therefore hope for that degradation; and again, he may himself fear to lose power, grace, honour, or reputation because of his neighbour's advancement, and may therefore be miserable at that advancement; and again, he may feel himself injured by his neighbour, and wish to be revenged, so that he sets himself to seek out the other's hurt.

DANTE

Lord, I perceive my soul deeply guilty of envy. . . . I had rather thy work were undone than done better by another than by myself! . . . Dispossess me, Lord, of this bad spirit, and turn my envy into holy competition; . . . yea, make other men's gifts to be mine, by making me thankful to thee for them.

★ THOMAS FULLER

The flowers of the earth do not grudge at one another, though one be more beautiful and fuller of virtue than another; but they stand kindly one by another, and enjoy one another's virtue.

BOEHME

Although I am far from Thee, may no one else be far from Thee.

HAFIZ

Lord of the world, I beg of you to redeem Israel. And if you do not want to do that, then redeem the Gentiles.

PRAYER OF RABBI ISRAEL OF KOZNITZ

To reflect that another human being, if at a distance of ten thousand years from the year 1883, would enjoy one hour's more life, in the sense of fulness of life, in consequence of anything I had done in my little span, would be to me a peace of soul.

RICHARD JEFFERIES

Now may every living thing, feeble or strong, omitting none, tall or middle-sized or short, subtle or gross of form, seen or unseen, those dwelling near or far away,—whether they be born or yet unborn—may every living thing be full of bliss.

THE BUDDHA

With everything, whether it is above or below, remote or near, visible or invisible, thou shalt preserve a relation of unlimited love without any animosity or without a desire to kill.

THE BUDDHA

What is a charitable heart? It is the heart of him who burns with pity for all creation—for every human being, every bird, every animal, every demon. He looks at the creatures or remembers them, and his eyes are filled with tears. His heart also is filled with deep compassion and limitless patience; it overflows with tenderness, and cannot bear to see or hear any evil or the least grief endured by the creature.

Therefore he offers his prayer constantly for the dumb creatures and for the enemies of truth and for those who do him harm, that they may be preserved and pardoned. And for the reptiles also he prays with great compassion, which rises without measure from the depths of his heart till he shines again and is glorious like God.

ST. ISAAK OF SYRIA

PROPOSITION: Hatred can never do good.

Proof: We endeavour to destroy the man whom we hate, that is, we endeavour to do something which is bad. Therefore, etc., *q.e.d.* . . .

Corollary I: Envy, derision, contempt, rage, revenge, and the other emotions which have reference to hatred or arise from it, are bad . . .

PROPOSITION: He who lives under the guidance of reason endeavours as much as possible to repay his fellow's hatred, rage, contempt, etc., with love and nobleness.

Proof: All emotions of hatred are bad: and therefore he who lives according to the precepts of reason will endeavour as much as possible to bring it to pass that he is not assailed by emotions of hatred, and consequently he will endeavour to prevent any one else from suffering those emotions. But hatred is increased by reciprocated hatred, and, on the contrary, can be demolished by love in such a way that hatred is transformed into love. Therefore he who lives under the guidance of reason will endeavour to repay another's hatred, etc., with love, that is, nobleness. *Q.e.d.*

Note: He who wishes to revenge injuries by reciprocal hatred will live in misery. But he who endeavours to drive away hatred by means of love, fights with pleasure and confidence: he resists equally one or many men, and scarcely needs at all the help of fortune. Those whom he conquers yield joyfully, not from want of force but increase thereof. All these things follow so clearly from the definitions alone of love and intellect that there is no need for me to point them out.

SPINOZA

The best thing then we can bring to pass, as long as we have no perfect knowledge of our emotions, is to conceive some manner of living aright or certain rules of life, to commit them to memory, and to apply them continuously to the individual things which come in our way frequently in life, so that our imagination may be deeply affected with them and they may be always ready for us. For instance, we placed among the rules of life . . . that hatred must be overcome by love or nobleness, not requited by reciprocated hatred. But in order that this rule may be always ready for us when we need it, we must often think and meditate on the common injuries done to men, and in what manner and according to what method they may best be avoided by nobility of character. For if we unite the image of the injury to the image of this rule, it will always be ready for us . . . when an injury is done to us.

SPINOZA

God is not my father in particular, or any man's father (horrible presumption and madness!), no, he is only father in the sense of father of all, and consequently only my father in so far as he is the father of all. When I hate some one or deny that God is his father—it is not he who loses, but me: for then I have no father.

KIERKEGAARD

The man who truly loves his neighbour, therefore loves also his enemy. . . . We think that it is impossible for a man to love his enemy, alas!, for enemies can hardly bear to look at each other. Oh, well, then close your eyes . . . and remember the commandment that *thou shalt love*, then you love—your enemy? No, then you love your neighbour, for you do not see that he is your enemy.

KIERKEGAARD

The branches of anger and envy are these: hatred, evil suspicion, despising, unreasonable blaming, unkindness, and back-biting against them that despise thee or speak evil of thee or against thee; a gladness of their trouble, and a fury against sinful men and others that will not do as thou thinkest they should do; with a great desire of thine heart under colour of charity and righteousness that they were well punished and chastised for their sin.

★ WALTER HYLTON

Look and bethink thee how Christ loved Judas, who was both His deadly enemy and a sinful villain. How goodly Christ was to him, how benign, how courteous, and how humble to him that He knew damnable. And nevertheless He chose him to be His Apostle, and sent him to preach with the other Apostles. He gave him power to work miracles, He showed to him the same good cheer in word and in deed as He did to the other Apostles, He washed his feet, and preached to him as He did to the other Apostles; He despised him not nor spake any evil of him; and yet though he had done all these he had said but the truth. And more: when Judas took him He kissed him and called him His friend. And all this charity showed Christ to Judas whom he knew to be damnable; in no manner pretending nor flattering, but in truly good love and clean charity.

★★ WALTER HYLTON

[Christ has appeared on earth for a few moments during the terror of the Inquisition. The Grand Inquisitor has had Him flung into prison, and now reviles him bitterly and tells Him he will burn him on the morrow.]

When the Inquisitor ceased speaking he waited some time for his Prisoner to answer him. His silence weighed down upon him. He saw that the Prisoner had listened intently all the time, looking gently in his face and evidently not wishing to reply. The old man longed for Him to say something, however bitter and terrible. But He suddenly approached the old man in silence and softly kissed him on his bloodless aged lips. That was all his answer. The old man shuddered. His lips moved. He went to the door, opened it, and said to Him: "Go, and come no more . . . come not at all, never, never!" And he let Him out into the dark alleys of the town. The Prisoner went away.

DOSTOEVSKY

Never listen to accounts of the frailties of others; and if any-one should complain to you of another, humbly ask him not to speak about him at all.

ST. JOHN OF THE CROSS

Our souls may lose their peace and even disturb other people's if we are always criticising trivial actions which often are not real defects at all, but we construe them wrongly through ignorance of their motives.

ST. TERESA

It is the part of wisdom—and this is true of the Christian life as well as in general—not to be over-exacting of human nature.

FATHER YELCHANINOV

It is not because Angels are holier than men or devils that makes them Angels, but because they do not expect holiness from one another, but from God alone.

BLAKE

It is a moral imperative that we should rise above suspicion and morbid imagination, and never suspect anybody of anything. To suspect evil in others always means being blind to evil in oneself. Not to succumb to suspiciousness and evil imaginings is the first rule of moral and mental hygiene.

BERDYAEV

Believe nothing against another but upon good authority. Nor report what may hurt another, unless it be a greater hurt to others to conceal it.

WILLIAM PENN

When you speak evil of another man, Satan will compel you to be his witness against the object of your words. Would you become Satan's assistant? Blame the fault, not the man.

RABBI PINHAS OF KORETZ

Darts, barbëd arrows, iron-headed spears,
However deep they penetrate the flesh,
May be extracted; but a cutting speech,
That pierces, like a javelin, to the heart,
None can remove; it lies and rankles there.

THE MAHA-BHARATA

Do not despise others because, as it seems to you, they do not possess the virtues you thought they had: they may be pleasing to God for other reasons which you cannot discover.

ST. JOHN OF THE CROSS

No man can justly censure or condemn another, because indeed no man truly knows another. This I perceive in my self; for I am in the dark to all the world, and my nearest friends behold me but in a cloud. Those that know me but superficially, think less of me than I do of my self; those of my neer acquaintance think more; God, who truly knows me, knows that I am nothing . . . Further, no man can judge another, because no man knows himself: for we censure others but as they disagree from what we fancy laudable in our selves, and commend others but for that wherein they seem to consent with us.

★ SIR THOMAS BROWNE

Everything that is unconscious in ourselves we discover in our neighbour, and we treat him accordingly. We no longer subject him to the test of drinking poison; we do not burn him or put screws on him; but we injure him by means of moral verdicts pronounced with the deepest conviction. What we combat in him is usually our own inferior side.

C. G. JUNG

One has only to grow older to become more tolerant. I see no fault that I might not have committed myself.

GOETHE

We all make mistakes, but everyone makes different mistakes.

THE DYING BEETHOVEN

Forgiving love is a possibility only for those who know they are not good, who feel themselves in need of divine mercy, who . . . know that the differences between the good man and the bad man are insignificant in [God's] sight.

REINHOLD NIEBUHR

When your brother sins against you in any way—for instance, if he speaks ill of you—do not be angered against him, but seek to find in him those good qualities which undoubtedly exist in every man, and dwell lovingly on them, despising his evil calumnies concerning you as not worth attention. The gold-diggers do not pay attention to the quality of sand and dirt in the gold-dust, but only look for the grains of gold; and though they are but few, they value this small quantity, and wash it out of heaps of useless sand.

Every person that does any evil is sufficiently punished by the evil he has committed: it would therefore be insane and most inhuman to nourish anger against such a man; it would be the same as to drown a sinking man, or push into the fire a person who is already being devoured by the flame. To such a man, as to one in danger of perishing, we must show double love, and pray fervently to God for him; not judging him, not rejoicing at his misfortune.

★★ JOHN OF CRONSTADT

Almighty God, have mercy on N and N and on all that bear me evil will, and would me harm, and their faults and mine together, by such easy, tender, merciful means as Thine infinite wisdom best can divine, vouchsafe to amend and redress, and make us saved souls in heaven together where we may ever live and love together with thee and thy blessed saints, O glorious Trinity, for the bitter passion of our sweet saviour Christ, amen.

ASCRIBED TO SIR THOMAS MORE

Most merciful and loving Father,
We beseech Thee most humbly, even with all our hearts,
To pour out upon our enemies with bountiful hands what-
soever things Thou knowest may do them good.
And chiefly a sound and uncorrupt mind,
Where-through they may know Thee and love Thee in true
charity and with their whole heart,
And love us, Thy children, for Thy sake.
Let not their first hating of us turn to their harm,
Seeing that we cannot do them good for want of ability.
Lord, we desire their amendment and our own.
Separate them not from us by punishing them,
But join and knot them to us by Thy favourable dealing with
them.
And, seeing we be all ordained to be citizens of the one ever-
lasting city,
Let us begin to enter into that way here already by mutual love,
Which may bring us right forth thither.

AN ELIZABETHAN PRAYER FOR OUR ENEMIES

VII

A brother asked Abbâ Poemen, saying, "Tell me, why it is that when I say I am sorry to a brother who is angry with me I do not see him pleased with me?" The Abbâ said unto him, "Tell me truly: when thou sayest thou art sorry, dost thou think thou art doing it, not because thou hast sinned against him, but because Christ so commanded?" And the brother said unto him "It is even thus." The Abbâ said unto him, "Because of this God doth not permit him to be pleased with thee, and because thou dost not say thou art sorry in fulfilment of thine own desire, but as if thou hadst not sinned against him, but he had sinned against thee."

★ THE PARADISE OF THE FATHERS

[This takes place at a monastery of which Abbâ (Father) Poeman is head: the "brothers" are the monks.]

On one occasion three old men went to the Abbâ, and on one of them rested some small suspicion of evil; and one of them said unto him, "Father, make me a fishing-net," and he replied, "I will not make thee a net." Then another said unto him, "Do us an act of grace, and make us a net, so that we may be able to keep thee in remembrance in our monastery"; and the Abbâ said again, "I am not at leisure to do so." Then the third brother, on whom rested the suspicion of evil, also said unto him, "Father, make me a net which I can possess direct from thy hands"; and the Abbâ answered straightaway, and said unto this man, "I will make one for thee." And afterwards the other two brethren said unto him privately: "Consider how much we entreated thee, and yet thou wouldst not be persuaded to make a net for us, and thou didst say to this man, 'I will make thee one immediately!'" The Abbâ said unto them, "I told you that I would not make one, and ye were not grieved, because I had not the leisure; but if I had not made one for this man, he would have said, 'It was because the Abbâ had heard about my sins that he was unwilling to make a net for me.' "

★ THE PARADISE OF THE FATHERS

An aged man, whom Abraham hospitably invited to his tent, refused to join him in prayer to the one spiritual God. Learning that he was a fire-worshipper, Abraham drove him from his door. That night God appeared to Abraham in a vision and said: "I have borne with that ignorant man for seventy years; could you not have patiently suffered him one night?"

THE TALMUD

I went up to Heaven in a dream and stood at the Gates of Paradise in order to observe the procedure of the Heavenly Tribunal. A learned Rabbi approached and wished to enter. "Day and night," he said, "I studied the Scriptures." "Wait," said the Angel. "We will investigate whether your study was for its own sake or whether it was as a matter of profession or for the sake of honours."

A man famed for his piety next approached. "I constantly fasted," he said. "Wait," said the Angel, "until we have completed our investigation to learn whether your motives were pure."

Then a tavern-keeper drew near. "I kept an open door and fed without charge every poor man who came to my inn," he said.

The Heavenly Portals were opened to him. No investigation was required.

RABBI AARON LIEB OF PRIMISHLAN

A thief in his old age was unable to play his "trade" and was starving. A wealthy man, hearing of his distress, sent him food. Both the rich man and the thief died on the same day. The trial of the magnate occurred first in the Heavenly Court; he was found wanting and sentenced to Purgatory. At the entrance, however, an Angel came hurrying to recall him. He was brought back to the Court and learned that his sentence had been reversed. The thief whom he had aided on earth had stolen the list of his iniquities.

THE YEHUDI

A Rabbi ordered his Warden to gather ten men together to chant Psalms for the recovery of a sick man. When they entered, a friend of the Rabbi exclaimed: "I see among them notorious thieves."

"Excellent," retorted the Rabbi. "When all the Heavenly Gates of Mercy are closed, it requires experts to open them."

HASIDIC STORY

[According to the old Hebrew ritual, a prayer recited by at least ten men was as if recited by the whole of Israel.]

A coachman sought the Rabbi of Berditchev's advice as to whether he should give up his occupation because it interfered with regular attendance at the synagogue.

"Do you carry poor travellers free of charge?" asked the Rabbi.

"Yes," answered the coachman.

"Then you serve the Lord in your occupation just as faithfully as you would by frequenting the synagogue."

HASIDIC STORY

The wife of the Rabbi of Roptchitz said to him: "Your prayer was lengthy to-day. Have you succeeded in bringing it about that the rich should be more generous in their gifts to the poor?"

158

The Rabbi replied: "Half of my prayer I have accomplished. The poor are willing to accept them."

HASIDIC STORY

When Rabbi Levi Yitzhak accepted the call to become Rabbi of Berditchev he stipulated that he should be invited to participate only in those meetings when new regulations were to be decided. Once it was resolved to vote upon a prohibition against house-to-house begging by the poor. It was suggested that a public fund should be substituted to aid them. The Rabbi was called, but he protested, saying: "Why do you summon me upon an old matter?" "But it is new," they said.

"You are mistaken," was his reply. "It is as old as Sodom and Gomorrah, where direct aid to the poor was forbidden. Perhaps they also had a public fund, the object of which was that the wealthy should be freed from the necessity of coming face to face with the poor."

HASIDIC STORY

Rabbi Mendel was accustomed to restrain an angry rebuke until he had investigated the *Shulchan Arukh* to learn whether anger is permissible in the particular instance. But how much genuine anger could he feel after completing his search?

HASIDIC STORY

[The *Shulchan Arukh* is a list of many hundreds of commands and prohibitions incumbent on Jews.]

When you speak evil of another man, Satan will compel you to be his witness against the object of your words. Do you wish to become Satan's assistant?

RABBI PINHAS OF KORETZ

He who gives a penny to a poor man receives six blessings: he who shows his sympathy with the poor man receives eleven blessings.

RABBI NAHMAN OF BRATZLAV

An opponent of Rabbi Shmelke wished to shame him in public. He sent him a flask of very old and strong wine on the day before the Day of Atonement in the hope that he would become drunk from it. The Rabbi tasted a little and perceived the sender's intention. When he was reciting Psalms after the Services, he repeated several times the verse: "By this I know that Thou delightest in me, that mine enemy doth not triumph over me," and translated it thus: "By this I shall know that Thou art pleased with me, that those who wished to disgrace me receive no harm because of me."

HASIDIC STORY

A father complained to the Baalshem that his son had forsaken God. "What, Rabbi, shall I do?"

"Love him more than ever," was the Baalshem's reply.

HASIDIC STORY

A king had a son and a friend. Six times the son sinned against his father, and six times the friend obtained forgiveness for him. The seventh time the friend dared not intercede again. What, then, did the king? He gave his forgiveness without being asked for it.

EDMOND FLEG (from a Midrash)

Rabbi Rafael used always to warn people against applying the measuring-rod in their dealings with one another: A surplus of love is necessary to fill up what is lacking of love in this world.

MARTIN BUBER

[The less love others show us the more we should show them, so as to right the balance. What is wanted, to make the world pleasanter, is the opposite of tit for tat.]

To sin against a fellow-man is worse than to sin against the Creator. The man you harmed may have gone to an unknown place, and you may lose the opportunity to beg his forgiveness. The Lord, however, is everywhere and you can always find Him when you seek Him.

A HASIDIC RABBI

Rabbi Shmelke once had no money to give to a beggar. He ransacked his wife's drawer, took from it a ring and gave it to the destitute man. His wife returned, saw that the drawer was open and that her ring was missing. She raised a hue and cry, and when her husband explained his action she asked him to run after the beggar, since the ring was worth fifty thalers.

The Rabbi ran swiftly in pursuit, and, catching up with the beggar, said: "I have just learned that the ring is worth fifty thalers. Let no one cheat you by giving you less than its value."

HASIDIC STORY

It may sometimes happen that thine own hand inadvertently strikes thee. Wouldst thou take a stick and chastise thy hand for its heedlessness, and thus add to thy pain? It is the same when thy neighbour, whose soul is one with thine, because of insufficient understanding does thee harm: shouldst thou retaliate, it would be thou who wouldst suffer.

RABBI SHMELKE OF NIKOLSBURG

Rabbi Wolf of Zbarazh once saw thieves robbing his home. He remained still and murmured: "I do not wish to cause you to be guilty of a sin, and therefore I make you a gift of everything you take."

In a moment he noticed that they were taking a jar containing medicine. He then approached them and said: "Do not fear to take away whatever you can place in your bag, for I am presenting these things to you as gifts; but, I beg of you, do not consume the contents of the jar you have included. It is medicine and may harm you."

HASIDIC STORY

Love the wicked man. Why? Because he will then love you, and love will unite his soul and yours. As a consequence, inasmuch as you hate wickedness you will transfer your hate to him, thereby causing him to repent and turn from evil to good.

RABBI RAFAEL OF BERSHAD

Cherish no hate for thy brother who offends, because you have not offended like him. If your fellow-man possessed your nature, he might not have sinned. If you possessed his nature, you might have offended as he has done. A man's transgressions depend not entirely upon his free choice, but often upon many other circumstances.

A HASIDIC RABBI

I hate nobody. How could we hate men who believe that they control that which drives them, that driving fate which will hold us as long as this earth has breath?

Believe me, it is hard not to hate—only the realisation of the compulsion behind compulsion in men's lives gives us knowledge and makes us wise and understanding.

ERNST TOLLER

[By "the compulsion" in a man's life Toller means, I take it, those perhaps inescapable influences (such as a bad upbringing)

162

that may explain his shortcomings: and by "the compulsion behind the compulsion" he probably means (to take the case of a bad upbringing) those influences on his father or mother that may explain the bad upbringing. See, on this connection, the passage starting at the bottom of page 227.]

ONE IN THE PUBLIC GALLERY

The Seraph scanned the murderer in the dock—
The motionless Judge, beneath the court-room clock,
The listening jury, warders, counsel, Clerk;
Ay, one and all who shared that deepening dark:
    And then, as I shunned to see,
He turned his burning eyes and looked at me.

WALTER DE LA MARE

VIII

§ 1

He who sustains God's creatures is as though he had created them.

TANHUMA

In every act the good man seeks to save.

MENANDER

Him who destroys one human life, the Scripture regards as if he had destroyed the whole world.

THE TALMUD

The life and destiny of the least of human beings has an absolute meaning in respect of eternity; his life and his destiny are everlasting. For that reason one may not do away with a single human creature and escape punishment; we must consider the divine image and likeness in every one, from the most noble to the most despicable.

BERDYAEV

The Scriptures relate that God bade Abraham offer his son as a burnt-offering, and Abraham prepared to obey. But an angel stopped him and instantly he heeded the angel's voice even though God had not himself revoked his command. What the Scriptures teach us thereby is this: None but God can command us to destroy a man, and if the very smallest angel comes after the command has been given and cautions us: "Lay not thy hand upon . . ." we must obey him.

RABBI MENDEL OF KOSOV

CAPITAL PUNISHMENT

The more attention one gives to the punishment of death, the more he will be inclined to adopt the opinion of Beccaria —that it ought to be disused. Whence originated the prodigal fury with which the punishment of death has been inflicted? It is the effect of an imbecility of soul, which finds in the rapid destruction of convicts the great advantage of having no further occasion to concern oneself about them.

JEREMY BENTHAM

And thou, man, who by these my labours dost look upon the marvellous works of nature, if thou judgest it to be an atrocious act to destroy the same, reflect that it is an infinitely atrocious act to take away the life of man.

LEONARDO DA VINCI

A deep reverence for human life is worth more than a thousand executions in the prevention of murder; and is, in fact, the great security of human life. The law of capital punishment, whilst pretending to support this reverence, does in fact tend to destroy it.

JOHN BRIGHT

Blood demands blood. Does it? The system of compensation might be carried on ad infinitum—an eye for an eye and a tooth for a tooth, as by the old Mosaic Law. Why, because you lose your eye, is that of your opponent to be extracted? Where is the reason for the practice? Knowing that revenge is not only evil but useless we have given it up on minor points. Only to the last we stick firm. I came away from Snow Hill that morning with a disgust for murder, but it was for the murder I saw done.

I pray to Almighty God to cause this disgraceful sin to pass from among us, and to cleanse our land of blood.

THACKERAY (from *On Going to See a Man Hanged*)

So, for instance, during my stay in Paris, the sight of an execution revealed to me the instability of my superstitious belief in progress. When I saw the head part from the body, and how they thumped separately into the box, I understood, not with my mind but with my whole being, that no theory of the reasonableness of our present progress could justify this deed; and that though everybody from the creation of the world, on whatever theory, had held it to be necessary, I knew it to be unnecessary and bad; and therefore the arbiter of what is good and evil is not what people say and do, nor is it progress, but it is my heart and I.

TOLSTOY

Criminals do not die by the hands of the law. They die by the hands of other men.

Assassination on the scaffold is the worst form of assassination, because there it is invested with the approval of society.

It is the deed that teaches, not the name we give it. Murder and capital punishment are not opposites that cancel one another, but similars that breed their kind.

BERNARD SHAW

I think if she had been spared she could have become a very good woman.

HIGH PRISON OFFICER
(*of Mrs. Thompson, who was executed.*)

The final scene must always be a haunting and imperishable memory—the dreadful hooded figure on the scaffold, the thud

166

of the falling drop, the awful plunge into the yawning pit, and the jerk as the rope tautens and sways. No one can leave the slaughter-shed without a deep sense of humiliation, horror and shame.

S. R. GLANVILLE MURRAY, *Prison Chaplain*

Now with the rack and tortures and so on—you suffer terrible pain of course; but then your torture is bodily pain only (although no doubt you have plenty of that) until you die. But *here* I should imagine the most terrible part of the whole punishment is, not the bodily pain at all—but the certain knowledge that in an hour—then in ten minutes, then in half a minute, then now —this very *instant*—your soul must quit your body and that you will no longer be a man—and that this is certain, *certain!* That's the point—the certainty of it. Just that instant when you place your head on the block and hear the iron grate over your head—then—*that* quarter of a second is the most awful of all.

This is not my own fantastical opinion—many people have thought the same; but I feel it so deeply that I'll tell you what I think. I believe that to execute a man for murder is to punish him immeasurably more dreadfully than is equivalent to his crime. A murder by sentence is far more dreadful than a murder committed by a criminal. The man who is attacked by robbers at night, in a dark wood, or anywhere, undoubtedly hopes and hopes that he may yet escape until the very moment of his death. There are plenty of instances of a man running away, or imploring for mercy—at all events hoping on in some degree—even after his throat was cut. But in the case of an execution, that last hope—having which it is so immeasurably less dreadful to die—is taken away from the wretch and *certainty* substituted in its place! There is his sentence, and with it that terrible certainty that he cannot possibly escape death—which, I consider, must be the most dreadful anguish in the world. You may place a soldier before a cannon's mouth in battle, and fire upon him—and he will still hope. But read to that same soldier his death-sentence, and he will either go mad or burst into tears. Who dares to say that any man can suffer this without going mad? No, no! it is an abuse, a shame—it is unnecessary—why should such a thing exist? Doubtless there may be men who have been sentenced, who have suffered this mental anguish for a while and then have been reprieved; perhaps such men may have been able to relate their feelings afterwards. Our Lord Christ spoke of this anguish and dread. No! no! no! No man should be treated so, no man, no man!

DOSTOEVSKY (from *The Idiot*)

To mutilate a human body by hanging a man is to affront the God Who made it.

RASHI

O Lord God our heavenly Father, put love into our hearts, we beseech thee, for all who lie in prison, and especially for those who are under sentence of death; and grant that our love may bring them some measure of relief. Through the infinite merits of Him who bade us not to judge and Himself condemned not, and in whose Suffering on the Cross all men are brothers.

ANONYMOUS

§ 3

CRIMINALS AND PRISONS

Therefore thou art inexcusable, O man, whosoever thou art that judgest: for wherein thou judgest another, thou condemnest thyself; for thou that judgest doest the same things.

ROMANS

Consider too that thou doest many a wrong thing thyself and art much as others are, and if thou dost refrain from certain wrong-doings, yet hast thou a disposition inclinable thereto even supposing that through cowardice or a regard for thy good name or some such base consideration thou dost not actually commit them.

MARCUS AURELIUS

The evil for which we punish others is of the same substance as the evil in our own thinking and feeling.

DAVID ABRAHAMSEN

For no man is voluntarily bad; but the bad become bad by reason of an ill disposition of the body and bad education, things which are hateful to every man and happen to him against his will.

PLATO

Every Criminal [was once] an Infant Love.

BLAKE

When, in 1925, I started my clinical clerkship at the Royal Norwegian University Clinic in Oslo, we were one day making the rounds with our professor. He was at that time in his sixties and we considered him old, although thinking today of my own age I believe he was young. The professor was comfortably seated in a chair while we were standing around listening to him, when we suddenly heard high screams in the corridor. We all rushed out and saw a young fellow running toward us with two men in close pursuit. The frightened young man took refuge behind us. At that point the professor asked what was the matter.

169

The pursuers explained that the young man was a criminal whom they had been trailing for several days. They had seen him walking into the hospital and had orders to take him to the police station.

One of the detectives started to walk behind us to catch the man, but the professor shot out like lightning and placed himself between them. "This man is a criminal," said the detective in a determined voice and made a grab for him. The professor stood straight as a ramrod and retorted, "I have no criminals here, I have only sick people". And pointing, he added one word: "Go!" The detectives looked at each other, turned around and left slowly.

DAVID ABRAHAMSEN

Once admit that if I do something wicked to you we are quits when you do something equally wicked to me, and you are bound to admit also that the two blacks make a white. Our criminal system is an organized attempt to produce white by two blacks. Common sense should doggedly refuse to believe that evil can by abolished by duplicating it.

BERNARD SHAW

The first prison I ever saw had inscribed on it *Cease to do evil: learn to do well*; but as the inscription was on the outside, the prisoners could not read it. It should have been addressed to the self-righteous free spectator in the street, and should have run *All have sinned, and fallen short of the glory of God*.

BERNARD SHAW

Sometimes one would know a man for years in prison and despise him and think that he was not a human being but a brute. And suddenly a moment will come by chance when his soul will suddenly reveal itself in an involuntary outburst, and you see in it such wealth, such feeling, such heart, such a vivid understanding of its own suffering, and of the suffering of others, that your eyes are open and for the first moment you can't believe what you have seen and heard yourself.

DOSTOEVSKY (from *The House of the Dead*)

Rabbi Baroka was walking one day through the crowded market-place of his town, and met Elijah. "Who of all this multitude has the best claim to Heaven?" asked the Rabbi. The prophet pointed to a disreputable, weird-looking creature, a jailer. "That man yonder, because he is considerate to his prisoners."

THE TALMUD

Every Christian must reject with detestation that covert propaganda for cruelty which tries to drive mercy out of the world by calling it names such as "Humanitarianism" and "Sentimentality".

C. S. LEWIS

IX

Be like a tree. The tree gives shade even to him who cuts off its boughs.

SRI CHAITANYA

[The following extracts are taken from the Meditations of the Roman Emperor Marcus Aurelius. They are addressed to himself, and it is always himself that he means when he says "Thou" etcetera.

For decades now I have found these Meditations the best of all bedside books: a convenient edition is published by Heinemann in the Loeb Classics.]

Say to thyself at daybreak: I shall come across the busy-body, the thankless, the overbearing, the treacherous, the envious, the unneighbourly. All this has befallen them because they know not good from evil. But I, in that I have comprehended the nature of the Good that it is beautiful, and the nature of Evil that it is ugly, and the nature of the wrong-doer himself that it is akin to me, not as partaker of the same blood and seed but of intelligence and a morsel of the Divine, can neither be injured by any of them—for no one can involve me in what is debasing —nor can I be angry with my kinsman and hate him. For we have come into being for co-operation, as have the feet, the hands, the eyelids, the rows of upper and lower teeth. Therefore to thwart one another is against Nature; and we do thwart one another by showing resentment and aversion.

.   .   .   .

If a man's armpits are unpleasant, art thou angry with him? If he has foul breath? What would be the use? The man has such a mouth, he has such armpits. Some such effluvium was bound to come from such a source. *But the man has sense*, thou retortest. *With a little attention he could see wherein he offends.*

172

I congratulate thee! Well, thou too hast sense. By a rational attitude, then, in thyself evoke a rational attitude in him, enlighten him, admonish him. If he listen, thou shalt cure him, and have no need of anger.

.   .   .   .

When thou wouldst cheer thine heart, think upon the good qualities of thy associates; as for instance, this one's energy, that one's modesty, the generosity of a third, and some other trait of a fourth. For nothing is so cheering as the images of the virtues mirrored in the characters of those who live with us, and presenting themselves in as great a throng as possible. Have these images then ever before thine eyes.

.   .   .   .

It is a man's especial privilege to love even those who stumble. And this love follows as soon as thou reflectest that they are of kin to thee and that they do wrong involuntarily and through ignorance, and that within a little while both they and thou will be dead; and this, above all, that the man has done thee no hurt; for he has not made thy ruling Reason worse than it was before.

["Ruling Reason" is a translation of the Greek word *hege-monikon*, by which the writer means two things that are really one and the same: namely the "still, small voice" within us which tells us how we ought to behave (or our conscience); and our individual essence, or that which, being different in each of us, makes each of us what we are.]

.   .   .   .

Does a man do thee wrong? Go to and mark what notion of good and evil was his that did the wrong. Once perceive that and thou wilt feel compassion, not surprise or anger. For thou hast still thyself either the same notion of good and evil as he or another not unlike. Thou needst must forgive him then.

But if thy notions of good and evil are no longer such, all the more easily shalt thou be gracious to him that sees awry.

．　　．　　．　　．　　．　　．　　．

If he did wrong, with him lies the evil. But maybe he did no wrong.

．　　．　　．　　．　　．　　．　　．

Enter into every man's ruling Reason, and give every one else an opportunity to enter into thine.

．　　．　　．　　．　　．　　．　　．

If a man makes a slip, enlighten him with loving-kindness, and shew him wherein he hath seen amiss. Failing that, blame thyself or not even thyself.

．　　．　　．　　．　　．　　．　　．

Does another's wrong-doing shock thee? Turn to thyself and bethink thee what similar wrong-doing there is of thine own, such as deeming money to be a good or pleasure or a little cheap fame and the like. For by marking this thou wilt quickly forget thy wrath.

．　　．　　．　　．　　．　　．　　．

A branch cut off from its neighbour branch cannot but be cut off from the whole plant. In the very same way a man severed from one man has fallen away from the fellowship of all men. Now a branch is cut off by others, but a man separates himself from his neighbour by his own agency in hating him or turning his back upon him; and is unaware that he has thereby sundered himself from the whole civic community. But mark the gift of God, who established the law of fellowship. For it is in our power to grow again to the neighbour branch, and again to make perfect the whole. But such a break constantly repeated makes it difficult for the seceding part to unite again and resume its former condition. And in general the branch that from the first has shared in

174

the growth of the tree and lived with its life is not like that which has been cut off and afterwards grafted on to it, as the gardeners are apt to tell you. Be of one bush, but not of one mind.

As those who withstand thy progress along the path of right reason will never be able to turn thee aside from sound action, so let them not wrest thee from a kindly attitude towards them; but keep a watch over thyself in both directions alike, not only in steadfastness of judgment and action but also in gentleness towards those who endeavour to stand in thy path or be in some other way a thorn in thy side. For in fact it is a sign of weakness to be angry with them, no less than to shrink from action and be terrified into surrender. For they that do the one or the other are alike deserters of their post, the one as a coward, the other as estranged from a natural kinsman and friend.

★ MARCUS AURELIUS

X

Mutual Forgiveness of each Vice,
Such are the Gates of Paradise.

BLAKE

And Throughout all Eternity
I forgive you, you forgive me.
As our dear Redeemer said:
"This the Wine & this the Bread."

BLAKE

In Heaven the only Art of living
Is Forgetting & Forgiving . . .

BLAKE

If I should dare to lay my finger on a grain of sand
In way of vengeance, I punish the already punish'd. O whom
Should I pity if I pity not the sinner who is gone astray?

BLAKE

The hand of Vengeance sought the bed
To which the purple tyrant fled;
The iron hand crush'd the tyrant's head,
And became a tyrant in his stead.

Until the tyrant himself relent,
The tyrant who first the black bow bent,
Slaughter shall heap the bloody plain:
Resistance and War is the tyrant's gain.

But the tear of love—and forgiveness sweet,
And submission to death beneath his feet—
The tear shall melt the sword of steel,
And every wound it has made shall heal.

BLAKE

The great secret of morals is love; or a going out of our own nature, and an identification of ourselves with the beautiful which exists in thought, action, or person, not our own. A man, to be greatly good, must imagine intensely and comprehensively; he must put himself in the place of another and of many others; the pains and pleasures of his species must become his own. The great instrument of moral good is the imagination.

SHELLEY

I think of every single person who has been kind to me in my prison life . . . down to the poor thief who, recognising me as we tramped round the yard at Wandsworth, whispered to me in the hoarse prison voice men get from long and compulsory silence: "I am sorry for you; it is harder for the likes of you than it is for the likes of us."

OSCAR WILDE

I was walking along the street . . . I was stopped by a decrepit old beggar.

Bloodshot, tearful eyes, blue lips, coarse rags, festering wounds. . . . Oh, how hideously poverty had eaten into this miserable creature!

He held out to me a red, swollen, filthy hand. He groaned, he mumbled of help.

I began feeling in all my pockets. . . . No purse, no watch, not even a handkerchief. . . . I had taken nothing with me. And the beggar was still waiting . . . and his outstretched hand feebly shook and trembled.

Confused, abashed, I warmly clasped the filthy, shaking hand. . . . "Don't be angry, brother; I have nothing, brother."

The beggar stared at me with his bloodshot eyes; his blue lips smiled; and he in his turn gripped my chilly fingers.

"What of it, brother?" he mumbled; "thanks for this, too. That is a gift too, brother."

I knew that I too had received a gift from my brother.

TURGENEV

XI

[Nothing could offend more against Charity than an attitude of prejudice towards people of a nation, race or colour not our own. This is what the quotations in this short but very important section are about.

In the first of them Isaiah, greatest of the Israelite prophets before Christ, is saying that not only will perfect harmony be established between Egypt, Assyria and Israel—traditional enemies, like the Germans and French—but that God will put Israel third. There can of course be no first, second or third in the Unity: Isaiah was simply protesting, in the vividest language he could find, against the idea that God could put any one nation (even Israel, "His inheritance") above any other. Israel was God's "inheritance" in the sense that He had chosen them: and what He had chosen them for was precisely to proclaim His Unity—a Unity in which there can be neither first nor third.

In the second of the extracts below Sir Thomas Browne, a seventeenth-century physician, denounces an outrage as prevalent, apparently, in his own day as in ours: namely, that of applying some offensive label or other to a whole nation. He gives a pretty selection, and anyone can vary it for himself. "The Jews", for instance, you often hear people say (or it may the Scots) "think of nothing but money": "the Irish" are "wild": "the Italians", when up against it in a battle, "always run away": and a certain nasty habit was at one time described as "the English vice" by Frenchmen and "the French vice" by Englishmen—though in fact only a trifling minority of either people ever practised it. All this may sound very funny: but such nonsense, by poisoning the international atmosphere, can help to ruin the world.

A particularly bad example of it occurred during the second world war. Lord Vansittart, who had been a high Foreign Office official, wrote a pamphlet called *Black Record*, which had an enormous sale and convinced a great number of ignorant people. Going back to a remote period of history, he told us, in effect, that it was overwhelmingly "the Germans" who had been the curse of the world. For with the exception of a very small and ineffective minority, "the Germans" in general had always been butchers or willing acquiescers in butchery: it was always "the Germans", we were led to infer, who had been the aggressors. *Black Record*, in a review of "history" from Julius Cæsar to Hitler, made no single mention of aggressors other than German, except for a passing reference to the Mongols of the thirteenth century: and the European wars of 1864, 1866 and 1870, the near-wars of 1905 and 1911, and the world wars of 1914-1918 and 1939-1945, were simply the culmination of a consistent German aggressiveness that went back to before Christ. "Hitler is the natural and continuous product of a breed which from the dawn of history has been predatory and bellicose". It was in the innate evil of the "German" character—the character of the German people as a whole—that the world's greatest problem consisted.

In the last two sentences of *Black Record*, even the very small and ineffective minority of "good" Germans, previously admitted as a half-hearted matter of form, disappears. *No* German, it seems, can be a Christian. "On the British people has been laid an honour, far greater than *any German* can ever dream, of sharing—in their still, small way—the sacrifice of Hitler's enemy, Christ".

Now every schoolboy will know all this for the nonsense it is. Lord Vansittart, for instance, talked a lot about Frederick the Great: about Napoleon he said not a word. And yet "Since the eleventh century", wrote a British Ambassador, and he was speaking the truth, "France and England have been fighting on the same battlefields. Mostly as enemies, sometimes as allies; always to a certain extent rivals." But every time they fought as enemies, one or other of them must have been the aggressor.

Now Lord Vansittart was neither evil nor stupid: on the contrary, he was clever and good. The fact is that the wickedness of *Black Record* sprang from something of great excellence in its author: passionately hating Nazism, which was proper, he hated the Nazis, which was primitive, saw a Nazi in every German,

179

which was blind, and branded Germany as the everlasting aggressor, which was ludicrous. As for the idea that no German could be a follower of Christ, some of them were following Christ, in the hardest and most practical way, at the very moment he was writing: they were being tortured in prisons and concentration camps for their opposition to "Hitler, Christ's enemy".

I have written at some little length about this, because it is terribly easy, and terribly dangerous for the world, to "fall for" Vansittartism, not about Germany in particular but about foreigners in general. I was once swindled by a Frenchman and, to my horror, caught myself thinking "The French are crooks". The great thing to remember is that such expressions as "the French", "the Germans", "the English", or "the Jews" are meaningless. There is no such thing as "the Jews": there was Rothschild, who thought a lot about money, and Einstein, who thought as little about it as Christ. There is no such thing as "the Germans": there was Hitler, who was ferocious, and Schiller, who was as gentle as a lamb. And so one could go on for ever.]

In that day shall there be a highway out of Egypt to Assyria, and the Assyrian shall come into Egypt, and the Egyptians shall serve with the Assyrians.

In that day shall Israel be the third with Egypt and with Assyria, even a blessing in the midst of the land:

Whom the Lord of hosts shall bless, saying, Blessed be Egypt my people, and Assyria the work of my hands, and Israel mine inheritance.

ISAIAH

There is another offence unto Charity, which no Author hath ever written of, and few take notice of; and that's the reproach, not of whole professions and trades, but of whole nations, wherein by opprobrious epithets we miscall each other, and, by an uncharitable logic, from a disposition in a few conclude a habit in all.

> The mutinous English, the blustering Scots,
> The ruffianly Italians, the mad French,
> The cowardly Rumanians, the thieving Gascons,
> The arrogant Spaniards, the drunken Germans.

St. Paul, that calls the Cretans liars, doth it but indirectly, and upon quotation of their own poet. It is as bloody a thought in one way, as Nero's was in another; for by a word we wound a thousand, and at one blow assassine the honour of a nation.

★ SIR THOMAS BROWNE

The words, "I am proud to be a German" or "I am proud to be a Jew" sounded ineffably stupid to me. As well say, "I am proud to have brown eyes."

Must I then join the ranks of the bigoted and glorify my Jewish blood now, not my German? Pride and love are not the same thing, and if I were asked where I belonged I should answer that a Jewish mother had borne me, that Germany had nourished me, Europe had formed me, my home was the earth, and the world my fatherland.

ERNST TOLLER

Christ showed me that the fifth temptation which deprives me of welfare is the separation we make of our own from other nations. I cannot but believe this, and therefore if in a moment of forgetfulness feelings of enmity towards a man of another nation may arise within me, yet in my calm moments I can no longer fail to acknowledge that feeling to be a false one, and I cannot justify myself, as I used to do, by claiming the superiority of my own people to others, basing this on the errors, cruelties, and barbarities of another nation, nor can I, at the first reminder of this, fail to try to be more friendly to a foreigner than to a compatriot.

But not only do I now know that my separation from other nations is an evil, ruining my welfare, but I also know the temptation that led me into that evil, and I can no longer, as I did formerly, consciously and quietly serve it. I know that that temptation lies in the delusion that my welfare is bound up only with that of the people of my own nation, and not with that of all the peoples of the earth. I now know that my union with other people cannot be severed by a line of frontier and by Government decrees about my belonging to this or that nation. I now know that all men everywhere are equals and brothers. Remembering now all the evil I have done, suffered, and seen, resulting from the enmity of nations, it is clear to me that the cause of it all lay in the gross fraud called patriotism and love of one's country. Remembering my education, I now see that a feeling of hostility to other nations, a feeling of separation from them, was never really natural to me, but that all these evil feelings were artificially inoculated into me by an insane education. I now understand the meaning of the words: Do good to your enemies; behave to them as to your own people. You are all children of one Father; so be like your Father, i.e. do not make distinctions between your own people and other peoples; be the same with them all. I now understand that my welfare is only possible if I acknowledge my unity with all the people of the world without exception. I believe this. And that belief has changed my whole valuation of what is good and evil, lofty and mean. What seemed to me good and lofty—love of fatherland, of one's own people, of one's State, and service of it to the detriment of the welfare of other peoples, the military achievements of men, all this now appears to me repulsive and pitiable. What seemed to me bad and shameful—rejection of fatherland, and cosmopolitanism—now appears to me, on the contrary, good and noble.

TOLSTOY

[We have] to depose ignoble patriotism, and enthrone the noble kind of patriotism which aims at ends that are worthy of the whole of mankind.

ALBERT SCHWEITZER

THE LITTLE BLACK BOY

My mother bore me in the southern wild,
   And I am black; but oh, my soul is white!
White as an angel is the English child,
   But I am black, as if bereaved of light.

My mother taught me underneath a tree,
   And, sitting down before the heat of day,
She took me on her lap and kissed me,
   And, pointing to the East, began to say:

"Look on the rising sun: there God does live,
   And gives His light, and gives His heat away,
And flowers and trees and beasts and men receive
   Comfort in morning, joy in the noonday.

"And we are put on earth a little space,
   That we may learn to bear the beams of love,
And these black bodies and this sunburnt face
   Are but a cloud, and like a shady grove.

"For, when our souls have learned the heat to bear
   The cloud will vanish, we shall hear His voice,
Saying, 'Come out from the grove, My love and care,
   And round My golden tent like lambs rejoice.' "

Thus did my mother say, and kissed me,
   And thus I say to little English boy.
When I from black, and he from white cloud free,
   And round the tent of God like lambs we joy,

I'll shade him from the heat till he can bear
   To lean in joy upon our Father's knee;
And then I'll stand and stroke his silver hair,
   And be like him, and he will then love me.

BLAKE

XII

An Indian greeted a soldier who, at the time of the Indian Mutiny, was about to put a bayonet into his body, with the words, "And thou too art divine".

Quoted by REINHOLD NIEBUHR

The Chief Rabbi of Lyons was a Jewish chaplain to the French forces in the 1914-1918 war. One day a wounded man staggered into a trench and told the Rabbi that a Roman Catholic was on the point of death in no-man's-land, and was begging that his padre should come to him with a crucifix. The padre could not quickly be found. The Jew rapidly improvised a cross, ran out with it into no-man's-land, and was seen to hold it before the dying man's eyes. He was almost immediately shot by a sniper; the bodies of the Catholic and the Jew were found together.

FROM MEMORY

Pte. Clifford Elwood, of High Street, Nantyfyllon, Bridgend, Glamorganshire, and Bugler Robert Hunt, of King Street, Mansfield Woodhouse, Nottinghamshire, both stretcher-bearers, were returning to their lines on the Arakan front with a casualty when they heard a rustling in the bushes and the click of a rifle-bolt.

Out into their path stepped a 6-ft. Japanese with his rifle at the ready. He looked at the two men and the third man they carried on the stretcher, and then without a word or gesture dropped the muzzle of his rifle and stepped back into the jungle.

LEICESTER EVENING MAIL, May 19th, 1944

Mr. and Mrs. J. Gaines, of Fifteenth Avenue, Tong Road, Leeds, have received a letter from their son, Private Harry Gaines, who was wounded in the invasion and is in Worcester

Royal Infirmary on this, his 19th birthday. He has wounds in both legs and the right arm.

He tells of the kindness of a German prisoner in a Red Cross hospital in Normandy in succouring him when he fell wounded: "He carried me for 70 yards to the beach, then looked down at me, smiled, put a cigarette in my mouth, lit it, and put his lighter in my pocket. Then he took off his white shirt, tore it into shreds and dressed my wounds. Having done this, he kissed me, with tears in his eyes, and then walked away to attend to other wounded."

YORKSHIRE EVENING POST, June 13th, 1944

The following is an extract from a letter received from an Austrian Jew now in the British Pioneer Corps in the B.L.A. He is attached to a hospital receiving German wounded. He had been for nine months in the concentration camps of Dachau and Buchenwald: he had been hung by the wrists to a tree and had once nearly died of gangrene, Jews at that time not being allowed medical attention in concentration camps. He also has reason to believe that his old mother was taken to Poland two years ago:

"This is being written in the solitude of a ward in which I am guarding wrecked members of the people that calls itself Lord of Creation. It is so strange a situation that I can hardly describe what I am feeling. Loneliness is perhaps the only word for it. These are men who set out to conquer the world, and they and their kind have done unspeakable things to me and my kind, and I am supposed to hate them with all my strength, and would be right to do so according to recognised standards of human behaviour. But I cannot hate, or is it that in the face of suffering hatred is silent? So it happens that the guard is turned into a nurse, and if a man, from losing too much blood, goes out of his mind and stammers incoherently, I have to talk him to sleep again. And it sometimes happens that men try to hold my hand when I have helped them. That makes me feel lonely.

"Only a few lines. It is midnight, and I am going off duty after having had a busy time with that man who lost so much blood that he went crackers. He had an operation and blood transfusion, and I was the only one able to talk to him. In the end he obeyed my orders instantly with 'Jawohl, Herr Doktor!' Once he said 'Sie sind so ein feiner Mensch'[1] and then 'Sie sind zu mir wie ein Vater.'[2] What shall I make of that? I can only draw one conclusion, which is that I am a terribly bad soldier and I am somehow glad about it."

LEFT NEWS, November 1944

Elizabeth Pilenko came from a wealthy land-owning family in the south of Russia. She went to the Women's University of St. Petersburg and began at the age of eighteen, while still a student, to teach in the evening courses at the great Putilov factory. She published two books of poems and was a close friend of some of the best-known younger Russian poets.

She became a keen socialist revolutionary, and during the years 1914-1917 her life was taken up with revolutionary activities. After the October Revolution she worked with extraordinary skill and audacity in rescuing victims from the Terror. Later she became Mayor of her own home town, working for justice between the Whites and the Reds, both of whom had resorted to violence against their opponents. She was denounced as a Bolshevist, tried and acquitted.

In 1923 she went to Paris. The excesses of the Revolution as it developed revolted her, though she remained to her death a staunch advocate of its principles. She found her way back to religious faith largely under the influence of Serge Bulgakov, who had been a Marxist. She presented herself to the authorities of the Russian Church in Paris and announced that she wished to become a nun, "beginning at once, to-day", and to found a convent. She had her way, but she was not the traditional Russian Orthodox nun. She was accused by some of neglecting

[1] "You are a good man!"   [2] "You are like a father to me."

the long services and the traditional contemplation. "I must go my way," she said. "I am for the suffering people." In the early morning she was at the markets buying cheap food for the people she fed, bringing it back in a sack on her back. She was a familiar figure in the slum, in her poor black habit and her worn-out men's shoes.

The many Russian refugees in France in those days were stateless persons, many of them poverty-stricken, without privilege, without claim on any of the services which the country provided for the poor. Mother Maria worked among the poorest. She discovered that Russians who contracted tuberculosis were lying in a filthy hovel on the banks of the Seine into which the Paris police used to throw those syphilitic wrecks which they picked up along the riverside. With ten francs in her pocket she bought a château and opened a sanatorium.

Then she found that there were hundreds of Russians in lunatic asylums all over Europe. They had just "disappeared" into these institutions, where no questions were asked about them. She raised a public outcry and got many of them released. In those days the Russian congregations in and around Paris were living examples of what the early Christian communities must have been. They were real homes for the poor and the unwanted. Russians living in tenements could find there comfort and friendship. The Churches had their own labour exchanges, clinics and many other services, and the convent, over which Mother Maria presided, was central to their life.

When the German occupation took place Mother Maria summoned her chaplain and told him that she felt that her particular duty was to render all possible assistance to persecuted Jews. She knew that this would mean imprisonment and probably death, and she gave him the option of leaving. He refused. For a month the convent was a haven for Jews. Women and children were hidden within its walls. Money poured in to enable them to escape from France and hundreds were got away. At the end of a month the Gestapo came. Mother Maria was arrested and sent to the concentration camp at Ravensbruck. Her chaplain was sent to Buchenwald, where he died of starvation and overwork.

The story of her life in the camp is only now being pieced together. She was known even to the guards as "that wonderful Russian nun", and it is doubtful whether they had any intention of killing her. She had been there two and a half years when a new block of buildings was erected in the camp, and the prisoners were told that these were to be hot baths [but knew that they were to be gas-chambers]. A day came when a few dozen prisoners from the women's quarters were lined up outside the buildings. One girl became hysterical. Mother Maria, who had not been selected, came up to her. "Don't be frightened," she said. "Look, I shall take your turn," and, in line with the rest, she passed through the doors. It was Good Friday, 1945.

CHRISTIAN NEWS LETTER, April 17th, 1946

XIII

RELIGION AND POLITICS

[The long section now nearing its end is entitled "The Relation of Man to Man": and it is clear that to omit any reference to politics would be to make nonsense of it. On the other hand, any systematic treatment of the subject would be as clearly out of place. All I can do is to gather together a few extracts that illuminate, as vividly as possible, some basic attitudes that are clearly implied in the general outlook of this anthology.

I have printed nothing that touches directly on the difficult question of socialism versus capitalism, for there is room for quite honest differences of opinion here among people who genuinely care for the values I have been trying to unfold. I have myself always believed, and still believe, that the Judaeo-Christian tradition, if true to itself, must reach its climax (so far as mere institutions, mere ways of organizing ourselves, are concerned) in socialism or rather Christian communism: by which I mean, not anything remotely resembling the so-called socialism of Western Labour Parties or the so-called communism of Soviet Russia, but "having all things in common" on the model, more or less, of the early Church, and of the *Kibbutzim*, or collective settlements, in contemporary Israel. Albert Schweitzer, on the other hand, whose whole life has been an exemplification of Christianity, and who is as worthy of attention and respect as anyone now living, has categorically stated (see page 450) that "in the question of possession, the ethic of reverence for life is outspokenly individualist, in the sense that wealth acquired or inherited must be placed at the service of the community, not through any measures taken by society, but through the absolutely free decision of the individual". And few could be so arrogant as to insist that they are certainly right and Schweitzer certainly wrong.

For the rest, here are some indispensables:]

Everything begins in mysticism and ends in politics.

CHARLES PÉGUY

[The beginning is a sense of communion with God or the Whole: the end is the working out of that communion in terms of social and national life.]

Are not Religion and Politics the same thing? Brotherhood is Religion!

BLAKE

It would be atrociously dishonest and wrong to wait for social improvement to follow man's moral perfecting; we must work actively for the reform of society.

BERDYAEV

[Berdyaev is referring to the numerous people who say "First change human nature" (or, alternatively, First make the individual better) "and the evils of society will automatically disappear".]

It is vain to assert the dignity of human beings if we do not strive to transform the conditions that oppress them: strive to deal so that men can live worthily and gain their bread in honour.

★ JACQUES MARITAIN

[It may be thought that, in the now prosperous countries of Britain and America, no one is "oppressed" or lives unworthily or gains his bread otherwise than in honour. It is astonishing that such an idea could enter anyone's head. See the last extract in this section, Tagore's "Money and Power", written decades ago, but now more urgent than ever: and remember that this concentration on money is by no means confined to magnates and millionaires, but affects a large and (in Britain) increasing percentage of the entire population. Consider, also, the growth of violence, of crime, of juvenile delinquency, not to mention the preoccupation with atomic warfare. And remember, finally, that a *majority* of the world's population is living on the verge of starvation, and quite a considerable proportion a long way over it: and that we in Britain and America, who could transform the whole situation by an act of genuine self-sacrifice, do only the very minimum our self-interest appears to demand.]

Wherever there is lost the consciousness that every man is an object of concern for us just because he is a man, civilisation and morals are shaken, and the advance to fully developed inhumanity is only a question of time.

ALBERT SCHWEITZER (1923)

A proneness to think of society as some entity other than its individual members . . . cannot be too severely condemned.

H. D. LEWIS

[What does the word "society" mean? Does it signify something that really *exists* with an independent existence of its own, as John and Mary, Charles and Janet—flesh-and-blood men and women—do really and independently exist? Nothing of the kind. The word "society" is the merest shorthand, a way of indicating, without actually enumerating, all the Charleses and Janets—all the breathing, rejoicing, suffering, *concrete* individuals —who together constitute the society in question.

But we carelessly *think* of "society" as if it really did exist in its own right, the way a person exists: we personalize an abstract expression, and with it a lot of other abstract expressions. We say, for instance, that "society" or "the law", backed by "public opinion", hangs "murderers". But in fact twelve particular jurymen find a particular man guilty of murder, a particular judge sentences him, a particular hangman pinions him, and a particular prison official pulls the lever—all with the passive consent or active approval of particular you's and me's.

We similarly personalize nations or countries, and thereby depersonalize *men*. There is no such thing, in the sense of its being a real living entity, as "England" or "Germany". There are so many Englishmen or Germans, an individual, every one of them, like you and me: these, and the physical territory in which they live, the mountains and valleys and pastures, the cities and townships and villages, of their several homelands. That is all: unless you care to add the non-human creatures, every one of them again individual, and the works of art and historical monuments and ruins—and something we call the national character or maybe the national tradition, something we have to be terribly careful about in our thinking and feeling. For "the national character", also, is devoid of independent existence: it does not float about in a vacuum, divorced from the solid people who partake of or exhibit it. In brief, there is nothing but the physical landscape—and men. Individual men, individual Englishmen or Germans: for to talk about "The English" or "The Germans" is only another way of talking about "England" or "Germany".

Now the fact that we have forgotten all this (or have never realized it, owing to our easy acceptance, from earliest childhood, of labels that personalize abstractions) allows us to commit such unspeakable abominations against our fellow human beings as might otherwise have been impossible. I remember being most vividly aware of this during the recent world war. Night after night that dreadful voice on the air, either coldly matter-of-fact or with the faintest ring of triumph in it, advised us that so many tons of high-explosive or incendiary bombs had been dropped on Germany. Germany! They had been dropped, not on that mythical entity, not on that figment of the imagination or rather of thoughtlessness, but on German men, German women and German children (never mind the cities and houses, the bridges and docks): living torches, forty thousand of them, had been flinging themselves into the canal at Hamburg, fathers and mothers had been spattered with the brains of their children. But that was not how we thought of it, if we thought at all: we were doing it, as the announcer told us, to "Germany". And *we* were not doing it either, for the personalization works both ways: "England" was doing it. I am not suggesting that we consciously, or even unconsciously, adopted this alibi, though there may have been a few who did the one and a few who did the other, and there were a few of course also who understood the reality and refused to hoodwink themselves: what I am saying is that to the majority, taking "Germany" and "England" for granted, the thought of Germans and Englishmen, not to say of one particular, visualized German or of one particular, visualized Englishman, namely the listener himself, simply never occurred. Nor am I concerned with the question of whether the bombing of "Germany" was proper or necessary: I am concerned only to insist that individual men and women living in England did it to individual men and women living in Germany, and vice versa. For that is the dreadful reality: and it is realities, not labels, that matter.]

All our rational investigation and rational planning of the economic and political and social spheres is without meaning unless it is the means to one end—the living of the personal life of community in joy and freedom.

JOHN MACMURRAY

All that can be expected from the most perfect institutions is that they should make it possible for individual excellence to develop itself, not that they should produce the excellent individual. . . . The political life is but the means of the true life.

AMIEL

This "I and mine" causes the whole misery. With the sense of possession comes selfishness, and selfishness brings on misery. Every act of selfishness or thought of selfishness makes us attached to something, and immediately we are made slaves.

VIVEKANANDA

It is an easy thing to talk of patience to the afflicted,
To speak the laws of prudence to the houseless wanderer,
To listen to the hungry raven's cry in the wintry season
When the red blood is fill'd with wine & with the marrow of lambs.
It is an easy thing to laugh at wrathful elements,
To hear the dog howl at the wintry door, the ox in the slaughter house moan;
To see a god on every wind & a blessing on every blast;
To hear sounds of love in the thunder storm that destroys our enemies' house;
To rejoice in the blight that covers his field, & the sickness that cuts off his children,
While our olive & vine sing & laugh round our door, & our children bring fruits and flowers.
Then the groan & the dolor are quite forgotten, & the slave grinding at the mill,
And the captive in chains, & the poor in the prison, & the soldier in the field
When the shatter'd bone hath laid him groaning among the happier dead.
It is an easy thing to rejoice in the tents of prosperity. . . .

BLAKE

The present state of the world calls for a moral and spiritual revolution, revolution in the name of personality, of man, of every single person. This revolution . . . should place the value of human personality above the idols of production, technics, the state, the race or nationality.

BERDYAEV

MONEY AND POWER

In recent centuries a devastating change has come over our mentality with regard to the acquisition of money. Whereas in former ages men treated it with condescension, even with disrespect, now they bend their knees to it. That it should be allowed a sufficiently large place in society, there can be no question; but it becomes an outrage when it occupies those seats which are specially reserved for the immortals, by bribing us, tampering with our moral pride, recruiting the best strength of society in a traitor's campaign against human ideals, thus disguising, with the help of pomp and pageantry, its true insignificance. Such a state of things has come to pass because, with the help of science, the possibilities of profit have suddenly become immoderate. The whole of the human world, throughout its length and breadth, has felt the gravitational pull of a giant planet of greed, with concentric rings of innumerable satellites, causing in our society a marked deviation from the moral orbit. In former times the intellectual and spiritual powers of this earth upheld their dignity of independence and were not giddily rocked on the tides of the money market. But, as in the last fatal stages of disease, this fatal influence of money has got into our brain and affected our heart. Like a usurper, it has occupied the throne of high social ideals, using every means, by menace and threat, to seize upon the right, and, tempted by opportunity, presuming to judge it. It has not only science for its ally, but other forces also that have some semblance of religion, such as nation-worship and the idealising of organised selfishness. Its methods are far-reaching and sure. Like the claws of a tiger's paw, they are softly sheathed. Its massacres are invisible, because they are fundamental, attacking the very roots of life. Its plunder is ruthless behind a scientific system of screens, which have the formal appearance of being open and responsible to inquiries. By whitewashing its stains it keeps its respectability unblemished. It makes a liberal use of falsehood in diplomacy, only feeling embarrassed when its evidence is disclosed by others of the trade.

An unscrupulous system of propaganda paves the way for wide-spread misrepresentation. It works up the crowd psychology through regulated hypnotic doses at repeated intervals, administered in bottles with moral labels upon them of soothing colours. In fact, man has been able to make his pursuit of power easier today by his art of mitigating the obstructive forces that come from the higher region of his humanity. With his cult of power and his idolatry of money he has, in a great measure, reverted to his primitive barbarism.

TAGORE

FOURTH PART

I. ACCEPTANCE

[By the title of this section is meant our acceptance of everything that happens to us, and of everything around us that no human will can change, with tranquillity and, wherever possible, with joy.]

There was a man in the land of Uz, whose name was Job; and that man was perfect and upright, and one that feared God, and eschewed evil.

And there were born unto him seven sons and three daughters.

His substance also was seven thousand sheep, and three thousand camels, and five hundred yoke of oxen, and five hundred she asses, and a very great household; so that this man was the greatest of all the men of the east.

And his sons went and feasted in their houses, every one his day; and sent and called for their three sisters to eat and to drink with them.

And it was so, when the days of their feasting were gone about, that Job sent and sanctified them, and rose up early in the morning, and offered burnt offerings according to the number of them all: for Job said, It may be that my sons have sinned, and cursed God in their hearts. Thus did Job continually.

Now there was a day when the sons of God came to present themselves before the Lord, and Satan came also among them.

And the Lord said unto Satan, Whence comest thou? Then Satan answered the Lord, and said, From going to and fro in the earth, and from walking up and down in it.

And the Lord said unto Satan, Hast thou considered my servant Job, that there is none like him in the earth, a perfect and an upright man, one that feareth God, and escheweth evil?

Then Satan answered the Lord, and said, Doth Job fear God for nought?

Hast not thou made an hedge about him, and about his house, and about all that he hath on every side? thou hast blessed the work of his hands, and his substance is increased in the land.

But put forth thine hand now, and touch all that he hath, and he will curse thee to thy face.

And the Lord said unto Satan, Behold, all that he hath is in thy power; only upon himself put not forth thine hand. So Satan went forth from the presence of the Lord.

And there was a day when his sons and his daughters were eating and drinking wine in their eldest brother's house:

And there came a messenger unto Job, and said, The oxen were plowing, and the asses feeding beside them:

And the Sabeans fell upon them, and took them away; yea, they have slain the servants with the edge of the sword; and I only am escaped alone to tell thee.

While he was yet speaking, there came also another, and said, The fire of God is fallen from heaven, and hath burned up the sheep, and the servants, and consumed them; and I only am escaped alone to tell thee.

While he was yet speaking, there came also another, and said, The Chaldeans made out three bands, and fell upon the camels, and have carried them away, yea, and slain the servants with the edge of the sword; and I only am escaped alone to tell thee.

While he was yet speaking, there came also another, and said, Thy sons and thy daughters were eating and drinking wine in their eldest brother's house:

And, behold, there came a great wind from the wilderness, and smote the four corners of the house, and it fell upon the young men, and they are dead; and I only am escaped alone to tell thee.

Then Job arose, and rent his mantle, and shaved his head, and fell down upon the ground, and worshipped,

And said, Naked came I out of my mother's womb, and naked shall I return thither: the Lord gave, and the Lord hath taken away; blessed be the name of the Lord.

471 JOB

Then cometh Jesus with them unto a place called Gethsemane, and saith unto the disciples, Sit ye here, while I go and pray yonder.

And he took with him Peter and the two sons of Zebedee, and began to be sorrowful and very heavy.

Then saith he unto them, My soul is exceeding sorrowful, even unto death: tarry ye here, and watch with me.

And he went a little farther, and fell on his face, and prayed, saying, O my Father, if it be possible, let this cup pass from me; nevertheless not as I will, but as thou wilt.

And he cometh unto the disciples, and findeth them asleep, and saith unto Peter, What, could ye not watch with me one hour?

Watch and pray, that ye enter not into temptation: the spirit indeed is willing, but the flesh is weak.

He went away again the second time, and prayed, saying, O my Father, if this cup may not pass away from me, except I drink it, thy will be done.

And he came and found them asleep again: for their eyes were heavy.

And he left them, and went away again, and prayed the third time, saying the same words.

Then cometh he to his disciples, and saith unto them, Sleep on now, and take your rest: behold, the hour is at hand. and the Son of man is betrayed into the hands of sinners.

ST. MATTHEW

[The cup that Christ, in this passage, begs that he may not have to drink is his approaching Crucifixion.]

Rabbi Meir sat during the whole of the Sabbath-day in the School instructing the people. During his absence from the house his two sons died, both of them of uncommon beauty and enlightened in the Law. His wife bore them to her bed-chamber, and spread a white covering over their bodies. In the evening Rabbi Meir came home. "Where are my sons?" he asked. "I repeatedly looked round the School, and I did not see them there." She gave him a cup of wine. He praised the Lord at the going out of the Sabbath, drank, and again asked, "Where are my sons?" "They will not be afar off," she said, and placed food before him that he might eat. When he had said grace after the meal, she thus addressed him: "With thy permission, I would ask thee one question." "Ask it then," he replied. "A few days ago a person entrusted some jewels into my custody, and now he demands them of me; should I give them back again?" "This is a question," said the Rabbi, "which my wife should not have thought it necessary to ask. What! wouldst thou hesitate to restore to every one his own?" "No," she replied; "but yet I thought it best not to restore them without acquainting you therewith." She then led him to the chamber, and took the white covering from the dead bodies. "Ah, my sons! my sons!" loudly lamented the father. "My sons! the light of my eyes!" The mother turned away and wept bitterly. At length she took her husband by the hand, and said: "Didst thou not teach me that we must not be reluctant to restore that which was entrusted to our keeping? See—the Lord gave, and the Lord hath taken away; blessed be the name of the Lord!"

★ THE TALMUD

My teacher, the Baalshem, realising that he was on the point of death, exclaimed: "Lord of the Universe, I make Thee a gift of the remaining hours of my life."

RABBI PINHAS OF KORETZ

Rabbi Shmelke and his brother once begged their teacher, the Preacher of Mezeritz, to explain to them the words of the Talmud: "A man must bless God for the evil in the same way that he blesses Him for the good which befalls."

The Preacher replied: "Go to the House of Study, and you will find there a man smoking. He is Rabbi Zusya, and he will explain this to you."

When Rabbi Shmelke and his brother questioned Rabbi Zusya, he laughed and said: "I am surprised that the Rabbi sent you to me. You must go elsewhere, and make your inquiry from one who has suffered tribulations in his lifetime. As for me, I have never experienced anything but good all my days."

But Rabbi Shmelke and his brother knew full well that from

his earliest hour to the present he had endured the most grievous sorrows. Thereupon they understood the meaning of the words of the Talmud, and the reason their Rabbi had sent them to Rabbi Zusya.

HASIDIC STORY

I am content; and what should Providence add more?

SIR THOMAS BROWNE

The children of Israel did not find in the manna all the sweetness and strength they might have found in it; not because the manna did not contain them, but because they longed for other meat.

ST. JOHN OF THE CROSS

[After they had crossed the Red Sea, the children of Israel journeyed through the wilderness, where there was no food: so God sent "manna" to feed them—"a small round thing, as small as hoar frost"—which they found lying on the ground "when the dew was gone up". But they still cried out for the rich food that they had enjoyed in Egypt.]

He who is meek and contented . . . whose mind is filled with
    the fullness of acceptance and of rest;
He who has seen Him and touched Him, he is freed from all
    fear and trouble.

KABIR

Dispose of me according to the wisdom of thy pleasure: thy will be done, though to my own undoing.

★ SIR THOMAS BROWNE

Things are greater than we, and will not comply with *us*; we, who are less than things, must comply with *them*.

BENJAMIN WHICHCOTE

Sin is an attempt to *control* the unalterable laws of everlasting righteousness, goodness and truth, upon which the universe depends.

BENJAMIN WHICHCOTE

Rabbi Bunam was once walking outside the city with some of his disciples. He bent, picked up a speck of sand, looked at it, and put it back exactly where he had found it. "He who does not believe," he said, "that God wants this bit of sand to lie in this particular place, does not believe at all."

HASIDIC STORY

He who is in a state of rebellion cannot receive grace, to use the phrase of which the Church is so fond—so rightly fond, I dare say—for . . . the mood of rebellion closes up the channels of the soul, and shuts out the airs of heaven.

OSCAR WILDE

[I cannot imagine Oscar Wilde meaning that we should sit down and do nothing in the face of injustice, whether to ourselves or to others. On the contrary, we should fight against it to the end. But *how* we fight, that is the question. To fight against it in the spirit of Christ—"nevertheless not as I will, but as thou wilt"—is one thing: to fight against it in a mood of rebellion—in a general fury at the whole scheme of things, or in *personal* resentment at what has happened to *us*, is quite another. Acceptance, in the meaning intended throughout this section, is by no means inconsistent with an unwavering and unending struggle against any wrong that human wills can right: the struggle, indeed, is steadied and strengthened by the acceptance. And apart altogether from that, there are people who rebel, not because wilful injustice is in question, but because they or their dear ones—or their race or their nation—have been somehow unfortunate, or because, to repeat a phrase, they hate the whole scheme of things here below. It is this sort of rebellion, above all, that "shuts out the airs of heaven".]

Keep your heart in peace; let nothing in this world disturb it: all things have an end.

In all circumstances, however hard they may be, we should rejoice, rather than be cast down, that we may not lose the greatest good, the peace and tranquillity of our soul.

If the whole world and all that is in it were thrown into confusion, disquietude on that account would be vanity, because that disquietude would do more harm than good.

To endure all things with a steady and peaceful mind, not only brings with it many blessings to the soul, but also enables us, in the midst of our difficulties, to have a clear judgment about them, and to supply the fitting remedy for them.

★ST. JOHN OF THE CROSS

There lives no man on earth who may always have rest and peace without troubles and crosses, with whom things go always according to his will. There is always something to be suffered here, consider it as you will. And as soon as you are free of one adversity, perhaps two others come in its place. Therefore yield yourself willingly to them, and seek only that true peace of the heart, which none can take away from you, that you may overcome all adversity; the peace that breaks through all adversities and crosses, all oppression, suffering, misery, humiliation, and what more there may be of the like, so that a man may be joyful and patient therein, as were the beloved disciples and followers

of Christ. Now if a man were lovingly to give his whole dili-
gence and might thereto, he would very soon come to know that
true eternal peace which is God Himself, as far as it is possible
to a creature; insomuch that what was bitter to him before
would become sweet, and his heart would remain ever unmoved
among all things.

THEOLOGIA GERMANICA

Disquietude is the greatest evil which happens to the soul
except sin. For as the seditious and internal troubles of a State
ruin it entirely and prevent it from being able to resist the
foreigner, so our heart, being troubled and disquieted in itself,
loses not only the force to maintain the virtues it has acquired,
but more than this, even the means of resisting the temptations
of Satan, who thereupon makes all sorts of efforts to fish, as is
said, in troubled waters.

Disquietude arises from an immoderate desire to be freed
from an evil which we feel, or to gain the good which we hope
for. And yet there is nothing which makes the evil worse and
which removes the good to a greater distance than disquietude
and worry. Birds are caught in nets and snares because when
they find themselves entrapped they struggle and move im-
moderately to escape from it, and in doing so they entangle
themselves so much the more. When, then, you are pressed
with the desire of being freed from some evil, or of attaining
some good, before all things place your spirit in a state of repose and tranquillity, calm your judgment and your will. And
then, quite softly and gently, pursue the end of your desire,
taking in order the means which will be suitable. And when
I say quite softly, I do not wish to say negligently, but without
worry, trouble, and disquietude. Otherwise, in place of giving
effect to your desire, you will spoil everything, and will embarrass yourself very greatly.

★ ST. FRANCIS DE SALES

Nekhlyudov remembered how at Kuzminskoye he had meditated on his life and tried to solve the questions, what he ought
to do, and how he ought to do it; and he remembered how he
had become perplexed in these questions and had been unable
to decide them, so many were the considerations involved in
each. He now put to himself the same questions, and was
astonished how simple it all was. It was simple because he now
took no thought of what would happen to himself—that no
longer even interested him: he was thinking only of what he
ought to do. And strangely enough, while he was not considering his own needs, he knew without any doubt what he ought
to do for others. . . .

The black cloud had moved on till it stood right above him:
lightning lit up the whole courtyard and the thunder sounded
directly overhead. The birds had all ceased singing, the leaves
began to rustle, and the first flaws of the storm-wind reached
the steps where he sat. . . . Nekhlyudov went into the house.
"Yes, yes," he thought. "The work which is carried out by our
life, the whole work, the whole meaning of this work is dark
to me, and cannot be made intelligible. . . . Why should my
friend die, and I be left alive? . . . Why was Katyusha born?
. . . Why did this war come about? Of what use was my subse-
quent dissolute life? To understand all this, to understand the
whole work of the Master is not in my power; but to do his
will, written in my conscience, that is in my power, and that I
know without a doubt. And when I do this, then undoubtedly
I am at peace."

TOLSTOY (from Resurrection)

The important thing, the thing that lies before me, the thing
that I have to do, if the brief remainder of my days is not to be
maimed, marred, and incomplete, is to absorb into my nature
all that has been done to me, to make it part of me, to accept it
without complaint, fear, or reluctance.

OSCAR WILDE

[Oscar Wilde had been one of the most popular figures in London: but almost everyone turned against him and spat at him (in some cases almost literally) after he had been convicted of the offence for which he was imprisoned. He wrote the above in Reading Goal.]

We cannot change anything unless we accept it. Condemnation does not liberate, it oppresses. I am the oppressor of the person I condemn, not his friend and fellow-sufferer. I do not in the least mean to say that we must never pass judgment in the cases of persons whom we desire to help and improve. But if the doctor wishes to help a human being he must be able to accept him as he is. And he can do this in reality only when he has already seen and accepted himself as he is.

Perhaps this sounds very simple, but simple things are always the most difficult. In actual life it requires the greatest discipline to be simple, and the acceptance of oneself is the essence of the moral problem and the epitome of a whole outlook upon life. That I feed the hungry, that I forgive an insult, that I love my enemy in the name of Christ—all these are undoubtedly great virtues. What I do unto the least of my brethren, that I do unto Christ. But what if I should discover that the least amongst them all, the poorest of all the beggars, the most impudent of all the offenders, the very enemy himself—that these are within me, and that I myself stand in need of the alms of my own kindness—that I myself am the enemy who must be loved—what then? As a rule, the Christian's attitude is then reversed; there is no longer any question of love or long-suffering; we . . . condemn and rage against ourselves. . . .

Neurosis is an inner cleavage—the state of being at war with oneself. Everything that accentuates this cleavage makes the patient worse, and everything that mitigates it tends to heal the patient. What drives people to war with themselves is the intuition or the knowledge that they consist of two persons in opposition to one another. The conflict may be between the sensual and the spiritual man ... It is what Faust means when he says: "Two souls, alas, dwell in my breast apart." A neurosis is a dissociation of personality.

Healing may be called a religious problem. In the sphere of social or national relations, the state of suffering may be civil war, and this state is to be cured by the Christian virtue of forgiveness for those who hate us. That which we try with the conviction of good Christians to apply to external situations, we must also apply to the inner state in the treatment of neurosis. This is why modern man has heard enough about guilt and sin. He is sorely enough beset by his own bad conscience, and wants rather to learn how he is to reconcile himself with his own nature—how he is to love the enemy in his own heart ...

C. G. JUNG

[Parts of this may be unclear to some readers. They are explained in the Appendix—page 472.]

Out of evil, much good has come to me. By keeping quiet, repressing nothing, remaining attentive, and, hand in hand with that, by accepting reality—taking things as they are, and not as I wanted them to be—by doing all this, rare knowledge has come to me, and rare powers as well, such as I could never have imagined before. I always thought that, when we accept things, they overpower us in one way or another. Now this is not true at all, and it is only by accepting them that one can define an attitude toward them. So now I intend playing the game of life, being receptive to whatever comes to me, good and bad, sun and shadow that are for ever shifting, and, in this way, also accepting my own nature with its positive and negative sides. Thus everything becomes more alive to me. What a fool I was! How I tried to force everything to go according to my idea!

A PATIENT'S LETTER TO JUNG

[By defining an attitude to "things"—to what is *there* in the world, to what *happens* to us—the writer means, I think, establishing a positive relationship with them, living with them, so that they and we are no longer indifferent or hostile to one another. When we get friendly with some one, we "define our attitude" to him as one of friendship: but we cannot do so until we accept him.]

We receive everything, both life and happiness; but the *manner* in which we receive, this is what is still ours. Let us, then, receive trustfully without shame or anxiety. Let us humbly accept from God even our own nature, and treat it charitably, firmly, intelligently. Not that we are called upon to accept the evil and the disease in us, but let us accept *ourselves* in spite of the evil and the disease.

AMIEL

THE DEAF BEETHOVEN CONDUCTS

Beethoven mounted the conductor's platform, and the orchestra, knowing his deafness, found itself plunged into an anxious excitement, which was only too soon justified; for scarcely had the music begun before its creator offered a bewildering spectacle. At the *piano* passages he sank upon his knee, at the *forte* he leaped up; so that his figure, now shrinking into that of a dwarf, disappeared under the desk, and then stretched up far above it like a giant, his hands and arms working as though, with the beginning of the music, a thousand lives had entered every member. At first this happened without disturbance of the effect of the composition, for the disappearance and appearance of his body coincided with the dying away and swelling of the music; but, all at once, the genius ran ahead of the orchestra, and the composer disappeared at the *forte* passages and appeared again at the *piano*. Now danger was imminent, and, at the critical moment, the first fiddle took the commander's staff and indicated to the orchestra that he alone was to be followed. For a time Beethoven noticed nothing of the change. When he finally observed it a smile came to his lips which, if ever one which kind fate permitted me to see can be called so, deserved to be called "heavenly".

FRANZ WILD (who was present)

"I accept the universe," is reported to have been a favourite utterance of [the American authoress] Margaret Fuller; and when someone repeated this phrase to Thomas Carlyle, his sardonic comment is said to have been: "Gad! she'd better!" At bottom the whole concern of both morality and religion is with the manner of our acceptance of the universe. Do we accept it only in part and grudgingly, or heartily and altogether? Shall our protests against certain things in it be radical and unforgiving, or shall we think that, even with evil, there are ways of living that must lead to good? If we accept the whole, shall we do so as if stunned into submission—as Carlyle would have us—"Gad! we'd better!"—or shall we do so with enthusiastic assent? Morality pure and simple accepts the law of the whole which it finds reigning, so far as to acknowledge and obey it, but it may obey it with the heaviest and coldest heart, and never cease to feel it as a yoke. But for religion, in its strong and fully developed manifestations, the service of the highest never is felt as a yoke. Dull submission is left far behind, and a mood of welcome, which may fill any place on the scale between cheerful serenity and enthusiastic gladness, has taken its place.

WILLIAM JAMES

FOURTH PART

II. MAN'S DIGNITY AND RESPONSIBILITY

Arise, then, free man, stand forth in thy world. It is God's world. It is also thine.

JOSIAH ROYCE

O God, by whom the dignity of human nature was wondrously established.

FROM THE MASS

For thou hast made him a little lower than the angels, and hast crowned him with glory and honour.

FROM PSALM 8

I have said, Ye are gods; and all of you are children of the most High.

FROM PSALM 82

When God made man the innermost heart of the Godhead was put into man.

MEISTER ECKHART

God said to Moses, 'In every place where you find a trace of the feet of man, there am I before you.'

THE MEKILTA

Man was created so that he might lift up the Heavens.

RABBI MENDEL OF KOTZK

For He made Man (as it were) for his Play-fellow.

THOMAS VAUGHAN

THE SIXTH DAY OF CREATION

Now all things were already arrived at their own end: "the heaven and the earth," as Moses says, "were finished," and all things that lie between them; and the particular things were adorned with their appropriate beauty, the heaven with the rays of the stars, the sea and air with the living creatures that swim and fly, and the earth with all varieties of plants and animals, to all which, empowered by the Divine will, it gave birth together; the earth was full, too, of her produce, bringing forth fruits at the same time with flowers; the meadows were full of all that grows therein, and all the mountain ridges, and summits, and every hill-side, and slope, and hollow, were crowned with young grass, and with the varied produce of the trees, just risen from the ground, yet shot up at once into their perfect beauty; and all the beasts that had come into life at God's command were rejoicing, we may suppose, and skipping about, running to and fro in the thickets in herds according to their kind, while every sheltered and shady spot was ringing with the chants of the song-birds. And at sea, we may suppose, the sight to be seen was of the like kind, as it had just settled to quiet and calm in the gathering together of its depths, where havens and harbours spontaneously hollowed out on the coasts made the sea reconciled with the land; and the gentle motion of the waves vied in beauty with the meadows, rippling delicately with light and harmless breezes that skimmed the surface; and all the wealth of creation by land and sea was ready, and none was there to share it.

For not as yet had that great and precious thing, man, come into the world of being; it was not to be looked for that the ruler should appear before the subjects of his rule; but when his dominion was prepared, the next step was that the king should be manifested. When, then, the Maker of all had prepared beforehand, as it were, a royal lodging for the future king (and this was the land, and islands, and sea, and the heaven arching like a roof over them), and when all kinds of wealth had been stored in this palace (and by wealth I mean the whole creation, all that is in plants and trees, and all that has sense, and breath, and life; and if we are to account materials also as wealth—all that for their beauty are reckoned precious in the eyes of men, as gold and silver, and the substances of your jewels which men delight in—having concealed, I say, abundance of all these also in the bosom of the earth as in a royal treasure-house), he thus manifests man in the world, to be the beholder of some of the wonders therein, and the lord of others; that by his enjoyment he might have knowledge of the Giver, and by the beauty and majesty of the things he saw might trace out that power of the Maker which is beyond speech and language.

For this reason man was brought into the world last after the creation, not being rejected to the last as worthless, but as one whom it behoved to be king over his subjects at his very birth. And as a good host does not bring his guest to his house before the preparation of his feast, but, when he has made all due preparation, and decked with their proper adornments his house, his couches, his table, brings his guest home when things suitable for his refreshment are in readiness—in the same manner the rich and munificent Entertainer of our nature, when He had decked the habitation with beauties of every kind, and prepared this great and varied banquet, then introduced man, assigning to him as his task not the acquiring of what was not there, but the enjoyment of the things which were there; and for this reason He gives him as foundations the instincts of a two-fold organization, blending the Divine with the earthy, that by means of both he may be naturally and properly disposed to each enjoyment, enjoying God by means of his more divine nature, and the good things of earth by the sense that is akin to them.

ST. GREGORY OF NYSSA

FROM "ADMIRATION"

The lily and the rosy-train
    Which, scatter'd on the ground,
   Salute the feet which they surround,
Grow for thy sake, O Man; that like a chain
    Or garland they may be
       To deck ev'n thee:
       They all remain
    Thy gems; and bowing down their head
    Their liquid pearl they kindly shed
In tears; as if they meant to wash thy feet,
For joy that they to serve thee are made meet.

The sun doth smile, and looking down
    From the Heav'n doth blush to see
    Himself excellèd here by thee:
Yet frankly doth disperse his beams to crown
    A creature so divine;
      He loves to shine,
      Nor lets a frown
    Eclipse his brow, because he gives
    Light for the use of one that lives
Above himself. Lord! What is Man that he
Is thus admirèd like a Deity!

TRAHERNE

[I have been unable to discover the meaning of "rosy-train", a word, I am told, that occurs nowhere else in English literature. But I suspect that it means a cluster of pink-and-white daisies.]

THE SCRIBE

    What lovely things
      Thy hand hath made:
    The smooth-plumed bird
      In its emerald shade,

The seed of the grass,
　　The speck of stone
Which the wayfaring ant
　　Stirs—and hastes on!

Though I should sit
　　By some tarn in thy hills,
Using its ink
　　As the spirit wills
To write of Earth's wonders,
　　Its live, willed things,
Flit would the ages
　　On soundless wings
Ere unto Z
　　My pen drew nigh;
Leviathan told,
　　And the honey-fly:

And still would remain
　　My wit to try—
My worn reeds broken,
　　The dark tarn dry,
All words forgotten—
　　Thou, Lord, and I.

472　WALTER DE LA MARE

Beloved, now are we the sons of God, and it doth not yet appear what we shall be: but we know that, when he shall appear, we shall be like him; for we shall see him as he is.

I JOHN

§ 2

What is the worst thing that the Evil Inclination can achieve? To make man forget that he is the son of a King.

RABBI SHELOMO OF KARLIN

[The Evil Inclination is a sort of positive anticonscience, a Satanic perversity that automatically demands of us, on occasion, that we should do evil. Aldous Huxley describes it with perfect accuracy in *The Devils of Loudun:* "Every yes begets a corresponding no. . . . Even the well-balanced and the self-controlled are sometimes aware of a paradoxical temptation to do the exact opposite of what they know they ought to do. It is a temptation, very often, to an evil without point or profit, to a gratuitous and, so to say, disinterested outrage against common sense and common decency. Most of these inductive temptations are successfully resisted—most, but by no means all. Every now and then sensible and fundamentally decent people will embark, all of a sudden, on courses of which they themselves are the first to disapprove. In these cases the evil-doer acts as though he were possessed by some entity different from and malignantly hostile to his ordinary self. In fact, he is the victim of a neutral mechanism, which (as not uncommonly happens with machines) has got out of hand and, from being the servant of its possessor, has become his master. . . . Every collection of spiritual letters abounds in references to those frightful temptations against the faith and against chastity, to which the seekers after perfection are peculiarly subject. Good directors point out that such temptations are a normal and almost inevitable feature of the spiritual life and must not be permitted to cause undue distress."]

You may see the sun of Divinity quite clearly through the smoked glass of humanity, but no otherwise.

★ COVENTRY PATMORE

I believe in the human being, mind and flesh; form and soul.

RICHARD JEFFERIES

Not believing in the glory of our own soul is what the Vedanta calls atheism.

VIVEKANANDA

Strange is the vigour in a brave man's soul. The strength of his spirit and his irresistible power, the greatness of his heart and the height of his condition, his mighty confidence and contempt of dangers, his true security and repose in himself, his liberty to dare and do what he pleaseth, his alacrity in the midst of fears, his invincible temper, are advantages which make him master of fortune. His courage fits him for all attempts, makes him serviceable to God and man. . . .

TRAHERNE

> We never know how high we are
>   Till we are called to rise;
> And then, if we are true to plan,
>   Our statures touch the skies.
> The heroism we recite
>   Would be a daily thing,
> Did not ourselves the cubits warp
>   For fear to be a king.

472   EMILY DICKINSON

We carry with us the wonders we seek without us: there is all Africa and her prodigies in us; we are that bold and adventurous piece of Nature, which he that studies wisely learns in a compendious abridgement what others labour at in an endless volume.

★ SIR THOMAS BROWNE

Now for my life, it is a miracle of thirty years, which to relate, were not a history, but a piece of poetry, and would sound to common ears like a fable. . . . Men that look upon my outside, perusing only my condition and fortunes, do err in my altitude; for I am above Atlas's shoulders. There is surely a piece of Divinity in us, something that was before the elements, and owes no homage unto the sun. Nature tells me I am the Image of God, as well as Scripture: he that understands not thus much, hath not his introduction or first lesson, and is yet to begin the alphabet of man.

★ SIR THOMAS BROWNE

Never are we so poor as men want to make us. Always we have the wealth which we are, the beauty which we live.

ERNST TOLLER

O my God, the soul which thou gavest me is pure.

THE HEBREW MORNING SERVICE

Shall men, then, always walk in meekness? Not so, say the Rabbis. There are moments when haughtiness becomes a duty. When the Evil Inclination approaches, whispering in thine ear: "You are unworthy to fulfil the Law," say: "I am worthy."

HASIDIC SAYING

How often has the virtue of obedience and humility been distorted into humility in the face of evil, obedience to evil itself!

BERDYAEV

But you see that the mountain of Christian perfection is extremely high. Ah! my God, you say this: how then shall I be able to climb it? Courage, Philothea! When the little bees begin to take shape, they are called nymphs, and do not know yet how to fly over the flowers, or on the mountains, or on the neighbouring hills to gather honey. But little by little, nourishing themselves with the honey which their mothers have prepared, these little nymphs take wing and become strong, so that afterwards they fly to gather honey through the whole country. It is true that we are still little bees in devotion, we do not know how to climb as we would, which is nothing less than to attain the summit of Christian perfection. But if we begin to take shape by our desires and resolutions, our wings will begin to grow. We must therefore hope that one day we shall be spiritual bees, and shall fly. And meanwhile, let us live on the honey of the precepts which devout people of old have left us in so large quantity, and let us pray God that He will give us feathers like doves that not only shall we be able to fly in the time of the present life, but may also rest in the eternity of the future.

ST. FRANCIS DE SALES

I vow God is omnipotent, but he is impotent to thwart the humble soul with towering aspiration. And where I cannot master God and bend him to my will it is because I fail either in will or meekness. I say, and I would stake my life upon it, that by will a man might pierce a wall of steel, and accordingly we read about St. Peter that on catching sight of Jesus he walked upon the water in his eagerness to meet him.

MEISTER ECKHART

God is omnipotent—but powerless still
To stop my heart from wishing what it will.

ANGELUS SILESIUS

I ought, therefore I can.

KANT

As the appearance of the bow that is in the cloud in the day of rain, so was the appearance of the brightness round about. This was the appearance of the likeness of the glory of the Lord. And when I saw it, I fell upon my face, and I heard a voice of one that spake.

And he said unto me, Son of man, *stand upon thy feet*, and I will speak unto thee.

EZEKIEL

[The italics are mine: God is saying "Don't grovel to me".]

Live unto the dignity of thy nature, and leave it not disputable at last, whether thou hast been a man. Desert not thy title to a Divine particle and union with invisibles. Let true knowledge and virtue tell the lower world thou art a part of the higher. Let thy thoughts be of things which have not entered into the hearts of beasts; think of things long past, and long to come; acquaint thy self with the dancing-places of the stars, and consider the vast expansion beyond them. Ascend unto invisibles; fill thy spirit with spirituals, with the mysteries of faith, the wonders of religion, and thy life with the Honour of God; without which, though giants in wealth and dignity, we are but dwarfs and pygmies in humanity, and may hold a pitiful rank in that triple division of mankind into heroes, men and beasts. For though human souls are said to be equal, yet is there no small inequality in their operations; some maintain the allowable station of men; many are far below it; and some have been so divine, as to approach the pinnacle of their natures, and to be in the dwelling-place of Spirits.

★ SIR THOMAS BROWNE

A man who desires to help others by counsel or deed will refrain from dwelling on men's faults, and will speak but sparingly of human weaknesses. But he will speak at large of man's virtue

224

and power, and the means of perfecting the same, that thus men may endeavour joyously to live, so far as in them lies, after the commandment of reason.

SPINOZA

We should all confess our gratitude for the powers we possess. The wise man should dedicate his sagacity, the eloquent man should devote his excellence of speech to the praise of God in prose and verse; and, in general, the natural philosopher should offer his physics, the moralist his ethics, the artist and the man of science the arts and sciences they know. So, too, the sailor and the pilot will dedicate their favourable voyage, the husbandman his fruitful harvest, the herdsman the increase of his cattle, the doctor the recovery of his patients, the general his victory in fight, and the statesman or the monarch his legal chieftaincy or kingly rule. In a word, he who is no lover of self will regard God as the true cause of all the powers of body and soul, and of all external goods. Let no one, therefore, however humble and insignificant he be, despairing of a better fortune, scruple to become a suppliant of God. Even if he can expect nothing more, let him give thanks to the best of his power for what he has already received. Infinite are the gifts he has: birth, life, nature, soul, sensation, imagination, desire, reason. Reason is a small word, but a most perfect thing, a fragment of the world-soul, or, as for the disciples of the Mosaic philosophy it is more pious to say, a true impression of the Divine Image.

PHILO

The feeling that man is not a mere casual visitor at the palace-gate of the world, but the invited guest whose presence is needed to give the royal banquet its sole meaning, is not confined to any particular sect in India. Let me quote here some poems from a mediaeval poet of Western India—Jnândâs—whose works are nearly forgotten, and have become scarce from the very exquisiteness of their excellence. In the following poem he is addressing God's messenger, who comes to us in the morning light of our childhood, in the dusk of our day's end, and in the night's darkness:

> Messenger, morning brought you, habited in gold.
> After sunset, your song wore a tune of ascetic grey, and then came night.
> Your message was written in bright letters across the black.
> Why is such splendour about you, to lure the heart of one who is nothing?

This is the answer of the messenger:

> Great is the festival hall where you are to be the only guest.
> Therefore the letter to you is written from sky to sky,
> And I, the proud servant, bring the invitation with all ceremony.

And thus the poet knows that the silent rows of stars carry God's own invitation to the individual soul.

472   RABINDRANATH TAGORE

I say no man has ever yet been half devout enough,
None has ever yet adored or worship'd half enough,
None has begun to think how divine he himself is . . .

WALT WHITMAN

In a certain sense, every single human soul has more meaning and value than the whole of history with its empires, its wars and revolutions, its blossoming and fading civilisations.

BERDYAEV

Human personality and individuality written and signed by God on each human countenance—in so extraordinary a way, sometimes, on the face of a great man—is something altogether sacred . . . Every human face is a very special door to Paradise, which cannot possibly be confused with any other, and through which there will never enter but one soul.

LÉON BLOY

The evil of egoism, of a man regarding himself as the centre of everything, does not come from his unduly high opinion of himself, nor from his claim to unconditional importance and immeasurable worth. Since every individual human being can ultimately become perfect and, at any moment here and now, can receive absolute truth into his mind and introduce it into his life, he cannot be valued too highly. Seen rightly, every man has an absolute importance and value; he is irreplaceable, and therefore of immeasurable worth. (Is it not said in the Gospel: What shall a man give in exchange for his soul?) The failure of a man to recognise his own unconditional importance would be equivalent to his abdication from the dignity of man. Here is the root of all error, and the death of all faith. For how can a creature so poor and weak that it has lost faith even in itself, find the courage to believe in anything? No, the basic lie and evil do not come from the individual's self-awareness and self-esteem. They come from his unwillingness to extend to others the recognition of an absolute worth rightly perceived by him in himself, but wrongly refused to others when, seeing himself exclusively as a central fact in life, he banishes all others to the outer edge of his own existence, and ascribes to them only an accidental value dependent on himself.

★★ VLADIMIR SOLOVIEV

§ 3

[The present section of this anthology is called "Man's Dignity and Responsibility". The previous subsections have dealt with his

227

dignity: the subsection that follows, and the one after that, deal with his responsibility. There is obviously a very close connection between the two attributes dignity and responsibility. A man with no personal responsibility at all for a single one of his thoughts or actions or feelings; a man who couldn't possibly have thought or acted or felt, in the tiniest particular, otherwise than as he *has* thought or acted or felt: such a man would clearly be, not a man, but an automaton. And while an automaton has its own dignity as part of the Whole, its dignity is a dead sort of dignity, the dignity of just being *there*, not the living, breathing, from-the-inside sort of dignity which is what people mean by the word.

The question is, then, which *are* we, we human beings? Are we automata, directed from the outside? Or are we, or at any rate can we be, fully responsible creatures, directing ourselves from within? In the traditional phrase: Have we freedom of will, freedom, that is, to do what we wish? Or is everything pre-determined—has everything I am to do every moment been already determined, from outside me, in advance of my actually doing it? There is a famous Oxford limerick about predetermi-nation:

> There was a young man who said "Damn!
> It really does seem that I am
> Predestined to move
> In a pre-arranged groove:
> Not even a bus, but a tram!"

There is a lot to be said on both sides, and people have been saying it ever since this question of questions first arose for discussion, perhaps among the cave-men. The case for free will is, briefly, as follows. We *feel* ourselves free: indeed, it would not be too much to say that we *know* ourselves free, in the sense, beyond logic or argument, that we *know* we love someone or that we *know* twice two don't make five. In other words: we *experience* ourselves as responsible for what we do, for "our own" actions, exactly as a music-lover experiences his delight in a melody he thinks beautiful. It would be as useless to tell us that the responsibility doesn't exist, that we merely imagine it, or that the actions are in no sense "our own", as to tell the man who loves music that he feels no delight. We, and the music-lover, would dismiss the remarks as nonsensical.

Moreover: what really gives meaning to an action is not the action itself, but the fact that whoever performs it has deliberately *chosen* to perform it.[1] Or this at any rate is what strikes us if we pause to reflect for a moment. We may, of course, be mistaken: every human act may have a place in the total meaning of things, apart altogether from someone having chosen to do it. Or there may, after all, be no total meaning of things: there may be nothing but meaningless chaos. But neither assumption seems probable: and if there is only meaningless chaos, life seems hardly worth living, and this whole discussion a waste of time.

Finally: often, when we "come to a decision", something happens inside us which, hard though it is to describe, is easy to recognize. What happens is this: we act with unmistakable *spontaneity*. I mean that we suddenly *leap to* the decision as we might leap to save someone from drowning. It isn't a question of our brain prompting this, or our heart prompting that, or our moral sense prompting the other: we have just simply leapt to it with our whole very selves. And it is hard to believe that this feeling of spontaneity is bogus, that we have in fact had no choice, that we have been *compelled*, from the outside, to act in this way and no other.

So much for the case in favour of free will, and it is an exceedingly strong one; but the case against it has still to be told.

That our wills, if free at all, are not completely free, at all times and in all circumstances, seems obvious. First, take the question of heredity. We are *born* with certain characteristics, inherit them from our parents or grandparents or remote

---

[1] The crucifixion of Christ, for example, is, in itself, meaningless as well as horrible: but the fact that he *chose* crucifixion, rather than be false to his love of humanity, is full of meaning as well as of beauty.

ancestors: we cannot help being born with them: nor, whether we like it or not, can they fail to have some measure of influence on our manner of living. That is why, when we wish to excuse something evil a friend may have done, we often say "he has a bad heredity"; and it is right that we should say it. One person, for instance, may have been born with an exceptionally violent temperament, and another with an exceptionally gentle one; and though both may be free to resist a temptation to kill someone, resistance is harder for the first than the second. And there is an extreme case of this. A certain kind of lunatic, whether he has been born or become one, appears to have little, if any, freedom of will, and so can hardly, if at all, be responsible for his actions: he is shackled, bound, enslaved by his lunacy: but on the other hand even he may now and then do something, some act of kindness for instance, which suggests, because of its spontaneity, that freedom of will is, in spite of everything, at work, however dimly and partially, in his ruined person.

Then there are forms of mental illness, short of lunacy, that obviously compel a man to think or feel or act, in certain respects, this or that or the other way, whether he wants to or not. Take, for instance, claustrophobia, or the fear of being shut up in narrow spaces. As a man with a nervous 'tic', an automatic jerking of the head, cannot possibly stop it, so an extreme claustrophobic cannot possibly get into a lift until someone, probably a psychiatrist, has helped him to get rid of his illness by uncovering, and revealing to the patient himself, the remote and hidden cause of it. If someone shouts at him "Get into that lift!" or gently urges him to do so; or if he tries desperately, off his own bat, to conquer his fear: this may very well make matters not better but worse, if his mental illness has gone far enough. And if he's carried in by main force he goes mad with anxiety. In a word: the claustrophobic, in respect of his claustrophobia, is devoid of free will.

Then there is the effect of environment, of the atmosphere that surrounds us. If we live amidst violence, if violence is more or less taken for granted by our neighbours and is generally "the thing" (as in Hitler's Germany), we may become in some measure *predisposed* to it: and though, if we are old enough and have seen the greater beauty of gentleness, we may be free to choose the latter (as many in Hitler's Germany did), those of us on the other hand who are younger and less experienced, and inclined by the temperament they have been born with to do as everybody else does rather than to strike out for themselves, are in a very different position: then freedom of choice in this matter may practically vanish. And so I could go on. We may form certain habits, for instance, at so early an age that no reasonably sane person could think us responsible for forming them: and they become so much a part of our ordinary life that, when we want to shake them off, we find it, if not utterly impossible, then all but impossible to do so.

There is another thing: we may feel, at the moment, that we are acting in perfect freedom, but discover afterwards that this was not so. Here is an example, one of a type very common indeed. We may suddenly decide, after leaving the house, to return for a moment to make certain we securely fastened the front door. Now what could be freer, a matter more of our own choosing, than that? And then we remember that our parents, who made a tremendous impression on us in our childhood, were terribly afraid of burglars. So may it not be that, while we *seem* to be free, we should immediately recognize that everything about us has *really* been decided in advance, if we could only discover what, in each case, has decided it.

Finally, a word about "original sin". Original sin is a fact: but so is original virtue; and I could wish that people interested in human conduct would talk more of the second and less of the first. Original virtue is a prompting inside us, so strong that we can hardly resist it, to "do good": original sin is a similar prompting to "do evil". The frequency and strength, both of the one and of the other, vary as between individuals: but almost everyone, maybe actually everyone, experiences original sin (as well as, I must continue to insist, original virtue) at some time or other during the course of their lives. All that "original" means is that the promptings are thought of as part and parcel of human nature, as having been there from the beginning; and this may well be the case.

We think more about original sin than about original virtue for a very simple reason: there is something terrifying about feeling *bound* to do evil, or what strikes us as evil, and nothing terrifying at all about similarly feeling *bound* to do good, or what strikes us as good. And the experience of original sin can be very terrifying indeed. The most famous and vivid description of it is that of St. Paul: "For the good that I would, I do not: but the evil that I would not, that I do. Now if I do what I would not, it is no more I that do it but sin that dwelleth in me. I find then a principle[1] that, when I would do good, evil is present with me. For I delight in the law of God after the inward man [i.e. the real 'I', the whole heart and soul of me, loves goodness]; but I see another law in my members [i.e. in my body] warring against the law of my mind, and bringing me with captivity to the law of sin which is in my members. O wretched man that I am! who shall deliver me from the body of this death?"

Now there can be few adult and mature persons—persons, I mean, who have reached a certain stage in their development as dignified and responsible human beings—who have not risen from their beds, time out of number, to echo St. Paul's words with no less than St. Paul's agony. It is true that St. Paul was referring primarily to the "lusts of the flesh", to "sexual temptations", and that we no longer look at things quite like that. Drawing a rigid distinction between body and soul, St. Paul thought of our bodies, and particularly of our sexual instincts, as somehow evil—which was rather blasphemous of him, seeing that God has created the sex in us, not only for the begetting and bearing of children, so that the creation might continue, but also for our joy: whereas we, on the other hand, or most of us, think of body and soul as nothing but different aspects of a whole single man, different ways of fulfilling his life, like the two sides

---

[1] The meaning is clarified by the use at this point, as in the New English Bible, of "principle" rather than "law".

of one penny. But while differing from St. Paul about body and soul, some of us share his experience of being, on occasion, at deadly conflict with ourselves. We may, for instance, dearly love someone, and yet, if only for a second, find ourselves, from no will of our own, suddenly wishing him harm: or, hating jealousy from the bottom of our soul, we may harbour a jealousy for some rival which, however hard we try, we don't seem able to get rid of.

Some people, vividly aware of this original sin in them, imagine that it makes nonsense of the case for free will. If, they think, we can't *help* evil thoughts coming into our minds, how can we be free to choose good thoughts? But is there really much in this? St. Paul himself, a few verses after his outburst, explains how he conquers the compulsion to sin that so terrifies him. He conquers it by attempting to live like his Master, Jesus Christ: by attempting, indeed, to love his Master so much that the two, he and his Master, in a sense become one. And he finds this, he tells us, quite easy.

*   *   *

The time has come now for me to state—I was going to say my own belief in the matter, but prefer to call it my passionate conviction. Here it is then. We are largely *conditioned*: we largely think, feel or act as we *must*. But within the framework of that picture of our general condition, there is nevertheless an *area* of freedom. In every one of us (except, perhaps, the totally insane—and who can define total insanity?) there is the power—on certain occasions and in certain respects, which differ as between one individual and another—to leap, in full and genuine freedom, to decisions. And it is in such moments that we become godlike, for then we are creating as God creates. Such moments are worth everything else in our whole lifetime put together.

A word in conclusion. The rule for ourselves, in this whole matter, should not be the same as the rule for our neighbour. It is the responsibility, the ability to be and do good, that we must stress in our own case, though with great humility and a proper charity towards ourselves when we fail. But in the case of our neighbour the emphasis must be different: here it is original sin, or heredity, or adverse circumstances, or the force of environment, that we must keep ever in our minds, while striving none the less to inspire him, in Spinoza's words, with a sense of "man's virtue and power". And the more we keep aware of our own difficulties in these various respects, the more compassionately shall we sympathize with such difficulties in others.

*   *   *

The first two of the extracts that follow insist, in a grandly uncompromising fashion, on the complete responsibility of every human being for everything he does. Next comes a demand that everyone should use his own judgment, and not slavishly follow other people's: and this is followed by the statement of a plain fact, namely that a man's salvation or, as we might put it, his moral and spiritual improvement, can come only from within him. After that I am printing four extracts that deal, in their several ways, with various aspects of the matter.

Finally, Bossuet, a seventeenth-century divine, sums up the whole argument very much as I have myself summed it up in this note.]

And Moses returned unto the Lord, and said, Oh, this people have sinned a great sin, and have made them gods of gold.

Yet now, if thou wilt forgive their sin—; and if not, blot me, I pray thee, out of thy book which thou hast written.

And the Lord said unto Moses, Whosoever hath sinned against me, him will I blot out of my book.

EXODUS

[The dash, followed by a semi-colon, is a dramatic way of saying "well and good". Moses, after descending from the top of Mount Sinai with the Ten Commandments, finds that the Israelites have

234

fashioned a Golden Calf in his absence and are worshipping it; or, in other words, have turned to the worship of money. So he goes back and, for love of his people, begs leave to take the burden of their sin on his own shoulders.]

The word of the Lord came unto me again, saying,

What mean ye, that ye use this proverb concerning the land of Israel, saying, The fathers have eaten sour grapes, and the children's teeth are set on edge?

As I live, saith the Lord God, ye shall not have occasion any more to use this proverb in Israel.

Behold, all souls are mine; as the soul of the father, so also the soul of the son is mine: the soul that sinneth, it shall die.

But if a man be just, and do that which is lawful and right . . .

And hath not oppressed any, but hath restored to the debtor his pledge, hath spoiled none by violence, hath given his bread to the hungry, and hath covered the naked with a garment;

He that hath not given forth upon usury, neither hath taken any increase, that hath withdrawn his hand from iniquity, hath executed true judgment between man and man,

Hath walked in my statutes, and hath kept my judgments, to deal truly; he is just, he shall surely live, saith the Lord God.

If he beget a son that is a robber, a shedder of blood, and that doeth the like to any one of these things . . .

Hath oppressed the poor and needy, hath spoiled by violence, hath not restored the pledge, and hath lifted up his eyes to the idols, hath committed abomination,

Hath given forth upon usury, and hath taken increase: shall he then live? he shall not live: he hath done all these abominations; he shall surely die; his blood shall be upon him.

Now, lo, if he beget a son, that seeth all his father's sins which he hath done, and considereth, and doeth not such like . . .

That hath taken off his hand from the poor, that hath not received usury nor increase, hath executed my judgments, hath walked in my statutes; he shall not die for the iniquity of his father, he shall surely live. . . .

Yet say ye, Why? doth not the son bear the iniquity of the father? When the son hath done that which is lawful and right, and hath kept all my statutes, and hath done them, he shall surely live.

The soul that sinneth, it shall die. The son shall not bear the iniquity of the father, neither shall the father bear the iniquity of the son: the righteousness of the righteous shall be upon him, and the wickedness of the wicked shall be upon him.

But if the wicked will turn from all his sins that he hath committed, and keep all my statutes, and do that which is lawful and right, he shall surely live, he shall not die.

All his transgressions that he hath committed, they shall not be mentioned unto him: in his righteousness that he hath done he shall live . . .

Therefore I will judge you, O house of Israel, every one according to his ways, saith the Lord God. Repent, and turn yourselves from all your transgressions; so iniquity shall not be your ruin.

Cast away from you all your transgressions, whereby ye have transgressed; and make you a new heart and a new spirit: for why will ye die, O house of Israel?

For I have no pleasure in the death of him that dieth, saith the Lord God: wherefore turn yourselves, and live ye.

EZEKIEL

Yea, and why even of yourselves judge ye not what is right?

ST. LUKE

Work out your own salvation with fear and trembling.

PHILIPPIANS

["With fear and trembling" is not a threat, but a recognition that life is a serious business.]

It is at my own option not to have a good inclination and not to do a good action; but it is by no means within my power not to have the possibility of good. This possibility is inherent in me whether I will or no. Now the meaning of all this will be rendered clearer by an example or two. That we have the possibility of seeing with our eyes is no power of ours; but it is in our power that we make a good or a bad use of our eyes. So again that I may, by applying a general case in illustration, embrace all, the fact that we have the possibility of accomplishing every good thing by action, speech and thought comes from Him who endowed us with this possibility, and also assists it. Accordingly, whenever we say that a man can live without sin, we also give praise to God by our acknowledgment of the possibility which we have received from Him, Who has bestowed such power upon us.

★★ PELAGIUS

We contradict the Lord to His face when we say: It is hard, it is difficult; we cannot, we are men; we are encompassed with fragile flesh. O blind madness! O unholy audacity! We charge the God of all knowledge with a two-fold ignorance, that He does not seem to know what He has made nor what He has commanded, as though, forgetting the human weakness of which He is Himself the author, He imposed laws upon man which he cannot endure.

PELAGIUS

If what is commanded be not in the power of every one, all the numberless exhortations in the Scriptures, and also all the promises, threatenings, expostulations, reproofs, asseverations,

237

benedictions, and maledictions, together with all the forms of precepts, must of necessity stand coldly useless.

ERASMUS

[Erasmus is attacking Luther, the founder of Protestantism, who, while a strong "anti-freewill" man, was devoted to the Bible: and is pointing out that, if everything is indeed predetermined, then the ethical teaching of Moses, of the Hebrew prophets and of Jesus Christ—and, we might add, of Socrates and the Buddha and Mahatma Gandhi and anyone anywhere who has tried, at one time or another, to raise the general level of human morality—is so much waste of time.]

My freedom to do within certain limits what I have resolved to do is an immediate experience, something, that is, which I am aware of as I am aware of my own existence. Whether or not to call on a friend to-night, that is something I have to think about precisely because I am free to do it or not to do it. I can be expected to obey traffic regulations because it is known that I can follow them if I want to. Throughout our thinking everywhere there are ideas that make sense only if such freedom exists. Demands can be made only on a will known to be free.

It is often considered, however, that when I act with this apparent freedom I am myself but a link in a whole chain of causes and effects. If this is the case, then freedom of will is really only the freedom to do what I have decided to do. But it remains open why I decide to do this rather than that. Those who believe that every event is determined by some cause will then assume that my decision, too, has been determined by some cause, although the cause remains unknown to me. Thus, my will would "in reality" be unfree.

I do not know whether this theory is correct. I merely want to emphasise that it is a theory and not a matter of experience. It is a theory that will have to be tested, sooner or later, by observation and experiment. Let the causes that determine our actions be brought to light, and we shall believe in them. But the freedom which makes me what I am, that freedom is a matter of experience. To accept the fact that freedom is a matter of experience is not in itself enough to prove that determinism is false, for the truth may still be that our actions are determined, but by causes unknown to us. Equally, however, the discovery of what those causes are would not prove that freedom is false, in the sense I have been meaning. No theory of how our minds work can take from me the burden of the decisions I must make in life. As long as the uncertainty of the future is not in fact removed, a self-conscious being, a being who says "I", must make his choices, whether he believes them to be predetermined or not.

Moreover a human being, a rational creature, a creature that *reasons*, is not under the compulsion of *instinct*. The completely instinctive action is predetermined. If we subject an animal to a certain stimulus we can predict its reaction. We experience within ourselves the lack of freedom at those moments when we are at the mercy of our instincts. But rational action is free. Even in the case of an animal acting rationally, we are unable to predict which of several alternatives it will choose. For in rational action a choice is made *within* the individual, and no heredity nor tradition relieves it of that choice. If there are any determining motives, they are at any rate essentially unknown at the moment the choice is made.

Thus theories of determinism cannot in any way affect our experience of freedom: the only thing that can affect it is an experience of the *absence* of freedom, an experience we have, for instance, when we are acting under the compulsion of instinct . . .

★★ C. F. VON WEIZSÄCKER

I am, *in God's hands,* my own master.

BOSSUET

[The italics are mine.]

239

§ 4

[If we believe in the Unity of the whole, in the interconnect-
ness of all things, then clearly everything we think, feel or do
affects the whole universe, though we may actually see or understand very little of the result. This is expressed in a suitably
dramatic, not to say exaggerated, manner (for exaggeration can
be necessary, if people are to be really impressed) in the following
magnificent passages. Everything in the first of them will be
clear, once we have thought ourselves into the point of view of
an ancestral Hebrew. The Holy of Holies was that part of the
Temple in which the Spirit of God, though everywhere in the
universe, was thought specially to reside. "Three hundred and
fifty-four days" is not a printer's error or a mistake by the author:
this is the number of days in the old Hebrew calendar. The Holy
Torah means, in this passage, the first five books of our Bible
(but for a fuller explanation see p. 249). The business about
God's name, however, requires a little explanation.

God can really have no name, because to name a person or
thing is to particularise it, distinguish it from other persons or
things: you call a boy Jack because he isn't Henry and you call
a stone a stone because it isn't a star. But God is in Jack as well
as in Henry, in a star as well as in a stone: God is in everything,
and therefore distinguishable, as wholly other, from nothing. Or,
to put it conversely: everything is in God, and there is nothing
outside Him to distinguish Him from. This is by no means,
however, to say that God, as the pantheists believe, simply *is*
everything: I think of Him, rather, as the creative leaven in all
things—creative precisely because, as well as being in all things,
He remains eternally Himself.

*   *   *

The Deity, then, can have no name: but He has usually been
given one (in our own case, God) if only to avoid long and com-
plicated expressions, though there are other reasons too. The
Jews gave Him several, but one above all—a Name of Names:
this, commonly called the Tetragrammaton, consisted of four

letters, and could be pronounced, owing to the nature of Hebrew, in several different ways. The Tetragrammaton probably signifies "He who lives" or "He who is" or "He who brings into being", but some authorities interpret it differently.

Now any actual pronunciation of the Tetragrammaton, silently as well as aloud, was hedged about by all manner of restrictions, which varied, in severity and comprehensiveness, at different periods of Jewish history. At one time the correct pronunciation was virtually suppressed, and forgotten by the people at large: and the tradition of secrecy has persisted to this very day. The word (written YHVH and often transcribed as Jehovah or Jahveh) appears in our Bible as "the Lord", a translation, not of the Tetragrammaton, but of *Adonai*: and Jews, when they read or pray, substitute for it either *Adonai* or *Hashem* ("the Name").

The reason for all this is easier to feel than to explain. In a very deep sense, the name of a person *is* the person (that is why, when you call a prisoner No. 794 instead of Harry, you shamefully depersonalize him): and for creatures, as an everyday matter, to attempt a familiar identification with God, such as the voicing of His essence implies, would be an intolerable presumption against transcendent Holiness. And there was this special fear: that people might speak the Name when committing sin.

Magic may also have come into the matter. When you address a person by name—when you call, for instance, "Jack" rather than "Hi, you"—you establish a certain power over him by compelling his attention: and magical practices have often derived from the idea that by knowing the name of a god you could use him for your own purposes. But to use God at all—even for good ends—is illegitimate; and to use Him for evil ones would be the final abomination.

Pronunciation of the ineffable Name, for all that, might on occasion be, not merely permissible, but of high religious significance as an act of special communion; and the High Priest did in fact utter the Name in the Holy of Holies on the Day of Atonement.]

RABBI AZRAEL'S DISCOURSE FROM "THE DYBBUK"

The world of God is great and holy. In all the world the holiest land is the Land of Israel. In the Land of Israel the holiest city is Jerusalem; in Jerusalem the holiest place was the Holy Temple, and the holiest spot in the Temple was the Holy of Holies. (*He pauses.*) In the world there are seventy nations, and of them the holiest is Israel. The holiest of the people of Israel is the tribe of the Levites. The holiest of the Levites are the priests, and amongst the priests, the holiest is the High Priest. (*Pause.*) The year has three hundred and fifty-four days. Of these the holidays are the holiest. Holiest of the holidays are the Sabbaths and the holiest of the Sabbaths is the Day of Atonement, Sabbath of Sabbaths. (*Pause.*) There are in the world seventy tongues. The holiest of these is the holy tongue of Israel. The holiest of all things written in this tongue is the Holy Torah; of the Torah the holiest part is the Ten Commandments, and the holiest of all the words in the Ten Commandments is the Name of the Lord. (*Pause.*) At a certain hour, on a certain day of the year, all these four supreme holinesses met together. This took place on the Day of Atonement, at the hour when the High Priest entered the Holy of Holies and there revealed the Divine Name. And as this hour was holy and terrible beyond words, so also was it the hour of utmost peril for the High Priest, and for the entire commonweal of Israel. For if, in that hour (which God forbid), a sinful or a wayward thought had entered the mind of the High Priest, it would have brought the destruction of the world. (*Pause.*) Wherever a man stand to lift his eyes to heaven, that place is a Holy of Holies. Every human being created by God in His own image and likeness is a High Priest. Each day of a man's life is the Day of Atonement; and every word he speaks from his heart is the name of the Lord. Therefore the sin of any man, whether of commission or of omission, brings the ruin of a whole world in its train.

S. ANSKY

Every man who begets a free act projects his personality into the infinite. If he gives a poor man a penny grudgingly, that penny pierces the poor man's hand, falls, pierces the earth, bores holes in suns, crosses the firmament and compromises the universe. If he begets an impure act, he perhaps darkens thousands of hearts whom he does not know, who are mysteriously linked to him, and who need this man to be pure as a traveller dying of thirst needs the Gospel's draught of water. A charitable act, an impulse of real pity sings for him the divine praises, from the time of Adam to the end of the ages; it cures the sick, consoles those in despair, calms storms, ransoms prisoners, converts the infidel and protects mankind.

The whole of Christian philosophy lies in the unutterable importance of the free act and in the notion of an enveloping and indestructible mutual dependence.

LÉON BLOY

[A rough paraphrase might read somewhat as follows. Anyone who, by using his freedom of will, *creates* a thought, feeling or action, influences the whole universe. If he gives a penny to a beggar but grudges it (which is an insult to the beggar's dignity, and far worse than giving him nothing), the penny doesn't remain in the beggar's hand to relieve his suffering, but falls down, down, down through endless space until its poison, the poison that a single human being has put into it by his disrespect for others, has contaminated everything. Any deliberate impurity in our actions, anything we do with bad motives, such as selfishness or envy or greed, may result in unhappiness for thousands of people we have never heard of, but who are mysteriously linked to us as parts of a common Whole, and may need a purity in our actions that will spread through the universe as much as a traveller dying of thirst needs a cup of cold water. A loving act, on the other hand, an impulse of real pity, is as if its author were praising God in that moment—in a moment that included all moments—and so were helping the God of pity and love to increase pity and love everywhere. And the more pity and love

243

there is, the more, by an equal measure, will the sick be cured, the despairing consoled, prisoners set free, and humanity protected from evil.

The essence of Christianity is twofold. First, it is of unutterable importance that we should use our free will to the full. Secondly, everything is connected with everything else, and this interdependence, the dependence of everything upon everything, can never be destroyed.]

I understand, finally, why the love of God created men responsible for one another and gave them hope as a virtue. Since it made of each of them the ambassador of the same God, in the hands of each rested the salvation of all. No man had the right to despair, since each was the messenger of a thing greater than himself . . .

My [Christian] civilisation made each responsible for all, and all responsible for each. The individual was to sacrifice himself in order that by his sacrifice the community be saved; but this was no matter of idiotic arithmetic. It was a matter of the respect for Man present in the individual. What made my civilisation grand was that a hundred miners were called upon to risk their lives in the rescue of a single miner entombed. And what they rescued in rescuing that miner was Man.

ANTOINE DE SAINT-EXUPÉRY

§ 5

God addressed Adam, after creating him, thus: "The nature of all other beings is limited and confined within the bounds of laws prescribed by Us. Thou, confined by no limits, in accordance with thine own free will, in whose hand We have placed thee, shalt choose for thyself the limits of thy nature. We have made thee neither of heaven nor of earth, neither mortal nor immortal, so that with freedom of choice and with honour, as though the maker and moulder of thyself, thou mayest fashion thyself in whatever shape thou shalt prefer. Thou shalt have the power to degenerate into the lower forms of life, which are brutish. Thou shalt have the power, out of thy soul's judgment, to be reborn into the higher forms, which are divine."

O supreme generosity of God the Father, O highest and most marvellous felicity of man! To him it is granted to have whatever he chooses, to be whatever he wills! Beasts as soon as they are born bring with them from their mother's womb all they will ever possess: but on man, when he came into life, the Father conferred the seeds of all kinds and the germs of every way of life. Whatever seeds each man cultivates will grow to maturity and bear in him their own fruit. Who would not admire this our chameleon? Or who could more greatly admire aught else whatever?

★★ PICO DELLA MIRANDOLA

FOURTH PART

III. ACTIVITY

What doth it profit, my brethren, though a man say he hath faith, and have not works? can faith save him?

If a brother or sister be naked, and destitute of daily food,

And one of you say unto them, Depart in peace, be ye warmed and filled; notwithstanding ye give them not those things which are needful to the body; what doth it profit?

Even so faith, if it hath not works, is dead, being alone.

JAMES

[To say that you have "faith", that you "believe in" Jesus Christ, is quite profitless—does no good to you or to anyone else—unless your belief finds expression in "works": namely in doing everything possible for your fellow human beings, as instructed by the Christ you profess to believe in.]

All study of Torah without work must in the end be futile and become the cause of sin.

RABBAN GAMALIEL III

[Torah means a whole way of life revealed to Israel by God. Its rules—some of them recorded in the books of Exodus and Deuteronomy and some of them a matter of tradition—were given, it was believed, on Sinai to Moses, who transmitted them to the Israelites below. There have always been Jews who have spent their entire lives "studying" Torah, so as to make quite certain that even the smallest regulation has been exactly understood.]

Give me a knowledge that's fertile in performances, for theories without their effects are but Nothings in the dress of Things.

THOMAS VAUGHAN

Activity is the only road to knowledge.

BERNARD SHAW

I call heaven and earth to witness that whether it be Jew or heathen, man or woman, freeman or slave—only according to their acts does the Divine spirit rest upon them.

TANNA DEBE ELIYAHU

A man saves his soul not by assenting to metaphysical dogmas, but solely by love of God that fulfils itself in action.

★ CHASDAI CRESCAS

[Crescas is far from implying, however, that metaphysical dogmas—particular theories of the nature of things, such as the doctrine of the Trinity—are necessarily false, or that whether we believe in them or not is of little importance.]

Let a man first do good deeds, and then ask God for knowledge of Torah: let a man first act as righteous and upright men act, and then let him ask God for wisdom.

TANNA DEBE ELIYAHU

He whose wisdom exceeds his works, to what is he like? To a tree whose branches are many, but whose roots are few; and the wind comes and plucks it up and overturns it upon its face, as it is said, And he shall be like a lonely juniper tree in the desert, and shall not see when good cometh; but shall inhabit the parched places in the wilderness, a salt land and not inhabited. But he whose works exceed his wisdom, to what is he like? To a tree whose branches are few, but whose roots are many, so that even if all the winds in the world come and blow upon it, it cannot be stirred from its place, as it is said, And he shall be as a tree planted by the waters; and that spreadeth out its roots by the river, and shall not perceive when heat cometh, but his leaf shall be green; and shall not be troubled in the year of drought, neither shall cease from yielding fruit.

RABBI ELEAZER B. AZARIAH

Once I resolved to devote a whole day to the recitation of the entire Book of Psalms. When towards evening I was approaching the end, the Warden of my Rabbi came over to me, and said that the Rabbi wished to speak with me. I requested him to inform the Rabbi that I would see him as soon as I had finished.

But the Warden returned and bade me come immediately. The Rabbi asked me: "Why did you not obey my first summons?" I explained the reason.

The Rabbi replied: "I called you to make a collection for a poor Jew. Psalms can be chanted by the Angels as well, but mortal men are needed to aid the destitute. Charity is a greater duty than the chanting of Psalms, inasmuch as the Angels cannot perform charity."

A HASIDIC RABBI

[In reply to an old man who expressed anguish at not having yet atoned.] O my friend, you are thinking only of yourself. How about forgetting yourself and thinking of the world?

RABBI ELIEZER OF DZIKOV

I have understood that one who aimeth at his individual peace and happiness adopteth the Lower Path. But he who, from the very start, devoteth the merit of his love and compassion to the cause of others, I understand belongeth to the Higher Path.

MILAREPA

There is no quality and there is no power of man that was created to no purpose. . . . But to what end can the denial of God have been created? This too can be uplifted through deeds of charity. For if someone comes to you and asks your help, you shall not turn him off with pious words, saying: "Have faith and take your troubles to God!" You shall act as if there were no God, as if there were only one person in all the world who could help this man—only yourself.

RABBI MOSHE LEIB OF SASOV

§ 2

We should not go into holes, cloisters, cells and corners; for Christ saith: "Let your light shine before men, that your Father may have praise in your works."

BOEHME

The fascination of a purely contemplative life tempted St. Francis, and he asked himself if instead of preaching to the multitudes he would not do better to live quietly away from the world, and think only of communion between his soul and God.

This aspiration for the selfish repose of the cloister came back to him several times in his life; but love always won the victory. He was too much the child of his age not to be at times tempted by that happiness which the Middle Ages regarded as the supreme bliss of the elect in paradise—peace. His distinguishing peculiarity is that he never gave way to it.

★ PAUL SABATIER

[But it might as truly be said that a life devoid of prayer and meditation becomes dry and sterile.]

252

Christ was the greatest contemplative that ever lived, yet he was ever at the service of men, and never did his ineffable and perpetual contemplation diminish . . . his exterior activity.

RUYSBROECK

And Jesus went into the temple of God, and cast out all them that sold and bought in the temple, and overthrew the tables of the moneychangers, and the seats of them that sold doves. . . .

ST. MATTHEW

Christians are living in this sinful world and must bear its burden, they may not steal away from the battlefield.

BERDYAEV

Worrying about immortality is for people of rank, and especially ladies, who have nothing to do. But an able man, who has something regular to do here, and must toil and struggle to produce day by day, leaves the future world to itself, and is active and useful in this.

★ GOETHE

§ 3

The more perfection anything has, the more active and the less passive it is; and contrariwise, the more active it is, the more perfect it becomes.

SPINOZA

Activity is better than inertia. Act, but with self-control.

THE BHAGAVAD-GITA

You have the right to work, but for the work's sake only. You have no right to the fruits of work. Desire for the fruits of work must never be your motive in working. Never give way to laziness, either.

Perform every action with your heart fixed on the Supreme Lord. Renounce attachment to the fruits. Be even-tempered in success and failure. . . .

THE BHAGAVAD-GITA

[Consider three artists. The first, like Van Gogh, paints a chair because he *must* paint a chair: he *must* express his joy in the chair, and his gratitude for its creation, not only by painting it, but by painting it as perfectly as possible. Nothing else concerns him. The second paints a portrait with half an eye to the money he will get out of it. The third thinks only of the money. Now the first is an artist: the second is half a business man and half an artist: the third is a business man with the skill of an artist. And only the first, the Van Gogh, has painted with "his heart fixed on God": the other two have been "attached to the fruits" of their painting.]

The good man seeks nothing in his work; only slaves and hirelings ask anything for work, or work for the getting of something. If thou wouldst become righteous, have no ulterior purpose in thy work; nor fix thine eye on anything in time or in eternity, not reward nor happiness nor this nor that, for verily all such works are dead.

★★ MEISTER ECKHART

A man should direct his will and all his works to God and having only God in view go forward unafraid, not thinking, am I right or am I wrong? One who worked out all the chances ere starting his first fight would never fight at all. And if, going to some place, we must think how to set the front foot down we shall never get there. It is our duty to do the next thing: go straight on, that is the right way.

★ MEISTER ECKHART

Once when Rabbi Bunam honoured a man in his Synagogue by asking him to blow the ram's horn, and the fellow began to make lengthy preparations to concentrate on the meaning of the sounds, the Rabbi cried out: "Fool, go ahead and blow!"

HASIDIC STORY

[The Rabbi is saying very much what Meister Eckhart was saying just above. A ram's-horn trumpet, called a Shofar, is blown in synagogues on the Hebrew New Year (several times) and on the Day of Atonement (once), to signify or represent, on these solemn occasions, the voice of God on Mount Sinai, the repentance of a contrite heart, and possibly the ram sacrificed by Abraham in place of Isaac. The following delightful legend is quoted by Jung in his *Psychology and Religion, West and East*: "And I," cried Abraham, "swear that I will not go down from this altar until you have heard me. When you commanded me to sacrifice my son Isaac you offended against your word: 'In Isaac shall your descendants be named'. So if ever my descendants offend against you, and you wish to punish them, then remember that you are not without fault and forgive them." "Very well, then," replied the Lord, "there behind you is a ram caught in the thicket by his horns. Offer up that instead of your son Isaac. And if ever your descendants sin against me, and I sit in judgement over them on New Year's Day, let them blow the horn of a ram, that I may remember my words, and temper justice with mercy."

A Shofar-blower has to produce three standard types of noise —a piercing sort of call, a kind of trembling, and a rapid triplet— which are combined in various ways at each blowing: and to blow efficiently means, among other things, to put full "meaning" into these sounds—a sufficiently piercing quality, for instance,

255

into the "call". This is by no means easy: and an invitation to blow is considered a great honour.

There is always a large number of people in any congregation who regard themselves as experts in Shofar-blowing. You see them nodding or shaking their heads to express approval or disapproval of this sound or that. I remember how all this delighted me when I attended the Bayswater Synagogue as a boy.]

Enoch was a cobbler; with each stitch of his awl that drew together the top and bottom leather, he joined God and His Shekhinah.

HASIDIC SAYING

[This is surely a wonderful saying. According to an old Hebrew tradition, God, though a Unity, is divided into two: namely (a) His ultimate being, Elohut, remote from the imperfections of His creatures, and (b) His Shekhina, His Glory, His Presence, a perfection that dwells among us here below in the as yet very imperfect world of His creation, wandering astray and scattered. (Or, as we might put it far less picturesquely: There is a lot of goodness in the world, all mixed up with a lot of evil—a lot of *imperfect* goodness; but there couldn't be imperfect goodness unless *perfect* goodness existed, just as "rather liking a man" couldn't mean anything unless "completely liking him" meant something.) The exile of the Shekhina can be ended only when the world, through the actions and feelings of individual men and women, gets better: or, to put it positively, all good actions and feelings unite, or rather help in uniting, God with His Shekhina. And to do any piece of work, however "humble", with devotion and without thought of reward is a very good action indeed.]

I pray with my carpenter's bench.

RABBI ZALMAN OF LADI

It is not only prayer that gives God glory but work. Smiting on an anvil, sawing a beam, whitewashing a wall, driving horses, sweeping, scouring, everything gives God some glory if being in his grace you do it as your duty. To go to communion worthily gives God great glory, but to take food in thankfulness and temperance gives him glory too. To lift up the hands in prayer gives God glory, but a man with a dungfork in his hand, a woman with a slop-pail, give him glory too. He is so great that all things give him glory if you mean they should. So then, my brethren, live.

GERARD MANLEY HOPKINS

Duke Huan of Ch'i was reading a book at the upper end of the hall; the wheelwright was making a wheel at the lower end. Putting aside his mallet and chisel, he called to the Duke and asked him what book he was reading. "One that records the words of the Sages," answered the Duke. "Are those Sages alive?" asked the wheelwright. "Oh, no," said the Duke, "they are dead." "In that case," said the wheelwright, "what you are reading can be nothing but the lees and scum of bygone men." "How dare you, a wheelwright, find fault with the book I am reading? If you can explain your statement, I will let it pass. If not, you shall die." "Speaking as a wheelwright," he replied, "I look at the matter in this way: when I am making a wheel, if my stroke is too slow, then it bites deep but is not steady; if my stroke is too fast, then it is steady, but does not go deep. The right pace, neither slow nor fast, cannot get into the hand unless it comes from the heart. It is a thing that cannot be put into words; there is an art in it that I cannot explain to my son. That is why it is impossible for me to let him take over my work, and here I am at the age of seventy, still making wheels. In my opinion it must have been the same with the men of old. All that was worth handing on, died with them; the rest, they put into their books. That is why I said that what you were reading was the lees and scum of bygone men."

472 CHUANG TZU

If a man did only cast stones into the sea (if his brother be pleased with it, and he get his living by it) then he is as acceptable to God as a preacher in a pulpit.

BOEHME

Whom dost thou worship in this lonely dark corner of a temple with doors all shut? Open thine eyes and see thy God is not before thee!

He is there where the tiller is tilling the hard ground and where the pathmaker is breaking stones. He is with them in sun and in shower, and his garment is covered with dust. Put off thy holy mantle and even like him come down on the dusty soil! . . .

Come out of thy meditations and leave aside thy flowers and incense! What harm is there if thy clothes become tattered and stained? Meet him and stand by him in toil and in sweat of thy brow.

RABINDRANATH TAGORE

Our day of work is not our day of joy—for that we require a holiday; for, miserable that we are, we cannot find our holiday in our work. The river finds its holiday in its onward flow, the fire in its outburst of flame, the scent of the flower in its permeation of the atmosphere; but in our everyday work there is no such holiday for us. It is because we do not let ourselves go, because we do not give ourselves joyously and entirely up to it, that our work overpowers us.

O giver of thyself! at the vision of thee as joy let our souls flame up to thee as the fire, flow on to thee as the river, permeate thy being as the fragrance of the flower. Give us strength to love, to love fully, our life in its joys and sorrows, in its gains and losses, in its rise and fall. Let us have strength enough fully to see and hear thy universe and to work with full vigour therein. Let us fully live the life thou hast given us, let us bravely take and bravely give. This is our prayer to thee. Let us once for all dislodge from our minds the feeble fancy that would make out thy joy to be a thing apart from action, thin, formless, and unsustained. Wherever the peasant tills the hard earth, there does thy joy gush out in the green of the corn, wherever man displaces the entangled forest, smooths the stony ground, and clears for himself a homestead, there does thy joy enfold it in orderliness and peace.

RABINDRANATH TAGORE

§ 4

[Gautama Buddha lived in the sixth century before Christ. Observing the pain and unhappiness that human beings had to suffer during much of their lives, and being a man of abounding compassion, he sought for a way to bring them happiness and peace. He came to the conclusion that the root of all misery was Life itself—the activity, the longing and the struggle which is the very condition of human life here on earth, the life of separate, individual human beings. And death, he also concluded, could never of itself bring release, for so long as people continued to absorb themselves in earthly activities they would return after death in new bodies and start living again, and so it would go on and on. There was only one remedy. Let them give up all struggling and longing, all human activity, and they would achieve Nirvana—the final extinction of individual existence and absorption in the Whole. Eight stages of meditation and of withdrawal from the world were essential if Nirvana was to be won. But the Buddha also taught—and this was somewhat contradictory—that anyone who desired Nirvana must love his fellow-men in utter unselfishness and help them whenever he could.

Lowes Dickinson's *The Magic Flute* is a sort of imaginative interpretation of Mozart's opera. Tamino is seeking—he does not quite know for what: say for the meaning of existence. He has been examining various religions and philosophies, including

Christianity, and has gone to live, before the following scene, in a Buddhist monastery.]

And Tamino persevered, and entered the seventh stage [of the Buddhist road]. And there he was aware of nothing, and his soul was like nothing. And this state was beyond even peace, and he would have been glad to remain in it for ever. But as it so happened, on that day, he had gone out to meditate in the little wood that surrounded the monastery. And as he sat there by the way, lost in meditation, there passed a traveller. And thieves leapt out upon him and wounded and robbed him and left him for dead. He cried for aid to Tamino, but Tamino sat there unconscious, seeing and hearing nothing. And so the man lay bleeding on the ground, and there he was when Tamino returned to earth. Tamino was dazed and for a long time did not understand what he saw nor know what he had to do. But presently, as the current of his life in the flesh set in again, he went up to the man and bound up his wounds as best he could. But the man's blood had flowed too long. He looked at Tamino and died. And in his eyes, before he died, Tamino saw the look he had seen once on the battle field. And all his peace, so painfully won, fled from him. And he went back to the monastery, and passed over on to the island, and mounted to the topmost terrace, and there sat down beside one of the images of Gautama. It was evening, and the setting sun shone on the stone face, till it seemed to flush into life. And Tamino, looking into the eyes of the face, said:

'Lord Buddha, was your gospel true?'

And the image answered back:

'True and false.'

'What was true in it?'

'Selflessness and Love.'

'What false?'

'Flight from Life.'

'Must I go back to Life?'

But the light had faded from the face and it turned to stone again.

G. LOWES DICKINSON (from *The Magic Flute*)

FOURTH PART

IV. INTEGRITY

Become what thou art!

ORPHIC SAYING

It is the chiefest of good things for a man to be *himself*.

BENJAMIN WHICHCOTE

We can live—and many do—our entire life as the pale reflection of someone else, as a copy of someone else. The first, original meaning of living is to be oneself, rising to the transformation of oneself into the image and likeness of God.

FATHER YELCHANINOV

In the coming world they will not ask me: "Why were you not Moses?" They will ask me: "Why were you not Zusya?"

RABBI ZUSYA OF HANIPOL

A man's own natural duty, even if it seems imperfectly done, is better than work not naturally his own, even if this is well performed. When a man acts according to the law of his nature, he cannot be sinning. Therefore, no one should give up his natural work, even though he does it imperfectly. For all action is involved in imperfection, like fire in smoke.

THE BHAGAVAD-GITA

The apple tree never asks the beech how he shall grow; nor the lion, the horse, how he shall take his prey.

BLAKE

It blooms because it blooms, the pretty rose:
Why, or who looks, it neither asks nor knows.

ANGELUS SILESIUS

Every man's leading propensity ought to be call'd his leading virtue and his good Angel.

BLAKE

If the fool could persist in his folly he would become wise.

BLAKE

No bird soars too high, if he soars with his own wings.

BLAKE

Even a slug is a star, if it dares to be its horned and slimy self.

JOHN HARGRAVE

It is by that which he longs for that every man knows and apprehends the quality with which he has to serve God.

THE BAALSHEM

Every complexion of the inward man, when sanctified by humility, and suffering itself to be tuned and struck and moved by the Holy Spirit of God, according to its particular frame and turn, helps mightily to increase that harmony of divine praise, thanksgiving and adoration which must arise from different instruments, sounds and voices. To condemn this variety in the servants of God or to be angry at those who have not served Him in the way that we have chosen for ourselves is but too plain a sign that we have not enough renounced the elements of selfishness, pride and anger.

WILLIAM LAW

When I thus rest in the silence of contemplation, Thou, Lord, makest reply within my heart, saying: Be thou thine and I too will be thine. . . . Thou, Lord, canst not be mine if I be not mine own.

NICHOLAS OF CUSA

§ 2

Lieh Tzu asked Kuan Yin, saying "The Man of Extreme Power . . . can tread on fire without being burnt. Walk on the top of the whole world and not stagger. May I ask how he attains to this?" "He is protected," said Kuan Yin, "by the purity of his breath. Knowledge and skill, determination and courage could never lead to this. . . . When a drunk man falls from his carriage, however fast it may be going he is never killed. His bones and joints are not different from those of other men; but his susceptibility to injury is different from theirs. This is because his soul is intact.[1] He did not know that he was riding; he does not know that he has fallen out. Neither death nor life, astonishment nor fear can enter into his breast; therefore when he bumps into things, he does not stiffen with fright. If such integrity of the spirit can be got from wine, how much greater must be the integrity that is got from Heaven?"

CHUANG TZU

[In reply to disciples who asked why he was watching a rope dancer so absorbedly.] This man is risking his life, and I cannot say why. But I am quite sure that while he is walking the rope he is not thinking of the fact that he is earning a hundred gulden by what he is doing, for if he did he would fall.

RABBI HAYYIM OF KROSNO

[1] Is impervious to disturbances from outside (*note by Arthur Waley*).

265

When he has no lust, no hatred,
A man walks safely among the things of lust and hatred.

THE BHAGAVAD-GITA

After the death of Rabbi Uri of Strelisk, one of his Hasidim came to Rabbi Bunam. The latter welcomed him and asked him what particular trait of character it was Rabbi Uri's main purpose to instil in his Hasidim. The Hasid replied: "I believe Rabbi Uri sought to make his Hasidim very humble. The Rabbi would order a rich Hasid to draw water at the pump, and to bring in the pail on his shoulder—a thing the man would never have done at home."

Rabbi Bunam remarked: "My way is different; I will explain it to you by a parable: Three men were convicted of a crime, and were lodged in a dark dungeon. Two of them were men of intelligence, but the third was a witless person. When food was lowered in the dark, the witless one did not know how to take his share, and would break the plate, or cut himself with the knife. One of his fellow-prisoners sought to aid him by rehearsing with him the necessary behaviour, but the next day a different arrangement of the food would baffle him again. One of the prisoners then remarked: 'Why waste time teaching this fellow every time? Help me to bore a hole in the wall to admit light, and then he will know how to eat unaided.' Likewise, I attempt to admit into the soul of a man the love of God. This is a light whereby a man can learn wise conduct in its entirety, and not trait by trait."

HASIDIC STORY

Pleasing to God are all a good man's ways:
As pleasing when he drinks as when he prays.

ANGELUS SILESIUS

God wants the heart.

THE TALMUD

EVENING ON CALAIS BEACH

It is a beauteous evening, calm and free,
  The holy time is quiet as a Nun
  Breathless with adoration; the broad sun
Is sinking down in its tranquillity;
The gentleness of heaven broods o'er the sea:
  Listen! the mighty Being is awake,
  And doth with his eternal motion make
A sound like thunder—everlastingly.
Dear Child! dear Girl! that walkest with me here,
  If thou appear untouch'd by solemn thought,
  Thy nature is not therefore less divine:
Thou liest in Abraham's bosom all the year;
  And worshipp'st at the Temple's inner shrine,
  God being with thee when we know it not.

WORDSWORTH

["And it came to pass, that the beggar died, and was carried by the angels into Abraham's bosom"—Luke. Abraham was in heaven.

Utter integrity is always unconscious of itself. The moment a man knows that he is a man of integrity, he proves that he is not. Many children are creatures of almost perfect integrity, whatever their faults and imperfections. That is doubtless why Christ asked that the little children should come unto him: like desires like.]

Nothing is so beautiful as a child going to sleep while he is
  saying his prayers, says God.
I tell you nothing is so beautiful in the world. . . .
And yet I have seen beautiful sights in the world.
And I know something about it. My creation is overflowing
  with beauty.

267

My creation overflows with marvels.

There are so many that you don't know where to put them.

I have seen millions and millions of stars rolling under my feet
     like the sands of the sea.

I have seen days as scorching as flames,

Summer days of June and July and August.

I have seen winter evenings spread out like a cloak.

I have seen summer evenings as calm and soft as something
     shed by Paradise,

All studded with stars.

I have seen those slopes of the Meuse and those churches which
     are my own houses,

And Paris and Reims and Rouen and cathedrals which are my
     own palaces and my own castles,

So beautiful that I am going to keep them in heaven.

I have seen the capital of the kingdom and Rome the capital
     of Christendom.

I have heard mass sung and triumphant vespers.

And I have seen the plains and vales of France,

And they are more beautiful than anything.

I have seen the deep sea, and the deep forest, and the deep
     heart of man.

I have seen hearts devoured by love

During whole lifetimes

Lost in love

Burning like flames. . . .

And I have seen looks of prayer, looks of tenderness,

Lost in love,

Which will gleam for all eternity, nights and nights.

And I have seen whole lives from birth to death,

From baptism to viaticum,

Unrolling like a beautiful skein of wool.

But I tell you, says God, that I know of nothing so beautiful
     in the whole world

As a little child going to sleep while he is saying his prayers

Under the wing of his guardian angel

And laughs happily as he watches the angels and begins to go
    to sleep;
And is already mixing his prayers together and no longer knows
    what they are all about;
And sticks the words of *Our Father* among the words of *Hail,*
  Mary, all in a jumble,
While a veil is already coming down over his eyelids,
The veil of night over his gaze and over his voice.
I have seen the greatest saints, says God. But I tell you
I have never seen anything so funny and I therefore know of
    nothing so beautiful in the world
As that child going to sleep while he says his prayers
(As that little creature going to sleep in all confidence)
And getting his *Our Father* mixed up with his *Hail, Mary.*
Nothing is so beautiful . . .

472   CHARLES PÉGUY

[Some knowledge of Jewish practice is necessary for an understanding of the following passage. By the Days of Awe is meant
the period, a very solemn one, between New Year and the Day
of Atonement. A Jewish boy is confirmed at the age of thirteen.
Jews fast, and attend a synagogue, throughout the Day of Atonement. The Additional Service comes between the morning and
the afternoon prayers.]

A villager, who year after year prayed in the Baalshem's
House of Prayer on the Days of Awe, had a son who was so
dull-witted that he could not even grasp the shapes of the letters,
let alone the meaning of the holy words. On the Days of Awe
his father did not take him to town with him, because he did
not understand anything. But when he was thirteen and of age
according to the laws of God, his father took him along on the
Day of Atonement, for fear the boy might eat on the fast-day
simply because he did not know any better.

Now the boy had a small whistle which he always blew when

he sat out in the fields to herd the sheep and the calves. He had taken this with him in the pocket of his smock and his father had not noticed it. Hour after hour, the boy sat in the House of Prayer and had nothing to say. But when the Additional Service began, he said: "Father, I have my little whistle with me. I want to sing on it". The father was greatly perturbed and told him to do no such thing, and the boy restrained himself. But when the Afternoon Service began, he said again: "Father, do let me blow my little whistle". The father became angry and said: "Where did you put it?" And when the boy told him, he laid his hand on his pocket so that the boy could not take it out. But now the Closing Prayer began. The boy snatched his pocket away from his father's hand, took out the whistle and blew a loud note. All were frightened and confused. But the Baalshem went on with the prayer, only more quickly and easily than usual. Later he said: "The boy made things easy for me."

HASIDIC STORY

A little farmer boy, having been left an orphan at an early age, was unable to read, but had inherited a large, heavy prayer book from his parents. On the Day of Atonement he brought it into the synagogue, laid it on the reading desk, and, weeping, cried out: "Lord of Creation! I do not know how to pray; I do not know what to say—I give Thee the entire prayer book."

HASIDIC STORY

An ignorant villager, having heard it is a good religious deed to eat and drink on the day before the Day of Atonement, drank himself into a stupor. He awoke late at night, too late for the opening service. Not knowing the prayers by heart, he devised a plan. He repeated the letters of the alphabet over and over, beseeching the Almighty to arrange them into the appropriate words of the prayers. The following day he attended the synagogue at Kotzk. After the closing service the Rabbi summoned him to inquire the cause of his absence the evening before. The villager confessed his transgression and asked whether his manner of reciting the prayers could be pardoned. The Rabbi replied: "Your prayer was more acceptable than mine because you uttered it with the entire devotion of your heart."

HASIDIC STORY

§ 4

[What the following seven extracts come to is this: Whatever you do or whatever you feel, do or feel it with all your heart and with all your soul if you are to do or feel it at all. God, someone has said, prefers a great sinner to a man of wishy-washy virtue. For while nothing is impossible, the first is far likelier than the second to become a great saint.]

I know thy works, that thou art neither cold nor hot: I would thou wert cold or hot.

So then because thou art lukewarm, and neither cold nor hot, I will spue thee out of my mouth.

REVELATION

He who can burn with enmity can also burn with love for God, but he who is coldly hostile will always find the way closed.

RABBI YAAKOV YITZHAK OF LUBLIN

'Tis death, my Soul, to be indifferent:
Set forth thy self unto thy whole extent.

TRAHERNE (from *Another*)

There is a story to the effect that a poor man asked his rich brother: "Why are you wealthy, and I am not?" The other answered: "Because I have no scruples against doing wrong." The poor brother began to misconduct himself, but he remained poor. He complained of this to his elder brother, who answered: "The reason your transgressions have not made you wealthy is that you did them, not from the conviction that it makes no matter whether we do good or evil, but solely because you desired riches."

How much more applicable is this to doing good with the proper intention!

THE BAALSHEM

If ye keep not Sabbath for the whole week, ye shall not see the Father.

ATTRIBUTED TO CHRIST (from the Oxyrhynchus Papyri)

[The Sabbath is a day set aside for communion with God— for quietly losing ourselves in the Whole. But only when *every* day is such a Sabbath can the communion be complete.]

The old-time rabbis used to teach that the kingdom of God would come if only the whole of Israel would really keep a single Sabbath simultaneously.

ALBERT SCHWEITZER

And a certain ruler asked him, saying, Good Master, what shall I do to inherit eternal life?

And Jesus said unto him, Why callest thou me good? none is good, save one, that is, God.

Thou knowest the commandments, Do not commit adultery, Do not kill, Do not steal, Do not bear false witness, Honour thy father and thy mother.

And he said, All these have I kept from my youth up.

Now when Jesus heard these things, he said unto him, Yet lackest thou one thing: sell all that thou hast, and distribute unto the poor, and thou shalt have treasure in heaven: and come, follow me.

And when he heard this, he was very sorrowful: for he was very rich.

ST. LUKE

§ 5

[To be genuine and *real* in any action or feeling is to do or feel it for its own sake and not with any thought of the consequences, any hope of reward or fear of punishment or loss. To do a thing, on the other hand, with ulterior motives is to be a sort of liar. If we really and whole-heartedly love someone, for instance, our love cannot possibly be affected, one way or the other, by the question of whether he loves us in return: we either love him in all possible circumstances or don't genuinely love him at all. If we love him on condition that he loves us, we are loving not him but ourselves: we want something *out of* our love. Of course it is delightful to be loved in return, but that is something extra.

Everyone knows the difference between a pure act—as in solving a mathematical problem because it's wonderful to solve it—and an impure one—as in solving the same problem because we want better marks. We feel the joy of being really and truly ourselves when we do a pure act—a joy that makes us rejoice in the joy of everyone round us. An impure act, on the other hand, strikes us, in comparison, as rather "cheap".

That is the substance of the present subsection.]

When Rabbi Baer's wife pressed her starving child to her bosom, the Rabbi heaved a sigh of rebellion against their

273

unhappy fate. Forthwith a voice from Heaven thundered into his ear: "Thou hast lost thy share in Paradise".

"It matters not," said the Rabbi joyfully. "The slavery of reward has gone; henceforth I will serve God as a freeman."

HASIDIC STORY

While absorbed in his devotions, the Rabbi of Ladi was heard to say. "My Lord and God, I do not desire Thy Paradise; I do not desire the bliss of the After World; I desire only Thee Thyself."

HASIDIC STORY

Spirit raves not for a goal.

GEORGE MEREDITH (from *A Faith on Trial*)

[Spirit—what is spiritual or godlike in a man, the quality that *makes* him a man—isn't like a long-distance runner that's panting to *get* somewhere: it is good and sufficient in itself, for its own sake.]

He who loves God cannot endeavour to bring it about that God should love him in return.

SPINOZA

This being so, we may, with reason, regard as a great absurdity what many, who are otherwise esteemed as great theologians, assert, namely, that if no eternal life resulted from the love of God, then they would seek what is best for themselves: as though they could discover anything better than God! This is just as silly as if a fish (for which, of course, it is impossible to live out of the water) were to say: if no eternal life is to follow this life in the water, then I will leave the water for the land.

SPINOZA

Most seem to think that they are free in so far as they may give themselves up to evil living, and that they lose their natural right in so far as they are obliged to live according to the divine laws. They therefore think that piety and religion are burdens which after death they will lay aside, and hope to receive a reward for their servitude, that is, their piety and religion. Not by this hope alone, but also, and even principally, by the fear of suffering dreadful punishments after death, are they induced to live, as far as their feebleness and weak-mindedness allows them, according to the divine laws; and if this hope or fear were not in men, but, on the other hand, if they thought that their minds were buried with their bodies, and that there did not remain for the wretches worn out with the burden of piety the hope of longer life, they would return to life according to their own ideas, and would direct everything according to their evil desires. This seems no less absurd to me than if a man, when he discovered that he could not keep his body alive for ever with wholesome food, should straightway seek to glut himself with poison and deadly foods; or that a man, when he discovered that his mind was not eternal or immortal, should prefer to live without any mind at all: this all seems so absurd to me that it scarcely deserves to be refuted.

★ SPINOZA

[Suppose] that there is no reality other than the events which make up the life of man in the present world. Even the most devout should not find it very hard to make this supposition, for it is a belief that is actually held by many more persons than those who profess any profound religious convictions in Western countries to-day. There is nothing blatantly contradictory about it, no palpable absurdity. In that case we may suppose for a moment that the unbeliever is right. But would it not still be true that we ought to treat our neighbour in one way rather than another? Should we not still succour the needy, alleviate pain and avoid the infliction of it, seek a fair distribution of material goods, cultivate our talents, and generally so conduct ourselves that the fleeting spell of man's life on earth should be as full of richness and wonder and the glow of affection as it is possible for it to be? Admitting, as the present writer is most ready to admit, that life would be full of frustration and lack the only salve that will bring genuine easement to the mind of man, it would still be true, to limit ourselves to the obvious, that cruelty would merit condemnation and kindness praise. Indeed, these virtues and vices might reveal their nature all the more clearly in the glow of a purely secular light [in the light, that is to say, of a belief that God and the spiritual do not exist, and that when we die there is nothing beyond]. And may not the understanding acquired in this way prove in the end a means of enrichment and sanity in the religious life itself?

H. D. LEWIS

[Erasmus is referring in the following passage to monks of various orders.]

Most of them place their greatest hope for salvation on a strict performance of their foolish ceremonies, and a belief in their legendary traditions. They fancy that by doing and believing, in these respects, more even than God has commanded they acquire so much merit that one heaven can never be an adequate reward for the excellence of their life; little thinking that the Judge of all the earth at the last day shall put them off, with a "Who hath required these things at your hands?", and call them to account only for their loyal fulfilment of the precept he left them, which was that of charity and love. It will be pretty to hear their pleas before the great tribunal: one will brag how he mortified his bodily appetite by feeding only upon fish; another will urge that he spent most of his time on earth in the divine exercise of singing psalms: a third will tell how many days he fasted, and what severe penance he imposed on himself for the bringing his body into subjection: another shall produce in his own behalf as many ceremonies as would load a fleet of merchant-men: a fifth shall plead, that in three-score years he never as much as touched a piece of money, except he fingered it through a thick pair of gloves: a sixth, to testify his former humility, shall bring along with him his sacred monk's-hood, so old and nasty, that any seaman had rather stand bare-headed on the deck, than put it on to defend his ears from the sharpest storms: the next that comes to answer for himself shall plead that for fifty years together he had lived like a sponge upon the same place, and was content never to change his homely habitation: another shall whisper softly, and tell the judge he has lost his voice by a continual singing of holy hymns and anthems: and the last shall intimate that he has forgot to speak, by having always kept silence, in obedience to the injunction of taking heed lest he should have offended with his tongue. But amidst all their fine excuses our Saviour shall interrupt them with this answer, Woe unto you, scribes and pharisees, hypocrites, verily I know you not; I left you but one precept, of loving one another, which I do not hear any one plead he has faithfully discharged: I told you plainly in my gospel, without any parable, that my father's kingdom was prepared, not for such as should lay claim to it by austerities, prayers, or fastings, but for those who should render themselves worthy of it by the exercise of faith, and the performance of charity: I cannot own as my disciples such as depend on their own merits without a reliance on my mercy: as many of you therefore as trust to the broken reeds of your own deserts, may even go search out a new heaven, for you shall never enter into that, which from the foundations of the world was prepared only for such as are true of heart.

★★ ERASMUS

Six hundred and thirteen commandments were given to Moses. Then David came and reduced them to eleven. Then came Isaiah, and reduced them to six. Then came Micah, and reduced them to three. Then Isaiah came again, and reduced them to two, as it is said, "Keep ye judgment and do

277

righteousness." Then came Amos, and reduced them to one, as it is said, "Seek ye me and live."

RABBI SIMLAI

[What is necessary for "salvation"—for being saved from a half-dead sort of existence when life to the brim can be ours— is not the observance of religious ceremonies or doing this and avoiding that because God has so ordered, but a pure love of the Creator and His creation, and, above all, of our fellow human beings.]

To my Divine Mother I prayed only for pure love. I offered flowers at Her Lotus Feet and prayed: "Mother, here is Thy virtue, here is Thy vice. Take them both and grant me only pure love for Thee. Here is Thy knowledge, here is Thy ignorance. Take them both and grant me only pure love for Thee. Here is Thy purity, here is Thy impurity. Take them both, Mother, and grant me only pure love for Thee."

SRI RAMAKRISHNA

[In Ramakrishna's religion the Deity, the creative spirit of the universe, was thought of as a woman.]

He who acts out of the pure love of God, not only does he not perform his actions to be seen by men, but does not do them even that God may know of them. Such an one, if he thought it possible that his good works might escape the eye of God, would still perform them with the same joy, and in the same pureness of love.

ST. JOHN OF THE CROSS

The Best should be the dearest of all things to us! And in our love of it, neither advantage nor injury, gain nor loss, honour nor dishonour, praise nor blame, nor anything of the kind should be regarded; but what is in truth the Noblest and Best should be also the dearest of all things, and that for no other cause than that it is the Noblest and Best. Hereby should a man order his life, within and without!

★★ THEOLOGIA GERMANICA

So long as a man seeks his best as *his*, and for his own sake, he will never find it. For so long as he does this, he seeks himself, and imagines that he is himself the Best; and seeing that he is not the Best, he seeks not the Best, so long as he seeks himself. But whosoever seeks, loves, and pursues the Good for the sake of the Good and for nothing but the love of the Good, he will find it, for he seeks it aright. And they who seek it otherwise, err.

★★ THEOLOGIA GERMANICA

O God, if I worship Thee from hope of Paradise, exclude me from it. But if I worship Thee for Thyself alone, then withhold not Thyself from me.

RABI'A

We read in the gospel that our Lord went into the temple and cast out all them that sold and bought. Now consider who they were that sold and bought therein and who they are still. Lo, they are merchants all who, while avoiding mortal sin and wishing to be virtuous, do good works to the glory of God, fasts, for example, prayers, etc., all of them excellent, but do them with a view to God's giving them somewhat, doing to them somewhat, they wish for in return. All such are merchants.

★★ MEISTER ECKHART

Blessedness is not the reward of virtue, but virtue itself.

SPINOZA

[To be blessed with something is to have something excellent conferred on us by God. We may be blessed, for instance, with perfect health, or beautiful children, or the love of friends. But we may also be blessed, not with this or that, but generally: and, in that event, we are in a state of blessedness. What Spinoza is saying is that blessedness is not a reward for being good: being good *is* blessedness. "Virtue is its own reward".]

Put an end once for all to this discussion of what a good man should be, and be one.

MARCUS AURELIUS

§ 5

[Many of us have only one calling, one way of living to which God has specifically called us, as He called Moses to be His prophet and Beethoven to write, not just music in general, but the particular music he actually wrote. If we have such a calling we may discover it early in life, as when a schoolboy suddenly tells himself "I *must* be a scientist"; or by the process of trial and error, as when it dawned upon Gauguin, the French painter, after he had spent years as a merchant, that he *must* be an artist; or sometimes, alas, on our deathbeds, when as we look back on the life that is going we think remorsefully "If only I had been a doctor! I see now that that's what I ought to have been." No need to explain how we discover our calling: a voice within us says "That and no other". And if we disobey the voice for whatever reason: if, for example, we reject our calling as too difficult, or choose something else that we can make more money by, we are losing ourselves, what we are, what we are endowed with, the thing so real in us that it can be thought of as still existing in the universe when our bodies are dead.

This is what George Borrow is saying in the first of the next four passages: and de la Mare finds grandeur in even a scarecrow that faithfully performs what it was made for. The other two poems—Wordsworth's "Resolution and Independence" and the passage from Ibsen's "Peer Gynt"—are about callings in a rather different sense. Not by any means everyone is born to be something specific: but *any* work that honourably comes to us is also a calling, and if we do it with whole-hearted resolution we fulfil the dignity of human nature.]

O ye gifted ones, follow your calling, for however various your talents may be, ye can have but one calling. Let neither obstacles nor temptations induce you to leave it; bound along if you can; if not, on hands and knees follow it, perish in it, if needful; but ye need not fear that; no one ever yet died in the true path of his calling before he had attained the pinnacle. Turn into other paths, and for a momentary advantage or gratification ye have sold your inheritance, your immortality.

★ GEORGE BORROW

THE SCARECROW

All winter through I bow my head
    Beneath the driving rain;
The North Wind powders me with snow
    And blows me back again;
At midnight in a maze of stars
    I flame with glittering rime,
And stand, above the rubble, stiff
    As mail at morning-prime.
But when that child, called Spring, and all
    His host of children, come,
Scattering their buds and dew upon
    These acres of my home,

281

Some rapture in my rags awakes;
    I lift void eyes and scan
The skies for crows, those ravening foes,
    Of my strange master, Man.
I watch him striding lank behind
    His clashing team, and know
Soon will the wheat swish body high
    Where once lay sterile snow;
Soon shall I gaze across a sea
    Of sun-begotten grain,
Which my unflinching watch hath sealed
    For harvest once again.

472   WALTER DE LA MARE

RESOLUTION AND INDEPENDENCE

I

There was a roaring in the wind all night;
The rain came heavily and fell in floods;
But now the sun is rising calm and bright;
The birds are singing in the distant woods;
Over his own sweet voice the Stock-dove broods;
The Jay makes answer as the Magpie chatters;
And all the air is filled with pleasant noise of waters.

II

All things that love the sun are out of doors;
The sky rejoices in the morning's birth;
The grass is bright with rain-drops;—on the moors
The hare is running races in her mirth;
And with her feet she from the plashy earth
Raises a mist; that, glittering in the sun,
Runs with her all the way, wherever she doth run.

III

I was a Traveller then upon the moor;
I saw the hare that raced about with joy;
I heard the woods and distant waters roar;
Or heard them not, as happy as a boy:
The pleasant season did my heart employ:
My old remembrances went from me wholly;
And all the ways of men, so vain and melancholy.

IV

But, as it sometimes chanceth, from the might
Of joy in minds that can no further go,
As high as we have mounted in delight
In our dejection do we sink as low;
To me that morning did it happen so;
And fears and fancies thick upon me came;
Dim sadness—and blind thoughts, I knew not, nor could
name.

V

I heard the sky-lark warbling in the sky;
And I bethought me of the playful hare:
'Even such a happy Child of earth am I;
Even as these blissful creatures do I fare;
Far from the world I walk, and from all care;
But there may come another day to me—
Solitude, pain of heart, distress, and poverty.'

VIII

Now, whether it were by peculiar grace,
A leading from above, a something given,
Yet it befell that, in this lonely place,
When I with these untoward thoughts had striven,
Beside a pool bare to the eye of heaven
I saw a Man before me unawares:
The oldest man he seemed that ever wore grey hairs.

IX

As a huge stone is sometimes seen to lie
Couched on the bald top of an eminence;
Wonder to all who do the same espy,
By what means it could thither come, and whence;
So that it seems a thing endued with sense;
Like a sea-beast crawled forth, that on a shelf
Of rock or sand reposeth, there to sun itself;

X

Such seemed this Man, not all alive nor dead,
Nor all asleep—in his extreme old age:
His body was bent double, feet and head
Coming together in life's pilgrimage;
As if some dire constraint of pain, or rage
Of sickness felt by him in times long past,
A more than human weight upon his frame had cast.

XI

Himself he propped, limbs, body, and pale face,
Upon a long grey staff of shaven wood:
And, still as I drew near with gentle pace,
Upon the margin of that moorish flood
Motionless as a cloud the old Man stood,
That heareth not the loud winds when they call;
And moveth all together, if it move at all.

XII

At length, himself unsettling, he the pond
Stirred with his staff, and fixedly did look
Upon the muddy water, which he conned,
As if he had been reading in a book:
And now a stranger's privilege I took;
And, drawing to his side, to him did say,
"This morning gives us promise of a glorious day."

XIII

A gentle answer did the old Man make,
In courteous speech which forth he slowly drew:
And him with further words I thus bespake,
"What occupation do you there pursue?
This is a lonesome place for one like you."
Ere he replied, a flash of mild surprise
Broke from the sable orbs of his yet-vivid eyes.

XIV

His words came feebly, from a feeble chest,
But each in solemn order followed each,
With something of a lofty utterance drest—
Choice word and measured phrase, above the reach
Of ordinary men; a stately speech;
Such as grave Livers do in Scotland use,
Religious men, who give to God and man their dues.

XV

He told, that to these waters he had come
To gather leeches, being old and poor:
Employment hazardous and wearisome!
And he had many hardships to endure:
From pond to pond he roamed, from moor to moor;
Housing, with God's good help, by choice or chance;
And in this way he gained an honest maintenance.

XVI

The old Man still stood talking by my side;
But now his voice to me was like a stream
Scarce heard; nor word from word could I divide;
And the whole body of the Man did seem
Like one whom I had met with in a dream;
Or like a man from some far region sent,
To give me human strength, by apt admonishment.

XVII

My former thoughts returned: the fear that kills;
And hope that is unwilling to be fed;
Cold, pain, and labour, and all fleshly ills;
And mighty Poets in their misery dead.
—Perplexed, and longing to be comforted,
My question eagerly did I renew,
"How is it that you live, and what is it you do?"

XVIII

He with a smile did then his words repeat;
And said that, gathering leeches, far and wide
He travelled; stirring thus about his feet
The waters of the pools where they abide.
"Once I could meet with them on every side;
But they have dwindled long by slow decay;
Yet still I persevere, and find them where I may."

XIX

While he was talking thus, the lonely place,
The old Man's shape, and speech—all troubled me:
In my mind's eye I seemed to see him pace
About the weary moors continually,
Wandering about alone and silently.
While I these thoughts within myself pursued,
He, having made a pause, the same discourse renewed.

XX

And soon with this he other matter blended,
Cheerfully uttered, with demeanour kind,
But stately in the main; and, when he ended,
I could have laughed myself to scorn to find
In that decrepit Man so firm a mind.
"God," said I, "be my help and stay secure;
I'll think of the Leech-gatherer on the lonely moor!"

472 WORDSWORTH

THE SERMON BY THE GRAVE

The Priest:

Now, when the soul has gone to meet its doom,
and here the dust lies, like an empty pod,—
now, my dear friends, we'll speak a word or two
about this dead man's pilgrimage on earth.

He was not wealthy, neither was he wise,
his voice was weak, his bearing was unmanly,
he spoke his mind abashed and faltering,
he scarce was master at his own fireside;
he sidled into church, as though appealing
for leave, like other men, to take his place.

It was from Gudbrandsdale, you know, he came.
When here he settled he was but a lad;—
and you remember how, to the very last,
he kept his right hand hidden in his pocket.

That right hand in the pocket was the feature
that chiefly stamped his image on the mind,—
and therewithal his writhing, his abashed
shrinking from notice wheresoe'er he went.

But, though he still pursued a path aloof,
and ever seemed a stranger in our midst,
you all know what he strove so hard to hide,—
the hand he muffled had four fingers only.—

I well remember, many years ago,
one morning; there were sessions held at Lundë.
'Twas war-time, and the talk in every mouth
turned on the country's sufferings and its fate.

I stood there watching. At the table sat
the Captain, 'twixt the Bailiff and the sergeants;
lad after lad was measured up and down,
passed, and enrolled, and taken for a soldier.
The room was full, and from the green outside,
where thronged the young folks, loud the laughter rang.

A name was called, and forth another stepped,

287

one pale as snow upon the glacier's edge.
They bade the youth advance; he reached the table;
we saw his right hand swaddled in a clout;—
he gasped, he swallowed, battling after words,—
but, though the Captain urged him, found no voice.
Ah yes, at last! Then with his cheek aflame,
his tongue now failing him, now stammering fast,
he mumbled something of a scythe that slipped
by chance, and shore his finger to the skin.

Straightway a silence fell upon the room.
Men bandied meaning glances; they made mouths;
they stoned the boy with looks of silent scorn.
He felt the hail-storm, but he saw it not.
Then up the Captain stood, the grey old man;
he spat, and pointed forth, and thundered "Go!"

And the lad went. On both sides men fell back,
till through their midst he had to run the gauntlet.
He reached the door; from there he took to flight;—
up, up he went,—through wood and over hillside,
up through the stone-slips, rough, precipitous.
He had his home up there among the mountains.—

It was some six months later he came here,
with mother, and betrothed, and little child.
He leased some ground upon the high hillside,
there where the waste lands trend away towards Lomb.
He married the first moment that he could;
he built a house; he broke the stubborn soil;
he throve, as many a cultivated patch
bore witness, bravely clad in waving gold.
At church he kept his right hand in his pocket,—
but sure I am at home his fingers nine
toiled every bit as hard as others' ten.—
One spring the torrent washed it all away.

Their lives were spared. Ruined and stripped of all,
he set to work to make another clearing;
and, ere the autumn, smoke again arose

from a new, better-sheltered, mountain farm-house.
Sheltered? From torrent—not from avalanche;
two years, and all beneath the snow lay buried.

But still the avalanche could not daunt his spirit.
He dug, and raked, and carted—cleared the ground—
and the next winter, ere the snow-blasts came,
a third time was his little homestead reared.

Three sons he had, three bright and stirring boys;
they must to school, and school was far away;—
and they must clamber where the hill-track failed,
by narrow ledges through the headlong cliff.
What did he do? The eldest had to manage
as best he might, and, where the path was worst,
his father cast a rope round him to stay him;—
the others on his back and arms he bore.

Thus he toiled, year by year, till they were men.
Now might he well have looked for some return.
In the New World, three prosperous gentlemen
their school-going and their father have forgotten.

He was short-sighted. Out beyond the circle
of those most near to him he nothing saw.
To him seemed meaningless as cymbals' tinkling
those words that to the heart should ring like steel.
His race, his fatherland, all things high and shining,
stood ever, to his vision, veiled in mist.

But he was humble, humble, was this man;
and since that sessions-day his doom oppressed him,
as surely as his cheeks were flushed with shame,
and his four fingers hidden in his pocket.—
Offender 'gainst his country's laws? Ay, true!
But there is one thing that outshines the law,
sure as the snow-white tent of Glittertind
has clouds, like higher rows of peaks, above it.
No patriot was he. Both for church and state
a fruitless tree. But there, on the upland ridge,
in the small circle where he saw his calling,

there he was great, because he was himself.
His inborn note rang true unto the end.
His days were as a lute with muted strings.
And therefore, peace be with thee, silent warrior,
that fought the peasant's little fight, and fell!

It is not ours to search the heart and soul;—
that is no task for dust, but for its ruler;—
yet dare I freely, firmly, speak my hope:
he scarce stands crippled now before his God!

★ IBSEN (from *Peer Gynt*)

§ 6

Truth is a divine thing, a friend more excellent than any human friend.

ST. THOMAS AQUINAS

The essence of man lies in this, in his marvellous faculty for seeking truth, seeing it, loving it, and sacrificing himself to it.

GUISEPPE PREZZOLINI

Now I, Callicles, am persuaded of the truth of these things, and I consider how I shall present my soul whole and undefiled before the judge in that day. Renouncing the honours at which the world aims, I desire only to know the truth, and to live as well as I can, and, when I die, to die as well as I can. And, to the utmost of my power, I exhort all other men to do the same. And, in return for your exhortation of me, I exhort you also to take part in the great combat, which is the combat of life, and greater than every other earthly conflict.

PLATO

And yet, my friend, I would rather that the whole world should be at odds with me, and oppose me, than that I myself should be at odds with myself, and contradict myself.

PLATO

The Devil is compromise.

IBSEN

Talk nonsense, but talk your own nonsense. . . . To go wrong in one's own way is better than to go right in someone else's.

DOSTOEVSKY

Do always what you believe right, Brother; and if that is wrong, repent of it afterwards.

A FRANCISCAN (*in a Housman play*)

If God were able to backslide from truth I would fain cling to truth and let God go.

MEISTER ECKHART

Christ likes us to prefer truth to him because, before being Christ, he is truth. If one turns aside from him to go towards the truth, one will not go far before falling into his arms.

SIMONE WEIL

He who does not bellow the truth when he knows the truth makes himself the accomplice of liars and forgers.

CHARLES PÉGUY

If only they were to forsake me, and observe my teachings!

WORDS PUT INTO THE MOUTH OF GOD

(from the Talmud)

The least one can demand of people who judge any doctrine is that they should judge of it in the sense in which the teacher himself understood it. And Christ understood his teaching not as a distant ideal for humanity, obedience to which is impossible, nor as a mystical poetic fantasy wherewith he captivated the simple-minded inhabitants of Galilee. He understood his teaching as a real thing, and a thing which would save mankind. And he did not dream on the cross but died for his teaching, and many others are dying and will yet die. Of such a teaching one cannot say that it is a dream!

Every true doctrine is a dream to those in error. We have come to this, that there are many people (of whom I was one) who say that this teaching is visionary because it is not natural to man. It is not in accord, they say, with man's nature to turn the other cheek when one cheek is struck; it is not natural to give what is one's own to another; it is unnatural to work for others instead of for oneself. It is natural to man, they say, to defend his safety and the safety of his family and his property: in other words, it is natural for man to struggle for his own existence. The learned jurists prove scientifically that man's most sacred duty is to defend his rights, that is—to struggle.

But it is sufficient to free oneself for a moment from the thought that the order which exists and has been arranged by men is the best and is sacrosanct, for the objection that Christ's teaching is not accordant with man's nature to turn against the objector. Who will deny that to murder or torture, I will not say a man, but to torture a dog or kill a hen or calf is contrary and distressing to man's nature? (I know people who live by tilling the land, and who have given up eating meat merely because they had themselves to kill their own animals.) Yet the whole structure of our lives is such that each man's personal advantage is obtained by inflicting suffering on others, which is contrary to human nature. The whole order of our life and the whole complex mechanism of our institutions, designed for the infliction of violence, witness to the extent to which violence is contrary to human nature. Not a single judge would decide to strangle with a rope the man he condemns to death from the bench. Not a single magistrate would make up his mind himself to take a peasant from his weeping family and shut him up in prison. None of our generals or soldiers, were it not for discipline, oaths of allegiance, and declarations of war, would, I will not say kill hundreds of Turks and Germans and destroy their villages, but even wound a single man. All this is only done thanks to a very complex state and social machinery the purpose of which is so to distribute the responsibility for the evil deeds that are done that no one should feel the unnaturalness of those deeds. Some men write the laws; others apply them; a third set drill men and habituate them to discipline, that is to say, to senseless and implicit obedience; a fourth set—the people who are disciplined—commit all sorts of deeds of violence, even killing people, without knowing why or wherefore. But a man need only, even for a moment, free himself mentally from this net of worldly organisation in which he is involved to understand what is really unnatural to him.

TOLSTOY

FOURTH PART

V. HUMILITY AND GRATITUDE

O Saviour, pour upon me thy Spirit of meekness and love,
Annihilate the Selfhood in me, be thou all my life,
Guide thou my hand which trembles exceedingly upon the rock
    of ages.

BLAKE

Lord, make me an instrument of Thy Peace. Where there is
hatred, let me sow love; where there is injury, pardon; where
there is doubt, faith; where there is despair, hope; where there
is darkness, light; where there is sadness, joy.

O Divine Master, grant that I may not so much seek to be
consoled, as to console; to be understood, as to understand;
to be loved, as to love. For it is in giving that we receive, it is
in pardoning that we are pardoned; it is in dying that we are
born to eternal life.

ST. FRANCIS OF ASSISI

Make me pure, Lord: Thou art holy;
Make me meek, Lord: Thou wert lowly;
Now beginning, and alway:
Now begin, on Christmas day.

GERARD MANLEY HOPKINS (fragment)

I am only the vessel in which the powers of life work, and
create; and I dare not but be humble at the little I can manage
to let come through.

ERNST TOLLER

[Or, in religious language: When God wishes to bring more
joy into the world, he can do so only through human beings: we
are his instruments for the purpose. For example, it is only
through *our* work for peace that peace can be won. But most of us
are poor instruments, and little of God's purpose gets through us.]

We cannot be too careful how we receive praise. For if we contemplate ourselves in a false glass we are sure to be mistaken about what is due to us; and because we are too apt to believe what is pleasing, rather than what is true, we may be too easily swelled beyond our just proportion by the windy compliments of men.

Make ever therefore allowances for what is said on such occasions, or thou exposest as well as deceivest thyself.

For an over-value of ourselves gives us but a dangerous security in many respects.

We expect more than belongs to us; take all that is given us though never meant us; and fall out with those that are not as full of us as we are of ourselves.

Be not fond therefore of praise, but seek virtue that leads to it.

And yet no more disparage thy merit than overrrate it. For though humility be a virue, a pretended one is not.

★WILLIAM PENN

It is my humility that gives God his divinity, and the proof of it is this. God's peculiar property is giving. But God cannot give if he has nothing to receive his gifts. Now I make myself receptive to his gifts by my humility, so I by my humility do make God giver; and since giving is God's own peculiar property, I do by my humility give God his property. The would-be giver must needs find a taker; without a taker he cannot be a giver, for it is the taker by his taking that makes the man a giver. So God, to be the giver, must discover a receiver. Now none but the humble can receive the gift of God. So God, to use his godlike power of giving, will also need my humility; without humility he cannot give man anything, for I without humility cannot accept his gift. Thus it is true that I by my humility do give God his divinity.

MEISTER ECKHART

Thinking which keeps contact with reality must look up to the heavens, it must look over the earth, and dare to direct its gaze to the barred windows of a lunatic asylum. Look to the stars and understand how small our earth is in the universe. Look upon earth and know how minute man is upon it. The earth existed long before man came upon it. In the history of the universe, man is on the earth for but a second. Who knows but that the earth will circle round the sun once more without man upon it? Therefore we must not place man in the centre of the universe. And our gaze must be fixed on the barred windows of a lunatic asylum, in order that we may remember the terrible fact that the mental and spiritual are also liable to destruction.

Only when thinking thus becomes quite humble can it set its feet upon the way that leads to knowledge. The more profound a religion is, the more it realises this fact—that what it knows through belief is little compared with what it does not know. The first active deed of thinking is resignation—acquiescence in what happens. Becoming free, inwardly, from what happens, we pass through the gate of recognition on the way to ethics.

The deeper we look into nature, the more we recognise that it is full of life, and the more profoundly we know that all life is a secret and that we are united with all life that is in nature. Man can no longer live his life for himself alone. We realise that all life is valuable and that we are united to all this life. From this knowledge comes our spiritual relationship to the universe.

ALBERT SCHWEITZER

§ 2

He who has a humble mind is regarded as if he had offered all the sacrifices of the Law.

RABBI JOSHUA B. LEVI

There is a very high rung on the ladder of life which only one man in a whole generation can reach: that of having learned all secret wisdom and then praying like a little child.

RABBI MENDEL OF RYMANOV

Be humble, if thou would'st attain to Wisdom. Be humbler still, when thou hast mastered Wisdom.

THE VOICE OF THE SILENCE

Humility is the garment of God: and every one who wears it truly resembles the One who descended from his heights and hid the valour of His greatness and covered His glory with humility, so that his creatures should not be scorched by the sight of Him. For they would not have been able to look at Him had He not taken part of them into Himself and thus begun to talk to them.

ST. ISAAC OF SYRIA

A king was told that a man of humility is endowed with long life. He attired himself in old garments, took up his residence in a small hut, and forbade anyone to show reverence before him. But when he honestly examined himself, the King found himself to be prouder of his seeming humility than ever before. A philosopher thereupon remarked to him: "Dress like a king; live like a king; allow the people to show due respect to you; but be humble in your inmost heart."

THE BAALSHEM

THE MONK WITH A BEAUTIFUL BEARD

In the time of Moses there was a dervish who spent days and nights in a state of adoration, yet experienced no feeling for spiritual things. He had a beautiful long beard, and often while praying would stop to comb it. One day, seeing Moses, he went to him and said: 'O Pasha of Mount Sinai, ask God, I pray you, to tell me why I experience neither spiritual satisfaction nor ecstasy'.

The next time Moses went up on Sinai he spoke to God about the dervish and God said, in a tone of displeasure: 'Although this dervish has sought union with me, nevertheless he is constantly thinking about his long beard'. When Moses came down he told the dervish what God had said. The dervish thereupon began tearing out his beard, weeping bitterly. Gabriel then came along to Moses and said: 'Even now your dervish is thinking about his beard. He thought of nothing else while praying, and is even more attached to it while he is tearing it out!'

FARID UD-DIN ATTAR

On one occasion they brought a man possessed of a devil to one of the monks, and entreated him to cast the devil out, but the old man was unwilling to do so; but since they urged him strongly he was persuaded, and he had mercy on the man, and he said to the devil, "Get thee out from that which God hath fashioned." Then the devil answered and said, "I am going out, but I would ask thee to tell me one thing: What is the meaning of that which is written in the Gospel, Who are the goats and who are the sheep?" The old man answered and said, "I myself am one of the goats, but God knoweth who the sheep are"; and when the devil heard this, he cried out with a loud voice, saying "Behold, I go forth because of thy humility", and straightway he left the man and departed.

THE PARADISE OF THE FATHERS

[At the Last Judgment, according to the words of Christ as recorded by St. Matthew, all human beings, whether living or dead, will be brought before the Throne of Glory and separated one from another as a shepherd divides his sheep from his goats, namely into good and bad: the sheep will be placed on the right hand and awarded heaven or "eternal life", and the goats will be placed on the left hand and awarded hell or "eternal punishment". The Last Judgment takes place when the world has been brought to an end and God's Kingdom has succeeded it.

A friend of mine, a biblical scholar, is persuaded, he tells me, that such references to the Last Judgment are not genuine sayings of Christ, but a take-over into the New Testament of current theories about the end of the world. I hope he is right, for I find it difficult to reconcile "hell" or "eternal punishment" with the concept of a loving God that was the core of Christ's gospel. But if my friend is wrong, then what Christ is really teaching, I should like to think, in the vivid and dramatic language he loved, is that any act of kindness, even the smallest, to a fellow human being—a crust of bread, for example, to relieve a man's hunger—is a bit of goodness everlastingly *there* in the sum total of things, however many centuries may pass, simply because, at what we think of as a moment of time, it has been created, come into existence: and that similarly no act of unkindness, such as the refusal of a crust, can ever pass away— though the harm we have done to ourselves by such a failure can be modified by repentance, and the harm we have done to our neighbour can be "made good" or balanced, in some measure, by greater charity in the future. As for the Last Judgment, all that it can really mean is our condition, maybe on our deathbeds, when we strip off all indifference or pretence about our feelings and actions, and nakedly face the truth. Every moment in which a man does that is his Last Judgment.]

Rabbi Moshe Leib of Sasov once gave his last coin to a man of evil reputation. His students reproached him for it. Whereupon he replied: "Shall I be more particular than God, who gave the coin to me?"

HASIDIC STORY

Once the Rabbi of Apt came to a city in which two men competed for the privilege of giving him lodgings. Both houses were equally roomy and comfortable and in both households all the rules and regulations of Judaism were observed with pious exactitude. But one of the men was in ill repute for his many love affairs and other sinful doings and he knew quite well that he was weak and thought little of himself. The other man, however, no one in the whole community could accuse of the slightest breach of conduct. With proud and stately steps he walked abroad, thoroughly aware of his spotless purity.

The rabbi selected the house of the man with a bad reputation. When he was asked for the reason for his choice, he answered: "Concerning the proud, God says: 'I and he cannot live together in this world.' And if God himself, blessed be he, cannot share a room with the proud, then how could I? We read in the Torah, on the other hand, '. . . who dwelleth with them in the midst of their uncleannesses'. And if God takes lodgings there, why shouldn't I?"

HASIDIC STORY

A man of piety complained to the Baalshem, saying: "I have laboured hard and long in the service of the Lord, and yet I have received no improvement. I am still an ordinary and ignorant person."

The Baalshem answered: "You have gained the realisation that you are ordinary and ignorant, and this in itself is a worthy accomplishment."

HASIDIC STORY

A young man was asked by Rabbi Yitzhak Meir of Ger if he had learned the Torah. "Just a little," replied the youth.

"That is all anyone ever has learned of the Torah," was the Rabbi's answer.

HASIDIC STORY

It was the habit of Rabbi David Talner to spend half an hour early each morning reading his letters in his private room. An intimate asked why he did this even before saying his prayers, which would normally come first. The Rabbi answered: "I wish to commence the day aright. As you know, the more important a man is, the harder are his struggles against his evil thoughts, since the Satan strives hardest to tempt him. Hence when I look over my letters and find myself addressed as a Leader, a Saint, and the like, I pray to the Lord: 'You and I know that I do not merit these titles of honour. But since so many good men believe them in all sincerity, I beseech Thee to aid me to avoid temptation, so that these men may not feel shame.' "

★ HASIDIC STORY

When Rabbi Phineas Hurwitz came to Frankfurt to take up the post of Rabbi, he received an overpowering welcome. Thousands of people surrounded his carriage. A friend asked how he felt in this hour of triumph. The Rabbi replied: "I imagined that I was a corpse, being borne to the cemetery in the company of multitudes attending the funeral."

HASIDIC STORY

When Rabbi Shmelke came to Nikolsburg to assume his duties as Rabbi, he locked himself in a room and began to pace back and forth. One of the welcoming party overheard him repeating again and again the many forms of greeting he anticipated. When the welcome was concluded, the man confessed that he had overheard Rabbi Shmelke, and inquired if the Rabbi would explain his odd action.

Rabbi Shmelke said: "I dislike intensely honours which tend to self-pride; therefore I rehearsed to myself all the words of welcome. No one appreciates self-praise, and after becoming accustomed to these words of acclaim by frequent repetition,

I no longer felt pride in hearing these very phrases uttered by the committee of welcome."

HASIDIC STORY

Everyone must have two pockets, so that he can reach into the one or the other, according to his needs. In his right pocket are to be the words: "For my sake was the world created", and in his left: "I am earth and ashes".

RABBI BUNUM OF PZHYSHA

BONTZYE SHWEIG[1]

[Bontzye Shweig has just died, and has gone to Heaven for judgement. The Hasidic fancy about judgement after death is described in the square-bracketed passage on page 38.]

Down here, in *this* world, Bontzye Shweig's death made no impression at all. Ask anyone you like who Bontzye was, *how* he lived, and what he died of; whether of heart failure, or whether his strength gave out, or whether his back broke under a heavy load, and they won't know. Perhaps, after all, he died of hunger.

If a tram-car horse had fallen dead, there would have been more excitement. It would have been mentioned in the papers, and hundreds of people would have crowded round to look at the dead animal—even the spot where the accident took place.

But the tramway horse would receive less attention if there were as many horses as men—a thousand million.

Bontzye lived quietly and died quietly. He passed through *our* world like a shadow.

No wine was drunk at Bontzye's circumcision, no healths were proposed, and he made no beautiful speech when he was confirmed. He lived like a little dun-coloured grain of sand on

[1] Shweig = silent.

305

the sea-shore, among millions of his kind; and when the wind lifted him and blew him over to the other side of the sea, nobody noticed it.

When he was alive, the mud in the street preserved no impression of his feet; after his death, the wind overturned the little board on his grave. The grave-digger's wife found it a long way off from the spot, and boiled a potful of potatoes over it. Three days after that, the grave-digger had forgotten where he had laid him.

If Bontzye had been given a tombstone, then, in a hundred years or so, an antiquarian might have found it, and the name "Bontzye Shweig" would have echoed once again in *our* air.

A shadow! His likeness remained photographed in nobody's brain, in nobody's heart; not a trace of him remained.

"No kith, no kin!" He lived and died alone!

Had it not been for the human commotion, someone might have heard Bontzye's spine snap under its load; had the world been less busy, someone might have remarked that Bontzye (also a human being) went about with two extinguished eyes and fearfully hollow cheeks; that even when he had no load on his shoulders, his head drooped earthward as though, while yet alive, he were looking for his grave. Were there as few men as tramway horses, someone might perhaps have asked: What has happened to Bontzye?

When they carried Bontzye into the hospital, his corner in the underground lodging was soon filled—there were ten of his like waiting for it, and they put it up to auction among themselves. When they carried him from the hospital bed to the dead-house, there were twenty poor sick persons waiting for the bed. When he had been taken out of the dead-house, they brought in twenty bodies from under a building that had fallen in. Who knows how long he will rest in his grave? Who knows how many are waiting for the little plot of ground?

A quiet birth, a quiet life, a quiet death, and a quieter burial.

But it was not so in the *other* world. *There* Bontzye's death made a great impression.

306

The blast of the great Messianic Shofar[1] sounded through all the seven heavens: Bontzye Shweig has left the earth! The largest angels with the broadest wings flew about and told one another: Bontzye Shweig is to take his seat in the Heavenly Academy! In Paradise there was a noise and a joyful tumult: Bontzye Shweig! Just fancy! Bontzye Shweig!

Little child-angels with sparkling eyes, gold thread-work wings, and silver slippers, ran delightedly to meet him. The rustle of the wings, the tap-tap of the little slippers, and the merry laughter of the fresh, rosy mouths, filled all the heavens and reached to the Throne of Glory, and God Himself knew that Bontzye Shweig was coming.

Abraham, our father, stood in the gate, his right hand stretched out with a hearty greeting, and a sweet smile lit up his old face.

What are they wheeling through heaven?

Two angels are pushing a golden arm-chair into Paradise for Bontzye Shweig.

What flashed so brightly?

They were carrying past a gold crown set with precious stones —all for Bontzye Shweig.

"Before the decision of the Heavenly Court has been given?" ask the saints, not quite without jealousy.

"O," reply the angels, "that will be a mere formality. Even the prosecutor won't say a word against Bontzye Shweig. The case will not last five minutes."

Just consider: Bontzye Shweig!

When the little angels had met Bontzye in mid-air and played him a tune; when Abraham, our father, had shaken him by the hand like an old comrade; when he heard that a chair stood waiting for him in Paradise, that a crown lay ready for his head, and that not a word would be lost over his case before the Heavenly Court—Bontzye, just as in the other world, was

[1] The coming of the Messiah, according to tradition, would be heralded by a blast on the Shofar (ram's-horn trumpet).

too frightened to speak. His heart sank with terror. He is sure it is all a dream, or else simply a mistake.

He is used to both. He often dreamt, in the other world, that he was picking up money off the floor—there were whole heaps of it—and then he woke to find himself as poor as ever; and more than once people had smiled at him and given him a friendly word and then turned away and spat out.

"It is my luck," he used to think. And now he dared not raise his eyes, lest the dream should vanish, lest he should wake up in some cave full of snakes and lizards. He was afraid to speak, afraid to move, lest he should be recognised and flung into the pit.

He trembles and does not hear the angels' compliments, does not see how they dance round him, makes no answer to the greeting of Abraham, our father, and—when he is led into the presence of the Heavenly Court, he does not even wish it "good morning!"

He is beside himself with terror, and his fright increases when he happens to notice the floor of the Heavenly Courthouse; it is all alabaster set with diamonds. "And my feet standing on it!" He is paralysed. "Who knows what rich man, what rabbi, what saint they take me for—he will come—and that will be the end of me!"

His terror is such, he never even hears the president call out: "The case of Bontzye Shweig!", adding, as he hands the deeds to the advocate, "Read, but make haste!"

The whole hall goes round and round in Bontzye's eyes, there is a rushing in his ears. And through the rushing he hears more and more clearly the voice of the advocate, speaking sweetly as a violin.

"His name," he hears, "fitted him like the dress made for a slender figure by the hand of an artist-tailor."

"What is he talking about?" wondered Bontzye, and he heard an impatient voice break in with:

"No similes, please!"

"He never," continued the advocate, "was heard to complain

308

to either God or man; there was never a flash of hatred in his eye; he never lifted it with a claim on heaven."

Still Bontzye does not understand, and once again the hard voice interrupts: "No rhetoric, please!"

"Job gave way—this one was more unfortunate——"

"Facts, dry facts!"

"When he was a week old, he was circumcised. . . ."

"We want no realism!"

"The doctor who circumcised him did not know his work——"

"Come, come!"

"And he kept silent," the advocate went on, "even when his mother died, and he was given a stepmother at thirteen years old—a serpent, a vixen."

"Can they mean me after all?" thought Bontzye.

"No insinuations against a third party!" said the president, angrily.

"She grudged him every mouthful—stale, mouldy bread, tendons instead of meat—and *she* drank coffee with cream."

"Keep to the subject," ordered the president.

"She grudged him everything but her finger nails, and his black-and-blue body showed through the holes in his torn and fusty clothes. Winter time, in the hardest frost, he had to chop wood for her, barefoot, in the yard, and his hands were too young and too weak, the logs too thick, the hatchet too blunt. More than once he nearly dislocated his wrist; more than once his feet were nearly frost-bitten, but he kept silent, even to his father."

"To that drunkard?" laughs the accuser, and Bontzye feels cold in every limb.

"He never even complained to his father," finished up the advocate.

"And always alone," he continued, "no playmates, no school, nor teaching of any kind—never a whole garment—never a free moment."

"Facts, please!" reminded the president.

"He kept silent even later, when his father seized him by

the hair in a fit of drunkenness, and flung him out into the street on a snowy winter's night. He quietly picked himself up out of the snow and ran whither his feet carried him.

"He kept silent all the way—however hungry he might be, he only begged with his eyes.

"It was a wild, wet night in spring time, when he reached the great town; he fell like a drop into the ocean, and yet he passed that same night under arrest. He kept silent and never asked why, for what. He was let out, and looked about for the hardest work. And he kept silent. Harder than the work itself was the finding of it—and he kept silent.

"Bathed in a cold sweat, crushed together under heavy loads, his empty stomach convulsed with hunger—he kept silent.

"Bespattered with mud, spat at, driven with his load off the pavement and into the street among the cabs, carts, and tramways, looking death in the eyes every moment—he kept silent.

"He never calculated how many pounds' burden go to a groschen, how many times he fell on an errand worth a dreier; how many times he nearly panted out his soul going after his pay; he never calculated the difference between other people's lot and his—he kept silent.

"And he never insisted loudly on his pay; he stood in the doorway like a beggar, with a dog-like pleading in his eyes— 'Come again later!' and he went like a shadow to come again later, and beg for his wage more humbly than before.

"He kept silent even when they cheated him of part, or threw in a false coin.

"He took everything in silence."

"They mean me after all," thought Bontzye.

"Once," continued the advocate, after a sip of water, "a change came into his life: there came flying along a carriage on rubber tyres drawn by two runaway horses. The driver already lay some distance off on the pavement with a cracked skull. The terrified horses foamed at the mouth, sparks shot from their hoofs, their eyes shone like fiery lamps on a winter's night—and in the carriage, more dead than alive, sat a man.

"And Bontzye stopped the horses. And the man he had saved was a charitable Jew, who was not ungrateful.

"He put the dead man's whip into Bontzye's hands, and Bontzye became a coachman. More than that—he was provided with a wife, and more still—with a child.

"And Bontzye kept silent!"

"Me, they mean me!" Bontzye assured himself again, and yet had not the courage to give a glance at the Heavenly Court.

He listens to the advocate further:

"He kept silent also when his protector became bankrupt and did not pay him his wages.

"He kept silent when his wife ran away from him, leaving him a child at the breast.

"He was silent also fifteen years later, when the child had grown up and was strong enough to throw him out of the house."

"Me, they mean me!" Now he is sure of it.

"He kept silent even," began the angelic advocate once more in a still softer and sadder voice, "when the same philanthropist paid all his creditors their due but him—and even when (riding once again in a carriage with rubber tyres and fiery horses) he knocked Bontzye down and drove over him.

"He kept silent. He did not even tell the police who had done for him."

"He kept silent even in the hospital, where one may cry out.

"He kept silent when the doctor would not come to his bed-side without being paid fifteen kopeks, and when the attendant demanded another five—for changing his linen.

"He kept silent in the death-struggle—silent in death.

"Not a word against God; not a word against men!

"*Dixi!*"[1]

Once more Bontzye trembled all over; he knew that after the

[1] I have spoken, I have finished.

advocate comes the prosecutor. Who knows what *he* will say?

Bontzye himself had remembered nothing of his life.

Even in the other world he forgot every moment what had happened in the one before. The advocate had recalled everything to his mind. Who knows what the prosecutor will not remind him of?

"Gentlemen," begins the prosecutor, in a voice biting and acid as vinegar—but he breaks off.

"Gentlemen," he begins again, but his voice is milder, and a second time he breaks off.

Then, from out the same throat, comes in a voice that is almost gentle:

"Gentlemen! *He* was silent! I will be silent, too!"

There is a hush—and there sounds in front a new, soft, trembling voice:

"Bontzye, my child," it speaks like a harp, "my dear child Bontzye!"

And Bontzye's heart melts within him. Now he would lift up his eyes, but they are blinded with tears; he never felt such sweet emotion before. "My child!" "My Bontzye!"—no one, since his mother died, had spoken to him with such words in such a voice.

"My child," continued the presiding judge, "you have suffered and kept silent; there is no whole limb, no whole bone in your body, without a scar, without a wound, not a fibre of your soul that has not bled—and you kept silent.

"There they did not understand. Perhaps you yourself did not know that you might have cried out, and that at your cry the walls of Jericho would have shaken and fallen. You yourself knew nothing of your hidden power.

"In the other world your silence was not understood, but *that* is the world of delusion; in the world of truth you will receive your reward.

"The Heavenly Court will not judge you; the Heavenly Court will not pass sentence on you; they will not apportion you a reward. Take what you will! Everything is yours!"

312

Bontzye looks up for the first time. He is dazzled; everything shines and flashes and streams with light.

"Really?" he asks shyly.

"Yes, really!" answers the presiding judge with decision; "really, I tell you, everything is yours; everything in heaven belongs to you. Because all that shines and sparkles is only the reflection of your hidden goodness, a reflection of your soul. You only take of what is yours."

"Really?" asks Bontzye again, this time in a firmer voice.

"Really, really, really!" they answer him from all sides.

"Well, if it is so," Bontzye smiles, "I would like to have every day, for breakfast, a hot roll with fresh butter."

The Court and the angels looked down, a little ashamed; the prosecutor laughed.

ISAAC LOEB PEREZ

TRUE AND FALSE HUMILITY

God does not do the same thing twice. Every man is unique, and his uniqueness is given to him so that he may unfold it and make it flower. No one ever lived who was the same as he; for had there ever been one who was the same as he there would have been no reason for him to exist. Each person is a new thing in the world, and he should bring to perfection what makes him unique.

But just as a man requires the everyday world to perform his actions in, so his uniqueness is unfolded by his way of living with others: and the more truly unique he is, the more he can give to those others. For the unique is not the Whole, but a part of the Whole: and the purer a man is and the more perfect, the more intensely is he aware of but being a part, of but having a place in the great community of his fellow human-beings. This is humility. To feel the universe as a sea, and oneself as a wave in it—this is humility.

But there is a false humility and a true humility. For a man to feel scorn of himself and to forget that by his works and behaviour he can bless the whole world—this is false humility.

"The greatest evil is to forget that you are the son of a king". The truly humble *feel* others as they feel themselves, they feel themselves *in* others. To be proud is, not to know one's own value, but to contrast oneself with others, to regard oneself as higher than the least of others, to measure up and make judgment of others.

True humility is not a virtue you can will yourself to practise: it is a state of mind, an expression of your whole personality. The truly humble man *lives* in every being; he knows the nature and virtue of each. Because everyone is as himself to him, he knows from within him that everyone has some hidden value, that everyone has his hour. Every soul stands bright and clear for him in the splendour of its own existence. He can condemn no one, for "he who judges another has judged himself".

To live with understanding of others is mere justice: to live *in* others, as in oneself, is love. And it is out of love that the humble help others, not out of pity: pity is but a sharp, quick pain that one wants to get rid of. The man who merely pities another is not suffering with him, is not carrying the other's sorrow in his own heart, as one might share in the life of a tree, in the dream of its roots and the desire of its trunk and the thousand movements of its boughs; or as one might share in the life of an animal, with its stretchings and clawings, and the joy of its sinews and limbs, and the dumb understanding of its brain. The man who only pities receives a sharp, quick pain from the mere outward manifestation of another's sorrow: a pain having nothing in common with the real sorrow of the sufferer.

The only help that exists in God's sight is the help that comes from living in others. Thus it is told of Rabbi Bunam that when a poor man excited his pity he first provided for his immediate needs; then, when he felt the pangs of pity assuaged, he absorbed himself in the other with calm and devoted love, till the other became as himself—and only then did he truly begin to help.

★★ MARTIN BUBER

II

Gratitude or thankfulness is another virtue of great lustre, and so esteemed by God and all good men. It is an acknowledgment of benefits received, to the honour of those that confer them. It is indeed a noble sort of justice, with this difference though, that since benefits exceed justice, the tie is greater to be thankful than to be just; and consequently there is something baser in ingratitude than injustice. So that though you are not obliged by law to repay, your virtue, honour, and humanity naturally pledge you to be thankful, and by how much the less you are under external ties, consider your inward ties so much the stronger.

★★ WILLIAM PENN

One day a good-natured king gave a rare and beautiful fruit to a slave, who tasted it and thereupon said that never in his life had he eaten anything to delicious. This made the king wish to try it himself, and he asked the slave for a piece. But when he put it into his mouth he found it very bitter and he raised his eyebrows in astonishment. The slave said: 'Sire, since I have received so many gifts at your hand how can I complain of one bitter fruit? Seeing that you shower benefits on me why should one bitterness estrange me from you?'

FARID UD-DIN ATTAR

Be grateful to the man you help, think of him as God. Is it not a great privilege to be allowed to worship God by helping your fellow-man?

VIVEKANANDA

It is more blessed to give than to receive; yet a noble nature can accept and be thankful.

STRINDBERG

The grateful soul of the wise man is the true altar of God.

PHILO

Gratitude is heaven itself.

BLAKE

THE QUESTION

I

I dreamed that, as I wandered by the way,
   Bare Winter suddenly was changed to Spring;
And gentle odours led my steps astray,
   Mixed with a sound of waters murmuring
Along a shelving bank of turf, which lay
   Under a copse, and hardly dared to fling
Its green arms round the bosom of the stream,
But kissed it and then fled, as thou mightest in dream.

II

There grew pied wind-flowers and violets;
   Daisies, those pearled Arcturi of the earth,
The constellated flower that never sets;
   Faint oxlips; tender bluebells, at whose birth
The sod scarce heaved; and that tall flower that wets—
Like a child, half in tenderness and mirth—
Its mother's face with Heaven's collected tears
When the low wind its playmate's voice it hears.

III

And in the warm hedge grew lush eglantine,
   Green cow-bind and the moonlight-coloured may,
And cherry-blossoms, and white cups whose wine
   Was the bright dew yet drained not by the Day;
And wild roses, and ivy serpentine,
   With its dark buds and leaves wandering astray;
And flowers, azure, black, and streaked with gold,
Fairer than any wakened eyes behold.

IV

And nearer to the river's trembling edge
   There grew broad flag-flowers, purple pranked with
      white,
And starry river-buds among the sedge,
   And floating water-lilies, broad and bright,
Which lit the oak that overhung the hedge
   With moonlight beams of their own watery light;
And bulrushes, and reeds of such deep green
As soothed the dazzled eye with sober sheen.

V

Methought that of these visionary flowers
   I made a nosegay, bound in such a way
That the same hues which in their natural bowers
   Were mingled or opposed, the like array
Kept these imprisoned children of the Hours
   Within my hand;—and then, elate and gay,
I hastened to the spot whence I had come,
That I might there present it—oh to whom?

472 SHELLEY

VI. FREEDOM

[What is personal freedom? It is essentially something *inside* a man: the presence of something in a man's soul, not the absence of such outer restrictions as the walls of a prison or Acts of Parliament that he must obey or take the consequences. To be free is to be at rest in the depths of one's being, whatever people and circumstances may be doing to one. But such inner serenity is by no means a sign of indifference, of "not caring": on the contrary, it is just because he cares so deeply for what is god-like in him—for the divine spark within him that nothing outside him can ever wholly extinguish—that the best sort of man remains calm and undisturbed in all circumstances, and thinks comparatively little of any discomfort or even agony he may suffer.

Consider actual imprisonment. People who go to prison for refusing to do something they think wrong—conscientious objectors, for instance—are far freer, in the deepest sense, than people who do something they think wrong for fear of going to prison. Or consider Socrates. He was sentenced to death by the Athenians for teaching what he believed to be true: but as he sat awaiting the cup of poison that would kill him, he continued to discuss philosophy with his friends in undiminished tranquillity. Contrast him with an unhappy murderer who struggles on his way to the scaffold. Both are prisoners: both, in full consciousness, are on the point of sudden death: but one is free, the other a slave.

It is even possible, for human beings of the rarest quality, to remain free under torture. I know of one or two who did so in a Nazi concentration camp: and Jesus Christ was so utterly free on the Cross (except, perhaps, for a passing moment of despair) that he could pray for his tormentors. No one, on the other hand, can possibly be free when the torturer is his own guilty conscience.

The meaning of inner freedom becomes clear if we think about its opposite, inner slavery. Inner slavery is nothing but preoccupation with self. A man totally preoccupied with himself is a total slave: he spends his entire life in a prison far narrower than any ever built of bricks and mortar or stone. We all know from our own experience that this is the case: we are all partially imprisoned, for none of us is completely free from the selfishness that *is* our imprisonment. Or certainly very few of us. But there are kinds, as well as degrees, of preoccupation with self, and they vary, or may vary, at different periods in our lives. There are two kinds in the main, though they easily fade into one another: namely the normal and the morbid.

The normal kind is ordinary selfishness and greed, the habit of thinking and acting as our own comfort, our own advantage, our own security (present or future) may dictate. But there are people who, in addition, are worried or tortured, sometimes or always, by a vague sort of terror or by feelings of guilt. This is to be morbidly preoccupied with self. A man feels guilty, not so much because something has been done, as because *he* has done it: a man feels terror, not so much because something may happen, but because something may happen to *him*. His spirit is like an ingrowing nail: it turns back on itself.

A free man's spirit, on the other hand, turns outward instead of inward: it gives itself, naturally and spontaneously, to the Whole. This is what Christ meant when he summed up all the wisdom we can ever have about freedom and slavery in the saying "He who loses his life will find it, and he that seeks to save his life will lose it". There is nothing vague or metaphorical about that: it is the literal truth, provided that by "living" one means something more than just keeping alive.

Inner slavery is at its climax in hatred. To hate a man is to withdraw oneself the greatest possible distance from him and then, shut up in oneself, to murder him in one's own heart. And inner freedom is, just as obviously, at its climax in love. To love is to go out into the Whole as a bird wings its way through the sky.

Nothing that I have said must be thought for a single moment to imply that to starve or annihilate one's self is even remotely desirable: people who interpret Christ's saying as meaning, for instance, that our self is somehow contemptible, something to be shackled, totally misunderstand him. The opposite is the case: the very heart of the matter is precisely this—that a man, far from attempting to mutilate his self, must preserve and perfect it. The self is that part or aspect of the whole sum of things, of *reality*, with which we do our work in that reality: we have nothing else to do it with: or, more accurately, it is only through the selves of each one of us that Reality can unfold and express itself—or that God, in more familiar language, can fulfil His purpose. So we must see to it that "our" self grows and blossoms, must preserve it from all outrage, and must submit it *only* to the purposes of the greater, Total Self—and that is not submission but freedom.

Or, to put it in the metaphorical language (as you may like to call it) of Hebrew mysticism: God, when he created the universe, radiated His spirit into the whole of it: therefore no living creature, or, for the matter of that, no stick or stone, can be without its own special "spark" of the Deity. So every human being is the guardian of that divine spark within him; and to preserve it unharmed, or rather to free it from all intervening corruption and restore it to its original integrity, is the essence of our duty to God. Anyone who submits to outrage against his self—anyone who allows others, for instance, to dictate to him what *he* is to think or what *he* is to feel—is not only a slave: he murders life. Equally, anyone who loves the enemy that attempts such or similar outrages is not only free: he increases life.

If all that I have been saying is true—if freedom is something within us, something spiritual, something infinitely precious—then the gravest of all our responsibilities is to do away, in so far as we can, with anything that may corrupt it: and we have only to look at the world around us, or, far more important, into our own hearts, to realise that freedom—inner, positive freedom—is habitually corrupted to a quite horrifying degree. It starts in the cradle, this corruption of freedom (maybe earlier: we do not know), and continues, in the majority of cases perhaps, throughout much of a man's life, and even at times to

323

the grave. I shall not stop to consider whether people are born, on the whole, with more freedom than slavery in them, or the other way about: a few remarks about this will be found on pages 227-234, and the question, though highly important in itself, is of little concern for our immediate purpose.

Corruption of inner freedom comes in the main from two sources: individual contacts and the general environment. To take individual contacts first: like for the most part elicits like. Assault a man with hatred or contempt, and he in turn assaults you: more, he begins to feel hatred or contempt for men and women in general. A slave yourself, you have now enslaved *him*. But this is not always the case: a minority—though a surprisingly large one, to the glory of human nature—can react in the way Socrates did, and a few even in the way Christ did. The reverse, however, is almost invariable. Meet a man with love, and he loves you in return: further, his whole nature becomes more loving. A free man yourself, you have now freed *him*. Assault by hatred can enslave a man who was once conspicuously free, and loving can free a man who was once conspicuously a slave. Or so life has taught me.

As to the general environment, there is little that needs saying about that. The more inner freedom the whole atmosphere breathes out, the more inner freedom we breathe in with it. That is why, other things being equal, a co-operative society, a society in which most people work, more or less as a matter of course, for public service or the good of the whole, is far better than a competitive society, a society in which most people work, also as a matter of course, for the highest wages or biggest profits. Again: a society that encourages people to think for themselves, instead of weakly following others, is far better than a society that encourages a dead level of conformity through fear of "public opinion", and infinitely better than a society that *imposes* conformity by terror or process of law.

A word about "outer" restraints on a man's freedom. If it is true that a prisoner can be inwardly free, it is also true that most prisoners are inwardly as well as outwardly enslaved by simply being in prison. Anything that a man feels as an assault on his liberty produces, in general but with exceptions, a feeling of hatred or at least of resentment: and that is to say that it inwardly enslaves him. Moreover: it focuses his whole attention on the struggle to free himself, and that again is to say that it inwardly enslaves him. The supreme charge against Hitler's and Stalin's concentration camps, and similar iniquities, is not that they enslaved people's bodies (though God knows that was evil enough), but that they enslaved people's souls by corrupting their birthright of inner freedom.

I have been compelled, as a publisher, to read a great deal about the Hitlerite concentration camps: and the most dreadful thing in that most dreadful of all literatures is not the physical torture, shudderingly awful though that was, nor even the fact that human beings, God forgive them, could commit such unspeakable atrocities: the most dreadful thing in that literature is the way in which, with Socratic or Christian exceptions, the victims were inwardly enslaved by what they suffered. Some inmates of Belsen and similar hells became more like wild beasts than men and women who had been made in God's image. That, I repeat, is the supreme charge against their unhappy tormentors.

To end with something less horrible: just as the best sort of society is a co-operative rather than a competitive one, so in the best sort of society outward restraints have been reduced to a minimum. The ideal society, in other words, is a society in which everyone freely co-operates: a society ruled, or unruled, by a kind of Christian anarchy. Nothing remotely of the sort is at the moment in sight: but that should be our goal.]

THE DEATH OF SOCRATES

[Socrates, awaiting the cup of poison in his cell, is talking to his friends about immortality.]

Socrates replied with a smile: O Simmias, what are you saying? I am not very likely to persuade other men that I do not regard my present situation as a misfortune, if I cannot even persuade you that I am no worse off now than at any other time in my life. Will you not allow that I have as much of the spirit of prophecy in me as the swans? For they, when they perceive that they must die, having sung all their life long, do then sing more lustily than ever, rejoicing in the thought that they are about to go away to the god whose ministers they are. But men, because they themselves are afraid of death, slanderously affirm of the swans that they sing a lament at the last, not considering that no bird sings when cold, or hungry, or in pain, not even the nightingale, nor the swallow, nor yet the hoopoe; which are said indeed to tune a lay of sorrow, although I do not believe this to be true of them any more than of the swans. But because they are sacred to Apollo, they have the gift of prophecy, and anticipate the good things of another world; wherefore they sing and rejoice in that day more than ever they did before. And I too, believing myself to be the consecrated servant of the same God, and the fellow-servant of the swans, and thinking that I have received from my master gifts of prophecy which are not inferior to theirs, would not go out of life less merrily than the swans.

*   *   *

I will do my best, replied Socrates. But you must first let me hear what Crito wants; he has long been wishing to say something to me.

Only this, Socrates, replied Crito: the attendant who is to give you the poison has been telling me, and he wants me to tell you, that you are not to talk much; talking, he says, increases heat, and this is apt to interfere with the action of the poison; persons who excite themselves are sometimes obliged to take a second or even a third dose.

Then, said Socrates, let him mind his business and be prepared to give the poison twice or even thrice if necessary; that is all.

I knew quite well what you would say, replied Crito; but I was obliged to satisfy him.

*   *   *

Now the hour of sunset was near, for a good deal of time had passed while he was within. When he came out, he sat down with us again after his bath, but not much was said. Soon the jailer, who was the servant of the Government, entered and stood by him, saying: To you, Socrates, whom I know to be the noblest and gentlest and best of all who ever came to this place, I will not impute the angry feelings of other men, who rage and swear at me, when, in obedience to the authorities, I bid them drink the poison—indeed, I am sure that you will not be angry with me; for others, as you are aware, and not I, are to blame. And so fare you well, and try to bear lightly what must needs be—you know my errand. Then bursting into tears he turned away and went out.

Socrates looked at him and said: I return your good wishes, and will do as you bid. Then turning to us, he said, How charming the man is: since I have been in prison he has always been coming to see me, and at times he would talk to me, and was as good to me as could be, and now see how generously he sorrows on my account. We must do as he says, Crito; and therefore, let the cup be brought, if the poison is prepared: if not, let the attendant prepare some.

Yet, said Crito, the sun is still upon the hill-tops, and I know that many a one has taken the draught late, and after the announcement has been made to him he has eaten and drunk, and enjoyed the society of his beloved; do not hurry—there is time enough.

Socrates said: Yes, Crito, and they of whom you speak are right in so acting, for they think that they will be gainers by the delay; but I am right in not following their example, for I do not think that I should gain anything by drinking the poison a little later; I should only be ridiculous in my own eyes for sparing and saving a life which is already forfeit. Please then to do as I say, and not to refuse me.

Crito made a sign to the servant, who was standing by; and he went out, and having been absent for some time, returned with the jailer carrying the cup of poison. Socrates said: You,

327

my good friend, who are experienced in these matters, shall give me directions how I am to proceed. The man answered: You have only to walk about until your legs are heavy, and then to lie down, and the poison will act. At the same time he handed the cup to Socrates, who in the easiest and gentlest manner, without the least fear or change of colour or feature, looking at the man with all his eyes, as his manner was, took the cup and said: What do you say about pouring a little out of this cup as an offering to any god? May I, or not? The man answered: We only prepare, Socrates, just so much as we deem enough. I understand, he said: but I may and must ask the gods to prosper my journey from this to the other world—even so—and so be it according to my prayer. Then raising the cup to his lips, quite readily and cheerfully he drank off the poison. And hitherto most of us had been able to control our sorrow; but now when we saw him drinking, and saw too that he had finished the draught, we could no longer forbear, and in spite of myself my own tears were flowing fast; so that I covered my face and wept, not for him, but at the thought of my own calamity in having to part from such a friend. Nor was I the first; for Crito, when he found himself unable to restrain his tears, had got up, and I followed; and at that moment Apollodorus, who had been weeping all the time, broke out in a loud and passionate cry which made cowards of us all. Socrates alone retained his calmness: What is this strange outcry? he said. I sent away the women mainly in order that they might not misbehave in this way, for I have been told that a man should die in peace. Be quiet then, and have patience. When we heard his words we were ashamed, and restrained our tears; and he walked about until, as he said, his legs began to fail, and then he lay on his back, according to the directions, and the man who gave him the poison now and then looked at his feet and legs; and after a while he pressed his foot hard, and asked him if he could feel; and he said, No; and then his leg, and so upwards and upwards, and showed us that he was cold and stiff. And he felt them himself, and said: When the poison reaches the heart, that will be the end. . . . In a minute or two a movement was heard, and the attendants uncovered him; his eyes were set, and Crito closed his eyes and mouth.

Such was the death of our friend; concerning whom I may truly say, that of all the men of his time whom I have known, he was the wisest and justest and best.

PLATO

When freedom is not an inner idea which imparts strength to our activities and breadth to our creations, when it is merely a thing of external circumstance, it is like an open space to one who is blindfolded.

TAGORE

§ 2

For God freedom is necessary.

VLADIMIR SOLOVIEV

God has laid upon man the duty of being free, of safeguarding freedom of spirit, no matter how difficult that may be, or how much sacrifice and suffering it may require.

BERDYAEV

All creation is for God a sharing of His very being: that is, He can only create free beings. He can only bring into existence beings that He calls upon to make themselves.

★ LOUIS LAVELLE

The glorious liberty of the children of God.

ROMANS

What have we, Sons of God, to do with law?

MILTON

Where the Spirit of the Lord is, there is liberty.

II CORINTHIANS

§ 3

Love—and do what you wish.

ST. AUGUSTINE

[If your nature is to love, if the freedom within you is perfect, any outer restraint on your actions is unnecessary, for everything you do will be right. The next three quotations express pretty much the same.]

> Serene will be our days and bright
> And happy will our nature be,
> When love is an unerring light,
> And joy its own security . . .

WORDSWORTH

Virtue consists, not in abstaining from vice, but in not desiring it.

BERNARD SHAW

It is a great liberty to be able not to sin; it is the greatest liberty to be unable to sin.

ST. AUGUSTINE

330

Freedom means the spirit of union.

BOSANQUET

[The next three quotations expand Bosanquet's saying. People who fight for themselves, instead of doing what their conscience tells them is best for the Whole, which is to say, doing God's will, have a bogus sort of freedom that is not really freedom at all, but lays them open to domination by others.]

Others gain authority over you if you possess a will distinct from God's will.

RABBI NAHMAN OF BRATZLAV

All those who allow themselves a wrong liberty make themselves their own aim and object.

HENRY SUSO

Christianity promises to make men free; it never promises to make them independent [of one another].

W. R. INGE

§ 5

For if righteousness come by the law, then Christ is dead in vain.

GALATIANS

[Christ died to teach people that obedience to law cannot of itself make them righteous.]

That which Jesus founded, that which will remain eternally his, allowing for the imperfections which mix themselves with everything realised by humanity, is the doctrine of the liberty of the soul.

RENAN

No Law, apart from a Lawgiver, is a proper object of reverence. It is mere brute fact; and every living thing, still more every person exercising intelligent choice, is its superior. The reverence of persons can be appropriately given only to that which itself is at least personal.

. . . . . .

Freedom is not absence of determination [i..e. of a definite direction towards a definite goal] . . . It is determination by what seems good as contrasted with determination by irresistible compulsion.

WILLIAM TEMPLE

A large liberty will be the law of a spiritual society, and the increase of freedom a sign of the growth of human society towards the possibility of true spiritualisation. To spiritualise in this sense a society of slaves, slaves of power, slaves of authority, slaves of custom, . . . slaves of all sorts of imposed laws which they live under rather than live by, slaves internally of their own weakness, ignorance and passions from whose worst effect they seek or need to be protected by another and external slavery, can never be a successful endeavour. They must shake off their fetters first in order to be fit for a higher freedom.

AUROBINDO

Freedom, understood as something positive and joined with creativeness, becomes creative energy. Formal freedom, by which each protects and defends himself, must be but the preliminary to true freedom, by means of which human society is creatively transformed.

★ BERDYAEV

Man is fettered and weighed down. He both longs for freedom and fears it . . . In order to preserve freedom and to struggle for it, one must in a sense be already free, have freedom within oneself. Those who are slaves to the very core of their being do not know the name of freedom and cannot struggle for it. Ancient taboos surround man on all sides and fetter his moral life. In order to free himself from their power man must first be conscious of himself as inwardly free and only then can he struggle for freedom outwardly. The inner conquest of slavery is the fundamental task of moral life.

BERDYAEV

[Taboos—traditional prohibitions—can be terribly powerful. For instance: I have never been able to free myself from the Jewish taboo, imposed on me by my parents and on my parents by their parents, against eating pork. Stupid though this is, it matters little. What really matter are the moral taboos, such as "You must never take an insult lying down"—whereas those who are inwardly free have no need to "stand up for themselves", and their freedom precludes, by its very nature, any thought of retaliation.]

What then is the meaning of freedom for modern man? Is there a state of positive freedom in which the individual exists as an independent self and yet is not isolated but united with the world, with other men, and nature?

We believe that there is a positive answer, that man can be free and yet not alone, independent and yet an integral part of mankind—making up, that is to say, with the rest of humanity a

333

harmonious whole. This freedom man can attain by the realization of his self, by being himself. What is realisation of the self? We believe that the realisation of the self is accomplished by the realisation of man's total personality, by the active expression of his emotional and intellectual potentialities, his capacity to think and feel. These potentialities are present in everybody; they become real only to the extent to which they are expressed. In other words, *positive freedom consists in the spontaneous activity of the total, integrated personality*—integrated in the sense that head does not fight against heart nor heart against head, but the two work harmoniously together.

Spontaneous activity is not the activity of the automaton, the thoughtless imitation of others. Spontaneous activity is free activity of the self; the Latin root of the word, *sponte*, means literally "of one's free will". By activity we do not mean "doing something", but the creative activity that can be expressed, not only by what one does, but also by what one wills to do, and by the way one uses one's brain, heart and senses. And only if a man's brain, heart and senses do not fight with one another is spontaneous activity possible.

Small children offer an instance of spontaneity. They have an ability to feel and think that which is really *theirs*; this spontaneity shows in what they say and think, in the feelings that are expressed in their faces. If one asks what makes for the attraction small children have for most people I believe that, apart from sentimental and conventional reasons, the answer must be that it is this very quality of spontaneity.

Most of us can observe at least moments of our own spontaneity which are at the same time moments of genuine happiness. Whether it be the fresh and spontaneous perception of a landscape, or the dawning of some truth as the result of our thinking, or some pleasure of the senses that has not become commonplace, or the welling up of love for another person—in these moments we all know what a spontaneous act is and may have some vision of what human life could be if these experiences were not such rare and uncultivated occurrences.

Why is spontaneous activity the answer to the problem of freedom? Because in the spontaneous realisation of the self man unites himself with the world—with man, nature, and himself. Love is the foremost component of such spontaneity; not love as the loss or disappearance of the self in another person, not love as the possession of another person, but love as spontaneous affirmation of others,[1] as the union of the individual with others on the basis of the preservation of the individual self. What makes love so powerful is the very fact that two contrasted elements are harmonized in it: that it springs from the need of overcoming separateness, that it leads to oneness—and yet that individuality is not eliminated. Work is the other component of such spontaneity: not work as a compulsive activity but work as creation in which man becomes one with nature in the act of creation. What holds true of love and work holds true of all spontaneous action, whether it be the realization of sensuous pleasure or participation in the political life of the community. It affirms the individuality of the self and at the same time it unites the self with man and nature.

In all spontaneous activity the individual embraces the world. Not only does his individual self remain intact; it becomes stronger and more solidified. *For the self is as strong as it is active.* There is no genuine strength in possession as such, neither of material property nor of mental qualities like emotions or thoughts. There is also no strength in use and manipulation of objects; what we use is not ours simply because we use it. Ours is only that to which we are genuinely related by our creative activity, be it a person or an inanimate object. Only those qualities that result from our spontaneous activity give strength to the self and thereby form the basis of its wholeness.

This implies that what matters is the activity as such, the process and not the result. In the life of our society the emphasis is just the reverse. We produce not for a concrete satisfaction but for the abstract purpose of selling our commodity; we feel that we can acquire everything material or immaterial by buying it,

[1] We affirm others when we say "Ah, he is there!" v. G.

and thus things become ours independently of any creative effort of our own in relation to them. In the same way we regard our personal qualities and the result of our efforts as commodities that can be sold for money, prestige, and power. The emphasis thus shifts from the present satisfaction of creative activity to the value of the finished product. Thereby man misses the only satisfaction that can give him real happiness—the experience of the activity of the present moment—and chases after a phantom that leaves him disappointed as soon as he believes he has caught it—the illusory happiness called success.

If the individual realises his self by spontaneous activity and thus relates himself to the world, he ceases to be an isolated atom; he and the world become part of one structuralised whole; he has his rightful place, and thereby his doubt concerning himself and the meaning of life disappears. This doubt sprang from his separateness and from the thwarting of life; when he can live neither compulsively nor automatically but spontaneously, the doubt disappears. He is aware of himself as an active and creative individual and recognises that *there is only one meaning of life: the act of living itself*.

Positive freedom as the realisation of the self implies the full affirmation of the uniqueness of the individual. Men are born equal, but they are also born different. The basis of this difference is the inherited equipment, physiological and mental, with which they start life, to which is added the particular combination of circumstances and experiences that they meet with. This individual basis of the personality is as little identical with any other as two organisms are ever identical physically. The genuine growth of the self is always a growth on this particular basis; it is an organic growth like the growth of an animal, the unfolding of a nucleus that is peculiar for this one person and only for him. The development of the automaton, in contrast, is not an organic growth. Organic growth is possible only under the condition of supreme respect for the peculiarity of the self of other persons as well as of our own self. This respect for the cultivation of the uniqueness of the self is the most valuable achievement of human culture, and it is this very achievement that is in danger to-day.

The uniqueness of the self in no way contradicts the principle of equality. The statement that men are born equal implies that they all share the same fundamental human qualities, that they share the basic fate of human beings, that they all have the same inalienable claim on freedom and happiness. It further-more means that their relationship is one of solidarity, not one of domination on the one hand and submission on the other. What the idea of equality does not mean is that all men are alike. Such an idea of equality is derived from the rôle that the individual plays in his economic activities to-day. In the relation between the man who buys and the one who sells, the concrete differences of personality are eliminated. In this situation only one thing matters, that the one has something to sell and the other has money to buy it. In economic life one man is not different from another; as real persons they are, and the cultivation of their uniqueness is the essence of individuality.

★★ ERICH FROMM

§ 6

FROM "AN ENEMY OF THE PEOPLE"

FROM ACT IV

[Dr. Stockmann, medical officer of the Baths in a small Norwegian town which are supposed to be curative, has dis-covered that in fact they are dangerous to health, and expects to be honoured for the discovery. But the prosperity of the town depends on people visiting it to be cured, and the "solid majority" —the average man in the street who always prefers to let well alone—wants the whole thing hushed up. Dr. Stockmann is dismissed. In the extract that follows he is addressing a meeting of his fellow-townsmen. Aslaksen is a printer, and a typical repre-sentative of the "solid majority".]

337

Dr. Stockmann. . . . I am about to make great revelations, my fellow-citizens! I am going to announce to you a far more important discovery than the trifling fact that our water-works are poisoned, and that our health-resort is built on pestilential ground. . . .

For *this* is the great discovery I made yesterday! (*In a louder tone.*) The most dangerous foe to truth and freedom in our midst is the solid majority. . . .

The majority is never right. Never, I say! That's one of the social lies a free, thinking man is bound to rebel against. Who make up the majority in any given country? Is it the wise men or the fools? I think we must agree that the fools are in a terrible, overwhelming majority, all the wide world over. . . .

I have said that I won't waste a word on the little, narrow-chested, short-winded crew that lie in our wake. Pulsating life has nothing more to do with them. I will rather speak of the few individuals among us who have made all the new, germinating truths their own. These men stand, as it were, at the outposts, so far in the van that the solid majority has not yet reached them—and *there* they fight for truths that are too lately born into the world's consciousness to have won over the majority. . . .

What sort of truths do the majority rally round? Truths that are decrepit with age. When a truth is so old as that it's in a fair way to become a lie, gentlemen. (*Laughter and jeers.*) Yes, yes, you may believe me or not, as you please; but truths are by no means the wiry Methuselahs some people think them. A normally-constituted truth lives—let me say—as a rule, seventeen or eighteen years; at the outside twenty; seldom longer. And truths so stricken in years are always shockingly thin; yet it's not till then that the majority takes them up and recommends them to society as wholesome food. I can assure you there's not much nutriment in that sort of fare; you may take my word as a doctor for that. All these majority-truths are like last year's salt pork; they're like rancid, mouldy ham, producing all the moral scurvy that devastates society. . . .

The truths acknowledged by the masses, the multitude, were certain truths to the vanguard in our grandfathers' days. We, the vanguard of to-day, don't acknowledge them any longer; and I don't believe there's any other certain truth but this— that no society can live a healthy life upon such old, marrowless truths as these. . . .

ASLAKSEN. Both as a citizen of this town and as a man, I am deeply shocked at what I have here had to listen to. Dr. Stockmann has unmasked himself in a manner I should never have dreamt of. I am reluctantly forced to subscribe to the opinion just expressed by some worthy citizens; and I think we ought to formulate this opinion in a resolution. I therefore beg to move, "That this meeting declares the medical officer of the Baths, Dr. Thomas Stockmann, to be an enemy of the people."

FROM THE END OF THE PLAY:

DR. STOCKMANN. . . . Just come here, Katrine; see how bravely the sun shines to-day! And how the blessed fresh spring air blows in upon me!

MRS. STOCKMANN. Yes, if only we could live on sunshine and spring air, Thomas!

DR. STOCKMANN. Well, you'll have to pinch and save where you can—and we'll get on all right. That's my least concern. Now what *does* trouble me is, that I don't see any man with enough independence and nobility of character to dare to take up my work after me.

PETRA. Oh! don't bother about that, father; you have time before you.—Why, see, there are the boys already.

(EILIF *and* MORTEN *enter from the sitting-room.*)

MRS. STOCKMANN. Have you had a holiday to-day?

MORTEN. No; but we had a fight with the other fellows in play-time——

EILIF. That's not true; it was the other fellows that fought us.

MORTEN. Yes, and then Mr. Rörlund said we'd better stop at home for a few days.

DR. STOCKMANN (*snapping his fingers and springing down from the table*). Now I have it, now I have it, on my soul! You shall never set foot in school again!

THE BOYS. Never go to school!

MRS. STOCKMANN. Why, Thomas——

DR. STOCKMANN. Never, I say. I'll teach you myself—that's to say, I won't teach you any blessed thing——

MORTEN. Hurrah!

DR. STOCKMANN. —but I'll try to make free, noble-minded men of you.—Look here, you'll have to help me, Petra.

PETRA. Yes, father, you may be sure I will.

DR. STOCKMANN. And we'll have our school in the room where they reviled me as an enemy of the people. But we must have more pupils. I must have at least twelve boys to begin with.

MRS. STOCKMANN. You'll never get them in this town.

DR. STOCKMANN. We shall see! (*To the boys.*) Don't you know any street urchins—any regular ragamuffins——?

MORTEN. Yes, father, I know lots!

DR. STOCKMANN. That's all right; bring me a few of them. I want to experiment with the street-curs for once; there are sometimes excellent heads among them.

MORTEN. But what are we to do when we've become free and noble-minded men?

DR. STOCKMANN. Drive all the wolves out to the far west, boys.

> (EILIF *looks rather doubtful;* MORTEN
> *jumps about, shouting* "*Hurrah!*")

MRS. STOCKMANN. If only the wolves don't drive you out, Thomas.

DR. STOCKMANN. Are you quite mad, Katrine? Drive *me* out! now that I'm the strongest man in the town!

MRS. STOCKMANN. The strongest—now?

DR. STOCKMANN. Yes, I venture to say this: that now I'm one of the strongest men upon earth.

MORTEN. I say, father!

DR. STOCKMANN (*in a subdued voice*). Hush! you mustn't speak about it yet; but I've made a great discovery.

MRS. STOCKMANN. What, again?

340

Dr. STOCKMANN. Yes, certainly. ((*Gathers them about him, and speaks confidentially*.) This is what I've discovered, you see: the strongest man upon earth is he who stands most alone.

MRS. STOCKMANN (*shakes her head, smiling*). Ah! Thomas——!

PETRA (*grasping his hands encouragingly*). Father!

★ IBSEN

IN PRAISE OF CHRISTIAN ANARCHY

[This is from *The Modern Symposium*, a dramatic dialogue in which a number of people—a Liberal, a Conservative, a Socialist and an Anarchist among them—discuss the nature of freedom.]

"Our city is not built with blue books, nor cemented with office dust; nor is it bonds of red-tape that make and keep it one. No! it is the attraction, uncompelled, of spirits made free; the shadowing into outward form of the eternal joy of the soul!"

He paused and seemed to collect himself; and then in a quieter tone: . . . "I know the terrors of that word [Anarchy]; but they are the terrors of an evil conscience; for it is only an order founded on iniquity that dreads disorder. Why do you fear for your property and lives, you who fear anarchy? It is because you have stolen the one and misdevoted the other; because you have created by your laws the man you call the criminal; because you have bred hunger, and hunger has bred rage. For this I do not blame you, any more than I blame myself. You are yourselves victims of the system you maintain, and your enemy, no less than mine, if you knew it, is goverment. For government means compulsion, exclusion, distinction, separation; while anarchy is freedom, union and love. Government is based on egotism and fear, anarchy on fraternity. It is because we divide ourselves into nations that we endure the oppression of armaments; because we isolate ourselves as individuals that we invoke the protection of laws. If I did not take what my brother needs I should not fear that he would take it from me; if I did not

341

shut myself off from his want, I should not deem it less urgent than my own. . . .

"Anarchy is not the absence of order, it is absence of force; it is the free outflowing of the spirit into the forms in which it delights; and in such forms alone, as they grow and change, can it find an expression which is not also a bondage. You will say this is chimerical. But look at history! Consider the great achievements of the Middle Age! Were they not the result of just such a movement as I describe? It was men voluntarily associating in communes and grouping themselves in guilds that built the towers and churches and adorned them with the glories of art that dazzles us still in Italy and France. The history of the growth of the state, of public authority and compulsion, is the history of the decline from Florence and Nuremberg to London and New York. As the power of the state grows the energy of the spirit dwindles; and if ever . . . the activity of the state should extend through and through to every department of life, the universal ease and comfort which may thus be disseminated throughout society will have been purchased dearly at the price of the soul. The denizens of that city will be fed, housed and clothed to perfection; only—and it is a serious drawback—only they will be dead. . . .

"To shatter material bonds that we may bind the closer the bonds of the soul, to slough dead husks that we may liberate living forms, to abolish institutions that we may evoke energies, to put off the material and put on the spiritual body, that . . . is the inspiration of our movement, that, and that only, is the true and inner meaning of anarchy. . . .

"There are anarchists who never made a speech . . . whom we know as our brothers, though perhaps they know not us. Two I will name who live for ever, Shelley, the first of poets, were it not that there is one yet greater than he, the mystic William Blake. . . . Who of our persecutors would believe that the song we bear in our hearts, some of us, I may speak at least for one, is the most inspired, the most spiritual challenge ever flung to your obtuse, flatulent, stertorous England:

342

'Bring me my bow of burning gold,
Bring me my arrows of desire,
Bring me my spear; O clouds unfold!
Bring me my chariot of fire!

'I will not cease from mental fight,
Nor shall my sword sleep in my hand,
Till I have built Jerusalem
In England's green and pleasant land.'

"England! No, not England, but Europe, America, the world!
Where is Man, the new Man, there is our country. But the new
Man is buried in the old; and wherever he struggles in his
tomb, wherever he knocks we are there to help to deliver him.
When the guards sleep, in the silence of the dawn, rises the
crucified Christ. And the angel that sits at the grave is the
angel of Anarchy."

472 G. LOWES DICKINSON

FROM "PROMETHEUS UNBOUND", ACT III

[The three chief characters in Shelley's play are the god
Jupiter, a despot who tyrannizes over the human race and in
particular deprives it of comforting and civilising fire; the Titan
Prometheus, grandchild of the marriage of Heaven and Earth,
who champions Jupiter's victims and in particular steals fire for
them; and Demogorgon or Eternity, whom we should call God.
Jupiter has chained Prometheus to a precipice in the Indian
Caucasus, where the vultures eat his liver: but eventually Demogorgon flings Jupiter into the bottomless pit, Prometheus is un-
chained, and mankind wins its freedom. The following passage
describes the transformation that ensues: but Shelley is really
describing, in a mythical form, what humanity would be like
(and may still be like) when freed from the last remnant of everything that at present enslaves it. My friend William Kean
Seymour, the poet, has been kind enough to prepare a prose
version, which will be found in the Appendix—page 472.]

343

SCENE IV.—*A Forest. In the Background a Cave.* PROMETHEUS,
ASIA, PANTHEA, IONE, *and the* SPIRIT OF THE EARTH

...... [*The* SPIRIT OF THE HOUR *enters.*

PROMETHEUS. We feel what thou hast heard and seen: yet
    speak.
SPIRIT OF THE HOUR. Soon as the sound had ceased whose
    thunder filled
The abysses of the sky and the wide earth,
There was a change: the impalpable thin air
And the all-circling sunlight were transformed,
As if the sense of love dissolved in them
Had folded itself round the spherèd world.
My vision then grew clear, and I could see
Into the mysteries of the universe . . .
. . . I floated to the earth:
It was, as it is still, the pain of bliss
To move, to breathe, to be; I wandering went
Among the haunts and dwellings of mankind,
And first was disappointed not to see
Such mighty change as I had felt within
Expressed in outward things; but soon I looked,
And behold, thrones were kingless, and men walked
One with the other even as spirits do,
None fawned, none trampled; hate, disdain, or fear,
Self-love or self-contempt, on human brows
No more inscribed, as o'er the gate of hell,
"All hope abandon ye who enter here";
None frowned, none trembled, none with eager fear
Gazed on another's eye of cold command,
Until the subject of a tyrant's will
Became, worse fate, the abject of his own,
Which spurred him, like an outspent horse, to death.
None wrought his lips in truth-entangling lines
Which smiled the lie his tongue disdained to speak;
None, with firm sneer, trod out in his own heart

344

The sparks of love and hope till there remained
Those bitter ashes, a soul self-consumed,
And the wretch crept a vampire among men,
Infecting all with his own hideous ill;
None talked that common, false, cold, hollow talk
Which makes the heart deny the *yes* it breathes,
Yet question that unmeant hypocrisy
With such a self-mistrust as has no name.
And women, too, frank, beautiful, and kind
As the free heaven which rains fresh light and dew
On the wide earth, passed; gentle radiant forms,
From custom's evil taint exempt and pure;
Speaking the wisdom once they could not think,
Looking emotions once they feared to feel,
And changed to all which once they dared not be,
Yet being now, made earth like heaven; nor pride,
Nor jealousy, nor envy, nor ill shame,
The bitterest of those drops of treasured gall,
Spoilt the sweet taste of the nepenthe, love.

Thrones, altars, judgement-seats, and prisons; wherein,
And beside which, by wretched men were borne
Sceptres, tiaras, swords, and chains, and tomes
Of reasoned wrong, glozed on by ignorance,
Were like those monstrous and barbaric shapes,
The ghosts of a no-more-remembered fame,
Which, from their unworn obelisks, look forth
In triumph o'er the palaces and tombs
Of those who were their conquerors: mouldering round,
These imaged to the pride of kings and priests
A dark yet mighty faith, a power as wide
As is the world it wasted, and are now
But an astonishment; even so the tools
And emblems of its last captivity,
Amid the dwellings of the peopled earth,
Stand, not o'erthrown, but unregarded now.

And those foul shapes, abhorred by god and man,—
Which, under many a name and many a form
Strange, savage, ghastly, dark and execrable,
Were Jupiter, the tyrant of the world;
And which the nations, panic-stricken, served
With blood, and hearts broken by long hope, and love
Dragged to his altars soiled and garlandless,
And slain amid men's unreclaiming tears,
Flattering the thing they feared, which fear was hate,—
Frown, mouldering fast, o'er their abandoned shrines:
The painted veil, by those who were, called life,
Which mimicked, as with colours idly spread,
All men believed or hoped, is torn aside;
The loathsome mask has fallen, the man remains
Sceptreless, free, uncircumscribed, but man
Equal, unclassed, tribeless, and nationless,
Exempt from awe, worship, degree, the king
Over himself; just, gentle, wise: but man
Passionless?—no, yet free from guilt or pain,
Which were, for his will made or suffered them,
Nor yet exempt, though ruling them like slaves,
From chance, and death, and mutability,
The clogs of that which else might oversoar
The loftiest star of unascended heaven,
Pinnacled dim in the intense inane.

SHELLEY

FROM "PROMETHEUS UNBOUND", ACT IV

[Demogorgon is speaking to Prometheus after liberating him.]

> To suffer woes which hope thinks infinite;
> To forgive wrongs darker than death or night;
>   To defy power which seems omnipotent;
> To love and bear; to hope till hope creates

From its own wreck the thing it contemplates;
    Neither to change, nor falter, nor repent;
This, like thy glory, Titan, is to be
Good, great, and joyous, beautiful and free;
This is alone Life, Joy, Empire, and Victory!

SHELLEY

§ 7

FREEDOM

God speaks:

When you love someone, you love him as he is.
I alone am perfect.
It is probably for that reason
That I know what perfection is
And that I demand less perfection of those poor people.
I know how difficult it is
And how often, when they are struggling in their trials,
How often do I wish and am I tempted to put my hand under
    their stomachs
In order to hold them up with my big hand
Just like a father teaching his son how to swim
In the current of the river
And who is divided between two ways of thinking.
For on the one hand, if he holds him up all the time and if he
    holds him up too much,
The child will depend on this and will never learn how to swim.
But if he doesn't hold him up just at the right moment
That child is bound to swallow more water than is healthy for
    him.
In the same way, when I teach them how to swim amid their
    trials
I too am divided by two ways of thinking.

Because if I am always holding them up, if I hold them up
 too often,
They will never learn how to swim by themselves.
But if I don't hold them up just at the right moment,
Perhaps those poor children will swallow more water than is
 healthy for them.
Such is the difficulty, and it is a great one.
And such is the doubleness itself, the two faces of the problem.
On the one hand, they must work out their salvation for them-
 selves. That is the rule.
It allows of no exception. Otherwise it would not be interesting.
 They would not be men.
Now I want them to be manly, to be men, and to win by themselves
Their spurs of knighthood.
On the other hand, they must not swallow more water than is
 healthy for them,
Having made a dive into the ingratitude of sin.
Such is the mystery of man's freedom, says God,
And the mystery of my government towards him and towards
 his freedom.
If I hold him up too much, he is no longer free
And if I don't hold him up sufficiently, I am endangering his
 salvation.
Two goods in a sense almost equally precious.
For salvation is of infinite price.
But what kind of salvation would a salvation be that was not free?
What would you call it?
We want that salvation to be acquired by himself,
Himself, man. To be procured by himself.
To come, in a sense, from himself. Such is the secret,
Such is the mystery of man's freedom.
Such is the price we set on man's freedom.
Because I myself am free, says God, and I have created man
 in my own image and likeness.
Such is the mystery, such the secret, such the price
Of all freedom.

That freedom of that creature is the most beautiful reflection
in this world
Of the Creator's freedom. That is why we are so attached to it,
And set a proper price on it.
A salvation that was not free, that was not, that did not come
from a free man could in no wise be attractive to us. What
would it amount to?
What would it mean?
What interest would such a salvation have to offer?
A beatitude of slaves, a salvation of slaves, a slavish beatitude,
how do you expect me to be interested in that kind of thing?
Does one care to be loved by slaves?
If it were only a matter of proving my might, my might has
no need of those slaves, my might is well enough known,
it is sufficiently known that I am the Almighty.
My might is manifest enough in all matter and in all events.
My might is manifest enough in the sands of the sea and in the
stars of heaven.
It is not questioned, it is known, it is manifest enough in
inanimate creation.
It is manifest enough in the government,
In the very event that is man.
But in my creation which is endued with life, says God, I
wanted something better, I wanted something more.
Infinitely better. Infinitely more. For I wanted that freedom.
I created that very freedom. There are several degrees to my
throne.
When you once have known what it is to be loved freely, sub-
mission no longer has any taste.
All the prostrations in the world
Are not worth the beautiful upright attitude of a free man as
he kneels. All the submission, all the dejection in the world
Are not equal in value to the soaring up point,
The beautiful straight soaring up of one single invocation
From a love that is free.

CHARLES PÉGUY

§ 8

Any morality which is against freedom is a bad morality.

JOHN MACMURRAY

People are happy who have no need of locks.

DOSTOEVSKY

I want nothing whatever. I am quite happy.

BLAKE

FIFTH PART

I. THE SELF

For this commandment which I command thee this day, it is not hidden from thee, neither is it far off.

It is not in heaven, that thou shouldest say, Who shall go up for us to heaven, and bring it unto us, that we may hear it, and do it?

Neither is it beyond the sea, that thou shouldest say, Who shall go over the sea for us, and bring it unto us, that we may hear it, and do it?

But the word is very nigh unto thee, in thy mouth, and in thy heart, that thou mayest do it.

DEUTERONOMY

Behold, the days come, saith the Lord, that I will make a new covenant with the house of Israel, and with the house of Judah:

Not according to the covenant that I made with their fathers in the day that I took them by the hand to bring them out of the land of Egypt; which my covenant they brake, although I was an husband unto them, saith the Lord:

But this shall be the covenant that I will make with the house of Israel; After those days, saith the Lord, I will put my law in their inward parts, and write it in their hearts; and will be their God, and they shall be my people.

JEREMIAH

And when he [Christ] was demanded of the Pharisees, when the kingdom of God should come, he answered them and said, The kingdom of God cometh not with observation:

Neither shall they say, Lo here! or, lo there! for, behold, the kingdom of God is within you.

ST. LUKE

[The correct rendering is probably not "within" but "among". No matter: "within" is equally true.]

We therefore conclude, finally, that, in order to make himself known to men, God can and need use neither words, nor miracles, not any other created thing, but only Himself.

SPINOZA

> The world was more in me than I in it.
> The King of Glory in my soul did sit.
> And to Himself in me he always gave
> All that he takes delight to see me have.
> For so my spirit was an endless sphere,
> Like God himself, and heaven and earth was there.

TRAHERNE (from Silence)

> His deepest wisdom harbours in thy side,
> In thine own bosom hides His utmost love.

WALTER DE LA MARE
(from The Imagination's Pride)

Begin to search and dig in thine own field for this pearl of eternity that lies hidden in it; it cannot cost thee too much, nor canst thou buy it too dear, for it is *all*; and when thou hast found it thou wilt know that all which thou hast sold or given away for it is as mere a nothing as a bubble upon the water.

WILLIAM LAW

We are potentially all things; our personality is what we are able to realise of the infinite wealth which our divine-human nature contains hidden in its depths.

⁴⁷⁴ W. R. INGE (interpreting Plotinus)

Be ye lamps unto yourselves.
Be your own reliance.
Hold to the truth within yourselves
as to the only lamp.

THE BUDDHA

Folly, to drink from puddles by the way
When here at home the crystal fountains play!

ANGELUS SILESIUS

A young Rabbi complained to his Master: "During the hours
when I am studying I feel filled with light and life, but as soon
as I cease to study this mood disappears. What ought I do?"

Thereupon the Rabbi replied: "It is like a man who journeys
through a forest on a dark night, and part of the way is accompanied by a companion who carries a lantern. At length they
come to a point where their paths divide, and they must go on
alone. If each carries his own lantern, he need fear no darkness."

HASIDIC STORY

We can never well be assured of Heaven, until we find it
rising up within ourselves and glorifying our own souls. When
true assurance comes, Heaven itself will appear upon the horizon of our souls, like a morning light chafing away all our dark
and gloomy doubtings before it. We shall not need then to light
up our candles to seek for it in corners; no, it will display its
own lustre and brightness so before us, that we may see it in its
own light, and ourselves the true possessors of it. Say not so
much, *Who shall ascend up into heaven*, to fetch it down from
thence? or *who shall descend into the deep*, to fetch it up from beneath? for in the growth of true internal goodness and in the progress of true religion it will freely unfold itself within us. Stay till
the grain of mustard-seed itself breaks forth from among the

clods that buried it, till through the descent of the heavenly dew
it sprouts up and reveals itself openly. This holy assurance is
indeed the budding and blossoming of felicity in our own souls;
it is the inward sense and feeling of the true life, spirit, sweetness and beauty of God powerfully expressing its own energy
within us.

★JOHN SMITH

Again, "Thou shalt love the Lord thy God with all thy heart,
with all thy soul, and with all thy strength, and thy neighbour
as thyself." Now these two precepts given by the written word
of God are an absolute demonstration of the first original perfection of man, and also a full and invincible proof that the same
original perfection is not quite annihilated, but lies in him as
an hidden, suppressed seed of goodness capable of being raised
up to its first perfection. For had not this divine unity, purity,
and perfection of love towards God and man been man's first
natural state of life, it could have nothing to do with his present
state. For had any other nature or measure or kind of love begun in the first birth of his life, he could only have been called
to that. For no creature has or can have a call to be above or
act above its own nature. Therefore, as sure as man is called to
this unity, purity, and perfection of love, so sure is it that it
was at first his natural heavenly state and still has its seed or
remains within him, as his only power and possibility of rising
up to it again. And therefore all that man is called to, every
degree of a new and perfect life, every future exaltation and
glory he is to have . . . , is a full proof that the same perfection
was originally his natural state and is still in him in such a seed
or remains of existence as to admit of a perfect renewal.

Now this mystery of an inward life hidden in man as his
most precious treasure, as the ground or origin of all that can
be great or good in him, . . . is a truth to which almost everything
in nature bears full witness. Look where you will, nothing appears
or works outwardly in any creature or in any effect of nature,

356

but what is all done from its own inward invisible spirit, not a spirit brought into it but its own inward spirit, which is an inward invisible mystery, till made known or brought forth by outward appearances. . . .

What a miserable mistake is it therefore to place religious goodness in outward observances . . . when every operation in nature and creature demonstrates that the Kingdom of Heaven must be all within us, or it never can possibly belong to us.

★ WILLIAM LAW

§ 2

[The next five extracts should be read together, the first three in the light of the fourth and fifth. We often find ourselves, particularly in early life, struggling against impulses and desires that we feel ashamed of, but in the end seem unable to resist. Our sense of shame is sometimes groundless, being merely the result of ideas about what is decent and proper that we have imbibed from our parents or the general atmosphere, though, if we really thought about it, we should realise that whatever we may be struggling against is as natural as eating or drinking, and indeed necessary for the development of our full personality. But sometimes we do right to feel ashamed, for we know that we have really damaged something in ourselves (spiritually, not physically) by our indulgence: we know that we are becoming somehow smaller than we might have been.

In such a situation, the worst thing we can do is to struggle against our desires in a negative sort of way. For by doing so we are concentrating our whole attention upon them, and so making them stronger rather than weaker: and if we succeed in suppressing them for the time being, we feel wretchedly frustrated until they arise to torment us once more.

What we have to do is to fight them in a positive way. At the root of them lies the energy, the creativity, the longing for fulfilment which is what makes us human beings, formed after the likeness of God: and the fruitful thing to do is to give it, this energy of ours, a direction that really does fulfil us, and so produces in the depths of our being an abiding sense of joy, instead of "putting us off" with an isolated bit of mere pleasure. There is only one way to do this: we have to immerse ourselves in what, as we know from our previous experience, can give us the kind of satisfaction, without flaw or taint in it, that will be followed by no troubling aftermath. Desires we don't much like tend to vanish if, being born poets, we write a poem, or, born mathematicians, we struggle with a mathematical problem: they seem, those desires, so trivial in comparison. And most if not all human beings are born *something*: if not poets or mathematicians, then say athletes or mechanics or readers or naturalists or climbers of mountains or hills. *Something* gives us flawless satisfaction, though we may often be able to follow our real avocation only as amateurs.]

Nothing is worse for the soul than struggling not to give play to feelings that it cannot control. This is called the Double Injury.

CHUANG TZU

Nature will force her way, and if you try to stifle her by drowning, she comes up, not the fairest part of her uppermost.

GEORGE MEREDITH (from *Diana of the Crossways*)

Sooner murder an infant in its cradle than nurse unacted desires.

BLAKE

One shall not kill "the evil impulse", the passion, in oneself, but one shall serve God *with* it.

MARTIN BUBER (interpreting Hasidism)

God wishes not to deprive us of pleasure; but He wishes to give us pleasure in its totality; that is to say, all pleasure. . . .

What greater pleasure is there than to find myself the one thing that I ought to be, and the whole thing that I ought to be? . . .

There is nothing pleasurable save what is uniform with the most inmost depths of the divine nature.

HENRY SUSO

§ 3

Freedom is to be in possession of oneself.

HEGEL

Anything is free when it spontaneously expresses its own nature to the full in activity.

JOHN MACMURRAY

Thus freedom in general is the experience which each thing has of the working of its own nature; and a distinction parallel to ours of freedom and unfreedom exists for the plant and for the stone or the atom. The plant undergoes the wind which bends it, or the air which sets its respiration at work. But it enjoys its own free act of respiration. The stone is passive to the freezing water that splits it, but free in its resilience to deformation.

474 SAMUEL ALEXANDER

The true self of any individual man is not something already fixed or determined, but something he has to aim at and work for.

★ JOSIAH ROYCE

That which it is the task of a human being to create is not something in some way external to himself and capable of taking on an independent existence: in reality it is himself.

★ GABRIEL MARCEL

Withdraw into yourself and look. And if you do not find yourself beautiful as yet, do as does the creator of a statue that is to be made beautiful; he cuts away here, he smooths there, he makes this line lighter, this other purer, until he has shown a beautiful face upon his statue. So do you also; cut away all that is excessive, straighten all that is crooked, bring light to all that is shadowed, labour to make all glow with beauty, and do not cease chiselling your statue until there shall shine out on you the godlike splendour of virtue, until you shall see the final goodness surely established in the stainless shrine.

And, when you have become this perfect work and see that it and you are one, nothing now remaining that can hinder your inner unity, nothing from without clinging to your inner self; now call up all your confidence, strike forward yet a step— you need a guide no longer—strain and see.

This is the only eye that sees Absolute Beauty. If the eye that tries to see it be dimmed by vice and unpurified, or weak and unable in its cowardly flinching to see the Uttermost Brightness, then it sees nothing, even though another point to what lies plain to see before it. To any vision must be brought an eye fitted to what is to be seen and having some likeness to it. Never did eye see the sun unless it had become sun-like, and never can soul see Beauty unless itself be beautiful. Therefore, first let each become godlike and each beautiful who cares to see God and Beauty.

★ PLOTINUS

[Plotinus was a follower of Plato, and in Plato's philosophy Absolute Beauty is indistinguishable from God. See p. 397.]

360

Beloved Pan, and all ye other gods who haunt this place, give me beauty in the inward soul; and may the outward and inward man be at one. May I reckon the wise to be the wealthy, and may I have such a quantity of gold as a temperate man and he only can bear and carry.—Anything more? The prayer, I think, is enough for me.

SOCRATES' PRAYER (from Plato's *Phaedrus*)

[Socrates was walking by the river Ilissus when he uttered this prayer: so he addresses it to Pan, god of the countryside.]

FROM MARCUS AURELIUS

Nothing can be more miserable than the man who goes through the whole round of things, and, as the poet says, *pries into the things beneath the earth*, and would gladly guess the thoughts in his neighbour's heart, if he could, while having no conception that he needs but to associate himself with the divine 'genius' in his own bosom, and to serve it truly.

[It will be remembered from previous passages that, according to the Hebrew mystics, God has put a fragment or "spark" of Himself into every human being. Marcus Aurelius believed much the same, and called it the divine 'genius'.]

．　．　．　．　．　．　．　．

Men seek out retreats for themselves in the country, by the seaside, on the mountains, and thou too art in the habit of longing above all for such things. But all this is unreasonable to the last degree, when thou canst at a moment's notice retire into thyself; for nowhere can a man find a retreat more full of peace or more free from care than his own soul. Make use then of this retirement continually and regenerate thyself.

．　．　．　．　．　．　．　．

Get rid of the opinion, *I am harmed*, and at once the feeling of being harmed disappears; get rid of the feeling, and the harm disappears at once.

That which does not make a man himself worse than before cannot make his life worse either, nor injure it whether from without or within.

. . . .

Be like a headland of rock on which the waves break incessantly; but it stands fast and around it the seething of the waters sinks to rest.

Ah, unlucky am I, that this has happened to me! Nay, but rather lucky am I that, though this has happened to me, yet am I still unhurt, neither crushed by the present nor dreading the future. Does what has happened to thee hinder thee one whit from being just, high-minded, chaste, sensible, deliberate, straightforward, modest, free, and from possessing all the other qualities, the presence of which enables a man's nature to come fully into its own? Forget not in future, when anything would lead thee to feel hurt, to take thy stand upon this axiom: *This is no misfortune, but to bear it nobly is good fortune.*

. . . .

Things of themselves cannot get the least grip on the soul, nor have any entry to her, nor turn her aside or move her; but the soul alone moves herself.

. . . .

When forced, as it seems, by things around thee to be utterly disquieted, return with all speed into thy self, staying in discord no longer than thou must. By constant recurrence to the harmony within, it will grow more natural to thee.

. . . .

Look within. Within is the fountain of Good, ready always to gush forth if thou wilt only dig deep enough.

. . . .

Pain is an evil either to the body—let the body then denounce it—or to the soul; but the soul can ensure her own fair weather and her own calm sea, and refuse to think of pain as an evil. For every conviction and impulse and desire and aversion is from within, and nothing climbs in thither.

. . . .

What if a man think scorn of me? That will be his affair. But it will be mine to refrain from doing or saying anything worthy of scorn. What if he hate me? That will be his affair. But I will be kindly and good-natured to everyone, and ready to shew even my enemy where he has seen amiss, not by way of rebuke nor with a parade of forbearance, but genuinely and chivalrously. For such should be the inner springs of a man's heart that the Gods see him angry at nothing and considering nothing a hardship. Why, what evil can happen to thee if thou thyself now doest what is congenial to thy nature, and welcomest what the Universal Nature now regards as well-timed, thou who art a man intensely eager that what is for the common interest should by one means or another be brought about?

. . . .

Often have I marvelled how each one of us loves himself above all men, yet sets less store by his own opinion of himself than by that of everyone else. At any rate, if a God or some wise teacher should come to a man and command him to admit no thought or design into his mind that he could not utter aloud as soon as conceived, he could not endure this order for a single day. So it is clear that we pay more attention to our neighbours' opinion than to our own.

★ MARCUS AURELIUS

THE LAKE OF BEAUTY

Let your mind be quiet, realising the beauty of the world, and
the immense the boundless treasures that it holds in store.

All that you have within you, all that your heart desires, all that your Nature so specially fits you for—that or the counterpart of it waits embedded in the great Whole, for you. It will surely come to you.

Yet equally surely not one moment before its appointed time will it come. All your crying and fever and reaching out of hands will make no difference.

Therefore do not begin that game at all.

Do not recklessly spill the waters of your mind in this direction and in that, lest you become like a spring lost and dissipated in the desert.

But draw them together into a little compass, and hold them still, so still;

And let them become clear, so clear—so limpid, so mirror-like;

At last the mountains and the sky shall glass themselves in peaceful beauty,

And the antelope shall descend to drink, and to gaze at his reflected image, and the lion to quench his thirst,

And Love himself shall come and bend over, and catch his own likeness in you.

EDWARD CARPENTER

§ 5

Who will justify him that sinneth against his own soul? and who will glorify him that dishonoureth his own life?

475   ECCLESIASTICUS

That action is ill, wherein we lose ourselves: and there is no recompense for the loss.

BENJAMIN WHICHCOTE

The soul is its own witness; yea, the soul
Itself is its own refuge; grieve thou not,
O man, thy soul, the great internal Witness.

475   THE CODE OF MANU

There is a self-love which we ought to have in accordance with God's will. We ought to love ourselves as God's creation and love the Divine image and likeness in us. We must love our neighbours as ourselves. This implies that we must love ourselves too and respect the image of God in us.

BERDYAEV

To love one's self in the right way [that is, unselfishly] and to love one's neighbour are at bottom one and the same. When selfishness has been taken from you, then you have learned to love yourself rightly.

When the busy man wastes his time and energy on vain and unimportant projects, is this not because he has not rightly learned to love himself? When the frivolous man abandons himself, almost as a mere nothing, to the folly of the moment, is not this because he does not rightly understand how to love himself? When the melancholy man wishes to be done with life, aye, with himself, is this not because he will not learn strictly and earnestly to love himself? When a man is self-torment thinks to do God a service by torturing himself, what is his sin except this, of not willing to love himself in the right way? Ah, and when a man presumptuously lays his hand upon himself, does not his sin precisely consist in not loving himself in the way in which a man *ought* to love himself? Oh, there is so much said in the world about treachery and faithlessness, and, God help us! this is unfortunately only too true, but let us still never forget that the most dangerous traitor of all is the one every man has in his own breast. This treachery (whether it consists in a man's loving himself in the wrong way, that is, selfishly, or selfishly refusing to love himself in the right way) this treachery is certainly a mystery because there is no outcry about it, as is usual in cases of treachery and faithlessness. But is it not therefore all the more important that we should repeatedly be reminded about the Christian teaching: that a man should love his neighbour as himself, that is, as he ought to love himself?

★★ KIERKEGAARD

365

The great law of love is to reverence one's self, for the reason that each of us is *this* creature who has been given *this* shape and has occupied *this* place in the order of creation. Reverence towards the self is reverence towards the mysterious reality with which God has endowed it. For our self is a holy temple of the Spirit, built by God's own hands, a wonderful inner universe with its own laws of gravity, still more marvellous than those we can see in the full vitality of the external universe with its infinity of mechanisms. But we are only entrusted to ourselves as works of art from the studio of an eternal Master. We are not our *own* master-pieces. That is why we are only given to ourselves as infinitely precious heirlooms, which we must treat as we would treat the treasure of our bliss.

★★ PETER WUST

Selfishness is not identical with self-love but with its very opposite. Selfishness is one kind of greediness. Like all greedi-ness, it contains an insatiability, as a consequence of which there is never any real satisfaction. Greed is a bottomless pit which exhausts the person in an endless effort to satisfy the need without ever reaching satisfaction. Close observation shows that while the selfish person is always anxiously concerned with himself, he is never satisfied, is always restless, always driven by the fear of not getting enough, of missing something, of being deprived of something. He is filled with burning envy of any-one who might have more. If we observe still closer . . . we find that this type of person is basically not fond of himself, but deeply dislikes himself.

The puzzle in this seeming contradiction is easy to solve. Selfishness is rooted in this very lack of fondness for oneself. The person who is not fond of himself, who does not approve of himself, is in constant anxiety concerning his own self. He has not the inner security which can exist only on the basis of genuine fondness and affirmation.

ERICH FROMM

366

I love my life supremely because Thou, O Lord, art my life's sweetness.

NICHOLAS OF CUSA

For if I ought to love myself in Thee who art my likeness, I am most especially constrained thereto when I see that Thou lovest me as Thy creature and Thine image.

NICHOLAS OF CUSA

§ 6

The idea of the perfect unity of all can at last be achieved, in real life, one way only: through the fullness of perfect individualities. Therefore the utlimate goal is inseparably twofold: namely the highest development of every individuality, and every individuality's fullest union with all. . . . The world needs us as much as we need it.

★★ VLADIMIR SOLOVIEV

FIFTH PART

II. INTIMATIONS

[There are moments in some people's lives when a veil seems suddenly drawn aside from the universe, and they see everything as divine. Such visions are always accompanied by a feeling of peculiar joy, and by a sense, very difficult to convey, of certainty, of inevitability, of everything being utterly "right".

It is often considered that experiences of this nature are a matter of over-sensitive nerves or of some other bodily change in us; or that they must be dismissed as an inexplicable illusion; and that anyhow there is nothing particularly "spiritual" about them. I find such reactions unsatisfying. To start with, who knows where the "physical" ends and the "spiritual" begins? They are inextricably mixed up with one another. It may happen, for example, that sexual attraction becomes suddenly love: but love is not sexual attraction, though sexual attraction is a prerequisite for one kind of love. Love is free or spiritual, and sexual attraction is instinctive or physical: but without the physical there could be, for bodily human beings, nothing spiritual, just as Traherne could never have seen "the dust and stones of the street" looking like gold, without eyes to see them with.

Secondly: the feeling of "rightness" and joy, a feeling like no other, that accompanies these experiences is sufficient evidence of their spiritual, or specially spiritual, nature for those who experience them (as several of the following extracts will show), though no evidence at all, of course, for those who do not.

It is also objected that identical or very similar sensations—the sensation of an unveiling as well as the sensation of joy—can be produced by swallowing the appropriate dose of an appropriate drug. I cannot say whether this is so, for I have never experimented with drugs. But if so, what of it? A drug may alter the body in such a way as to make it a better instrument for these visionary experiences.

It is objected, finally, that such experiences are characteristic of the ecstatic phases in manic depression. But again if so, what of it? Certain psychic intensifications, such as preclude the just balance of everyday sanity, may, on the other hand, encourage insights denied to the everyday sane. Beethoven, I imagine, was a manic depressive: but is anybody going to say that the *Es muss sein*, which unveils heaven, is therefore suspect? Anyhow, I prefer to call these phenomena, for my own part, intimations, or glimpses, of reality or eternity or divinity, or anything else of the kind you may wish.]

§ 1

And he [Moses] said, I beseech thee, shew me thy glory.

And he said, I will make all my goodness pass before thee, and I will proclaim the name of the Lord before thee; and will be gracious to whom I will be gracious, and will shew mercy on whom I will shew mercy.

And he said, Thou canst not see my face: for there shall no man see me, and live.

And the Lord said, Behold, there is a place by me, and thou shalt stand upon a rock:

And it shall come to pass, while my glory passeth by, that I will put thee in a cleft of the rock, and will cover thee with my hand while I pass by:

And I will take away mine hand, and thou shalt see my back parts: but my face shall not be seen.

EXODUS

Wherefore at certain times when the soul is least thinking of it and least desiring it, God is wont to give it these Divine touches, by causing it certain recollections of Himself.

ST. JOHN OF THE CROSS

Suppose a man in hiding and he stirs, he shows his whereabouts thereby; and God does the same. No one could ever have found God; he gave himself away.

MEISTER ECKHART

372

What is that which shines through me, and strikes upon my heart without hurting it? And I shudder and kindle: shudder, in as much as I am unlike it; kindle, in as much as I am like it. It is Wisdom, Wisdom's self which thus shines into me . . .

ST. AUGUSTINE

[In old theological literature the word Wisdom was sometimes used, as here, for God or Christ or the Trinity].

Everything visible conceals an invisible mystery, and the last mystery of all is God.

CHRISTOPHE ERNST LUTHARDT

This is none other but the house of God, and this is the gate of heaven.

GENESIS

For this world belongs as well to the Body or Corpus of God the Father, as the Heaven does.

Thou must not therefore think that the heavenly light in this world is quite extinct: No; there is only a duskishness or dim obscurity upon it, so that we cannot apprehend it with our corrupted eyes.

But if God did but once put away that duskishness, which moves about the light, and that thy eyes were opened, then in that very place where thou standest, sittest, or liest, thou shouldst see the glorious Countenance or Face of God and the whole heavenly Gate.

Thou needest not first to cast thine eyes up into Heaven, for it is written: 'The Word is near thee, namely on thy lips, and in thy heart'.

BOEHME

But what is Paradise? All things that are; for all that is, is good and joyous. Therefore it is called a Paradise, and is so indeed. It is said also that Paradise is an outer court of Heaven. Even so all that is, is verily an outer court of the Eternal and of Eternity, and especially what we may recognise and know of God and Eternity, in time and in temporal things and in creatures. For the creatures are a guide and a way to God and to Eternity. Thus all this is an outer court or forecourt of Eternity; and therefore it may well be called a Paradise, and be so in truth.

THEOLOGIA GERMANICA

And thus have you a Gate, in the prospect even of this world, whereby you may see into God's Kingdom.   TRAHERNE

The simple vision of pure love, which is marvellously penetrating, does not stop at the outer husk of creation: it penetrates to the divinity which is hidden within.   MALAVAL

Lo, these are but the outskirts of His ways: and how small a whisper do we hear of Him!   JOB

God keeps His holy mysteries
Just on the outside of man's dream.

ELIZABETH BARRETT BROWNING

If ye do not recognise God, at least recognise His signs.

AL-HALLAJ

What idea could we have of God without the sky?

GEORGE MACDONALD

> . . . objects recognised
> In flashes, and with glory not their own.
>
> WORDSWORTH

> A man that looks on glasse,
>   On it may stay his eye:
> Or if he pleaseth, through it passe,
>   And then the heav'n espie.
>
> GEORGE HERBERT

> As we see the sun but cannot look at it (for we see its light on all things but are blinded by its glare if we fix our eyes on it), so we may say of God that he is light and darkness, hidden and manifest. For we cannot see him, and if we raise our mind to behold him it is dazzled; yet we see him in all creation, which is resplendent with his light.
>
> LUIS DE LEON

> And Moses hid his face; for he was afraid to look upon God.
>
> EXODUS

> Our eyes shall see Thee, which before saw dust.
>
> GEORGE HERBERT

> I but open my eyes,—and perfection, no more and no less,
> In the kind I imagined, full-fronts me, and God is seen God
> In the star, in the stone, in the flesh, in the soul and the clod.
>
> BROWNING

> God is nearer to me than I am to myself: He is just as near to wood and stone, but they do not know it.
>
> MEISTER ECKHART

God is an angel in an angel, and a stone in a stone, and a straw in a straw.

JOHN DONNE

The tree of God is the skeleton of the Universe; it grows throughout the whole of Creation and spreads its branches through all its ramifications.

HEBREW DOCTRINE

The entire aggregate of existence springs from the divine world, in greater beauty There because There unmingled but mingled here.

PLOTINUS

All that is sweet, delightful, and amiable in this world, in the serenity of the air, the fineness of seasons, the joy of light, the melody of sounds, the beauty of colours, the fragrancy of smells, the splendour of precious stones, is nothing else but Heaven breaking through the veil of this world, manifesting itself in such a degree and darting forth in such variety so much of its own nature.

WILLIAM LAW

Nature is the living visible garment of God.

GOETHE

We may think of the Divine as a fire whose outgoing warmth pervades the Universe.

PLOTINUS

St. Francis ordered a plot to be set aside for the cultivation of flowers when the convent garden was made, in order that all who saw them might remember the Eternal Sweetness.

★THOMAS OF CELANO

What if earth
Be but the shadow of heaven . . . ?

MILTON

The devout man does not only believe but feels there is a
Deity. He has *actual sensations* of Him.

ADDISON

Our hearts were drunk with a beauty
Our eyes could never see . . .

A. E.

This made it the more likely that he had seen a true vision;
for instead of making common things look commonplace, as a
false vision would have done, it had made common things dis-
close the wonderful that was in them.

GEORGE MACDONALD

For now the unborn God in the human heart
Knows for a moment all sublimities . . .
Old people at evening sitting in the doorways
See in a broken window of the slum
The Burning Bush reflected, and the crumb
For the starving bird is part of the broken Body
Of Christ Who forgives us . . .

EDITH SITWELL (from *Holiday*)

["And the angel of the Lord appeared unto him in a flame of
fire out of the midst of a bush: and he looked, and, behold, the
bush burned with fire, and the bush was not consumed." Exodus.]

377

THE KINGDOM OF GOD

O World invisible, we view thee,
O World intangible, we touch thee,
O World unknowable, we know thee,
Inapprehensible, we clutch thee!

Does the fish soar to find the ocean,
The eagle plunge to find the air—
That we ask of the stars in motion
If they have rumour of thee there?

Not where the wheeling systems darken,
And our benumbed conceiving soars!—
The drift of pinions, would we hearken,
Beats at our own clay-shuttered doors.

The angels keep their ancient places;—
Turn but a stone, and start a wing!
'Tis ye, 'tis your estrangèd faces,
That miss the many-splendoured thing.

But (when so sad thou canst not sadder)
Cry;—and upon thy so sore loss
Shall shine the traffic of Jacob's ladder
Pitched betwixt Heaven and Charing Cross.

Yea, in the night, my Soul, my daughter,
Cry,—clinging Heaven by the hems;
And lo, Christ walking on the water,
Not of Gennesareth, but Thames!

475 FRANCIS THOMPSON

§ 2

I was in the Spirit on the Lord's day . . .

REVELATION

378

I still remember walking down the Notting Hill main road and observing the (extremely sordid) landscape with joy and astonishment. Even the movement of the traffic had something universal and sublime in it.

EVELYN UNDERHILL

It is only in exceptional moods that we realise how wonderful are the commonest experiences of life. It seems to me sometimes that these experiences have an 'inner' side, as well as the outer side we normally perceive. At such moments one suddenly sees everything with new eyes; one feels on the brink of some great revelation. It is as if we caught a glimpse of some incredibly beautiful world that lies silently about us all the time. I remember vividly my first experience of the kind when, as a boy, I came suddenly upon the quiet miracle of an ivy-clad wall glistening under a London street-lamp. I wanted to weep and I wanted to pray; to weep for the Paradise from which I had been exiled, and to pray that I might yet be made worthy of it. Such moments are rare, in my experience. But their influence is permanent. They import a tinge of unreality into our normal acceptances; we suspect them for the dull and purblind things that they are. There are analogous moments when one suddenly sees the glory of people. On some unforgettable evening one's friend is suddenly seen as the unique, irreplaceable, and utterly delightful being that he is. It is as if he had been freshly created. One is no longer concerned with his relations to oneself . . . He exists wholly in his own right; his significance is eternal, and the essential mystery of his being is as fathomless as that of God Himself.

J. W. N. SULLIVAN

The bright morning sun of summer heated the eastern parapet of London Bridge; I stayed in the recess to acknowledge it. The smooth water was a broad sheen of light, the built-up river flowed calm and silent by a thousand doors, rippling only where

379

the stream chafed against a chain. Red pennants drooped, gilded vanes gleamed on polished masts, black-pitched hulls glistened like a black rook's feathers in sunlight; the clear air cut out the forward angles of the warehouses, the shadowed wharves were quiet in shadows that carried light; far down the ships that were hauling out moved in repose, and with the stream floated away into the summer mist. There was a faint blue colour in the air hovering between the built-up banks, against the lit walls, in the hollows of the houses. The swallows wheeled and climbed, twittered and glided downwards. Burning on, the great sun stood in the sky, heating the parapet, glowing steadfastly upon me as when I rested in the narrow valley grooved out in prehistoric times. Burning on steadfast, and ever present as my thought. Lighting the broad river, the broad walls; lighting the least speck of dust; lighting the great heaven; gleaming on my finger-nail. The fixed point of day—the sun. I was intensely conscious of it; I felt it; I felt the presence of the immense powers of the universe; I felt out into the depths of the ether. So intensely conscious of the sun, the sky, the limitless space, I felt too in the midst of eternity then, in the midst of the supernatural, among the immortal . . . By these I saw my soul; by these I knew the supernatural to be more intensely real than the sun. I touched the supernatural, the immortal, there that moment.

RICHARD JEFFERIES

He never saw again what he saw that morning. The children on their way to school, the silvery grey pigeons that flew from the roofs to the pavement, the little loaves of bread that some invisible hand had put out, all seemed to him divine. Two little boys ran towards a pigeon and looked smilingly at Levin; the pigeon fluttered its wings and flew off, glistening in the sun, through the quivering snow-dust in the air; from a window came the odour of freshly-baked bread, as a few little rolls were laid on the sill. . . .

TOLSTOY (from *Anna Karenina*)

WAITING FOR A SEAT AT THE OPERA

It was not only a sense of expectation that made the waiting in Floral Street so happy, poignant beyond description though this was for one who was still very young, and only beginning to grow familiar with the masterpieces. To have heard a piece of music once or twice, to have it veiled in your consciousness and struggling to reveal itself, and to know that very soon, at a moment that inevitably must come, you will see it face to face —that is a felicity such as few other experiences can equal, and of the same nature, perhaps, as the quiet of expectation with which a saint awaits the beatific vision. But there were other elements in our happiness. We were a little community, for the "regulars" all knew one another, and we passed the time in keen and surprisingly expert discussion about the merits or demerits of recent performances: our sense of fellowship was almost conspiratorial. Yet for me something sacramental in Floral Street itself was perhaps the greatest felicity of all. In the narrow, rather sordid street, with opera house on one side and high blackened buildings (for they seemed immensely high) on the other, there would come, in the early evenings of that June or July weather, patches of sunlight from a sun itself unseen. And then, for all the bustle and noise in the world's greatest city, and for all, or perhaps because of, the distant traffic—distant, though in fact only just beyond our deep and narrow chasm—there would happen, in the interior castle of one's spirit, a lull, a suspension, a silence and a peace in which joy and sadness, both incomparably intense and yet of an utter tranquillity, were one. The late sun in cities has always had this effect on me. I suppose something of the kind was meant by Omar Khayyám, when he talked of "the brave music of a *distant* drum"; and many people experience it, I think, when faintly, in a sunlit street, they catch the tones of a penny whistle or barrel organ, or the singing of a human voice. There are days in Aix-en-Provence, its blazing streets empty as the sun goes down and then footsteps ringing out—footsteps, they might be, of the mailed soldiery in some long-dead Caesar's legions—, when the sadness would be unbearable were it not happiness as well; and I remember standing one August, as a boy of six or seven, on the little stone balcony of my home near Maida Vale, and feeling myself caught up I knew not whither as hussars came riding down from a neighbouring barracks, and the paving stones echoed to their horses' hooves, and the street was afire with the afternoon sun, and everything was silent. . . .

I shall not attempt to explain the experience of which I have been speaking, and which, I am certain, a great many people share: I shall only say of it, as of many other experiences which are bound up with sights and sounds, that any explanation in purely physical or "materialistic" terms is ludicrously beside the mark. So I shall content myself with repeating the word "sacramental". All physical things are sacraments, "outward and visible signs of an invisible mystery": and the world is so beautiful because it is a sacrament of the Supreme Beauty. To quote what Oscar Wilde himself quotes from Théophile Gautier, "I am one of those *pour qui le monde visible existe*": exists absolutely, but at the same time exists as an intimation. . . .

v. g. (from *My Dear Timothy*)

[Floral Street runs up the side of Covent Garden opera house: we used to wait there for a seat in the gallery.]

A YEAR OF WONDER

How shall I find the words to describe to you, my dear Timothy, what I felt in my year of wonder 1942? I had a heightened perception of everything, and everything was perceived as beautiful and good. But it was more than a perception; it was a meeting, for which I had gone out to the other and for which the other had gone out to me: a meeting with everything's self which at the same time was my self, but was nevertheless of a difference in selfhood which alone made the meeting a possibility. But the going out and the meeting were not different

382

things but the same thing, not successive but simultaneous; which is to say that they were not in time but in eternity. And the meeting, I say again, was with everything. With the greenness, the freshness, the slenderness, the littleness, the gentleness, the strength, the taperingness, the sun-acceptingness, the daisy-and-buttercup-enclosingness, of the benign and far-stretching grass. With the trees in their various species, and with every branch and every twig and every leaf of them. With stones and mould and air and sun and a deck-chair in the garden and a car down the lane and a spire on the downs and the wall of our house as I come in for lunch at one. And with people. I would sit, going up to London, in a crowded railway-compartment, and know myself as in every one of my fellow travellers, and know every one of them as in me.

I was in the Royal Automobile Club, of all places, on an afternoon that summer, and my eye happened to fall on a door. It was quite an ordinary door, in so far as any single thing in the universe is ordinary, with small panels and big panels and a knob; but I tell you that this door, and the look and the sound and the life of it, filled me with joy inexpressible. And I remember that on the same afternoon, in the same club, I suddenly saw something green through the doors of the winter garden, and saluted it with delighted recognition. . . .

v. g. (from *My Dear Timothy*)

FROM "THE CITY"

        . . . i know there lies
Open somewhere this hour a gate to Paradise,
Its blazing battlements with watchers thronged, O where?
I know not, but my flame-winged feet shall lead me there . . .
Or am I there already, and is it Paradise
To look on mortal things with an immortal's eyes?
Above the misty brilliance the streets assume
A night-dilated blue magnificence of gloom

Like many-templed Nineveh tower beyond tower;
And I am hurried on in this immortal hour.
Mine eyes beget new majesties: my spirit greets
The trams, the high-built glittering galleons of the streets . . .
Hurry with me, not all ignoble as we seem,
Lured by some inexpressible and gorgeous dream.
The earth melts in my blood. The air that I inhale
Is like enchanted wine poured from the Holy Grail.
What was that glimmer then? Was it the flash of wings
As through the blinded mart rode on the King of Kings?
O stay, departing glory, stay with us but a day,
And burning seraphim shall leap from out our clay,
And plumed and crested hosts shall shine where men have been,
Heaven hold no lordlier court than earth at College Green.
Ah, no, the wizardry is over; the magic flame
That might have melted all in beauty fades as it came.
The stars are far and faint and strange. The night draws down.
Exiled from light, forlorn, I walk in Dublin Town.
Yet had I might to lift the veil, the will to dare,
The fiery rushing chariots of the Lord are there,
The whirlwind path, the blazing gates, the trumpets blown,
The halls of heaven, the majesty of throne by throne,
Enraptured faces, hands uplifted, welcome sung
By the thronged gods, tall, golden-coloured, joyful, young.

A. E.

He did not stop on the steps either, but went quickly down; his
soul, overflowing with rapture, yearned for freedom, space, open-
ness. The vault of heaven, full of soft, shining stars, stretched vast
and fathomless above him. The Milky Way ran in two pale
streams from the zenith to the horizon. The fresh, motionless
still night enfolded the earth. The white towers and golden dome
of the cathedral gleamed out against the sapphire sky. The gorgeous autumn flowers, in the beds round the house, were slumber-
ing till morning. The silence of earth seemed to melt into the

silence of the heavens. The mystery of earth was one with the mystery of the stars. . . .

Alyosha stood, gazed, and suddenly threw himself down on the earth. He did not know why he embraced it. He could not have told why he longed so irresistibly to kiss it, to kiss it all. But he kissed it weeping, sobbing and watering it with his tears, and vowed passionately to love it, to love it for ever and ever. "Water the earth with the tears of your joy and love those tears," echoed in his soul.

What was he weeping over?

Oh! in his rapture he was weeping even over those stars, which were shining to him from the abyss of space, and "he was not ashamed of that ecstasy". There seemed to be threads from all those innumerable worlds of God, linking his soul to them, and it was trembling all over "in contact with other worlds". He longed to forgive everyone and for everything, and to beg forgiveness. Oh, not for himself, but for all men, for all and for everything. "And others are praying for me too", echoed again in his soul. But with every instant he felt clearly and, as it were, tangibly, that something firm and unshakable as that vault of heaven had entered into his soul. It was as though some idea had seized the sovereignty of his mind—and it was for all his life and for ever and ever. He had fallen on the earth a weak boy, but he rose up a resolute champion, and he knew and felt it suddenly at the very moment of his ecstasy. And never, never, all his life long, could Alyosha forget that minute.

"Someone visited my soul in that hour," he used to say afterwards, with implicit faith in his words.

Within three days he left the monastery in accordance with the words of his elder, who had bidden him "sojourn in the world".

DOSTOEVSKY (from *The Brothers Karamazov*)

I was crossing a little stream near Inchy Wood and actually in the middle of a stride from bank to bank, when an emotion never experienced before swept down upon me. I said, "That is what the devout Christian feels, that is how he surrenders his will to the will of God". I felt an extreme surprise, for my whole imagination was preoccupied with the pagan mythology of ancient Ireland, I was marking in red ink, upon a large map, every sacred mountain. The next morning I awoke near dawn, to hear a voice saying, "The love of God is infinite for every human soul because every human soul is unique, no other can satisfy the same need in God."

W. B. YEATS

One forenoon, when my terror and despair seemed to be at their height (if degrees can be spoken of in such a context, as they truly cannot), I set out for a walk with my wife. We went very slowly, my arm resting on hers: for my body was weak after a total insomnia that had lasted for twenty-two days, and every muscle and nerve in it ached. . . . About half an hour later we turned, sharply left, into a dark and narrow path that descended: and soon came out into a great open space—a sort of water-meadow, with herds grazing, and a high inland cliff just in front of us. There was dappled sunlight everywhere, and a slight breeze. I felt suddenly very still: and then I heard the inland cliff, and the grass and water and sky, say very distinctly to me "A humble and a contrite heart He will not despise". When I say I heard them say it I mean, quite literally, that I *heard* them say it: a voice came from them: but they were also themselves the voice, and the voice was also within me. . . . I said to my wife "The trouble is over": and that night I slept a little. The trouble, in one sense, was not over, for a year or two were to pass before it was more or less completely behind me: I was nevertheless right, because thenceforth, even at the worst moments, there was always a glimmer of light, however minute, at the end of the tunnel. . . . And now it is only by the greatest effort of will, if even so, that I can realise in recollection that terror and that despair, which have long appeared nothing to me; and when I live again in those days, as I often do, I live in the love that faithfully cared for me and saw me through to safety.

V. G. (of 1943)

[I am not sure whether, when I wrote the last sentence, I meant God's love or my wife's: but it makes no matter, for they are the same.]

From 1914 to 1918 I was not able to get away for any holidays, but in 1919 I spent Monday to Saturday several times in a remote cottage in the Lune Valley, reading, writing, and going for long solitary walks. One afternoon I had been walking along a seemingly endless country lane, little more than a grassy cart-track between hedges. It rose steadily for some time till it reached a point where a gap in the hedges gave a view over a wide stretch of open country. I had been curiously restless and expectant, and I sat down on a heap of stones overgrown with wild geranium, feeling that something—I did not know what—was going to happen. And here I will quote from an account written and published, in the form of a story, soon after:

'Suddenly I knew.'

'What did you know?'

'Everything. All there is to be known. The nature of reality and the meaning of life, and the secret that all the philosophers have desired to know since thought began. I can't tell you, of course. I have heard "unspeakable words" which it is not lawful for a man to utter. But one thing I will say. I knew in that moment that all life is one. Not only the life of men, and animals, and insects, and plants. No, the life that runs in the sides of the hills and beats like a great heart in the ribs of the mountains.'

PETER GREEN

I went out one afternoon for a walk alone. I was in the empty unthinking state in which one saunters along country lanes, simply yielding oneself to the casual sights around which give a town-bred lad with country yearning such intense delight. Suddenly I became conscious of the presence of someone else. I cannot describe it, but I felt that I had as direct perception of

387

the being of God all round about me as I have of you when we are together. It was no longer a matter of inference, it was an immediate act of spiritual (or whatever adjective you like to employ) apprehension. It came unsought, absolutely unexpectedly. I remember the wonderful transfiguration of the far-off woods and hills as they seemed to blend in the infinite being with which I was thus brought into relation. This experience did not last long. But it sufficed to change all my feeling. I had not found God because I had never looked for him. But he had found me.

JOSEPH ESTLIN CARPENTER

So did I feel one warm summer day lying idly on the hillside, not then thinking of anything but the sunlight, and how sweet it was to drowse there, when, suddenly, I felt a fiery heart throb, and knew it was personal and intimate, and started with every sense dilated and intent, and turned inwards, and I heard first a music as of bells going away, away into that wondrous underland whither, as legend relates, the Danaan gods withdrew; and then the heart of the hills was opened to me, and I knew there was no hill for those who were there, and they were unconscious of the ponderous mountain piled above the palaces of light, and the winds were sparkling and diamond clear, yet full of colour as an opal, as they glittered through the valley, and I knew the Golden Age was all about me, and it was we who had been blind to it but that it had never passed away from the world.

A. E.

I was no longer young: in fact I was well over sixty. The winter had been dark and tedious. For some reason or other I had not been able to read much, and I began to think there were signs of the coming end. Suddenly, with hardly any warning, spring burst upon us. Day after day we had clear, warm sunshine which deepened every contrast of colour, and at intervals we were blessed with refreshing rains. I spent most of my time out of doors on the edge of a favourite wood. All my life I had been a lover of the country, and had believed, if this is the right word, that the same thought, spirit, life, God, which was in everything I beheld, was also in me. But my creed had been taken over from books; it was accepted as an intellectual proposition. Most of us are satisfied with this kind of belief, and even call it religion. We are more content the more definite the object becomes, no matter whether or not it is in any intimate relationship with us, and we do not see that the moment God can be named he ceases to be God.

One morning when I was in the wood something happened which was nothing less than a transformation of myself and the world, although I 'believed' nothing new. I was looking at a great, spreading, bursting oak. The first tinge from the greenish-yellow buds was just visible. It seemed to be no longer a tree away from me and apart from me. The enclosing barriers of consciousness were removed and the text came into my mind, *Thou in me and I in thee*. The distinction of self and not-self was an illusion. I could feel the rising sap; in me also sprang the fountain of life up-rushing from its roots, and the joy of its outbreak at the extremity of each twig right up to the summit was my own: that which kept me apart was nothing. I do not argue; I cannot explain; it will be easy to prove me absurd, but nothing can shake me. *Thou in me and I in thee*. Death! what is death? There is no death: *in thee* it is impossible, absurd.

MARK RUTHERFORD

He remembered that during his epileptic fits, or rather immediately preceding them, he had always experienced a moment or two when his whole heart, and mind, and body seemed to wake up to vigour and light; when he became filled with joy and hope, and all his anxieties seemed to be swept away for ever; these moments were but presentiments, as it were, of the one final second (it was never more than a second) in which the fit came upon him. That second, of course, was inexpressible. When his attack was over, and the prince reflected on his symptoms, he used to say to himself: "These moments, short as they are, when I feel such extreme consciousness of myself, and consequently more of life than at other times, are due only to the disease—to the sudden rupture of normal conditions. Therefore they are not really a higher kind of life, but a lower." This reasoning, however, seemed to end in a paradox, and lead to the further consideration:—"What matter though it be only disease, an abnormal tension of the brain, if, when I recall and analyse the moment, it seems to have been one of harmony and beauty in the highest degree—an instant of deepest sensation, overflowing with unbounded joy and rapture, ecstatic devotion, and completest life?" Vague though this sounds, it was perfectly comprehensible to Muishkin, though he knew that it was but a feeble expression of his sensations.

That there was, indeed, beauty and harmony in those abnormal moments, that they uniquely revealed to him the wholeness of life, he could not doubt, nor even admit the possibility of doubt. He felt that they were quite dissimilar to the fantastic and unreal dreams due to intoxication by hashish, opium or wine. Of that he could judge, when the attack was over. These instants were characterized—to define it in a word—by an intense quickening of the sense of personality. Since, in the last conscious moment preceding the attack, he could say to himself, with full understanding of his words: "I would give my whole life for this one instant", then doubtless to him it really was worth a lifetime . . . What more unanswerable than a fact? And this fact had occurred. The prince had confessed unreservedly to himself that the feeling of intense beatitude in that crowded moment made the moment worth a lifetime. "I feel then," he said one one day to Rogojin in Moscow, "I feel then as if I understood those amazing words—'There shall be no more time.'" And he added with a smile: 'No doubt the epileptic Mahomet refers to that same moment when he says that he visited all the dwellings of Allah, in less time than was needed to empty his pitcher of water."

★ DOSTOEVSKY (from *The Idiot*)

390

When I went in the morning into the fields to work, the glory of God appeared in all His visible creation. I well remember we reaped oats, and how every straw and head of the oats seemed arrayed in a kind of rainbow glory, or to glow in the glory of God.

ANONYMOUS (*quoted by William James*)

On a certain spring morning I went out to walk. The fields were green, the birds sang, the dew glistened, the smoke was rising, here and there a man appeared; a light as of transfiguration lay on all things. It was only a little bit of the earth; it was only a moment of her existence; and yet as my look embraced her more and more it seemed to me not only so beautiful an idea, but so true and clear a fact, that she is an angel, an angel so rich and fresh and flower-like, and yet going her round in the skies so firmly and so at one with herself, turning her whole living face to Heaven and carrying me along with her into that Heaven, that I asked myself how the opinions of men could ever have so spun themselves away from life as to deem the earth only a dry clod, and to seek for angels above it or about it in the emptiness of the sky—only to find them nowhere.

GUSTAV THEODOR FECHNER

We wandered to the Pine Forest
    That skirts the Ocean's foam,
The lightest wind was in its nest,
    The tempest in its home.
The whispering waves were half asleep,
    The clouds were gone to play,
And on the bosom of the deep
    The smile of Heaven lay;
It seemed as if the hour were one
    Sent from beyond the skies,
Which scattered from above the sun
    A light of Paradise.

We paused amid the pines that stood
    The giants of the waste,
Tortured by storms to shapes as rude
    As serpents interlaced,
And soothed by every azure breath,
    That under Heaven is blown,
To harmonies and hues beneath,
    As tender as its own;
Now all the tree-tops lay asleep,
    Like green waves on the sea,
As still as in the silent deep
    The ocean woods may be.

How calm it was!—the silence there
    By such a chain was bound
That even the busy woodpecker
    Made stiller by her sound
The inviolable quietness;
    The breath of peace we drew
With its soft motion made not less
    The calm that round us grew.
There seemed from the remotest seat
    Of the white mountain waste,
To the soft flower beneath our feet,
    A magic circle traced,—
A spirit interfused around,
    A thrilling, silent life,—
To momentary peace it bound
    Our mortal nature's strife;
And still I felt the centre of
    The magic circle there
Was one fair form that filled with love
    The lifeless atmosphere.

SHELLEY

The snow hid all the grass, and all signs of vegetation, and the rocks showed themselves boldly everywhere, and seemed more stony than rock, or stone . . .

We lay sidelong upon the turf, and gazed on the landscape till it melted into more than natural loveliness . . .

As I lay down on the grass, I observed the glittering silver line on the ridge of the backs of the sheep, owing to their situation respecting the sun, which made them look beautiful, but with something of strangeness, like animals of another kind, as if belonging to a more splendid world.   DOROTHY WORDSWORTH

The clump of elms grew right over a deep and rugged hollow; their branches reached out across it, roofing in the cave.

Here was the spring, at the foot of a perpendicular rock, moss-grown low down, and overrun with creeping ivy higher. Green thorn bushes filled the chinks and made a wall to the well, and the long narrow hart's-tongue streaked the face of the cliff. Behind, the thick thorns hid the course of the streamlet, in front rose the solid rock, upon the right hand the sward came to the edge—it shook every now and then as the horses in the shade of the elms stamped their feet—on the left hand the ears of wheat peered over the verge. A rocky cell in concentrated silence of green things. . . . To this cell I used to come once now and then on a summer's day, tempted, perhaps, like the finches, by the sweet cool water, but drawn also by a feeling that could not be analysed. Stooping, I lifted the water in the hollow of my hand—carefully, lest the sand might be disturbed—and the sunlight gleamed on it as it slipped through my fingers. Alone in the green-roofed cave, alone with the sunlight and the pure water, there was a sense of something more than these. The water was more to me than water, and the sun than sun. The gleaming rays of the water in my palm held me for a moment, the touch of the water gave me something from itself. A moment, and the gleam was gone, the water flowing away, but I had had them. Beside the physical water and physical light I had received from them their beauty; they had communicated to me this silent mystery.   RICHARD JEFFERIES

Felpham is a sweet place for Study, because it is more Spiritual than London. Heaven opens here on all sides her golden Gates; her windows are not obstructed by vapours; voices of Celestial inhabitants are more distinctly heard, & their forms more distinctly seen; & my Cottage is also a Shadow of their houses.

BLAKE

"What," it will be Question'd, "When the Sun rises, do you not see a round disk of fire somewhat like a Guinea?" O no, no, I see an Innumerable company of the Heavenly Host crying, "Holy, Holy, Holy is the Lord God Almighty". I question not my Corporeal or Vegetative Eye any more than I would Question a Window concerning a Sight. I look thro' it & not with it.

475 BLAKE

The day before he died Rabbi Shneur Salomon asked his grandson "Is the ceiling still there?" When the boy said nothing, the Rabbi continued, in a voice quivering with joy, "I can see no ceiling or walls: I can only see the life of everything, and God creating everything and making everything live."

HASIDIC TRADITION

MUSIC AND THE BEATIFIC VISION

My introduction to music occurred on the first occasion that Mr. Pyatt invited me to dinner. . . . At the coffee stage we moved into another room, filled with very easy chairs and sofas, and containing a piano-player, a rather novel instrument at that time. Mr. Pyatt suggested trying a few rolls. . . . It so happened that the first one he put on was one of the mightiest and most immediately arresting of all compositions, Bach's great organ Toccata and Fugue in D minor. Even as arranged for the piano and played by a mechanical player it is, as I can testify, completely overwhelming. My first hearing of it was a cardinal experience in my life; perhaps, when all is summed up, it will prove to have been *the* cardinal experience of my life. For it was my first glimpse of those activities of the human spirit which are, I am convinced, the justification of life, and in which the meaning of life is to be found. Nothing that I had hitherto experienced belonged to that region. I experienced, quite literally, a revelation. All great art, I believe, is the record of a spiritual achievement, . . . of a degree of understanding, that cannot be communicated in other terms. But, for myself, it is only in certain great music that the revelation is complete and unambiguous. Such music is my substitute for the mystic vision. It is, perhaps, an experience that can never be satisfactorily rationalised, nor ever communicated to others. It is also an experience that can never be denied. No account of life that denies its supreme importance can be even remotely true. In this position, however much it may seem to conflict with my liking for clear reasoning based on verifiable premises, I am quite unshakable. I have heard, and I know.

I passed the rest of the evening in a sort of bewildered happiness. Several more rolls were played—too many for my untrained attention. I cannot remember what they were. After that first shock I listened but vaguely. But it was not until very late that I suddenly became conscious of fatigue and rose to go. Mr. Pyatt shook hands with a pleased smile, obviously finding his experiment completely successful, but, with a tact that could not be missed, he refrained from questioning me about my sensations. The bus-ride home was through a transfigured London. How I loved it all—the bright lights, the traffic, the dark trees of the park, the great, impressive buildings! I was in a dreamy ecstasy at the wonder of life, at its range and complexity, its infinite possibilities. Life! The scale of it! The diversity of it! The greatness of this adventure to which the spirit of man is committed! What undreamed-of possibilities lie before him, what new ways of thinking, what new knowledge, what new heights of experience! And there, as it seemed to me, amongst the farthest reaches of the spirit, lonely and prophetic, was music such as I had heard that night, music informed with the new understanding, the new degree of realisation, that has been achieved by the pioneers of our race.

J. W. N. SULLIVAN

§ 3

This is my delight, thus to wait and watch at the wayside where shadow chases light and the rain comes in the wake of the summer.

Messengers, with tidings from unknown skies, greet me and speed along the road. My heart is glad within, and the breath of the passing breeze is sweet.

From dawn till dusk I sit here before my door, and I know that of a sudden the happy moment will arrive when I shall see.

In the meanwhile I smile and I sing all alone. In the meanwhile the air is filling with the perfume of promise.

RABINDRANATH TAGORE

We are aware of evanescent visitations of thought and feeling, sometimes associated with place or persons, sometimes regarding our own mind alone, and always arising unforeseen and departing unbidden, but elevating and delightful beyond all expression . . . It is as it were the interpenetration of a diviner nature through our own; but its footsteps are like those of a wind over the sea, which the coming calm erases . . . These and corresponding conditions of being are experienced principally by those of the most delicate sensibility and the most enlarged imagination; and the state of mind produced by them is at war with every base desire. The enthusiasm of virtue, love, patriotism, and friendship, is essentially linked with such emotions; and whilst they last, self appears as what it is, an atom to a universe.

475 SHELLEY

THE COMING OF THE BUTTERFLIES

[According to Plato's philosophy, everything that we see on earth is what is called a "particular", as contrasted with its "Idea", which is "yonder" or "in Heaven". In every class of thing there are many particulars, but only one Idea. Thus every butterfly is a particular, and *the* Butterfly is its Idea. A particular butterfly *is* a butterfly because, in a way that Plato doesn't explain, it shares the nature of the Ideal Butterfly, being a sort of imperfect copy of, or derivative from, its perfect Original: without the Butterfly there could be no butterflies. We can understand this very well when we think, not of objects, but of qualities: the very imperfect goodness in a man is to the Goodness of God what a butterfly is to the Butterfly, the man being "here" or in time and God being "yonder" or in Eternity. The most important Ideas, of course, are those not of objects but of qualities, such as temperance, kindness, justice and so on; and the supreme Idea is that of Goodness (indistinguishable from Beauty), or, in other words, God.

The Platonic way of looking at things, when applied to butterflies or camels, lands us in difficulties: it is hard, for example, to imagine Ideal Mud or Ideal Ink (though Chesterton experienced the latter—see page 80). For all that, there is a profound truth behind this conception: the Butterfly is what all butterflies would be if everything about them was perfect from a butterfly point of view. Or say that the Butterfly is what all butterflies strive to be: and anything you strive to be must already exist—when you run a race the goal is *there*. As a matter of fact a lot of people, when exceptionally happy or even exceptionally sad (though that is a very inadequate way of putting it), have seen Ideal animals or even Ideal doors: look at Dorothy Wordsworth on page 393, and something I once wrote myself on page 383. To see a thing like that is to see it *sub specie aeternitatis*. That is a difficult expression to translate: a paraphrase might be "as God sees it, with all its dross and imperfections removed".

Charles Williams' superb novel "The Place of the Lion",

from which the following extract is taken, is about a time when the Ideas broke loose and appeared on earth.]

They ceased speaking, and remained leaning on the gate in silence. Anthony's eyes, passing over the garden, remained fixed where, two nights before, he had thought he saw the form of a lion. It seemed to him now, as he gazed, that a change had taken place. The smooth grass of the lawn was far less green than it had been, and the flowers in the beds by the house walls, on either side of the door, were either dying or already withered. Certainly he had not been in a state to notice much, but there had been left with him a general impression of growth and colour. Neither growth nor colour were now there: all seemed parched. Of course, it was hot, but still. . . .

There was a sudden upward sweep of green and orange through the air in front of him: he blinked and moved. As he recovered himself he saw, with startled amazement, that in the centre of the garden, almost directly above the place where he had seen the lion, there floated a butterfly. But—a butterfly! It was a terrific, a colossal butterfly, it looked as if it were two feet or more across from wing-tip to wing-tip. It was tinted and coloured with every conceivable brightness; green and orange predominating. It was moving upward in spiral flutterings, upward to a certain point, from which it seemed directly to fall close to the ground, then again it began its upward sweep, and again hovered and fell. Of the two men it seemed to be unaware; lovely and self-sufficient it went on with its complex manœuvres in the air. Anthony, after a few astonished minutes, took his eyes from it, and looked about him, first with a general gaze at all his surroundings, then more particularly at Mr. Tighe. The little man was pressed against the gate, his mouth slightly open, his eyes full of plenary adoration, his whole being concentrated on the perfect symbol of his daily concern. Anthony saw that it was no good speaking to him. He looked back at the marvel in time to see, from somewhere above his own head,

398

another brilliancy—but much smaller—flash through the air, almost as if some ordinary butterfly had hurled itself towards its more gigantic image. And another followed it, and another, and as Anthony, now thoroughly roused, sprang up and aside, to see the better, he beheld the air full of them. Those of which he had caught sight were but the scattered first comers of a streaming host. Away across the fields they came, here in thick masses, there in thinner lines, white and yellow, green and red, purple and blue and dusky black. They were sweeping round, in great curving flights; mass following after mass, he saw them driving forward from far away, but not directly, taking wide distances in their sweep, now on one side, now on another, but always and all of them speeding forward towards the gate and the garden beyond. Even as a sudden new rush of aerial loveliness reached that border he turned his head, and saw a cloud of them hanging high above the butterfly of the garden, which rushed up towards them, and then, carrying a whirl of lesser iridescent fragilities with it, precipitated itself down its steep descent; and as it swept, and hovered, and again mounted, silent and unresting, it was alone. Alone it went soaring up, alone to meet another congregation of its hastening visitors, and then again multitudinously fell, and hovered; and again alone went upward to the tryst.

Bewildered and distracted, Anthony caught his companion's arm. Mr. Tighe was by now almost hanging to the gate, his hands clutching frenziedly the topmost bar, his jaws working. Noises were coming from his mouth; the sweat stood in the creases of his face. He gobbled at the soft-glowing vision; he uttered little cries and pressed himself against the bars; his knees were wedged between them, and his feet drawn from the ground in the intensity of his apprehension. And over him faster and thicker the great incursion passed, and the air over the garden was filled with butterflies, streaming, rising, sinking, hovering, towards their centre, and faster now than Anthony's eyes could see the single host of all that visitation rose and fell, only whenever he saw it towards the ground, it turned upwards in a solitary magnificence and whenever, having risen, it dropped again, it went encircled by innumerable tiny bodies and wings.

Credulous, breathless, he gazed, until, after times unreckoned had passed, there seemed to be a stay. Lesser grew the clouds above; smaller the flights that joined them. Now there were but a score and now but twelve or ten—now only three tardy dancers waited above for the flight of their vision; and as again it rose, but one—coming faster than all the rest, reaching its strange assignation as it were at the last permitted moment, joining its summoning lord as it rose for the last time, and falling with it; and then the great butterfly of the garden floated idly in the empty air, and the whole army of others had altogether vanished from sight, and from knowledge. It also after a short while rose, curvetting, passed upward towards the roof of the house, settled there for a moment, a glowing splendour upon the red tiles, swept beyond it, and disappeared.

Anthony moved and blinked, took a step or two away, looked round him, blinked again, and turned back to Mr. Tighe. He was about to speak, but, seeing the other man's face, he paused abruptly. The tears were running down it; as his hands released the bars Anthony saw that he was trembling all over; he stumbled and could not get his footing upon the road. Anthony caught and steadied him.

"O glory, glory," Mr. Tighe said. "O glory everlasting!"

475   CHARLES WILLIAMS

REMEMBRANCE OF TRUE BEAUTY

[It was Plato's theory that all souls are immortal, and that every human being, before possessing a body, has lived, for a shorter or longer time, in "the other world"—the world of Reality or Ideas, as described on page 397—where he has seen Absolute Beauty together with Absolute Justice, Absolute Truth, and all the other Absolutes or Ideas, or, as they are called in this passage, "heavenly forms". Indeed, only a soul that has witnessed this splendour can pass, when given a body, into the form of a man: other souls may become animals (or perhaps trees or flowers—I do not remember about that). A man may have had many reincarnations as a man, or may, for lack of virtue, have become an animal at some time or other and then returned to his manhood: so that the date of his sojourn in "the other world" may be recent or remote.

A soul, when "yonder", has seen, as this passage expresses it, the beatific vision, and has been initiated into a mystery. To be initiated into a mystery is to be granted membership of a society that possesses some secret knowledge—the society of Freemasons, for instance. In the present case, the knowledge is that of Reality itself—of what life or existence really means, really *is*: and the beatific vision is the actual sight of that ineffable Reality —of that Reality whose surpassing wonder no words can express. As the Gospel puts it, the beatific vision is to see God, not through a glass darkly, but face to face.

Everything else in this passage follows naturally from the above. When we are suddenly transported with joy at the sight of a beautiful landscape, or a beautiful picture, or a beautiful human being, that is because, though we may not realise it, we are remembering the ideal, the inexpressible Beauty that we saw "yonder". The very word "transported" means "carried away" from one place to another.

The profound truth of Platonism (which is now very unfashionable) is expressed somewhat differently in other philosophies, religions and traditions. In the Judaeo-Christian tradition, for instance, we say, not that the soul once saw God, but that there is something of God in every soul: and that this something is specially at work in us during moments of enrapturing vision.]

Every soul of man has in the way of nature beheld true being; this was the condition of her passing into the form of man. But all souls do not easily recall the things of the other world; they may have seen them for a short time only, or they may have been unfortunate in their earthly lot, and, having had their hearts turned to unrighteousness through some corrupting influence, they may have lost the memory of the holy things which once they saw. Few only retain an adequate remembrance of them; and they, when they behold here any image of that other world, are rapt in amazement; but they are ignorant of what this rapture means . . . There was a time when with the rest of the happy band they saw beauty shining in brightness—we philosophers [among them]; and then we beheld the beatific vision and were initiated into a mystery which may be truly called most blessed, celebrated by us in our state of innocence, before we had any experience of evils to come, when we were admitted to the sight of realities innocent and simple and calm and happy, which we beheld shining in pure light, pure ourselves and not yet enshrined in that living tomb which we carry about, now that we are imprisoned in the body, like an oyster in his shell. Let me linger over the memory of scenes which have passed away.

But of beauty, I repeat again that we saw her there shining in company with the heavenly forms; and coming to earth we find her here too, shining in clearness through the clearest aperture of sense. For sight is the most piercing of our bodily senses . . . Now he who is not newly initiated, or who has become corrupted, does not easily rise out of this world to the sight of true beauty in the other; he looks only at her earthly namesake, and instead of being awed at the sight of her, he is given over to pleasure, and like a brutish beast he rushes on to enjoy and beget; he consorts with wantonness, and is not afraid or ashamed of pursuing pleasure in violation of nature. But he whose initiation is recent, and who has been the spectator of many glories in the other world, is amazed when he sees any one having a godlike face or form, which is the expression of divine beauty; and at first a shudder runs through him, and again the old awe steals over him; then looking upon the face of his beloved as of a god he reverences him, and if he were not afraid of being thought a downright madman, he would sacrifice to his beloved as to the image of a god.

★ PLATO (from the *Phaedrus*)

The Spiritual Universe, the Realm of the Divine Mind—
beautiful; the most beautiful of all; lying lapped in pure light and
in clear radiance; the original of which this beautiful world is a
shadow and an image; tranquil in the fullness of glory since in
it there is nothing devoid of intellect, nothing dark or out of rule;
a living thing in a life of blessedness—This must overwhelm with
awe any that has seen it, and penetrated it, to become a unit of it.

PLOTINUS

> The Soul that rises with us, our life's Star,
>   Hath had elsewhere its setting,
>   And cometh from afar:
>   Not in entire forgetfulness . . .

> . . . Hence in a season of calm weather
>   Though inland far we be,
> Our Souls have sight of that immortal sea
>   Which brought us hither. . . .

WORDSWORTH (from *Intimations*)

Most men in the course of their lives have known such Platonic
hours of initiation, when the sense of beauty has risen from a
pleasant feeling to a passion, and an element of strangeness and
terror has been mingled with their joy. In those hours the world
has seemed charged with a new vitality; with a splendour which
does not belong to it but is poured through it, as light through a
coloured window, grace through a sacrament, from that Perfect
Beauty which "shines in company with the celestial forms"
beyond the pale of appearance. In such moods of heightened
consciousness each blade of grass seems fierce with meaning, and
becomes a well of wondrous light: a "little emerald set in the City
of God". The seeing self is indeed an initiate thrust suddenly
into the sanctuary of the mysteries: and feels the "old awe and
amazement" with which man encounters the Real.

EVELYN UNDERHILL

SWANN'S PHRASE

[Proust, in what follows, is describing an experience common enough among music-lovers, but always freshly wonderful.

There are various pleasures to be had from listening to music. There is an intellectual pleasure: the pleasure of following a logical development; of grasping a structure; of noticing ingenuities of harmony or counterpoint, or happy subtleties of ornamentation, or occasional touches of humour, or the like. There is also a sensuous pleasure: the nerves react delightedly, or with horror or excitement or a sensation of lulling tranquillity (and all such reactions are pleasurable), to the drama and passion, the brief silences and gentle beginnings, the whole physical *sound* of the thing. But there are moments, and not only in listening to the works of the few supreme masters, when it is no longer a question of mere pleasure or even of happiness: it is a question of joy inexpressible. Wordsworth has perhaps expressed this experience better than any other writer in English: I gave the passage, and a paraphrase of it, on page 81, and shall repeat them here.

> "In such access of mind, in such high hour
>   Of visitation from the living God,
>   Thought was not: in enjoyment it expired.
>   No thanks he breathed, he proffered no request.
>   Rapt into still communion that transcends
>   The imperfect offices of prayer and praise,
>   His mind was a thanksgiving to the power
>   That made him; it was blessedness and love."

The expression is exact. Wordsworth, in those last two lines, is by no means saying that he was *giving* thanks, that he *knew* himself blessed, that he *felt* himself loving or loved. He is saying that "his mind"—namely he, himself, his whole being—*was* a thanksgiving, *was* blessedness, *was* love. He was "rapt": he was merged: for a moment any distinction had vanished between "the living God" and himself.

An experience of the kind obviously cannot, by its nature, be reflected upon at the moment of its occurrence: it just happens, and that's the end of the matter. But it can be reflected upon subsequently; and the following characteristics then emerge:

(1) To repeat what I said in an earlier note, the experience is, above all, one of *rightness* and *inevitability*, or, maybe one should say, of *inevitable rightness*. This rightness is experienced as above what we ordinarily call beautiful and what we ordinarily call good, though the good and the beautiful partake of it. And to hear this note of rightness is to know that all's well: this is one of the sources of the joy that engulfs one.

(2) To put it in a slightly different way, what is momentarily revealed—not through a glass darkly, but face to face—is reality. I do not of course mean that the *nature* of reality is revealed to one, in any way that could be even remotely explained or expressed to oneself or others. Rather, reality is for a moment *there*. Or more exactly, perhaps, one is for a moment *with* reality. (One responds, so to say, "that's reality".) And to be with it is to know again that all's well.

(3) One is not merely with it for a moment: one *is* it for a moment. There has been more than a visitation, there is communion: one is oneself part and parcel of the reality.

(4) The reality experienced must perforce be described as immaterial, in the sense that it presents itself as being of a totally different order from that of my body, or of the concert-hall, or of the catgut on the fiddler's violins. Of a totally different order: existent in another dimension. And yet, when I reflect upon the experience afterwards, I realise that without my ears and the concert-hall and the catgut—not to mention the food and drink, and the music-paper, and the lodgings, of Beethoven's Viennese existence—no such communion could have been mine.

(5) The whole moment—the reality, myself, and my communion with it, to distinguish what in truth cannot be distinguished—is outside time and place: it is happening everywhere and in eternity. And the reality is universal. It includes, or rather

it *is*, everything: everything that could possibly happen, everything that could conceivably *be*.

(6) The communion is also a recognition. One recognises something with a still but overwhelming delight: one greets it with a "Yes, this it is: this is what I know it to be, must ever know it to be, must ever have known it to be". And what is recognised is also the recogniser.

(7) Certain emotions, one realises later, have accompanied, or rather been bound up with, the moment. One's mind, in Wordsworth's phraseology, has been blessedness and tranquillity, gratitude and—above everything—love. But there has been something else. There has been awe: one has bowed the head and bent the knee.

The simplest way to put it is perhaps as follows. It is no longer a question of Beethoven composing something, making something: it is a question of his remembering, or overhearing, something that *exists*—"yonder", which is everywhere.]

So Swann was not mistaken in believing that the phrase of the sonata[1] did, really, exist. Human as it was from this point of view, it belonged, none the less, to an order of supernatural creatures whom we have never seen, but whom, in spite of that, we recognise and acclaim with rapture when some explorer of the unseen contrives to coax one forth, to bring it down from that divine world to which he has access to shine for a brief moment in the firmament of ours. This was what Vinteuil had done for the little phrase. Swann felt that the composer had been content (with the musical instruments at his disposal) to draw aside its veil, to make it visible, following and respecting its outlines with a hand so loving, so prudent, so delicate and so sure, that the sound altered at every moment, blunting itself to indicate a shadow, springing back into life when it must follow the curve of some more bold projection. And one proof that Swann

[1] As I have come across people, otherwise highly literate, who are unfamiliar with the commonest musical terms, I may be forgiven, perhaps, for explaining that a sonata is a particular kind of instrumental music—in the present case, for piano and violin: and that a phrase is a short passage in it that sometimes appears only once, but more often recurs.

was not mistaken when he believed in the real existence of this phrase, was that anyone with an ear at all delicate for music would at once have detected the imposture had Vinteuil, endowed with less power to see and to render its forms, sought to dissemble (by adding a line, here and there, of his own invention) the dimness of his vision or the feebleness of his hand.

The phrase had disappeared. Swann knew that it would come again at the end of the last movement, after a long passage which Mme. Verdurin's pianist always "skipped". . . . And his personality was now so divided that the strain of waiting for the imminent moment when he would find himself face to face, once more, with the phrase, convulsed him in one of those sobs which a fine line of poetry or a piece of alarming news will wring from us, not when we are alone, but when we repeat one or the other to a friend, in whom we see ourselves reflected, like a third person, whose probable emotion softens him. It reappeared, but this time to remain poised in the air, and to sport there for a moment only, as though immobile, and shortly to expire. And so Swann lost nothing of the precious time for which it lingered. It was still there, like an iridescent bubble that floats for a while unbroken. As a rainbow, when its brightness fades, seems to subside, then soars again and, before it is extinguished, is glorified with greater splendour than it has ever shewn; so to the two colours which the phrase had hitherto allowed to appear it added others now, chords shot with every hue in the prism, and made them sing. Swann dared not move, and would have liked to compel all the other people in the room to remain still also, as if the slightest movement might embarrass the magic presence, supernatural, delicious, frail, that would so easily vanish. But no one, as it happened, dreamed of speaking. The ineffable utterance of one solitary man, absent, perhaps dead (Swann did not know whether Vinteuil were still alive) . . . , sufficed to arrest the attention of three hundred minds, and made of that stage on which a soul was thus called into being one of the noblest altars on which a supernatural ceremony could be performed.

MARCEL PROUST

The dying Boehme had asked his son to open the door as he heard strains of distant music: William Blake welcomed death with joyful songs, saying to his wife: "My beloved, they are not mine—no—they are not mine."

MONA WILSON

Heard melodies are sweet, but those unheard
Are sweeter; therefore, ye soft pipes, play on;
Not to the sensual ear, but, more endear'd,
Pipe to the spirit ditties of no tone . . .

475   KEATS

ODE TO A COMPOSER

Calm grows the air around,
Arrayed in beauty and unwonted light,
Salinas, at the sound
Of music exquisite
That thy skilled hand doth cunningly indite.

And at that sound divine
My soul, that in forgetfulness hath lain,
With a new light doth shine
And unto memory plain
Of its first splendid origin attain . . .

Up through the fields of air
It wings, till in the highest sphere it dwells,
And a new music there
It hears, music that wells
Undying and all other kinds excels.

The great Master there it sees,
His hand upon the mighty lyre, with train
Of skilful cadences,
Create the holy strain
That this eternal temple doth sustain.

Through sea of melody
In rapture sweet the soul doth onward glide
And sinks there finally,
Until whate'er betide
Beyond it to its senses is denied . . .

LOUIS DE LEON

FROM "THE PRELUDE"

[Wordsworth has been describing how, with some friends, he crossed the Alps. The last line but two becomes clear if we think of God, Reality, Eternity (here called the Apocalypse or revelation) as a great word: the "Characters" being a few letters of it. See the extract from Coleridge that follows the Wordsworth.]

The immeasurable height
Of woods decaying, never to be decayed,
The stationary blasts of waterfalls,
And in the narrow rent at every turn
Winds thwarting winds, bewildered and forlorn,
The torrents shooting from the clear blue sky,
The rocks that muttered close upon our ears,
Black drizzling crags that spake by the way-side
As if a voice were in them, the sick sight
And giddy prospect of the raving stream,
The unfettered clouds and region of the Heavens,
Tumult and peace, the darkness and the light—
Were all like workings of one mind, the features
Of the same face, blossoms upon one tree;
Characters of the great Apocalypse,
The types and symbols of Eternity,
Of first, and last, and midst, and without end.

WORDSWORTH

My babe so beautiful! It thrills my heart
With tender gladness, thus to look at thee,
And think that thou shalt learn far other lore
And in far other scenes! For I was reared
In the great city, pent 'midst cloisters dim,
And saw nought lovely but the sky and stars.
But thou, my babe! shalt wander like a breeze
By lakes and sandy shores, beneath the crags
Of ancient mountain, and beneath the clouds,
Which image in their bulk both lakes and shores
And mountain crags; so shalt thou see and hear
The lovely shapes and sounds intelligible
Of that eternal language, which thy God
Utters, who from eternity doth teach
Himself in all, and all things in himself.
Great universal Teacher! he shall mould
Thy spirit, and by giving make it ask.

S. T. COLERIDGE

§ 4

The seer of Lublin, having served a poor traveller with a
meal, cleared away the dishes. He was asked why he troubled
to do this. "Surely," he replied, "carrying the utensils out of
the Holy of Holies was part of the duty of the High Priest."

HASIDIC TRADITION

FIFTH PART

III. THE MANY AND THE ONE

And Moses said unto God, Behold, when I come unto the children of Israel, and shall say unto them, The God of your fathers hath sent me unto you; and they shall say to me, What is his name? what shall I say unto them?

And God said unto Moses, I AM THAT I AM: and he said, Thus shalt thou say unto the children of Israel, I AM hath sent me unto you.

EXODUS

[The word rendered by the two words I AM is in the future tense: a tense however that indicates, not the future as distinct from the present or past, but eternal living. "Existence, timeless and personal" would be a correct paraphrase for I AM.

What God is saying to Moses is that He can have no name, because, as I wrote on page 240, "to name a person or thing is to particularize it, distinguish it from other persons or things: you call a boy Jack because he isn't Henry and you call a stone a stone because it isn't a star. But God is in Jack as well as in Henry, in a star as well as in a stone: God is in everything, and therefore distinguishable, as wholly other, from nothing". There is one everlasting Reality or Existence, without which there could be no 'many'—no human beings or stars or stones (in general), and no Henry or Jack or the planet Venus or some medium-sized quartz-pebble (in particular).

But the longer of the two phrases, namely I AM THAT I AM, says more than this. It says: "Existence *is* Existence". There's nothing *beyond* Existence, Reality, God: and therefore nothing to "explain" it—and indeed nothing to say about it at all, except that it just *is*. Or, to repeat a word I have used twice before, it is mysteriously inevitable—the very words I AM THAT I AM are full of mystery and awe: and not only inevitable, but, as we understand if we believe that "God is love", inevitably right.

It may be added that no one who, even once in a lifetime, has experienced inevitable rightness can ever again believe that the

413

universe is a sort of accident, with no meaning to it and no purpose behind it.

In the first of the quotations below, it should be noted that Christ says, not "I was", but "I am".]

Jesus said unto them, Verily, verily, I say unto you, Before Abraham was, I am.

ST. JOHN

Lift up the stone and there shalt thou find me: cleave the wood, and I am there.

ATTRIBUTED TO CHRIST
(from the Oxyrhynchus Papyri)

Nevertheless I live; yet not I, but Christ liveth in me.

GALATIANS

Behold, I stand at the door, and knock: if any man hear my voice, and open the door, I will come in to him, and will sup with him, and he with me.

REVELATION

Things are all the same in God: they are God himself.

MEISTER ECKHART

Fully awakened souls . . . realise that it is God who does everything.

There was a monastery in a certain place. The monks residing there went out daily to beg their food. One day a monk, while out for his alms, saw a landlord beating a man mercilessly. The compassionate monk stepped in and asked the landlord to stop.

But the landlord was filled with anger and turned his wrath against the innocent monk. He beat the monk till he fell unconscious on the ground. Someone reported the matter to the monastery. The monks ran to the spot and found their brother lying there. Four or five of them carried him back and laid him on a bed. He was still unconscious. The other monks sat around him sad at heart; some were fanning him. Finally someone suggested that he should be given a little milk to drink. When it was poured into his mouth he regained consciousness. He opened his eyes and looked around. One of the monks said, "Let us see whether he is fully conscious and can recognise us." Shouting into his ear, he said, "Revered sir, who is giving you milk?" "Brother," replied the holy man in a low voice, "he who beat me is now giving me milk."

SRI RAMAKRISHNA

But of a sudden, as God was about to speak to Moses on Mount Sinai, there was silence in all the universe. Not an ox lowed in all the earth, not a bird twittered in all the skies, the waters ceased their murmur, the flames their crackling; the thunder was muted, and every echo was dumb; the wings of the Cherubim ceased to beat, and the mouths of the Seraphim to sing: in order that, in the silence of all things, all things might know that outside God naught Is.

EDMOND FLEG (*from a Midrash*)

He who has gotten the whole world plus God has gotten no more than God by himself.

MEISTER ECKHART

For the eye of the highest Angel there is but a single image. He grasps as a unity all that his inferiors regard as manifold.

★ MEISTER ECKHART

It is told of a Hasidic Master, that in his hours of rapture he had to look at the clock in order to keep himself in this world, and of another, that when he wished to consider the phenomena of life, he had to put on spectacles in order to control his spiritual vision, "for otherwise he would have seen all the separate phenomena in the world as one".

MARTIN BUBER

All things are transparent for them, and there is nothing dark or impenetrable, but everyone shines clear to everyone internally, and all things shine clear; for light shines clear to light. For everyone has all things in himself and sees all things in another; so that all things are everywhere and all is all and each is all, and the glory is infinite.

⋆ PLOTINUS

[Plotinus is speaking of existence "yonder". See pp. 400-402.]

How all things weave themselves to one,
Working, living, each in other,
While up and down the angelic powers go,
Bearing the golden pitchers to and fro!
The splendour swings from hand to hand!
On wings of fragrance, on wings that bless
From heaven through all the world they press
Till all rings loud with their loveliness.

GOETHE (from *Faust*)

If the doors of perception were cleansed everything would appear to man as it is, infinite.

For man has closed himself up till he sees all things thro' narrow chinks of his cavern.

BLAKE

416

The people think that they pray before God. But it is not so. For the prayer itself is the essence of the Godhead.

RABBI PINHAS OF KORETZ

Prayer is no other but the revelation of the will or mind of God

JOHN SALTMARSH

He it is that desireth in thee, and He it is that is desired

WALTER HYLTON

God in the depths of us receives God who comes to us: it is God contemplating God.

RUYSBROECK

What else, Lord, is Thy seeing, when Thou beholdest me with pitying eye, than that Thou art seen by me? In beholding me Thou givest Thyself to be seen by me, Thou who art a hidden God. None can see Thee save in so far as Thou grantest a sight of Thyself, nor is that sight anything else than Thy seeing him that seeth Thee.

NICHOLAS OF CUSA

God is the fire in me, I am the glow in Him.

ANGELUS SILESIUS

I am a single drop; how can it be
That God, the whole ocean, floweth into me?

ANGELUS SILESIUS

God within, God without! Beyond compare!
A Being wholly here and wholly there!

ANGELUS SILESIUS

Put out my eyes, and I can see you still;
slam my ears to, and I can hear you yet;
and without any feet can go to you;
and tongueless, I can conjure you at will.
Break off my arms, I shall take hold of you
and grasp you with my heart as with a hand;
arrest my heart, my brain will beat as true;
and if you set this brain of mine afire,
then on my blood-stream I yet will carry you.

RAINER MARIA RILKE

The love of God for men and the love of human minds for God is one and the same thing.

★SPINOZA

In the knowledge of the minds that know Him, in the self-surrender of the hearts that love Him, it is no paradox to affirm that He knows and loves Himself. As He is the origin and inspiration of every true thought and pure affection, of every experience in which we forget and rise above ourselves, so it is with all these that we seek to find Him.

★ JOHN CAIRD

§ 2

The more we understand particular things, the more we understand God.

SPINOZA

The Infinite alone resides in definite and determinate identity.

BLAKE

[Infinity is not something *outside* definite and finite things, such as men or women, animals or stones, each with its own special characteristics: on the contrary, it is only *in* finite things that infinity exists.]

Circle in point, blossom in seedling lies;
Those who seek God within the world are wise.

ANGELUS SILESIUS

It is only through the manifestations of Being, and only through those with which I enter into relations, that my being has any intercourse with infinite Being. The devotion of my being to infinite Being means devotion of my being to all the manifestations of Being which need my devotion, and to which I am able to devote myself.

ALBERT SCHWEITZER

[We can know and love God only by knowing and loving the various concrete creatures and things, the chief of which are men and women, in which God reveals himself.]

"That violence whereby sometimes a man doteth upon one creature is but a little spark of that love, even towards all, which lurketh in his nature. When we dote upon the perfections and beauties of some one creature, we do not love that too much, but other things too little. Never was anything in this world loved too much, but many things have been loved in a false way, and all in too short a measure." Traherne might have added (what many poets and novelists have remarked) that, when "we dote upon the perfections and beauties of some one creature", we frequently find ourselves moved to love other creatures. Moreover, to be in love is, in many cases, to have achieved a state of being in which it becomes possible to have direct intuition of the essentially lovely nature of ultimate reality. "What a world would this be, were everything beloved as it ought to be!" For many people, everything is beloved as it ought to be only when they are in love with "some one creature." The cynical wisdom of the folk affirms that love is blind. But in reality, perhaps, the blind are those who are not in love and who therefore fail to perceive how beautiful the world is and how adorable.

475   ALDOUS HUXLEY

In this light my spirit soon saw through all things; and in all creatures, in herb and grass, knew God—who He is, how He is, and what is His will.

BOEHME

In all faces is seen the Face of faces, veiled, and in a riddle.

NICHOLAS OF CUSA

The rose that with your earthly eyes you see,
Has flowered in God from all eternity.

ANGELUS SILESIUS

THE SPARK

Calm was the evening, as if asleep,
But sickled on high with brooding storm,
Couched in invisible space. And lo!
I saw in utter silence sweep
Out of that darkening starless vault
A gliding spark, as blanched as snow,
That burned into dust, and vanished in

420

A hay-cropped meadow, brightly green.
A meteor from the cold of space,
Lost in Earth's wilderness of air?—
Presage of lightnings soon to shine
In splendour on this lonely place?—
I cannot tell; but only how fair
It glowed within the crystalline
Pure heavens, and of its strangeness lit
My mind to joy at sight of it.

Yet what is common as lovely may be:
The petalled daisy, a honey bell,
A pebble, a branch of moss, a gem
Of dew, or fallen rain—if we
A moment in their beauty dwell;
Entranced, alone, see only them.
How blind to wait, till, merely unique,
Some omen thus the all bespeak!

WALTER DE LA MARE

[The poet has seen a shooting star—a rare and lovely occurrence—and has rejoiced at the sight of it. But, he says in the last
verse, a daisy or a stone or a drop of dew can be just as beautiful,
if for a moment, in quiet rapture, we dwell only in its loveliness:
how stupid of us to wait for our joy till something rare, something "merely unique" comes along to "bespeak the all"—to
show us God!]

I am the sacred smell of the earth,
The light of the fire,
Life of all lives . . .
Know me, eternal seed
Of everything that grows:
The intelligence of those who understand,
The vigour of the active.

In the strong, I am strength . . .
I am all that a man may desire
Without transgressing
The law of his nature.

THE BHAGAVAD-GITA

[God is speaking.]

THE HYMN OF BEING

"This Earth is the honey of all Beings, and all Beings
Are the honey of this Earth . . . O bright immortal Lover
That is incarnate in the body's earth—
O bright immortal Lover Who is all!"

"This Water is the honey of all Beings, and all Beings
Are the honey of this Water . . . O the bright immortal
    Lover
That is in water and that is the seed
Of life . . . O bright immortal Lover Who is All!"

"This Fire is the honey of all Beings, and all Beings
Are the honey of this Fire . . . O bright immortal Lover
That is in fire and shines in mortal speech—
O bright immortal Lover Who is All!"

"This Air is the honey of all Beings, and all Beings
Are the honey of this Air . . . O bright immortal Lover
That is in air and is our Being's breath—
O bright immortal Lover Who is all!"

"This Sun is the honey of all Beings, and all Beings
Are the honey of this Sun . . . O bright immortal Lover
That is in the sun and is our Being's sight—
O bright immortal Lover Who is all!"

"This Thunder is the honey of all Beings, and all Beings
Are the honey of this Thunder . . . O the bright immortal
    Lover,
That is in thunder and all voices—the beasts' roar—
Thunder of rising saps—the voice of Man!
O bright immortal Lover Who is All!"

EDITH SITWELL (from *The Bee-keeper*)

Who sees his Lord
Within every creature,
Deathlessly dwelling
Amidst the mortal:
That man sees truly. . . .
Who sees the separate
Lives of all creatures
United in Brahman
Brought forth from Brahman,
Himself finds Brahman.

THE BHAGAVAD-GITA

[Brahman or Brahma, in Hinduism of a certain kind and
period, is the Divine Reality or God.]

Yes, we must become Brahma. We must not shrink from
avowing this. Our existence is meaningless if we never can expect
to realise the highest perfection that there is. If we have an aim
and yet can never reach it, then it is no aim at all.

But can it then be said that there is no difference between
Brahma and our individual soul? Of course the difference is
obvious . . . Brahma is Brahma, he is the infinite ideal of perfection. But we are not what we truly are; we are ever to become
true, ever to become Brahma. . . .

In the music of the rushing stream sounds the joyful assurance, "I shall become the sea". It is not a vain assumption; it is
true humility, for it is the truth. The river has no other alterna-
tive. On both sides of its banks it has numerous fields and forests,

villages and towns; it can serve them in various ways, cleanse them and feed them, carry their produce from place to place. But it can have only partial relations with these, and however long it may linger among them it remains separate; it never can become a town or a forest.

But it can and does become the sea. The lesser moving water has its affinity with the great motionless water of the ocean. It moves through the thousand objects on its onward course, and its motion finds its finality when it reaches the sea.

The river can become the sea, but she can never make the sea part and parcel of herself. If, by some chance, she has encircled some broad sheet of water and pretends that she has made the sea a part of herself, we at once know that it is not so, that her current is still seeking rest in the great ocean to which it can never set boundaries.

In the same manner, our soul can only become Brahma as the river can become the sea. Everything else she touches at one of her points, then leaves and moves on, but she never can leave Brahma and move beyond him. Once our soul realises her ultimate object of repose in Brahma, all her movements acquire a purpose. It is this ocean of infinite rest which gives significance to endless activities. It is this perfectness of being that lends to the imperfection of becoming that quality of beauty which finds its expression in all poetry, drama, and art.

RABINDRANATH TAGORE

[A distinction between "the perfectness of being" and "the imperfection of becoming" is common to several religions and philosophies. The word being is applied to the unchangeable: the word becoming to things that develop and decay. An act of pure love has being: but the man who performs it is a creature of becoming and change. The One has being: the many become.]

It fills me with great joy and a high hope for the future of humanity when I realise that there was a time in the remote past when our poet-prophets stood under the lavish sunshine of an Indian sky and greeted the world with the glad recognition of kindred . . . It was not seeing man reflected everywhere in grotesquely exaggerated images, and witnessing the human drama acted on a gigantic scale in nature's arena of flitting lights and shadows. On the contrary, it meant crossing the limiting barriers of the individual, to become more than man, to become one with the All . . . These ancient seers felt in the serene depth of their mind that the same energy, which vibrates and passes into the endless forms of the world, manifests itself in our inner being as consciousness; and there is no break in unity. For these seers there was no gap in their luminous vision of perfection. They never acknowledged even death itself as creating a chasm in the field of reality. They said, *His reflection is death as well as immortality*. They did not recognise any essential opposition between life and death, and they said with absolute assurance, "It is life that is death". They saluted with the same serenity of gladness "life in its aspect of appearing and in its aspect of departure"—*That which is past is hidden in life, and that which is to come*. They knew that mere appearance and disappearance are on the surface like waves on the sea, but life which is permanent knows no decay or diminution.

Everything is sprung from immortal life and is vibrating with life, for *life is immense*.

This is the noble heritage from our forefathers waiting to be claimed by us as our own, this ideal of the supreme freedom of consciousness. It is not merely intellectual or emotional, it has an ethical basis, and it must be translated into action. In the Upanishad it is said, *The supreme being is all-pervading, therefore he is the innate good in all*. To be truly united in knowledge, love, and service with all beings, and thus to realise one's self in the all-pervading God, is the essence of goodness, and this is the keynote of the teachings of the Upanishads: *Life is immense !*

RABINDRANATH TAGORE

[The Upanishads are Hindu scriptures.]

It costs me nothing to feel that I am; it is no burden to me. And yet if the mental, physical, chemical and other innumerable facts concerning all branches of knowledge which have united in myself could be broken up, they would prove endless. It is some untold mystery of unity in me, that has the simplicity of the infinite and reduces the immense mass of multitude to a single point.

This One in me knows the universe of the many. But, in whatever it knows, it knows the One in different aspects. It knows this room only because this room is One to it, in spite of the seeming contradiction of the endless facts contained in the single fact of the room. Its knowledge of a tree is the knowledge of a unity, which appears in the aspect of a tree.

This One in me is creative. Its creations are a pastime, through which it gives expression to an ideal of unity in its endless show of variety. Such are its pictures, poems, music, in which it finds joy only because they reveal the perfect forms of an inherent unity.

This One in me not only seeks unity in knowledge for its understanding and creates images of unity for its delight; it also seeks union in love for its fulfilment. It seeks itself in others. This is a fact, which would be absurd had there been no great medium of truth to give it reality. In love we find a joy which is ultimate because it is the ultimate truth. Therefore it is said in the Upanishads that the *advaitam* is *anantam*,—"the One is infinite"; that the *advaitam* is *anandam*,—"the One is Love."

To give perfect expression to the One, the Infinite, through the harmony of the many; to the One, the Love, through the sacrifice of self, is the object alike of our individual life and our society.

RABINDRANATH TAGORE

One day, in a small village in Bengal, an ascetic woman from the neighbourhood came to see me. She had the name "Sarvakhepi" given to her by the village people, the meaning of which is "the woman who is mad about all things". She fixed her star-like eyes upon my face and startled me with the question, "When are you coming to meet me underneath the trees?" Evidently she pitied me who lived (according to her) prisoned behind walls, banished away from the great meeting-place of the All, where she had her dwelling. Just at that moment my gardener came with his basket, and when the woman understood that the flowers in the vase on my table were going to be thrown away, to make place for the fresh ones, she looked pained and said to me, "You are always engaged reading and writing; you do not see". Then she took the discarded flowers in her palms, kissed them and touched them with her forehead, and reverently murmured to herself, "Beloved of my heart". I felt that this woman, in her direct vision of the infinite personality in the heart of all things, truly represented the spirit of India.

RABINDRANATH TAGORE

At midnight the would-be ascetic announced:

"This is the time to give up my home and seek for God. Ah, who has held me so long in delusion here?"

God whispered, "I", but the ears of the man were stopped.

With a baby asleep at her breast lay his wife, peacefully sleeping on one side of the bed.

The man said, "Who are ye that have fooled me so long?"

The voice said again, "They are God", but he heard it not.

The baby cried out in its dream, nestling close to its mother.

God commanded, "Stop, fool, leave not thy home", but still he heard not.

God sighed and complained, "Why does my servant wander to seek me, forsaking me?"

RABINDRANATH TAGORE

The Formless is in the midst of all forms. I sing the glory of forms.

KABIR

427

... One space spreads through all creatures equally—
    inner-world-space. Birds quietly flying go
    flying through us. O, I that want to grow,
    the tree I look outside at's growing in me!

    I have a house within when I need care.
    I have a guard within when I need rest.
    The love that I have had!—Upon my breast
    the beauty of the world clings, to weep there.

RAINER MARIA RILKE

ON THE BEACH AT NIGHT ALONE

On the beach at night alone,
As the old mother sways her to and fro singing her husky song,
As I watch the bright stars shining, I think a thought of the . . .
    universes and of the future.

A vast similitude interlocks all,
All spheres, grown, ungrown, small, large, suns, moons, planets,
All distances of place however wide,
All distances of time, all inanimate forms,
All souls, all living bodies though they be ever so different, or
    in different worlds,
All gaseous, watery, vegetable, mineral processes, the fishes, the
    brutes,
All nations, colours, barbarisms, civilisations, languages,
All identities that have existed or may exist on this globe, or
    any globe,
All lives and deaths, all of the past, present, future,
This vast similitude spans them, and always has spann'd,
And shall forever span them and compactly hold and enclose
    them.

WALT WHITMAN

Cease not to think of the Universe as one living Being, possessed of a single Substance and a single Soul; and how all things trace back to its single aliveness; and how it does all things by a single impulse; and how all existing things are joint causes of all things that come into existence; and how intertwined in the fabric is the thread and how closely woven the web.

★ MARCUS AURELIUS

All that is in tune with thee, O Universe, is in tune with me! Nothing that is in due time for thee is too early or too late for me! All that thy seasons bring, O Nature, is fruit for me! All things come from thee, live in thee, go back to thee. A poet has said *Dear City of Cecrops!* Wilt though not say *O dear City of God!*?

★ MARCUS AURELIUS

[Cecrops was the founder of Athens.]

§ 3

It is eternity now, I am in the midst of it. It is about me in the sunshine.

RICHARD JEFFERIES

The only strength for me is to be found in the sense of a personal presence everywhere, it scarcely matters whether it be called human or divine; a presence which only makes itself felt at first in this and that particular form and feature. . . . Into this presence we come, not by leaving behind what are usually called earthly things, or by loving them less, but by living more intensely in them, and loving more what is really loveable in them; for it is literally true that this world *is* everything to us, if only we choose to make it so, if only we "live in the present" *because* it is eternity. . . .

R. L. NETTLESHIP

429

FAUST.   The Spirit looks not forward, not behind,
         Here in the Present—
HELEN.   Here our joy we find.

GOETHE

Both the first day and the last are happening at the present instant yonder.

MEISTER ECKHART

This increasing exploitation of life, is it not a result of the centuries-long disparagement of the here-and-now? What madness, to divert us towards a Beyond, when here, where we are, we are surrounded with tasks and expectations and futures! What imposture, to pilfer from us pictures of earthly delight in order to sell them to Heaven behind our backs! . . . And, since no emptiness can persist, is not everything that is taken away from here replaced by an illusion,—are not towns full of so much ugly artificial light and noise just because the true splendour in the song has been delivered over to some Jerusalem to be entered later?

★RAINER MARIA RILKE

§ 4

                    I know
    That love makes all things equal: I have heard
    By mine own heart this joyous truth averred,—
    The spirit of the worm beneath the sod,
    In love and worship, blends itself with God.

SHELLEY (from *Epi sychidion*)

I LAY AMONG THE FERNS

I lay among the ferns,
Where they lifted their fronds, innumerable, in the greenwood
    wilderness, like wings winnowing the air;
And their voices went past me continually.

And I listened, and lo! softly inaudibly raining I heard not the
    voices of the ferns only, but of all living creatures:
Voices of mountain and star,
Of cloud and forest and ocean,
And of the little rills tumbling amid the rocks,
And of the high tops where the moss-beds are and the springs
    arise.
As the wind at mid-day rains whitening over the grass,
As the night-bird glimmers a moment, fleeting between the lonely
    watcher and the moon,
So softly inaudibly they rained,
Where I sat silent.

And in the silence of the greenwood I knew the secret of the
    growth of the ferns;
I saw their delicate leaflets tremble breathing an undescribed
    and unuttered life;
And, below, the ocean lay sleeping;
And round them the mountains and the stars dawned in glad
    companionship for ever.

And a voice came to me, saying:
In every creature, in forest and ocean, in leaf and tree and bird
    and beast and man, there moves a spirit other than its
    mortal own,
Pure, fluid, as air—intense as fire,
Which looks abroad and passes along the spirits of all other
    creatures, drawing them close to itself,
Nor dreams of other law than that of perfect equality;
And this is the spirit of immortality and peace.

And whatsoever creature hath this spirit, to it no harm may
  befall:
No harm can befall, for wherever it goes it has its nested home,
  and to it every loss comes charged with an equal gain;
It gives—but to receive a thousand-fold;
It yields its life—but at the hands of love;
And death is the law of its eternal growth.

And I saw that was the law of every creature—that this spirit
  should enter in and take possession of it,
That it might have no more fear or doubt or be at war within
  itself any longer.
And lo! in the greenwood all around me it moved,
Where the sunlight floated fragrant under the boughs, and the
  fern-fronds winnowed the air;
In the oak-leaves dead of last year, and in the small shy things
  that rustled among them;
In the songs of the birds, and the broad shadowing leaves overhead;
In the fields sleeping below, and in the river and the high
  dreaming air;
Gleaming ecstatic it moved—with joy incarnate.
And it seemed to me, as I looked, that it penetrated all these
  things, suffusing them;
And wherever it penetrated, behold! there was nothing left
  down to the smallest atom which was not a winged spirit
  instinct with life.

EDWARD CARPENTER

FROM "THE BOOK OF THEL"

[The angel Thel is sad because everything dies. The lily of
the valley answers her:]

                                          'I am a wat'ry weed,
And I am very small, and love to dwell in lowly vales,
So weak, the gilded butterfly scarce perches on my head.

Yet I am visited from heaven, and he that smiles on all
Walks in the valley, and each morn over me spreads his hand
Saying, Rejoice, thou humble grass, thou new-born lilly-flower,
Thou gentle maid of silent valleys and of modest brooks;
For thou shalt be clothed in light, and fed with morning manna,
Till summer's heat melts thee beside the fountains and the
    springs
To flourish in eternal vales . . .'

  [But Thel is not satisfied, so the Lily tells her to]
                        'ask the tender cloud,

And it shall tell thee why it glitters in the morning sky,
And why it scatters its bright beauty thro' the humid air.
Descend, O little cloud, and hover before the eyes of Thel.'
The Cloud descended, and the Lily bowed her modest head,
And went to mind her numerous charge among the verdant
    grass.
'O little Cloud', the virgin said, 'I charge thee tell to me
Why thou complainest not when in one hour thou fade away;
Then we shall seek thee, but not find . . .'
The cloud then shew'd his golden head and his bright form
    emerg'd,
Hovering and glittering on the air before the face of Thel . . .
                 . . . 'look'st thou on my youth,
And fearest thou because I vanish and am seen no more?
Nothing remains. O maid, I tell thee, when I pass away,
It is to tenfold life, to love, to peace, and raptures holy:
Unseen descending, weigh my light wings upon balmy flowers,
And court the fair-eyed dew, to take me to her shining tent.
The weeping virgin, trembling, kneels before the risen sun,
Till we arise link'd in a golden band and never part,
But walk united, bearing food to all our tender flowers . . .
                 . . . everything that lives
Lives not alone nor for itself: fear not, and I will call
The weak worm from its lowly bed, and thou shalt hear its voice.
Come forth, worm of the silent valley, to thy pensive queen.'

The helpless worm arose, and sat upon the Lilly's leaf,
And the bright Cloud sail'd on, to find his partner in the vale.
Then Thel astonish'd view'd the Worm upon its dewy bed.
'Art thou a Worm? Image of weakness, art thou but a Worm?
I see thee like an infant wrapped in the Lilly's leaf.
Ah weep not, little voice, thou canst not speak, but thou canst weep.
Is this a Worm? I see thee lay helpless and naked, weeping,
And none to answer, none to cherish thee with mother's smiles.'
The Clod of Clay heard the Worm's voice and rais'd her pitying
    head;
She bow'd over the weeping infant, and her life exhal'd
In milky fondness, then on Thel she fix'd her humble eyes.
                    '. . . We live not for ourselves.
Thou seest me the meanest thing, and so I am indeed.
My bosom of itself is cold, and of itself is dark,
But he that loves the lowly, pours his oil upon my head
And kisses me, and binds his nuptial bands around my breast,
And says: Thou mother of my children, I have loved thee,
And I have given thee a crown that none can take away,
But how this is, sweet maid, I know not, and I cannot know.
I ponder, and I cannot ponder; yet I live and love.'
The daughter of beauty wip'd her pitying tears with her white veil,
And said, 'Alas! I knew not this, and therefore did I weep;
That God would love a Worm I knew, and punish the evil foot
That wilful bruis'd its helpless form; but that He cherish'd it
With milk and oil I never knew, and therefore did I weep . . .'

475 BLAKE

EARTH AND A WEDDED WOMAN

[This is about the mysterious harmony that unites us with
Nature. It is more than the warmth on our skins that makes us
rejoice when the sun comes out. So in this poem Susan, once as
fresh as a water-meadow, has been parched and dry ever since,
three years ago, her husband left her for the wars: and her

drouth has sent a dull, dark longing for refreshment writhing
through her being. Then a drouth in the countryside suddenly
breaks: the rain comes pouring down: and, as Earth receives it
with a gurgle, deep, satisfied breathing comes from Susan,
Earth's kin. And now she can wait happily for her husband's
return.]

I

The shepherd, with his eye on hazy South,
Has told of rain upon the fall of day.
But promise is there none for Susan's drouth,
That he will come, who keeps in dry delay.
The freshest of the village three years gone,
She hangs as the white field-rose hangs short-lived;
       And she and Earth are one
       In withering unrevived.
Rain! O the glad refresher of the grain!
And welcome waterspouts, had we sweet rain!

II

Ah, what is Marriage, says each pouting maid,
When she who wedded with the soldier hides
At home as good as widowed in the shade,
A lighthouse to the girls that would be brides:
Nor dares to give a lad an ogle, nor
To dream of dancing, but must hang and moan,
       Her husband in the war,
       And she to lie alone.
Rain! O the glad refresher of the grain!
And welcome waterspouts, had we sweet rain!

IV

Now, shepherd, see thy word, where without shower
A borderless low blotting Westward spreads.
The hall-clock holds the valley on the hour;
Across an inner chamber thunder treads:

The dead leaf trips, the tree-top swings, the floor
Of dust whirls, dropping lumped: near thunder speaks,
    And drives the dames to door,
    Their kerchiefs flapped at cheeks.
Rain! O the glad refresher of the grain!
And welcome waterspouts of blessed rain!

V

Through night, with bedroom window wide for air,
Lay Susan tranced to hear all heaven descend:
And gurgling voices came of Earth, and rare,
Past flowerful, breathings, deeper than life's end,
From her heaved breast of sacred common mould;
Whereby this lone-laid wife was moved to feel
    Unworded things and old
    To her pained heart appeal.
Rain! O the glad refresher of the grain!
And down in deluges of blessed rain!

VI

At morn she stood to live for ear and sight,
Love sky or cloud, or rose or grasses drenched.
A lureful devil, that in glow-worm light
Set languor writhing all its folds, she quenched.
But she would muse when neighbours praised her face,
Her services, and staunchness to her mate:
    Knowing by some dim trace,
    The change might bear a date.
Rain! O the glad refresher of the grain!
Thrice beauteous is our sunshine after rain!

GEORGE MEREDITH
(one stanza omitted)

Heaven is so full of delight that, viewed in itself, it is nothing but blessedness and delight; for the Divine Good proceeding from the Lord's Divine Love constitutes heaven both in general and in particular with every one there; and Divine Love consists in desiring that all may be saved and made happy from their inmost being and in full perfection. So that it amounts to the same thing whether you say heaven or heavenly joy. . . .

How great the delight of heaven is, may be seen from this fact alone, that it is delightful to all in heaven to share their delights and blessings with others; and since all in heaven are of this character, it is plain how immense is the delight of heaven; for in the heavens there is a participation of all with each and each with all. Such community of life results from the two heavenly loves which, as was said, are love to the Lord and to the neighbour, and it is the nature of these loves to communicate their delight to others. Love to the Lord is of this character because the Lord's love is the love of communicating all that He has to all mankind, for He desires the happiness of all. There is a similar love in every one who loves Him, because the Lord is in them; and so the angels share their delights with one another. . . .

Certain spirits had conceived the idea in the world that heavenly happiness consists in leading an idle life and in being waited on by others; but they were told that happiness never consists in mere inaction, because in that case every one would wish to sacrifice the happiness of others to his own; thus each would desire what no one could obtain. Such a life would not be active but idle, and would stultify all the powers of life, and every one ought to know that without activity there can be no happiness, and that rest is only for the sake of recreation in order that a man may return with fresh vigour to the activity of his life. They were afterwards shown by much evidence that angelic life consists in doing the good works of charity . . . Those who had the idea that heavenly joy consists in leading a life of indolence and idly inhaling eternal joy, were allowed some experience of such a life, in order to make them ashamed; and they found that it was extremely sad, and that, all joy being destroyed, they would in a short time feel nothing for it but disgust and loathing.

Some spirits who believed themselves better informed than others, declared that they had believed in the world that heavenly joy would consist solely in praising and giving glory to God, and that thus they would lead an active life; but they were told, that to praise and give glory to God is not properly an active life, and that God has no need of praise and worship; but His will is that all should perform useful things and thus do the good works of charity. But they were unable to associate with such works any idea of heavenly joy, but only an idea of servitude; yet the angels testified that in the performance of such good works there is the fullest freedom, because it proceeds from inward affection and is attended by indescribable delight . . .

In no case is heaven exactly the same for one as for another, just as no man, spirit or angel, is ever exactly like another even in face. When I merely thought of two persons being exactly alike or identical, the angels were shocked and said that every whole is formed by the harmonious concurrence of various parts and derives its character from that concurrence; and that in this manner every society of heaven forms a whole and that all the societies of heaven also make a whole; and this is the work of the Lord alone by means of love . . .

I have spoken at times with spirits who had recently come from the world, about the state of eternal life, saying that it was of importance to know who was the Lord of the kingdom, and what kind and form of government it had. Just as nothing is more important to those entering another kingdom in the world, than to know who and what the king is, the nature of his government and many other particulars relating to his kingdom, so it must be far more important in that kingdom, in which they were to live to eternity. They were told, therefore, that it was the Lord who governs heaven and also the universe; for He who rules the one rules the other; thus, that the kingdom in which they now were was the Lord's and that the laws of this kingdom were eternal truths, founded on this single law, that they should love the Lord above all things and their neighbour as themselves. If, indeed, they were desirous to be like the angels, they ought to love their neighbour more than themselves. On hearing this, they could make no reply, because in the life of the body they had heard something of the kind, but had not believed it. They wondered that there should be such love in heaven, and that it could be possible for any one to love his neighbour more than himself. But they were told that every good increases immensely in the other life, and that while living in the body men could not do more than love the neighbour as themselves, because their minds were occupied with matters relating to the body; but that when these are laid aside their love becomes purer, and at length angelic, and then they love the neighbour more than themselves. For there is joy in heaven in doing good to another, and none in doing good to oneself, unless it be in order that the good may become another's, and consequently for the sake of others; this is what is meant by loving the neighbour more than oneself.

It was said, furthermore, that the possibility of such love is shown in the world by the marriage love of some who have suffered death to protect a married partner from injury; by the love of parents for their children, since a mother would rather suffer hunger than see her child in want of food; by sincere friendship, which prompts one friend to expose himself to danger for another; . . . lastly by the very nature of love, whose delight is to serve others, not for its own sake but for theirs. But these things were incomprehensible to those who loved themselves more than others, and who, in the life of the body, had been greedy of gain; and they were still more incomprehensible to the avaricious. . . .

Heavenly joy, in its essence, cannot be described, because it is in the inmost life of the angels, and therefore in every detail of their thought and affection, and thus in every detail of their speech and action. It is as if the inner mind were fully open and free to receive the delight and blessedness which are diffused into every fibre, and thus throughout their whole being. The perception and

439

sensation of this joy is indescribable; for commencing in the inmost parts, it flows into every particular derived from them, and diffuses itself with continual increase towards the exterior parts. When good spirits, who have not yet attained to that joy, because they are not yet raised up into heaven, perceive it in the sphere of love flowing from an angel, they are filled with such delight that they fall, as it were, into a delicious swoon. This sometimes occurs to those who desire to know what heavenly joy is. . . .

The inhabitants of heaven are continually advancing towards the spring-time of life, and the more thousands of years they live, the more delightful and happy is the spring to which they attain, and this to eternity, with an increase according to the increase and degree of their love, charity and faith. Women who have died old and worn out with age, if they have lived in faith in the Lord, in charity to the neighbour and in happy marriage love with a husband, come in process of time more and more into the flower of youth and early womanhood, and attain to a beauty which exceeds every conception of beauty ever seen on the earth. Goodness and charity mould their form, presenting in it a likeness of themselves, and causing the joy and beauty of charity to shine forth from every feature of their countenance, so that they are the very forms of charity itself. Some who have beheld them have been overwhelmed with astonishment . . . Charity itself is what portrays and is portrayed, and in such a manner that the whole angel, and especially the face, is as it were an evident and clearly perceptible personification of charity. This form is indescribably beautiful to behold, and affects with charity the inmost life of the mind. In a word, to grow old in heaven is to grow young. Those who have lived in love to the Lord and in charity to their neighbour, become, in the other life, such forms of beauty. All angels are such forms, with innumerable variety; and of these heaven is composed.

SWEDENBORG

"THIS IS THE GATE OF HEAVEN"

God made the universe and all the creatures contained therein as so many glasses wherein He might reflect His own glory. He hath copied forth Himself in the creation; and in this outward world we may read the lovely characters of the Divine goodness, power, and wisdom. Good men may easily find every creature pointing out to that Being whose image it bears, and climb up from those darker resemblances of the Divine wisdom and goodness, shining out in different degrees upon several creatures, till they sweetly repose themselves in the bosom of the Divinity; and while they are thus conversing with this lower world they find God many times secretly flowing into their souls, and leading them silently out of the court of the temple into the Holy Place. It is nothing but a thick mist of pride and self-love that hinders men's eyes from beholding that sun which gives its light to them and all things else. . . . A good man is no more troubled whether this or that good thing be mine, or whether my perfections exceed the measure of this or that particular creature; for whatsoever good he beholds anywhere, he enjoys and delights in it as much as if it were his own, and whatever he beholds in himself, he looks not upon it as his property, but as a common good; for all these beams come from one and the same Fountain and Ocean of light in whom he loves them all with an universal love. Thus may a man walk up and down the world as in a garden of spices, and suck a Divine sweetness out of every flower. True religion never finds itself out of the infinite sphere of the Divinity; it beholds itself everywhere in the midst of that glorious unbounded Being who is indivisibly everywhere. A good man finds every place he treads upon holy ground; to him the world is God's temple; he is ready to say with Jacob, "How dreadful is this place! this is none other than the house of God, this is the gate of heaven."

★JOHN SMITH

The One remains, the many change and pass;
    Heaven's light for ever shines, earth's shadows fly;
Life, like a dome of many-coloured glass,
    Stains the white radiance of eternity . . .

SHELLEY

It is surely inconceivable that any living thing could be
beautiful, were there not a Life Absolute of a wonderful, an
ineffable beauty.

PLOTINUS

TO END

As in my own will-to-live there is a longing for wider life and for the mysterious exaltation of the will-to-live which we call pleasure, with dread of annihilation and of the mysterious encroachment of the will-to-live which we call pain; so is it also in the will-to-live all around me, whether it can express itself before me, or remains dumb.

Ethics consist, therefore, in my experiencing the compulsion to show all will-to-live the same reverence as I do to my own. There we have given us that basic principle of the moral which is a necessity of thought: It is good to maintain and to promote life; it is bad to destroy life or to obstruct it . . .

A man is truly ethical only when he obeys the compulsion to help all life which he is able to assist, and shrinks from injuring anything that lives. He does not ask how far this or that life deserves one's interest as being valuable, nor, beyond that, whether and how far it can appreciate such interest. Life as such is sacred to him. He tears no leaf from a tree, plucks no flower and takes care to crush no insect. If in summer he is working by lamplight, he prefers to keep the window shut and breathe a stuffy atmosphere rather than see one insect after another fall with singed wings upon his table.

If he goes into the street after a shower and sees an earthworm which has strayed on to it, he bethinks himself that it must get dried up in the sun, if it does not get back soon enough to ground into which it can burrow, and so he lifts it from the deadly stone surface, and puts it on the grass. If he comes across an insect which has fallen into a puddle, he stops a moment in order to hold out a leaf or a stalk on which it can save itself.

He is not afraid of being laughed at as sentimental. It is the fate of every truth to be a subject for laughter until it is generally recognised. Once it was considered folly to assume that men of colour were really men and ought to be treated as such, but the folly has become an accepted truth. To-day it is thought to be going too far to declare that constant regard for everything that lives, down to the lowest manifestations of life, is a demand made by rational ethics. The time is coming, however, when people will be astonished that mankind needed so long a time to learn to regard thoughtless injury to life as incompatible with ethics.

Ethics are responsibility without limit towards all that lives . . . Sympathy is too narrow to rank as the essence of the ethical. It denotes, of course, only interest in the suffering will-to-live. But ethics include also feeling as one's own all the circumstances and all the aspirations of the will-to-live, its pleasure, too, and its longing to live itself out to the full, as well as its urge to self-perfecting . . .

Arising, as it does, from an inner compulsion, the ethic of reverence for life . . . need give no answer to the question of what significance the ethical man's work for the maintenance, promotion, and exalting of life can have in the total happenings of the course of nature. It does not let itself be misled by the calculation that the maintaining and completing of life which it practises is hardly worth consideration beside the tremendous, unceasing destruction of life that goes on through natural forces. Having the will to action, it can leave on one side all the problems of the success of its work. Full of significance for the world is the fact in itself that in the ethically developed man there has made its appearance in the world a will-to-live which is filled with reverence for life and devotion to life . . .

The world is a ghastly drama of will-to-live divided against itself. One existence makes its way at the cost of another; one destroys the other . . . [But] if I save an insect from the puddle, life has devoted itself to life, and the division of life against itself is got rid of . . .

*   *   *   *   *   *

Why do I forgive anyone? Ordinary ethics say, because I feel sympathy with him. They allow men to seem to themselves, when they pardon others, frightfully good, and allow them to practise a style of pardoning which is not free from humiliation of the other. They thus make forgiveness a sweetened triumph of self-devotion.

The ethic of reverence for life does away with this unpurified view. All acts of forbearance and of pardon are, for this ethic, acts forced from one by truth towards oneself. I must practise unlimited forgiveness because, if I did not, I should be wanting in truth to myself, for it would be acting as if I myself were not guilty in the same way as the other has been guilty towards me. Because my life is so liberally spotted with falsehood, I must forgive falsehood which has been practised upon me; because I myself have been in so many cases wanting in love, and guilty of hatred, slander, deceit, or arrogance, I must pardon any want of love, and all hatred, slander, deceit, or arrogance which have been directed against myself. I must forgive quietly and without drawing attention to it; in fact I do not really pardon at all, for I do not let things develop to any such act of judgment . . . We have to carry on the struggle against the evil that is in mankind not by judging others, but by judging ourselves. Struggle with oneself and truth towards oneself are the means by which we work upon others . . .

*   *   *   *   *   *

But what is the relation between ethics and reverence for life in the conflicts which arise between inward compulsion to devote myself to others, and necessary self-assertion?

I too am subject to division of my will-to-life against itself. In a thousand ways my existence stands in conflict with that of others. The necessity to destroy and to injure life is imposed upon me. If I walk along an unfrequented path, my foot brings destruction and pain upon the tiny creatures which populate it. In order to preserve my own existence, I must defend myself against the existence which injures it. I become a hunter of the mouse which inhabits my house, a murderer of the insect which wants to have its nest there, a mass-murderer of the bacteria which may endanger my life. I get my food by destroying plants and animals. My happiness is built upon injury done to my fellow-men.

How does our ethic assert itself in the tragic necessity to

which I am subjected through the division of my will-to-live against itself? . . .

It allows to rank as good only the maintenance and promotion of life. . . . It does not abolish for man all ethical conflicts, but compels him to decide for himself in each case how far he can remain ethical and how far he must submit himself to the necessity for destruction of and injury to life, and therewith incur guilt . . . No one can lay down for him at what point, on each occasion, lies the extreme limit of possibility for his persistence in the preservation and promotion of life. He alone has to decide, by letting himself be guided by a feeling of the highest possible responsibility towards other life . . .

*   *   *   *   *   *

What does reverence for life say about the relations between men and the animal world?

Whenever I injure life of any sort, I must be quite clear whether it is necessary. Beyond the unavoidable, I must never go, not even with what seems insignificant. The farmer who has mown down a thousand flowers in his meadow to feed his cows, must be careful on his way home not to strike off in thoughtless pastime the head of a single flower by the roadside, for he thereby commits a wrong against life without being under the pressure of necessity.

Those who experiment with operations or the use of drugs upon animals, or inoculate them with diseases, so as to be able to bring help to mankind with the results gained, must never quiet any misgivings they feel with the general reflexion that their gruesome proceedings aim at a valuable result. They must first have considered in each individual case whether there is a real necessity to force upon any animal this sacrifice for the sake of mankind, and they must take the most careful pains to ensure that the pain inflicted is made as small as possible. How much wrong is committed in scientific institutions through neglect of anæsthetics, which to save time or trouble are not administered! How much, too, through animals being subjected to torture merely to give to students a demonstration of perfectly understood

448

phenomena. By the very fact that animals have been subjected to experiments, and have by their pain won such valuable results for suffering men, a new and special relation of solidarity has been established between them and us. From that springs for each one of us a compulsion to do to every animal all the good we possibly can. By helping an insect when it is in difficulties I am thereby attempting to cancel part of man's ever new debt to the animal world. Whenever an animal is in any way forced into the service of man, every one of us must be concerned with the suffering which it has thereby to undergo. None of us must allow any suffering to take place for which he himself is not responsible, if he can hinder it in any way, at the same time quieting his conscience with the reflexion that he would be mixing himself up in something which does not concern him. No one must shut his eyes and regard as non-existent the sufferings of which he spares himself the sight. Let no one regard as light the burden of his responsibility. While so much ill-treatment of animals goes on, while the moans of thirsty animals in railway trucks sound unheard, while so much brutality prevails in our slaughter-houses, while animals have to suffer in our kitchens painful death from unskilled hands, while animals have to endure intolerable treatment from heartless men, or are left to the cruel play of children, we all share the guilt.

We are afraid of making ourselves conspicuous, if we let it be noticed how we feel for the sufferings which man brings upon the animals. We think at the same time that others have become more "rational" than we are, and that they take as being usual, and as a matter of course, what we are excited about. Yet suddenly they will let slip a word which shows us that they too have not yet learnt to acquiesce. And now, though they are strangers, they are quite near us. The mask in which we misled each other falls off. We know now, from one another, that we are alike in being unable to escape from the gruesome proceedings that are taking place unceasingly around us. What a happy making of a new acquaintance!

The ethic of respect for life guards us from letting each other believe through our silence that we no longer experience what, as thinking men, we must experience. It prompts us to keep each other sensitive to what distresses us, and to talk and to act together without any feeling of shyness, just as the responsibility we feel moves us to. It makes us keep on the look-out together for opportunities of bringing some sort of help to animals, to make up for the great misery which men inflict on them, and thus to step for a moment out of the incomprehensible horror of existence.

*   *   *   *   *   *

In the matter also of our relation to other men, the ethic of reverence for life throws upon us a responsibility so unlimited as to be terrifying.

Here again it offers us no rules about the extent of the self-maintenance which is allowable; again, it bids us in each case come to terms with the absolute ethic of self-devotion. I have to decide, in accordance with the responsibility of which I am conscious, how much of my life, my possessions, my rights, my happiness, my time, and my rest I must devote to others, and how much of them I may keep for myself.

In the question of possession, the ethic of reverence for life is outspokenly individualist, in the sense that wealth acquired or inherited must be placed at the service of the community not through any measures taken by society, but through the absolutely free decision of the individual. It expects everything from a general increase in the feeling of responsibility. Wealth it regards as the property of society left in the sovereign control of the individual. One man serves society by carrying on a business in which a number of employees earn their living; another by giving away his wealth in order to help his fellows. Between these two extreme kinds of service let each decide according to the responsibility which he finds determined for him by the circumstances of his life. Let no one judge his neighbour. The one thing that matters is that each shall value what he possesses as means to action. Whether this is accomplished by his keeping and increasing his wealth, or by surrender of it, matters little. Wealth must reach the community in the most varied ways, if the latter is to profit by it in the best way.

Those who possess little wealth to call their own are most in danger of holding what they have in a purely selfish spirit. There is profound truth in the parable of Jesus which makes the servant who had received least the least loyal to his duty.

The ethic of reverence for life does not allow my rights, either, to belong to me. It forbids me to quiet my conscience with the reflexion that as the stronger, but by quite legitimate means, I am advancing myself at the cost of one who is weaker than I. In what law and public opinion allow me it sets a problem before me. It bids me think of others, and makes me ponder whether I can allow myself the inward right to pluck all the fruit that my hand can reach. Thus it may happen that in obedience to consideration for the existence of others I do what seems to ordinary opinion to be folly. Yes, it may even show itself to be folly by the fact that my renunciation has not been of the slightest benefit to him for whom it was made. And yet I was right. Reverence for life is the highest court of appeal. What it commands has its own significance, even if it seems foolish or useless . . .

Nor will reverence for life grant me my happiness as my own. At the moments when I should like to enjoy myself without restraint, it wakes in me reflexion about misery that I see or suspect, and it does not allow me to drive away the uneasiness thereby caused to me. Just as the wave cannot exist for itself, but is ever a part of the heaving surface of ocean, so must I never live my life for itself, but always in the experience which is going on around me. It is an uncomfortable doctrine which the true ethic whispers into my ear. You are happy, it says; therefore you are called upon to give much. Whatever more than others you have received in health, natural gifts, working capacity, success, a beautiful childhood, harmonious family circumstances, you must not accept as being a matter of course. You must pay a price for them. You must show more than average devotion of life to life.

451

To the happy the voice of the true ethic is dangerous, if they venture to listen to it. When it calls to them, it never damps down the irrational which glows within it. It assails them to see whether it can get them out of their rut and turn them into adventurers of self-devotion, people of whom the world has too few. . . .

Reverence for life is an inexorable creditor! If it finds anyone with nothing to pledge but a little time and a little leisure, it lays an attachment on these. But its hardheartedness is good, and sees clearly. The many modern men who as industrial machines are engaged in callings in which they can in no way be active as men among men, are exposed to the danger of merely vegetating in an egoistic life. Many of them feel this danger, and suffer under the fact that their daily work has so little to do with spiritual and ideal aims and does not allow them to put into it anything of their human nature. Others acquiesce; the thought of having no duties outside their daily work suits them very well.

But that men should be so condemned or so favoured as to be released from responsibility for devotion as men to men, the ethic of reverence for life will not allow to be legitimate. It demands that every one of us in some way and with some object shall be a man for men. To those who have no opportunity in their daily work of giving themselves as man to men, and have nothing else that they can give, it suggests their offering something of their time and leisure, even if these have been granted to them in scanty measure. Find for yourselves some secondary work (it says to them), an inconspicuous one, perhaps a secret one. Open your eyes and look for a human being or some work devoted to human welfare which needs from some one a little time or friendliness, a little sympathy, or sociability, or work. There may be a solitary or an embittered fellow-man, an invalid or an inefficient person to whom you can be something. Perhaps it is an old person or a child. Or some good work needs volunteers who can offer a free evening, or run errands. Who can enumerate the many ways in which that costly piece of fixed capital, a human being, can be employed! More of him is wanted everywhere! Hunt, then, for some situation for your humanity, and do not be frightened away if you have to wait, or to be taken on trial. And do not be disturbed by disappointments. Anyhow, do not be without some secondary work in which you give yourself as a man to men. There is one that is marked out for you, if you only truly will to have it. . . .

Thus does the true ethic speak of those who have only a little time and a little human nature to give. Well will it be with them if they listen to it, and are preserved from becoming stunted natures, because they have neglected this devotion of self to others.

But to everyone, in whatever state of life he finds himself, the ethic of respect for life does this: it forces him ever and again to be inwardly concerned with all the human destinies and all the other life-destinies which are going through their life-course around him, and to give himself, as man, to the man who needs a fellow-man. It will not allow the learned man to live only for his learning, even if his learning makes him very useful, nor the artist to live only for his art, even if by means of it he gives something to many. It does not allow the very busy man to think that with his professional activities he has fulfilled every demand upon him. It demands from all and every that they devote a portion of their life to their fellows. In what way and to what extent this is laid down for him the individual must gather from the thoughts which arise in him, and from the destinies in which his life moves. One man's sacrifice is outwardly unpretentious. He can accomplish it while continuing to live a normal life. Another is called to some conspicuous devotion, and must therefore put aside regard for his own progress. But let neither judge the other. The tasks of men have to be decided in a thousand ways to let the good become actual. What he has to bring as an offering is the secret of each individual. But one with another we have all to recognise that our existence reaches its true value only when we experience in ourselves something of the truth of the saying: "Whoever shall lose his life, the same shall find it" (St. Matt. x. 39).

*   *   *   *   *   *

453

The ethical conflicts between society and the individual arise out of the fact that the latter has to bear not only a personal but also a supra-personal responsibility. When my own person only is concerned, I can always be patient, always forgive, use all possible considerations, always be tenderhearted. But each of us comes into a situation when he is responsible not for himself only, but also for some undertaking, and then is forced into decisions which conflict with personal morality.

The industrialist who manages a business, however small, and the musician who undertakes public performances, cannot be men in the way they would like to be. The one has to dismiss a worker who is incapable or given to drink, in spite of any sympathy he has for him and his family; the other cannot let a singer whose voice is the worse for wear perform any longer, although he knows what distress he thus causes.

The more extensive a man's activities, the oftener he finds himself in the situation of having to sacrifice something of his humanity to his supra-personal responsibility. Out of this conflict consideration brings the average person to the decision that the wider responsibility does, as a matter of principle, annul the personal. It is with this idea that society addresses the individual. For the quieting of consciences for which this decision is too categorical, it perhaps lays down a few principles which undertake to determine, in a way that is valid for everybody, how far in any case personal morality can have a say in the matter.

To the current ethic no course remains open but to sign this capitulation. It has no means of defending the fortress of personal morality, because it has not at its disposal any absolute notions of good and evil. Not so the ethic of reverence for life. That possesses, as we can see, what the other lacks. It therefore never surrenders the fortress, even if the latter is permanently besieged. It feels itself in a position to persevere in holding it, and by continual sorties to keep the besiegers on the *qui vive*.

Only the most universal and absolute determination to maintain and promote life, which is the objective aimed at by reverence for life, is ethical. All other necessity or expediency is not ethical, but only a more or less necessary necessity, or a more or less expedient expediency. In the conflict between the maintenance of my own existence and the destruction of, or injury to, another, I can never put the ethical and the necessary together to form a relative ethical; I must choose between ethical and necessary, and, if I choose the latter, must take it upon myself to be guilty through an act of injury to life. Similarly I am not at liberty to think that in the conflict between personal and suprapersonal responsibility I can balance the ethical and the expedient to make a relative ethical, or even annul the ethical with the purposive [i.e. with something that serves a good purpose at the cost of damaging another's life]. I must choose between the two. If under the pressure of the supra-personal responsibility I yield to the expedient, I become guilty in some way or other through failure in reverence for life.

The temptation to combine with the ethical into a relative ethical the expedient which is commanded me by the suprapersonal responsibility is especially strong, because it can be shown, in defence of it, that the person who complies with the demand of this supra-personal responsibility acts unegoistically. It is not to his individual existence or his individual welfare that he sacrifices another existence or welfare, but he sacrifices an individual existence and welfare to what forces itself upon him as expedient in view of the existence or the welfare of a majority. But ethical is more than unegoistic. Ethical is nothing but the reverence felt by my will-to-live for every other will-to-live. Whenever I in any way sacrifice or injure life, I am not within the ethical, but I become guilty, whether it be egoistically guilty for the sake of maintaining my own existence or welfare, or unegoistically guilty for the sake of maintaining a greater number of other existences or their welfare.

This so easily made mistake of accepting as ethical a violation of reverence for life if it is based upon unegoistic considerations, is the bridge by crossing which ethics enter unintentionally the territory of the non-ethical. The bridge must be broken down.

Ethics go only so far as humanity does, humanity meaning respect for the existence and the happiness of individual human beings. Where humanity ends false ethics begin. The day on which this boundary is once for all universally recognised, and marked out so as to be visible to everyone, will be one of the most important in the history of mankind. Thenceforward it can no longer happen that ethics which are not ethics at all are accepted as real ethics, and deceive and ruin individuals and peoples.

The ethics hitherto current have hindered us from becoming as earnest as we must be by the fact that they have utterly deceived us as to the many ways in which each one of us, whether through self-assertion, or by actions justified by supra-personal responsibility, become guilty again and again. True knowledge consists in being gripped by the secret that everything around us is will-to-live and seeing clearly how again and again we incur guilt against life.

Fooled by false ethics, man stumbles about in his guilt like a drunken man. If he becomes instructed and earnest he seeks the road which leads him least into guilt.

We are all exposed to the temptation of lessening the guilt of humanity which comes from our working under supra-personal responsibility, by withdrawing as far as possible into ourselves. But such freedom from guilt is not honestly obtained. Ethics . . . forbid us to be like the housewife who leaves the killing of the eels to her cook, and compel us to undertake all duties involving supra-personal responsibility which fall to us, even if we should be in a position to decline them for reasons more or less satisfactory.

Each one of us, then, has to engage, so far as he is brought to it by the circumstances of his life, in work which involves supra-personal responsibility, but we must do it not in the spirit of the collective body, but in that of the man who wishes to be ethical. In every individual case we struggle therefore to preserve as much humanity as is ever possible in such work, and in doubtful cases we venture to make a mistake on the side of humanity rather than on that of the object in view. When we have become instructed and earnest, we think of what is usually forgotten: that all public activity of whatever sort has to do not with facts only, but also with the creation of that spirit and temper which is desirable in the collective body. The creation of such a spirit and temper is more important than anything directly attained in the facts. Public work, in which the utmost possible effort is not made to preserve humanity, ruins the disposition. He who under the influence of supra-personal responsibility simply sacrifices men and human happiness when it seems commanded, accomplishes something. But he has not reached the highest level. He has only outward, not spiritual influence. We have spiritual influence only when others notice that we do not decide coldly in accordance with principles laid down once and for all, but in each individual case fight for humanity. There is too little among us of this kind of struggling. From the smallest who is something in the smallest business, right up to the political ruler who holds in his hands the decision for peace or war, we act too much as men who in any given case can prepare without effort to be no longer men, but merely the executive of general interests. Hence there is no longer among us any trust in a righteousness lighted up with human feeling. Nor have we any longer any real respect for one another. We all feel ourselves in the power of a mentality of cold, impersonal, and usually unintelligent opportunism, which stiffens itself with appeals to principle, and in order to carry out small interests is capable of the greatest inhumanity and the greatest folly. We therefore see among us one temper of impersonal opportunism confronting another, and all problems are executed in a useless conflict of force against force because there is nowhere at hand such a spirit and temper as will make them solvable.

Only through our struggles for humanity can forces which work in the direction of the truly rational and expedient become powerful, while the present spirit and temper prevails. Hence the man who works under supra-personal responsibilities has to feel himself answerable not only for the successful result which is to be realised through him, but for the general spirit and temper which has to be created.

We therefore serve society without losing ourselves in it. We do not allow it to be our guardian in the matter of ethics. That would be as if the solo violinist allowed his bowing to be regulated by that of the double-bass player. Never for a moment do we lay aside our mistrust of the ideals established by society, and of the convictions which are kept by it in circulation. We always know that society is full of folly and will deceive us in the matter of humanity. It is an unreliable horse, and blind into the bargain. Woe to the driver if he falls asleep!

All this sounds too hard. Society serves ethics by giving legal sanction to its most elementary principles, and handing on the ethical principles of one generation to the next. That is much, and it claims our gratitude. But society is also something which checks the progress of ethics again and again, by arrogating to itself the dignity of the ethical teachers. To this, however, it has no right. The only ethical teacher is the man who thinks ethically, and struggles for an ethic. The conceptions of good and evil which are put in circulation by society are paper-money, the value of which is to be calculated not by the figures printed upon it, but by its relation to its exchange value in gold of the ethic of reverence for life. But so measured, its exchange value reveals itself as that of the paper-money of a half-bankrupt state.

The collapse of civilisation has come about through ethics being left to society. A renewal of it is possible only if ethics become once more the concern of thinking human beings, and if individuals seek to assert themselves in society as ethical personalities. In proportion as we secure this, society will become, instead of the [unspiritual kind of thing] that it naturally is, an ethical one. Previous generations have made the terrible mistake of idealising society as ethical. We do our duty to it by judging it critically, and trying to make it, so far as is possible, more ethical. Being in possession of an absolute standard of the ethical, we no longer allow ourselves to make acceptable as ethics principles of expediency or even of the vulgarest opportunism. Nor

458

do we remain any longer at the low level of allowing to be current, as in any way ethical, meaningless ideals of power, of passion, or of nationalism, which are set up by miserable politicians and maintained in some degree of respect by bewildering propaganda. All the principles, dispositions, and ideals which make their appearance among us we measure . . . with a rule on which the measures are given by the absolute ethic of reverence for life. We allow currency only to what is consistent with the claims of humanity. We bring into honour again regard for life and for the happiness of the individual. Sacred human rights we again hold high; not those which political rulers exalt at banquets and tread underfoot in their actions, but the true ones. We call once more for justice, not that . . . about which demagogues of all shades of colour shout themselves hoarse, but that which is filled to the full with the value of each single human existence. The foundation of law and right is humanity.

Thus we bring the principles, dispositions, and ideals of the collective body into agreement with humanity. At the same time we shape them in accordance with reason, for only what is ethical is truly rational. Only so far as the current disposition of men is animated by ethical convictions and ideals is it capable of truly purposive activity [i.e. of activity inspired by a truly creative purpose].

The ethic of reverence for life puts in our hands weapons for fighting false ethics and false ideals, but we have strength to use them only so far as we—each one in his own life—preserve our humanity. Only when those men are numerous who in thought and action bring humanity to terms with reality, will humanity cease to be current as a mere sentimental idea and become what it ought to be, a leaven to transform the spirit and temper of individuals and of society.

ALBERT SCHWEITZER

FROM THE CONVERSATIONS AND
EXHORTATIONS OF FATHER ZOSSIMA

Young man, be not forgetful of prayer. Every time you pray, if your prayer is sincere, there will be new feeling and new meaning in it, which will give you fresh courage, and you will understand that prayer is an education. Remember, too, every day, and whenever you can, repeat to yourself, "Lord, have mercy on all who appear before Thee to-day." For every hour and every moment thousands of men leave life on this earth, and their souls appear before God. And how many of them depart in solitude, unknown, sad, dejected that no one mourns for them or even knows whether they have lived or not! And behold, from the other end of the earth perhaps, your prayer for their rest will rise up to God though you knew them not nor they you. How touching it must be to a soul standing in dread before the Lord to feel at that instant that, for him too, there is one to pray, that there is a fellow creature left on earth to love him too! And God will look on you both more graciously, for if you have had so much pity on him, how much will He have pity Who is infinitely more loving and merciful than you! And He will forgive him for your sake.

Brothers, have no fear of men's sin. Love a man even in his sin, for that is the semblance of Divine Love and is the highest love on earth. Love all God's creation, the whole and every grain of sand in it. Love every leaf, every ray of God's light. Love the animals, love the plants, love everything. If you love everything, you will perceive the divine mystery in things. Once you perceive it, you will begin to comprehend it better every day. And you will come at last to love the whole world with an all-embracing love. Love the animals: God has given them the rudiments of thought and joy untroubled. Do not trouble it, don't harass them, don't deprive them of their happiness, don't work against God's intent. Man, do not pride yourself on superiority to the animals; they are without sin, and you, with your greatness, defile the earth by your appearance on it, and leave the traces of your foulness after you—alas, it is true of almost every one of us! Love children especially, for they too are sinless like the angels; they live to soften and purify our hearts and as it were to guide us. Woe to him who offends a child! Father Anfim taught me to love children. The kind, silent man used often on our wanderings to spend the farthings given us on sweets and cakes for the children. He could not pass by a child without emotion. That's the nature of the man.

At some thoughts one stands perplexed, especially at the sight of men's sin, and wonders whether one should use force or humble love. Always decide to use humble love. If you resolve on that once for all, you may subdue the whole world. Loving humility is marvellously strong, the strongest of all things, and there is nothing else like it.

Every day and every hour, every minute, walk round yourself and watch yourself, and see that your image is a seemly one. You pass by a little child, you pass by, spiteful, with ugly words, with wrathful heart; you may not have noticed the child, but he has seen you, and your image, unseemly and ignoble, may remain in his defenceless heart. You don't know it, but you may have sown an evil seed in him and it may grow, and all because you were not careful before the child, because you did not foster in yourself a careful, actively benevolent love. Brothers, love is a teacher; but one must know how to acquire it, for it is hard to acquire, it is dearly bought, it is won slowly by long labour. For we must love not only occasionally, for a moment, but for ever. Everyone can love occasionally, even the wicked can.

My brother asked the birds to forgive him; that sounds senseless, but it is right; for all is like an ocean, all is flowing and blending; a touch in one place sets up movement at the other end of the earth. It may be senseless to beg forgiveness of the birds, but birds would be happier at your side—a little happier, anyway—and children and all animals, if you were nobler than you are now. It's all like an ocean, I tell you. Then you would pray to the birds too, consumed by an all-embracing love, in a sort of transport, and pray that they too will forgive you your sin. Treasure this ecstasy, however senseless it may seem to men.

My friends, pray to God for gladness. Be glad as children, as the birds of heaven. And let not the sin of men confound you in your doings. Fear not that it will wear away your work and hinder its being accomplished. Do not say, "Sin is mighty, wickedness is mighty, evil environment is mighty, and we are lonely and helpless, and evil environment is wearing us away and hindering our good work from being done." Fly from that dejection, children! There is only one means of salvation, then take yourself and make yourself responsible for all men's sins, that is the truth, you know, friends, for as soon as you sincerely make yourself responsible for everything and for all men, you will see at once that it is really so, and that you are to blame for everyone and for all things. But throwing your own indolence and impotence on others you will end by sharing the pride of Satan and murmuring against God.

Of the pride of Satan what I think is this: it is hard for us on earth to comprehend it, and therefore it is so easy to fall into error and to share it, even imagining that we are doing something grand and fine. Indeed, many of the strongest feelings and movements of our nature we cannot comprehend on earth. Let not that be a stumbling-block, and think not that it may serve as a justification to you for anything. For the Eternal Judge asks of you what you can comprehend and not what you cannot. You will know that yourself hereafter, for you will behold all things truly then and will not dispute them. On earth, indeed, we are as it were astray, and if it were not for the precious image of Christ before us, we should be undone and altogether lost, as was the human race before the flood. Much on earth is hidden from us, but to make up for that we have been given a precious mystic sense of our living bond with the other world, with the higher heavenly world, and the roots of our thoughts and feelings are not here but in other worlds. That is why the philosophers say that we cannot apprehend the reality of things on earth.

God took seeds from different worlds and sowed them on this earth, and His garden grew up and everything came up that could come up, but what grows lives and is alive only through the feeling of its contact with other mysterious worlds. If that feeling grows weak or is destroyed in you, the heavenly growth will die away in you. Then you will be indifferent to life and even grow to hate it. That's what I think. . . .

Remember particularly that you cannot be a judge of anyone. For no one can judge a criminal, until he recognises that he is just such a criminal as the man standing before him, and that he perhaps is more than all men to blame for that crime. When he understands that, he will be able to be a judge. Though that sounds absurd, it is true. If I had been righteous myself, perhaps there would have been no criminal standing before me. If you can take upon yourself the crime of the criminal your heart is judging, take it at once, suffer for him yourself, and let him go without reproach. And even if the law itself makes you his judge, act in the same spirit so far as possible, for he will go away and condemn himself more bitterly than you have done. If, after your kiss, he goes away untouched, mocking at you, do not let that be a stumbling-block to you. It shows his time has not yet come, but it will come in due course. And if it come not, no matter; if not he, then another in his place will understand and suffer, and judge and condemn himself, and the truth will be fulfilled. Believe that, believe it without doubt; for in that lies all the hope and faith of the saints.

Work without ceasing. If you remember in the night as you go to sleep, "I have not done what I ought to have done", rise up at once and do it. If the people around you are spiteful and callous and will not hear you, fall down before them and beg their forgiveness; for in truth you are to blame for their not wanting to hear you. And if you cannot speak to them in their bitterness, serve them in silence and humility, never losing hope. If all men abandon you and even drive you away by force, then when you are left alone fall on the earth and kiss it, water it with your tears and it will bring forth fruit even though no one has seen or heard you in your solitude. Believe to the end, even if all men went astray and you were left the only one faithful; bring

463

your offering even then and praise God in your loneliness. And if two of you are gathered together—then there is a whole world, a world of living love. Embrace each other tenderly and praise God, for if only in you two His truth has been fulfilled.

If you sin yourself and grieve even unto death for your sins or for your sudden sin, then rejoice for others, rejoice for the righteous man, rejoice that if you have sinned, he is righteous and has not sinned.

If the evil-doing of men moves you to indignation and overwhelming distress, even to a desire for vengeance on the evildoers, shun above all things that feeling. Go at once and seek suffering for yourself, as though you were yourself guilty of that wrong. Accept that suffering and bear it and your heart will find comfort, and you will understand that you too are guilty, for you might have been a light to the evil-doers, even as the one man sinless, and you were not a light to them. If you had been a light, you would have lightened the path for others too, and the evil-doer might perhaps have been saved by your light from his sin. And even though your light was shining, yet you see men were not saved by it, hold firm and doubt not the power of the heavenly light. Believe that if they were not saved, they will be saved hereafter. And if they are not saved hereafter, then their sons will be saved, for your light will not die even when you are dead. The righteous man departs, but his light remains. Men are always saved after the death of the deliverer. Men reject their prophets and slay them, but they love their martyrs and honour those whom they have slain. You are working for the whole, you are acting for the future. Seek no reward, for great is your reward on this earth: the spiritual joy which is only vouchsafed to the righteous man. Fear not the great nor the mighty, but be wise and ever serene. Know the measure, know the times, study that. When you are left alone, pray. Love to throw yourself on the earth and kiss it. Kiss the earth and love it with an unceasing, consuming love. Love all men, love everything. . . .

DOSTOEVSKY

Wisdom is radiant and fadeth not away; and easily is she beheld of them that love her, and found of them that seek her. She forestalleth them that desire to know her, making herself first known. He that riseth up early to seek her shall have no toil, for he shall find her sitting at his gates. For to think upon her is perfectness of understanding, and he that watcheth for her sake shall quickly be free from care. Because she goeth about, herself seeking them that are worthy of her, and in their paths she appeareth unto them graciously, and in every purpose she meeteth them. For her true beginning is desire of discipline; and the care for discipline is love of her; and love of her is observance of her laws; and to give heed to her laws confirmeth incorruption; and incorruption bringeth near unto God; so then desire of wisdom promoteth to a kingdom. . . .

I myself also am mortal, like to all, and am sprung from one born of the earth, the man first formed, and in the womb of a mother was I moulded into flesh in the time of ten months, being compacted in blood of the seed of man and pleasure that came with sleep. And I also, when I was born, drew in the common air, and fell upon the kindred earth, uttering, like all, for my first voice, the selfsame wail: in swaddling clothes was I nursed, and with watchful cares. For no king had any other first beginning; but all men have one entrance into life, and a like departure. For this cause I prayed, and understanding was given me: I called upon God, and there came to me a spirit of wisdom. I preferred her before sceptres and thrones, and riches I esteemed nothing in comparison of her. Neither did I liken to her any priceless gem, because all the gold of the earth in her presence is a little sand, and silver shall be accounted as clay before her. Above health and comeliness I loved her, and I chose to have her rather than light, because her bright shining is never laid to sleep. But with her there came to me all good things together, and in her hands innumerable riches: and I rejoiced over them all because wisdom leadeth them; though

I knew not that she was the mother of them. As I learned without guile, I impart without grudging; I do not hide her riches. For she is unto men a treasure that faileth not, and they that use it obtain friendship with God, commended to him by the gifts which they through discipline present to him. . . .

For there is in her a spirit quick of understanding, holy, alone in kind, manifold, subtil, freely moving, clear in utterance, unpolluted, distinct, unharmed, loving what is good, keen, unhindered, beneficent, loving toward men, steadfast, sure, free from care, all powerful, all-surveying, and penetrating through all spirits that are quick of understanding, pure, most subtil: for wisdom is more mobile than any motion; yea, she pervadeth and penetrateth all things by reason of her pureness. For she is a breath of the power of God, and a clear effluence of the glory of the Almighty; therefore can nothing defiled find entrance into her. For she is an effulgence from everlasting light, and an unspotted mirror of the working of God, and an image of his goodness. And she, being one, hath power to do all things; and remaining in herself, reneweth all things: and from generation to generation passing into holy souls she maketh men friends of God and prophets. For nothing doth God love save him that dwelleth with wisdom. For she is fairer than the sun, and above all the constellations of the stars: being compared with light, she is found to be before it; for to the light of day succeedeth night, but against wisdom evil doth not prevail. . . .

Her I loved and sought out from my youth, and I sought to take her for my bride, and I became enamoured of her beauty. She glorifieth her noble birth in that it is given her to live with God, and the Sovereign Lord of all loved her. For she is initiated into the knowledge of God, and she chooseth out for him his works. But if riches are a desired possession in life, what is richer than wisdom, which worketh all things? And if understanding worketh, who more than wisdom is an artificer of the things that are? And if a man loveth righteousness, the fruits of wisdom's labour are virtues, for she teacheth soberness and understanding, righteousness and courage; and there is nothing

466

in life for men more profitable than these. . . . When I am come into my house, I shall find rest with her; for converse with her hath no bitterness, and to live with her hath no pain, but gladness and joy. When I considered these things in myself, and took thought in my heart how that in kinship unto wisdom is immortality, and in her friendship is good delight, and in the labours of her hands is wealth that faileth not, and in assiduous communing with her is understanding, and great renown in having fellowship with her words, I went about seeking how to take her unto myself. Now I was a child of parts, and a good soul fell to my lot; nay rather, being good, I came into a body undefiled. But perceiving that I could not otherwise possess wisdom except God gave her me (yea and to know by whom the grace is given, this too came of understanding), I pleaded with the Lord and besought him, and with my whole heart I said,

O God of the fathers, and Lord who keepest thy mercy, who madest all things by thy word; and by thy wisdom thou formedst man, that he should have dominion over the creatures that were made by thee, and rule the world in holiness and righteousness, and execute judgement in uprightness of soul; give me wisdom, her that sitteth by thee on thy throne; and reject me not from among thy servants: because I am thy bondman and the son of thy handmaid, a man weak and short-lived, and of small power to understand judgement and laws. For even if a man be perfect among the sons of men, yet if the wisdom that cometh from thee be not with him, he shall be held in no account. Thou didst choose me before my brethren to be king of thy people, and to do judgement for thy sons and daughters. Thou gavest command to build a sanctuary in thy holy mountain, and an altar in the city of thy habitation, a copy of the holy tabernacle which thou preparedst aforehand from the beginning. And with thee is wisdom, which knoweth thy works, and was present when thou wast making the world, and which understandeth what is pleasing in thine eyes, and what is right according to thy commandments. Send her forth out of the holy heavens, and from the throne of thy glory bid her come, that being present with me she may toil with me, and that I may learn what is well-pleasing before thee. For she knoweth all things and hath understanding thereof, and in my doings she shall guide me in ways of soberness, and she shall guard me in her glory. And so shall my works be acceptable, and I shall judge thy people righteously, and I shall be worthy of my father's throne. For what man shall know the counsel of God? Or who shall conceive what the Lord willeth? For the thoughts of mortals are timorous, and our devices are prone to fail. For a corruptible body weigheth down the soul, and the earthy frame lieth heavy on a mind that is full of cares. And hardly do we divine the things that are on earth, and the things that are close at hand we find with labour; but the things that are in the heavens who ever yet traced out? And who ever gained knowledge of thy counsel, except thou gavest wisdom, and sentest thy holy spirit from on high? And it was thus that the ways of them which are on earth were corrected, and men were taught the things that are pleasing unto thee; and through wisdom were they saved.

THE WISDOM OF SOLOMON

The wolf also shall dwell with the lamb, and the leopard shall lie down with the kid; and the calf and the young lion and the fatling together; and a little child shall lead them.

And the cow and the bear shall feed; their young ones shall lie down together: and the lion shall eat straw like the ox.

And the sucking child shall play on the hole of the asp, and the weaned child shall put his hand on the cockatrice' den.

They shall not hurt nor destroy in all my holy mountain: for the earth shall be full of the knowledge of the Lord, as the waters cover the sea.

ISAIAH

THE END

Blessed art thou, O Lord our God, King of the Universe, who has kept us in life, and hast preserved us, and hast enabled us to reach this season.

Christmas Eve, 1960

APPENDIX

Page 31: The Flood. Asswaged = grew less.

Pages 32, 33: Sodom. Peradventure = perhaps. Left communing = finished talking.

Page 33: Nineveh. A gourd is a sort of tree that grows very rapidly.

Page 37: Juliana of Norwich. Longeth = belongs. Proper = special.

Page 39: William Law. To communicate = to give a share of.

Page 61: Psalm 104. A cony = a small thick-skinned animal found in Syria. Leviathan = sea-monster.

Page 66: St. Francis. Similitude = likeness. Hath us in rule = guides us.

Pages 69, 70: The Song of Solomon. Turtle = turtle-dove. The mandrake is a plant. Contemned = despised.

Pages 72-74: Traherne. Virgin = unspoiled. Angelical and wholly celestial = like an angel in heaven. By intuition = without thinking about it. Contentions = quarrels. Exaction = forcing people to do things. Orient = shining like the dawn. Talked with my expectation = made me expect something wonderful.

Page 77: Wordsworth. Grain-tinctured = the colour of corn. Empyrean = fiery.

Page 106: George Herbert. I have inserted inverted commas to make the meaning clearer.

Page 123: Leigh Hunt. Accord = harmony. Cheerly = cheerily.

Page 133: Isaiah. Rereward = rearguard. Putting forth the finger = pointing to people with scorn.

Page 139: Romans. Give place unto = give way to. Heap coals of fire, etc. = produce remorse. Overcome of = defeated by.

Page 139: Colossians. Bowels of mercy = inner feelings of mercy. Is the bond of perfection = binds people together in a perfect way.

Page 141: James. Easy to be intreated = easily prevailed upon or persuaded.

Page 199: Job. Eschewed = abstained from.

Page 208: Jung. Epitome = a short way of expressing. A neurosis is a mental illness, as when we falsely imagine that everyone hates us and is persecuting us. By the conflict between the sensual and the spiritual man Jung means the conflict between our "body", which bids us, for instance, eat as much as we want to while others are starving, and our "spirit", which bids us, on the contrary, feed the others first. Dissociation of personality = a lack of unity inside us.

Page 219: Walter de la Mare. Tarn = lake. Reeds: the poet is using a reed as a pen.

Page 221: Emily Dickinson. Cubits = height, stature.

Page 226: Tagore. Habited = clothed. Ascetic = sombre.

Page 257: Chuang Tzu. Lees and scum = dregs, sediment, refuse.

Page 269: Péguy. Viaticum = Holy Communion when administered to the dying.

Pages 281, 282: Walter de la Mare. Rime = hoar frost. Mail = a suit of armour. Void = empty.

Page 286: Wordsworth. I have omitted two stanzas, and have put five lines of stanza V into inverted commas to make the meaning clearer.

Pages 316, 317: Shelley. Arcturi = the multitude of stars in the constellation Boötes. Pranked = decked out.

Page 342: Lowes Dickinson. Sterterous = stupid, puffed up, always snoring.

Page 343: Shelley. Here is William Kean Seymour's prose version:

The thunder ceased, which had been echoing around the earth and shaking the abysses of the sky. Suddenly there was a change, and in that moment the impalpable thin air and the all-pervading sunlight were transformed. It was as if the sense of love dissolved between them had cast a shining mantle over the wide world. The vision then grew clear, and I could see into the complex mysteries of the universe. . . .

I floated to the earth on languid plumes, dizzy with such delight that as I neared the hemispheres it was, as it still is, a blissful pain to move, to breathe, to be myself. After the first slow, hesitant approach to that strange world I wandered off among the haunts and dwellings of mankind; and at the first was disappointed at the difference between my inward glow of expectation and what lay spread before me.

But then I looked with clearer sight and understanding at those outward things. I saw that thrones were vacant where kings once had sat; that mortal men walked one with the other even as spirits do. I gazed on free men, not on slaves and trampling tyrants; and upon their brows no longer could be read the evil signs of hate, disdain or fear, self-love or self-contempt. These were not men who in their time had faltered despairing to hell's gate and read with burning eyes, 'All hope abandon, ye who enter here!' That was the Past of Man; but here none frowned, none trembled before another's eye of cold command. No tyrant satisfied his lust for power by rendering others abject to themselves, spurring them on, like outspent horses, to their death.

Nor did I once encounter men whose smiles convey a lie while their skilful tongues utter a half-pretence of truth. Nor those who torture their weak souls with sneers, treading the sparks of love and hope to bitter ashes, and in their agony of self-destruction infecting all who come their way.

None used a cynic tongue in false and hollow talk that makes the heart doubt its long-cherished faith without a word of protest. I saw no hypocrites wretched with self-mistrust.

And I saw women there, whose beauty matched their kindness, frank as the open skies and free as heaven. And as they passed, radiant and gentle, pure from any taint of caste and custom, I heard them speaking wisdom which before they could not think. They showed emotions which of old they feared to feel; and each and all had changed to beings that one time they dared not dream of. I had the sense of heaven there on earth; for no one harboured jealousy, or envy or false shame—that blackest gall that spoils the taste of love.

Thrones were still there, with altars, judgement-seats and prisons; but desolate and neglected, like barbaric shapes of old iniquities long since forgotten; for who remembers now their

473

might and purpose in the dark past when wretched men served them or succumbed to their power? One by one I passed them, thinking of the hideous waste they symbolised, when kings and priests held sway in dark millenniums of war and ignorance, misdirected faith and superstition. Yet now they stand for all to wonder at, the tools of Man's captivity long disused.

And those foul shapes assumed by Jupiter, the tyrant of the world; those monstrous images to which the panic-stricken nations bowed in ceaseless sacrifice of blood from hearts broken by ruined hopes and desecrated love: those life-consuming altars now stand soiled and garlandless, where once men flattered the dark thing they feared—the thing called Hate! Those were the Tyrant's shrines, now mouldering as I passed.

These men I met saw Truth with fearless eyes; for they had torn aside the painted veil which earlier generations thought was life. The loathsome mask of hate and superstition is stripped away. Man stands erect and free, classless and equal, tribeless and nationless. He lives on earth exempt from awe and worship and observance; paying no heed to rank and precedence, for all are equal in the common good, each man himself the king that each man serves. I saw Man just and gentle, true and wise.

But is Man passionless? No; yet free from the guilt and pain of centuries of misrule to which he had himself consented until he broke his chains. Passionless? No; for change, and chance, and death still test his courage, strength and vigilance; and he must be their master, they his slaves. For were it not for chance and death and mutability the bright spirit might pass unhindered beyond the loftiest star of unascended heaven pinnacled dim in in the intense Infinity.

Page 354: Inge. Realise = get through into our lives.

Page 359: Alexander. Resilience to deformation = struggle against losing its shape.

Page 364: Ecclesiasticus. Justify = excuse, acquit of wrong-doing. Glorify = do honour to.

Page 364: Code of Manu. Is its own witness = gives evidence for or against itself.

Page 378: Francis Thompson. The wheeling systems = the stars and planets, as seen in the night skies, vastly remote. By "our benumbed conceiving" is meant our numb attempt to understand the mystery of things as we stare up into the darkness. The drift of pinions = the flight of wings. The traffic of Jacob's Ladder = the angels going up and down on it. Estranged = unable, with our mere human eyes, to see clearly. Christ walked on the waters near Gennesareth.

Page 394: Blake. Corporeal or vegetative = bodily.

Page 396: Shelley. Evanescent = quickly vanishing. Interpenetration of a divine nature through our own = entry of a divine nature into our own and spreading through it.

Pages 398-400: Charles Williams. Plenary = absolute. Multitudinously = accompanied by the multitude of ordinary butterflies. Tryst = an appointment to meet: assignation means the same. Credulous is used in its old sense of "ready to believe what is true", and not in the modern one of "ready to believe anything, true or false". A horse that leaps in a particular way is said to curvet.

Page 408: Keats. Sensual = physical.

Page 420: Huxley. Direct intuition = knowledge that comes in a flash, and not as a result of any thinking or reasoning.

Page 432: Shelley. I have inserted inverted commas to make the meaning clearer.

NOTES ON WRITERS AND
BOOKS, SOURCES AND
ACKNOWLEDGMENTS, AND
INDEX

NOTES ON WRITERS
AND BOOKS

Aaron Leib of Primishlan. Hasidic Rabbi, 18th century. For Hasidic see p. 38.

Abélard, Peter. French philosopher, 1079–1142.

Abrahamsen, David. Contemporary American psychiatrist.

Addison, Joseph. British essayist, poet and man of letters, 1672–1719.

A. E. Pseudonym of George Russell, Irish poet, writer and painter, 1867–1935.

al-Hallaj. Mystic of Islam, executed for blasphemy in 922.

Alexander, Samuel. British philosopher, 1859–1938.

Amiel, Henry Frédéric. Swiss philosopher and critic, 1821–81.

Angelus Silesius. Pseudonym for Johann Scheffler, German physician and mystical poet, 1624–77.

Ansky, S. Jewish writer, 1863–1920.

Aquinas, St. Thomas. Philosopher and theologian, born in Southern Italy about 1225.

Arika, Abba ("Rab"). Rabbi. A.D. 160–247.

Augustine, St. Theologian, 354–430.

Aurobindo, Sri. Indian philosopher and teacher, 1872–1950.

Baalshem, The. See p. 38.

Bentham, Jeremy. British philosopher and jurist, 1748–1832.

Berdyaev, Nicholas. Russian philosopher and theologian, 1874–1948.

Bhagavad-Gita, The. Perhaps the most famous book in Hindu religious literature, probably of some date between the 5th and 2nd centuries B.C.

Bloy, Léon Marie. French writer and mystic, 1846–1917.

Boehme, Jakob. German mystic, 1575–1624.

Borrow, George Henry. British traveller and writer, 1801–81.

Bosanquet, Bernard. British philosopher, 1848–1923.

Bossuet, Jacques Bénigne. French divine, orator and writer, 1627–1704.

Bright, John. British statesman, 1811–1880.

Brontë, Emily. British poet and novelist, 1818–1848.

Browne, Sir Thomas. British physician and writer, 1605–82.

Buber, Martin. Contemporary Israeli philosopher and theologian.

Buddha, The. See p. 259.

Bunam of Pzhysha. Hasidic Rabbi, d. 1827.

Caird, John. British divine and philosopher, 1820–98.

Carpenter, Edward. British man of letters and social reformer, 1844–1929.

Chaitanya, Sri. Indian mystic, 1485–1533.

Chuang Tzu. Chinese thinker of the 4th and 3rd centuries B.C.

Clement of Alexandria. Christian philosopher, probably born about A.D. 150.

Crashaw, Richard. British poet, 1613 ?–49.

Crescas, Chasdai. Jewish philosopher, 1340–1410.

Dickinson, Emily. American poet, 1830–86.

Dickinson, G. Lowes. British man of letters, 1862–1932.

Dionysius the Areopagite. Christian philosopher writing probably in the 5th century A.D.

Donne, John. British poet and divine, 1573–1631.

Dostoevsky. Russian novelist, 1821–1881.

Ecclesiasticus. A book written perhaps a hundred years or so before Christ. At one time it got near to being included in the Bible.

Eckhart, Meister. German mystic, 1260 ?–1327.

Eleazer b. Azariah, Rabbi. 2nd century A.D.

Eliezer of Dzikov. Hasidic Rabbi, 18th–19th centuries.

Elimelekh of Lizhensk. Hasidic Rabbi, d. 1786.

Erasmus. Dutch philosopher and theologian, ?1466–1536.

Farid ud-din Attar. Persian poet and mystic, 1119–1229.

Fechner, Gustav Theodor. German psychologist, 1801–87.

Fénelon, François de Salignac de la Motte. French writer, Archbishop of Cambrai. 1651–1715.

Fleg, Edmond. Contemporary French writer on Jewish themes.

Fromm, Erich. Contemporary American psychologist.

Fuller, Thomas. British historian and divine, 1608–61.

Gamaliel III, Rabban. Rabbi, 3rd century A.D.

Goethe. German poet, 1749–1832.

Gregory of Nyssa, St. A Father or Head of the Eastern Church,
about 331 to about 396.

Green, Peter. Contemporary British divine.

Hafiz. Persian (Mohammedan) poet and mystic, d. 1388.

Hanokh of Alexander. Hasidic Rabbi, d. 1870.

Hargrave, John. Contemporary British writer.

Hayyim of Krosno. Hasidic Rabbi, a disciple of the Baalshem.

Hegel, Georg Wilhelm Friedrich. German philosopher, 1770–1831.

Herbert, George. British poet, 1593–1633.

Hopkins, Gerard Manley. British poet, 1844–89.

Hunt, Leigh. British poet and essayist, 1784–1859.

Huxley, Aldous. Contemporary British novelist and man of letters.

Hylton, Walter. British mystic; probably d. 1396.

Ibsen, Henrik. Norwegian dramatist, 1828–1906.

Inge, W. R. British philosopher and divine, 1860–1954.

Isaak of Syria, St. A Father or Head of a community of monks,
6th century A.D.

Israel of Koznitz. Hasidic Rabbi, d. 1814.

Israel of Rizhyn. Hasidic Rabbi, d. 1850.

Jalalu D-Din Rumi. Persian poet and mystic, 1207–73.

James, Henry. Anglo-American novelist, 1843–1916.

James, William. American philosopher, 1842–1910.

Jefferies, Richard. British novelist and writer on the countryside,
1848–87.

Jerome, St. Christian scholar, about 340–420.

Johanan, Rabbi. Died A.D. 279.

John of Cronstadt. Father John Sergieff, 1829–1908. Russian parish priest.

John of the Cross, St. Spanish mystic, 1542–91.

Joshua b. Levi, Rabbi. 3rd century A.D.

Juliana of Norwich. British mystic, 14th and 15th centuries.

Jung, C. G. Contemporary Swiss psychologist and psychiatrist.

Kabir. Indian mystic, born probably about 1440.

Kierkegaard, Sören. Danish philosopher and theologian, 1813–55.

Lavelle, Louis. French philosopher, 1883–1951.

Law, William. British divine and mystic, 1686–1761.

Leon, Luis de. Spanish poet and mystic, 1527–91.

Lewis, C. S. Contemporary British philosopher and writer.

Lewis, H. D. Contemporary British philosopher.

Luthardt, Christophe Ernst. Professor of Theology at the University of Leipzig, d. 1902.

Macdonald, George. British novelist and poet, 1824–1905.

Macgregor, G. H. C. Contemporary British theologian.

MacLeod, George F. Presbyterian divine, and leader of the Iona Community.

Macmurray, John. Contemporary British philosopher.

Malaval, François. French mystic, 1627–1719.

Maha-Bharata, The. One of the two great Hindu epics.

Manu, The Code of. An ancient compilation of Hindu rules, moral teaching, etc.

Marcel, Gabriel. Contemporary French philosopher.

Marcus Aurelius Antoninus. Roman Emperor. A.D. 121–80.

Mare, Walter de la. British poet, 1873–1956.

Maritain, Jacques. Contemporary French philosopher, theologian and sociologist.

Meir, Rabbi. 2nd century A.D.

Mekilta, The. A pre-Talmudic commentary on Exodus.

Menander. Greek comic poet, flourished in the 4th century B.C.

Mendel of Kosov. Hasidic Rabbi, d. 1825.

Mendel of Kotzk. Hasidic Rabbi, d. 1859.

Mendel of Rymanov. Hasidic Rabbi, d. 1815.

Meredith, George. British poet and novelist, 1828–1909.

Meynell, Alice. British poet, 1849–1922.

Midrash, The. Rabbinic commentaries on the Bible, 3rd–10th centuries. Sifra and Tanhuma are Midrashic treatises.

Milarepa. Tibetan mystic, about 1052–1135.

Mirror of Perfection, The. Probably a 14th-century compilation by followers of St. Francis of Assisi.

Molinos, Miguel de. Spanish divine, 1640–97.

More, Sir Thomas. British statesman, 1478–1535. Author of 'Utopia'.

Moshe Leib of Sasov. Hasidic Rabbi, d. 1807.

Nahman of Bratzlav. Hasidic Rabbi, d. 1810.

Nettleship, Richard Lewis. British philosopher, 1846–92.

Nicholas of Cusa. Philosopher and mystic, born at Cues on the Moselle in 1401. Became Cardinal.

Niebuhr, Reinhold. Contemporary American theologian and sociologist.

Origen. With Augustine, one of the two greatest theologians of the ancient church. About A.D. 185 to about A.D. 254.

Orphism. A Greek cult, of which Orpheus was the legendary founder.

Oxyrhynchus papyri. Two papyri found at Oxyrhynchus in 1897 and 1903. Third century A.D.

Paracelsus, Theophrastus Bombast von Hohenheim. German physician and chemist (of a sort), about 1490–1541.

Paradise of the Fathers, The. A history of a group of monks who lived in the Egyptian desert between about 250 and 400 A.D.

Patmore, Coventry. British poet, 1823–96.

Péguy, Charles. French author, poet, Catholic, republican, socialist, patriot and champion of the falsely accused Jew Dreyfus. 1873–1914.

Pelagius. British theologian, about A.D. 360 to about A.D. 420.

Penn, William. British Quaker, 1644–1718.

Perez, Isaac Loeb. Jewish writer, 1851–1915.

Peter the Lombard. Bishop of Paris. Died 1160.

Philo. Jewish philosopher of Alexandria, born about the beginning of the Christian era.

Pico della Mirandola, Giovanni. Italian philosopher, theologian and expert in Jewish mysticism, 1463–94.

Pinhas of Koretz. Hasidic Rabbi, died 1791.

Plato. The greatest of Greek philosophers (or some would say one of the two greatest).

Plotinus. Philosopher and mystic, born in Egypt A.D. 204 or 205, died 270. Plato's greatest disciple.

Prezzolini, Guiseppe. Contemporary Italian-American critic.

Proust, Marcel. French novelist, 1871–1922.

Rabi'a A woman mystic of Islam, died 801.

Rafael of Bershad. Hasidic Rabbi, d. 1816.

Ramakrishna, Sri. Indian mystic, 1836–86.

Rashdall, Hastings. British philosopher and theologian, 1858–1924.

Rashi. A Jewish scholar, 1040–1105.

Renan, Ernest. French philosopher and orientalist, 1823–92.

Rilke, Rainer Maria. German poet, 1875–1926.

Rolland, Romain. French man of letters, 1866–1944.

Royce, Josiah. American philosopher, 1855–1916.

Rutherford, Mark. Pseudonym of William Hale White, British author, 1829–1913.

Ruysbroeck, Jan van. Dutch mystic, 1293–1381.

Sabatier, Paul. French theologian and historian, 1858–1928.

Saint-Exupéry, Antoine de. French writer and aviator, 1900–45.

Sales, St. Francis de. Bishop of Geneva. 1567–1622.

Saltmarsh, John. Chaplain in Sir Thomas Fairfax's army during the Civil War.

Schiller. German poet, dramatist and philosopher, 1759–1805.

Schweitzer, Albert. Contemporary German doctor, musician, theologian and servant of humanity.

Seraphim of Sarov, St. Russian monk, b. 1750–60, d. 1833.

Shelomo of Karlin. Hasidic Rabbi, d. 1792.

Shmelke of Nikolsburg. Hasidic Rabbi, d. 1778.

Sifra. See Midrash.

Simlai, Rabbi. Third century A.D.

Sitwell, Edith. Contemporary British poet.

Smith, John. Christian and Platonist, 1618–52.

Solomon, Wisdom of. A book that just failed to be included in the Bible.

Soloviev, Vladimir. Russian philosopher and theologian, 1853–1900.

Spinoza, Baruch. Dutch philosopher, 1632–77.

Strindberg, August. Swedish dramatist and man of letters, 1849–1912.

Suso, Heinrich. German mystic, about 1300–66.

Suttie, Ian. British psychologist and psychiatrist, 1889–1935.

Sullivan, J. W. N. Irish man of letters, 1886–1937.

Swedenborg. Swedish scientist, philosopher and mystic, 1688–1772.

Tagore, Rabindranath. Indian poet and writer, 1861–1941.

Talmud, The. A great collection of Rabbinical treatises, etc., reduced to writing in the early centuries of our era.

Tanhuma. See Midrash.

Tanna debe Eliyahu. Midrashic compilation of the second half of the tenth century, embodying much older material.

Tao Tê Ching. The classic of Taoism, a system of Chinese philosophy, said to date from the 6th century B.C.

Temple, William. Archbishop of Canterbury. 1881–1944.

Teresa, St. Spanish mystic, 1515–82.

Theologia Germanica. One of the most beautiful works of German mysticism, written perhaps in the second half of the 14th century.

Thomas of Celano. A follower of St. Francis of Assisi (whom he joined probably about 1214) and his biographer.

Thompson, Francis. British poet, 1859–1907.
Toller, Ernst. German playwright, 1893–1939.
Traherne, Thomas. British poet, 1637?–74.
Turgenev, Ivan, Russian novelist, 1818–83.

Underhill, Evelyn. British writer on mysticism, 1875–1941.
Upanishads, The. Hindu scriptures, 800–600 B.C.
Uri of Strelisk. Hasidic Rabbi, d. 1826.

Vaughan, Thomas. British mystic, 1622–66.
Vivekananda, Swami. Indian philosopher and teacher, 1863–1902.
Voice of the Silence, The. A book of extracts, chosen by
    Madame Blavatsky, from a body of precepts current among
    mystic students in the East.

Weil, Simone. French writer and servant of humanity, 1909–43.
Waley, Arthur. Contemporary British poet, writer and trans-
    lator from the Chinese and Japanese.
Weizsäcker, Carl Friedrich von. Contemporary physicist.
Whichcote, Benjamin. British philosopher, 1609–83.
Whitman, Walt. American poet, 1819–92.
Wild, Franz. Singer, contemporary with Beethoven.
Williams, Charles. British poet and novelist, 1886–1945.
Wust, Peter. German philosopher. Professor of Philosophy at
    the University of Cologne, time of first World War.

Yaakov Yitzhak of Lublin. Hasidic Rabbi, d. 1815.
Yehudi, The. Hasidic Rabbi, d. 1814.
Yelchaninov, Father. A leader of the Russian Christian Student
    Movement in exile. 1881–1934.
Yerahmiel of Pzhysha. Hasidic Rabbi, son of the Yehudi.
Yitzhak Meir of Ger. Hasidic Rabbi, d. 1866.

Zalman of Ladi. Hasidic Rabbi, d. 1813.
Zohar, The. A great work of Jewish mysticism. Perhaps 1290.
Zusya of Hanipol. Hasidic Rabbi, d. 1800.

SOURCES AND
ACKNOWLEDGMENTS

My debt to my wife, in all the circumstances that produced the original *Year of Grace*, is one which (in the words, I think, of Oscar Wilde) "can happily never be repaid."

As for the present work, I am under a deep debt of gratitude to Sheila Hodges, Diana Collins, Rosemary Watt, James Parkes, William Kean Seymour, and Colonel Moses.

*   *   *   *   *   *

THE BIBLE. For the Old and New Testaments the Authorized Version has been used, except for *Hear, O Israel* (p. 15) and possibly one other instance, and except that chapter and verse numbers are not given, italics have been romanized, and the word 'Lord' is not printed in capitals. The Authorized Version is Crown Copyright, and is used by permission. For *Hear, O Israel* I have used the Authorized Daily Prayer Book of the United Hebrew Congregations of the British Empire (which was translated by the late Rev. S. Singer). For the Apocrypha the Revised Version has been used, by permission of the University Presses of Oxford and Cambridge.

THE HEBREW PRAYER BOOK. The extracts are from the Authorized Daily Prayer Book (see above) and are printed by permission of the Singer Prayer Book Publication Committee.

*   *   *   *   *   *

The citing of the names of authors, publishers and translators below will please be understood as acknowledging kind permission to reprint the relevant passages in the Anthology. The letter following a page number refers to the position of the passage on the page: thus 7a means the first passage that *begins* on page 7.

*   *   *   *   *   *

ABÉLARD. The passage is quoted by Hastings Rashdall in *The Idea of Atonement in Christian Theology* (Macmillan), and was no doubt translated by him. I thank the Executors as well as Messrs Macmillan for permission.

ABRAHAMSEN, DAVID. From *Who are the Guilty?* (Gollancz).

A.E. From *The Selected Poems of A.E.* (Macmillan), reproduced by permission also of Mr. Diarmuid Russell. The passage on p. 90 is an extract from *Ancestry*; p. 377 from *The Unknown God*. The prose extract on p. 388 is from *The Candle of Vision*. I thank Mr. Diarmuid Russell.

ALEXANDER, SAMUEL. From *Space, Time and Deity* (Macmillan). I thank the author's Executors for permission.

AL-HALLAJ. From Sufism by A. J. Arberry (Allen & Unwin).

AMIEL. From his *Journal*, tr. by Mrs. Humphry Ward (Macmillan).

ANGELUS SILESIUS. With two exceptions, the verses have been rhymed by me from prose translations made by my friend Dr. W. A. M. Rose. The exceptions are pp. 59 and 420, which are from *The Spiritual Maxims of Angelus Silesius*, tr. by Henry Bett (Epworth Press).

ANONYMOUS. The extract on p. 124 from the *Ancren Riwle*, is tr. by James Morton. The passage on p. 391 is quoted by William James in *Varieties of Religious Experience*.

ANSKY, S. From *The Dybbuk*, tr. by Henry G. Alsberg and Winifred Katzin. I thank Messrs. Curtis Brown for permission on behalf of Messrs. Liveright, New York.

AQUINAS, ST. THOMAS. The passage on p. 31 is from the *Summa Theologica*, in a translation made by Fathers of the English Dominican Province (Burns Oates and Washbourne). The passage on p. 290 is from *Commentary, I. Ethics,* tr. by Thomas Gilby in *Philosophical Texts of St. Thomas Aquinas* (Oxford University Press).

ARIKA, ABBA. Quoted in *A Short Survey of the Literature of Rabbinical and Mediaeval Judaism* by W. O. E. Oesterley and G. H. Box (S.P.C.K.).

AUROBINDO. The passage on p. 332 is from *The Human Cycle,* and is reproduced by kind permission of the Sri Aurobindo Ashram, Pondicherry. I thank Messrs. Dutton of New York for Canadian permission.

BERDYAEV, NICHOLAS. Pp. 53, 91, 164 are from *Dostoevsky,* tr. by Donald Attwater (Sheed and Ward). P. 116 is from *The End of our Time,* tr. by Donald Attwater (Sheed and Ward). Pp. 194, 222, 226, 329, 332, are from *The Fate of Man in the Modern World* tr. by Donald A. Lowrie (S.C.M. Press). Pp. 190, 253 are from *Christianity and Class War,* tr. by Donald Attwater (Sheed and Ward). Pp. 117a, b, 333, are from *Freedom and the Spirit,* tr. by Oliver Fielding Clarke (Bles). Pp. 125, 152, 365 are from *The Destiny of Man,* tr. by Natalie Duddington (Bles).

BHAGAVAD-GITA. I have used the translation (published by Phoenix House under the title *The Song of God*) by Swami Prabhavananda and Christopher Isherwood.

BLAKE, WILLIAM. I have sometimes followed the text—with occasional modification—in *Poetry and Prose of William Blake,* ed. by Geoffrey Keynes (Nonesuch Press) and sometimes other texts.

BLOY, LÉON. In all cases but one, from *Pilgrim of the Absolute, a Selection of his Writings edited by Raïssa Maritain,* tr. by John

489

Coleman and Harry Lorin Binsse (Eyre & Spottiswoode). I thank Pantheon Books (New York) for Canadian permission. P. 117 is quoted by Berdyaev in *Freedom and the Spirit* (Bles).

BOEHME. The passages on pp. 147, 252, and 258 are from *The Threefold Life of Man*, tr. by J. Sparrow, the translation having been corrected and amended (Watkins). The passage on p. 420 is translated by Willard Trask and quoted in Bernhart's Introduction to the *Theologia Germanica* (q.v.).

BOSANQUET, BERNARD. From *The Value and Destiny of the Individual*. I thank Mrs. Ellen Bosanquet for permission.

BROWNE, SIR THOMAS. From *Religio Medici* and *Christian Morals*. I have used the text of the six-volume edition prepared by Geoffrey Keynes and published by Faber and Faber.

BUBER, MARTIN. Pp. 25, 89, 358 are from *Hasidism* (Philosophical Library, New York). See also under "Hasidic Legends and Stories". P. 160 is from *Mamre* (Melbourne University Press). Pp. 313, 416 are from *Jewish Mysticism and the Legends of Baalshem*, tr. by Lucy Cohen (Dent).

BUDDHA, THE. The passages on pp. 143, 148(b) are from *Some Sayings of the Buddha*, tr. by F. L. Woodward (World's Classics, Oxford University Press). P. 148(c) is quoted in Tagore's *Sadhana*, and presumably translated by him.

CARPENTER, EDWARD. From *Towards Democracy* (Allen & Unwin).

CARPENTER, JOSEPH ESTLIN. From *Joseph Estlin Carpenter* by C. H. Herford (Clarendon Press).

CHESTERTON, G. K. Quoted in *Gilbert Keith Chesterton* by Maisie Ward (Sheen & Ward).

CHRISTIAN NEWS LETTER. I thank the Christian Frontier Council for permission.

CHUANG TZU. Translated by Arthur Waley in *Three Ways of Thought in Ancient China* (Allen & Unwin).

CLEMENT OF ALEXANDRIA. From the *Protreptikos*.

CRESCAS, CHASDAI. Included in *A Book of Jewish Thoughts* by the late Chief Rabbi, Dr. J. H. Hertz. I thank Mr. Samuel Hertz for permission.

DANTE. From the *Purgatorio*. I have used the version in Charles Williams' *The New Christian Year* (Oxford University Press).

DICKINSON, EMILY. From the Poems of Emily Dickinson (Cape).

DICKINSON, G. LOWES. P. 260 is from *The Magic Flute* (Allen & Unwin). P. 341 is from *A Modern Symposium* (Allen & Unwin).

DIONYSIUS THE AREOPAGITE. From *The Divine Names*, tr. by C. E. Rolt (S.P.C.K.).

DOSTOEVSKY. The extracts on pp. 124, 167, 389 are from *The Idiot*, tr. by Eva M. Martin (Everyman, Dent). The extracts on pp. 151, 384, 460 are from *The Brothers Karamazov*, tr. by Constance Garnett (Heinemann). The extract on p. 170 is from *The House of the Dead*, tr. by Constance Garnett (Heinemann). The extracts on pp. 291, 350 are from *Crime and Punishment*, tr. by Constance Garnett (Heinemann).

ECKHART, MEISTER. From the two-volume edition tr. by C. de B. Evans (Watkins), except in the cases of pp. 52, 375, which are quoted in Evelyn Underhill's *Mysticism* (Methuen) and are translated by Margaret Robinson.

ELEAZER b. AZARIAH. From *Ethics of the Fathers* in the Hebrew Prayer Book (q.v.).

ELIEZER, RABBI. From Martin Buber's *Tales of the Hasidim*. I thank Messrs. Thames and Hudson for permission.

FARID UD-DIN ATTAR. From *The Conference of Birds*, tr. by S. C. Nott (Janus Press).

FECHNER, GUSTAV THEODOR. Quoted in *The Centaur* by Algernon Blackwood (Macmillan) and presumably translated by him. I thank the Owner of the Copyright.

FLEG, EDMOND. From *The Life of Moses*, tr. by Stephen Haden Guest (Gollancz).

FROMM, ERICH. The passages are from *The Fear of Freedom* (Kegan Paul).

GAMALIEL III, RABBAN. From *Ethics of the Fathers* in the Hebrew Prayer Book (q.v.).

GOETHE. The passages on pp. 87, 253 are from *Eckermann's Conversations*, tr. by John Oxenford (Everyman's Library, Dent). The passages on pp. 101 (from *Goethes Gespräche*, Biedermann), 154 (from *Maximen und Reflexionen* published by the Goethe-Gesellschaft, Weimar), 416, 430 are translated in *Goethe and Faust* by F. M. Stawell and G. Lowes Dickinson (Bell).

GREEN, PETER. From *Our Lord and Saviour* (Longmans).

HAFIZ. From *Selection from the Rubaiyat and Odes of Hafiz*

rendered into English Verse by a Member of the Persia Society of London (Watkins).

HANOKH OF ALEXANDER, RABBI. From *The Hasidic Anthology* (see next item).

HASIDIC LEGENDS AND STORIES, AND SAYINGS OF HASIDIC RABBIS. The sources of these are *Tales of the Hasidim: the Early Masters* by Martin Buber, tr. by Olga Marx (Schocken Books, New York); *Tales of the Hasidim: the Later Masters* (same author, translator and publisher); the 800-page *The Hasidic Anthology*, translated, selected, compiled and arranged by Louis I. Newman, in collaboration with Samuel Spitz; and *Hasidim* by Martin Buber (Philosophical Library, New York). I owe the beautiful saying on p. 410 to Martin Buber, who quotes it in one of his essays.

HEBREW DOCTRINE. From *Major Trends in Jewish Mysticism* by Gershom Scholem (Schocken, Jerusalem).

HEBREW MORNING SERVICE. From the Hebrew Prayer Book (q.v.).

HIGH PRISON OFFICER. Reported by Margery Fry in a statement sent to Sir Ernest Gowers' Royal Commission on the Death Penalty.

HOPKINS, GERARD MANLEY. From *Poems of Gerard Manley Hopkins*, 3rd ed. (Oxford University Press). The prose passage on p. 257 is from *Note-books and Papers of Gerard Manley Hopkins*, ed. by Humphry House (Oxford University Press).

HUXLEY, ALDOUS. From *Ends and Means* (Chatto & Windus).

HYLTON, WALTER. From *The Scale of Perfection, newly edited from M.S. Sources by Evelyn Underhill* (Watkins).

IBSEN. The translation of *Peer Gynt* is by William and Charles Archer; that of *An Enemy of the People* by Mrs. E. Marx-Aveling. (Both Heinemann). P. 291 from *Brand*.

INGE, W. R. From *The Philosophy of Plotinus* (Longmans).

JALALU D-DIN RUMI. The passage is my own adaptation of some sentences, put together in my own way, from the *Masnavi*. I have used as a basis (by kind permission of the publisher, Mr. Arthur Probsthain) Professor C. E. Wilson's version, but I alone am responsible for the adaptation.

JAMES, HENRY. I thank Messrs. Paul R. Reynolds and Son of New York. From *The Golden Bowl*.

JAMES, WILLIAM. The passages are from *The Varieties of Religious Experience*. I thank Messrs. Paul R. Reynolds and Son of New York for permission.

JEWISH LEGENDS. That on p. 69 is from Fleg's (q.v.) *Life of Moses*; that on p. 113 is quoted in Erich Fromm's (q.v.) *Man for Himself*.

JOHANAN, RABBI. Included in *A Rabbinic Anthology* by C. G. Montefiore and H. Loewe (Macmillan).

JOHN OF CRONSTADT. From *My Life in Christ*, tr. by Goulaeff (Cassell).

JOHN OF THE CROSS, ST. The passages on pp. 152, 153, 203, 205, 278, are from *The Living Flame of Love*, tr. by David Lewis (Thomas Baker); that on p. 372 from *The Ascent of Mount Carmel*, in Professor Allison Peer's translation of the works (Burns Oates and Washbourne).

JOSHUA b. LEVI, RABBI. Included in *A Rabbinic Anthology* by C. G. Montefiore and H. Loewe (Macmillan).

JULIANA OF NORWICH. P. 52 is from *Juliana of Norwich: an Appreciation and an Anthology* by P. Franklin Chambers (Gollancz). I thank Mr. Chambers.

JUNG, C. G. The passages on pp. 154, 208 are from *Modern Man in Search of a Soul*, tr. by W. S. Dell and Cary F. Baynes (Kegan Paul). The patient's letter on p. 209 is from *The Secret of the Golden Flower*, tr. and explained by Richard Wilhelm with a European Commentary by C. G. Jung; tr. into English by Cary F. Baynes (Kegan Paul).

KABIR. From *One Hundred Poems of Kabir*, tr. Rabindranath Tagore assisted by Evelyn Underhill (Macmillan). I thank the Trustees of Rabindranath Tagore as well as Messrs. Macmillan for permission.

KIERKEGAARD. The passage on p. 150(a) is from the *Journals*, tr. by Alexander Dru (Oxford University Press); those on pp. 150(b) and 365 from *Works of Love*, tr. by David F. Swenson and Lillian Marvin Swenson (Oxford University Press and Princeton University Press).

LAVELLE, LOUIS. The passage is quoted in Paul Foulquié's *Existentialism*, tr. by Kathleen Raine (Dennis Dobson).

LAW, WILLIAM. From *Selected Mystical Writings of William Law*, ed. by Stephen Hobhouse, published by Barrie and Rockliff (Barrie Books Ltd.).

LEON, LUIS DE. P. 375 is from *The Names of Christ*, tr. by a Benedictine of Stanbrook. P. 408 is from *The Lyrics of Luis de Leon*, tr. Aubrey Bell. Both books published by Burns, Oates.

LEONARDO DA VINCI. From *The Notebooks of Leonardo da Vinci*, tr. Edward MacCurdy (Cape).

LEWIS, C. S. From *The Problem of Pain* (Bles).

LEWIS, H. D. From *Morals and the New Theology* (Gollancz).

MACDONALD, GEORGE. From *George Macdonald: An Anthology* by C. S. Lewis (Bles).

MACGREGOR, G. H. C. From *The New Testament Basis of Pacifism* (Fellowship of Reconciliation).

MACMURRAY, JOHN. The passages on p. 24 are from *The Clue to History* (S.C.M. Press); that on p. 193 from *Reason and Emotion* (Faber and Faber); those on pp. 350, 359 from *Freedom in the Modern World* (Faber and Faber).

MAHA-BHARATA. From *Indian Wisdom* by Sir Monier Monier-Williams (Luzac).

MALAVAL. Quoted by Evelyn Underhill in *Mysticism* (Methuen). The translation may be her own, or may be from *A Simple Method of Raising the Soul to Contemplation*, tr. by Lucy Menzies (Dent).

MANU, CODE OF. From *Indian Wisdom* by Sir Monier Monier-Williams (Luzac).

MARCEL, GABRIEL. The passage is quoted in Foulquié's *Existentialism*, tr. by Kathleen Raine (Dennis Dobson).

MARCUS AURELIUS. From the translation by C. R. Haines in the Loeb Classical Library, published by Heinemann.

MARE, WALTER DE LA. From the *Collected Poems* (Faber & Faber). P. 77 is from *O Lovely England* (Faber & Faber) and is entitled "Why then comes in . . ." I thank the Literary Trustees of Walter de la Mare and the Society of Authors as their representative.

MARITAIN, JACQUES. From *True Humanism*, tr. by M. R. Adamson (Bles).

MEIR, RABBI. The passage is quoted in Oesterley and Box (see Arika).

MEKILTA, THE. Quoted in *The Rabbinic Anthology*, ed. C. G. Montefiore and H. Loewe (Macmillan).

MENANDER. Quoted in the Loeb edition of *Clement of Alexandria* (Heinemann).

MEREDITH, GEORGE. I thank the Trustees as well as Messrs. Constable for permission.

MEYNELL, ALICE. I thank Sir Francis Meynell for permission.

MILAREPA. From *Tibet's Great Yogi Milarepa* by his disciple Rechung, tr. by Lama Kazi Dawa-Sandup, ed. by W. Y. Evans-Wentz (Oxford University Press).

MIRROR OF PERFECTION. From *"The Little Flowers" and the Life of St. Francis with the "Mirror of Perfection"* (Everyman's Library, Dent). The *Mirror* is translated by Robert Steele.

MOLINOS. The abridgement is from *The Varieties of Religious Experience* by William James, q.v.

MORE, SIR THOMAS. Included in Charles Williams' *The New Christian Year* (Oxford University Press).

NETTLESHIP, R. L. From *Richard Lewis Nettleship, Lectures and Memories* (Macmillan). I thank Mr. David John for permission.

NICOLAS OF CUSA. From *The Vision of God*, tr. by Emma Gurney Salter (Dent).

NIEBUHR, REINHOLD. The passage on p. 154 is from *An Interpretation of Christian Ethics* (S.C.M. Press). The story on p. 184 is quoted in *Moral Man and Immoral Society* from James B. Pratt's *India and its Faiths* (Constable).

NIETZSCHE. From *Thus Spake Zarathustra*, ed. by Dr. Oscar Levy, and tr. by Thomas Common. I thank Mrs. Maud Rosenthal.

OXYRHYNCHUS PAPYRI. From *The Apocryphal New Testament,* tr. by M. R. James (Clarendon Press).

PARADISE OF THE FATHERS. Translated by Sir E. A. Wallis Budge (Chatto & Windus).

PÉGUY. From *Basic Verities,* tr. by Ann and Julian Green (Kegan Paul).

PELAGIUS. The first passage on p. 237 is from the *Pro Libero Arbitrio,* and is to be found in *The Anti-Pelagian Works of St. Augustine,* tr. by Dr. Peter Holmes (T. & T. Clark). The second passage on p. 237 is quoted by Niebuhr in *An Interpretation of Christian Ethics* (S.C.M. Press).

PEREZ, ISAAC LOEB. From *Stories and Pictures,* tr. by Helena Frank (Jewish Publication Society of America).

PHILO. Included in *A Book of Jewish Thoughts* (See Crescas).

PICO DELLA MIRANDOLA. From the *Oration on the Dignity of Man,* tr. by Elizabeth Livermoore Forbes in *The Renaissance Philosophy of Man,* ed. by Ernst Cassirer etc. (University of Chicago Press).

PLATO. The translation of all passages is by Benjamin Jowett.

PLOTINUS. The passage on p. 360 is from the first Ennead, tr. by Stephen Mackenna. I am grateful to Sir Ernest Debenham for permission. The passage on p. 416 is from the fifth Ennead, and is, I think, translated by Dean Inge, in whose *The Philosophy of Plotinus* (Longmans) it is cited. The passages on pp. 376, 403, 442 are from Stephen Mackenna's translation, sometimes as it stands, sometimes modified. My thanks are due to Messrs. Faber & Faber. P. 89 is quoted in Inge's *The*

Philosophy of Plotinus (Longmans) and is probably translated by him.

PREZZOLINI. From an article in *La Voce* of April 13th 1911.

PROUST. From *Swann's Way*, tr. by C. K. Scott Moncrieff (Chatto & Windus).

RAMAKRISHNA. From *Ramakrishna: Prophet of New India* (the abridged *Gospel*), tr. by Swami Nikhilananda (Rider).

RASHDALL, HASTINGS. From *The Idea of Atonement in Christian Theology* (Macmillan). I am grateful to the Executors as well as to Messrs. Macmillan for permission.

RENAN, ERNEST. From *The Life of Jesus*, tr. by C. E. Wilbour (Everyman, Dent).

RILKE. P. 83 is from a letter quoted in *Requiem and Other Poems*, tr. by J. B. Leishman (Hogarth Press). P. 418 is from *Poems from the Book of Hours*, tr. by Babette Deutsch (Vision Press). P. 428 is from *Later Poems*, tr. by J. B. Leishman (Hogarth Press). P. 430 is from imaginary letter "On God", quoted in *Later Poems*.

ROLLAND, ROMAIN. From the translation of *Jean-Christophe* by Gilbert Cannan (Heinemann).

ROYCE, JOSIAH. From *The World and the Individual* (Macmillan, New York). I am grateful to Mr. Stephen Royce for permission.

RUTHERFORD, MARK. From *More Pages from a Journal* (Oxford University Press). I thank Mrs. D. V. White.

SABATIER, PAUL. From *The Life of St. Francis of Assisi*, tr. Louise Seymour Houghton (Hodder).

SAINT-EXUPÉRY, ANTOINE DE. From *Flight to Arras* (Heinemann). I am grateful to Messrs. Harcourt, Brace of New York for Canadian permission.

SALES, ST. FRANCIS DE. P. 99 is from *Letters to Persons in Religion*, quoted in *The Spirit of Love* by C. F. Kelley (Longmans). I thank Messrs. Harpers Brothers of New York for Canadian permission. The rest are from *Introduction to the Devout Life*, tr. by the Rev. Thomas Barns (Methuen).

SCHWEITZER, ALBERT. Pp. 183, 191, 272 are from *The Decay and Restoration of Civilization*, tr. by C. T. Campion (Black). P. 299 is from *Religion in Modern Civilization* (The Christian Century, Chicago). Pp. 419, 445 are from *Civilization and Ethics*, tr. by C. T. Campion (Black).

SERAPHIM OF SAROV, ST. From *St. Seraphim of Sarov*, tr. by A. F. Dobbie-Bateman (S.P.C.K.).

SHAW, BERNARD. Pp. 166, 250, 330 are from *Man and Superman*. P. 170 is from his Preface to *English Prisons under Local Government* by Sidney and Beatrice Webb. I thank the Public Trustee and the Society of Authors.

SIMLAI, RABBI. Included in *A Rabbinic Anthology* by C. G. Montefiore and H. Loewe (Macmillan).

SITWELL, EDITH. From *The Canticle of the Rose* (Macmillan).

SOLOVIEV. The passage on p. 329 is from *Lectures on Godmanhood*, with introduction by Peter Zouboff (Dennis Dobson). The other passages are from *The Meaning of Love*, and have been translated by Julia de Beausobre (Mrs. Namier).

SPINOZA. Pp. 87, 101, 149, 253, 274(c), 275, 279, 418 are from the *Ethics*, tr. by A. Boyle (Everyman's Library, Dent). Pp. 274(d), 354 are from the *Short Treatise on God, Man, and his Well-Being*, tr. by Dr. A. Wolf (Black).

STRINDBERG. From *The Road to Damascus*, tr. by Graham Rawson (Cape).

SULLIVAN, J. W. N. From *But for the Grace of God.* (Cape).

SUSO, HEINRICH. From *The Life of Blessed Henry Suso by Himself*, tr. by T. F. Knox (Methuen).

SUTTIE, IAN. From *The Origins of Love and Hate* (Kegan Paul).

SWEDENBORG. From *Heaven and Hell.* I have used the revised translation by F. Bayley, on the basis of the F'cap 8vo edition issued by the Swedenborg Society (Everyman, Dent).

TAGORE, RABINDRANATH. Pp. 81(a), (b), 258(b), 396 are from *Gitanjali* (Macmillan). Pp. 81(c), 258(c), 423, 424 are from *Sadhana* (Macmillan). Pp. 195, 225, 329, 426 are from *Creative Unity* (Macmillan). P. 427 is from *The Gardener* (Macmillan). I am grateful to the Trustees as well as to Messrs. Macmillan for permission.

TALMUD. The passages on pp. 37, 164, 266 are included in *A Rabbinic Anthology* by C. G. Montefiore and H. Loewe (Macmillan); and those on pp. 157, 171, 201 in *A Book of Jewish Thoughts* by the late Chief Rabbi, Dr. J. H. Hertz. I thank Mr. Samuel Hertz for permission. The passage on p. 292 is quoted in *Israel and the World* by Martin Buber.

TALMUDIC LEGEND. This is quoted by Ouspensky in *A New Model of the Universe* (Routledge & Kegan Paul) from *Agada* by Ravnitsky and Bialik.

TANHUMA. Included in *A Rabbinic Anthology* by C. G. Montefiore and H. Loewe (Macmillan).

TANNA DEBE ELIYAHU. The passage on p. 250(b) is included in *A Book of Jewish Thoughts* by the late Chief Rabbi, Dr. J. H. Hertz. I thank Mr. Samuel Hertz. The passage on p. 250(d) is from *A Rabbinic Anthology* by C. G. Montefiore and H. Loewe (Macmillan).

TAO-TÊ-CHING. From the translation by W. G. Old entitled *Lao Tze: The Tao-Teh-King* (Rider).

TEMPLE, WILLIAM. From *Nature, Man and God* (Macmillan). I am grateful to Mrs. William Temple for permission.

TERESA, ST. From *The Interior Castle*. I am grateful to the Right Reverend the Lady Abbess of Stanbrook Abbey for permission to use this version.

THEOLOGIA GERMANICA. From the edition with Susanna Winkworth's translation revised by Willard Trask to accord with Bernhart's version (Gollancz). I thank Pantheon Books, New York, for Canadian permission.

THOMAS OF CELANO. From *Legenda Prima*, quoted in Evelyn Underhill's *Mysticism* (Methuen) and possibly translated by her.

THOMPSON, FRANCIS. I am grateful to Sir Francis Meynell for permission.

TOLLER, ERNST. The passages on pp. 162, 222, 297, are from *Letters from Prison*, tr. by R. Ellis Roberts (Bodley Head); that on p. 181 from *I was a German* (Bodley Head).

TOLSTOY. The passage on p. 166, is from *A Confession*, tr. by Aylmer Maude (World's Classics, Oxford University Press); pp. 181, 292 are from *What I Believe*, tr. by Aylmer Maude (World's Classics, Oxford University Press). The passage on p. 207 was "Englished" by Robert Bridges from a literal translation by Nevill Forbes, and is included in *The Spirit of Man* (Longmans). P. 380 is from *Anna Karenina*, tr. by Rochelle S. Townsend (Everyman, Dent).

TRAHERNE. I thank the Clarendon Press for permission to reproduce these extracts. For the poems I have used the Dobell text.

TURGENEV. From *Dream Tales and Prose Poems*, tr. by Constance Garnett (Heinemann).

UNDERHILL, EVELYN. P. 379 is from *The Letters of Evelyn Underhill* (Longmans). P. 403 is from *Mysticism* (Methuen).

VIVEKANANDA. The works of Vivekananda from which the extracts are taken are published by the Advaita Ashrama, India.

WEIL, SIMONE. From *Waiting on God*, tr. by Emma Craufurd (Routledge and Kegan Paul).

WEIZSÄCKER, C. F. VON. From *The History of Nature*, tr. by Fred D. Wieck (University of Chicago Press).

WELLS, H. G. I am grateful to Mr. H. G. Wells' Executors for permission.

WILD, FRANZ. The story about Beethoven conducting is quoted in *Beethoven: the Search for Reality* by W. J. Turner (Dent) from Wild's autobiography. Spohr gives exactly the same account of this concert.

WILDE, OSCAR. From *De Profundis*—the complete version (Methuen). I am grateful to Mr. Vyvyan Holland for permission.

WILLIAMS, CHARLES. *The Place of the Lion* has been republished by Faber and Faber. I am grateful to Pearn, Pollinger and Higham, the late author's literary agents, for permission.

WILSON, MONA. From *A Life of William Blake* (Hart-Davis).

WORDSWORTH, DOROTHY. From *The Journals of Dorothy Wordsworth*, ed. de Selincourt (Macmillan).

WUST, PETER. From *Peter Wust on the Nature of Piety* in *Being and Having* by Gabriel Marcel, tr. by Katherine Farrer (Dacre Press).

YEATS. From *Autobiographies* (Macmillan). I thank Mrs. Yeats.

YELCHANINOV, FATHER. From his *Diary*, tr. by Helen Iswolsky and included in *A Treasury of Russian Spirituality*, ed. G. P. Fedotov (Sheed and Ward).

ZOHAR. The passage on p. 60 is included in *A Book of Jewish Thoughts* by the late Chief Rabbi, Dr. J. H. Hertz. I thank Mr. Samuel Hertz for permission. The passage on p. 118 is included in Fleg's (q.v.) *Life of Moses*.

INDEX

High Prison Officer, 166
Hopkins, Gerard Manley, 107, 257, 297
Hunt, Leigh, 123
Huxley, Aldous, 94, 419
Hylton, Walter, 100, 150, 151, 417

Ibsen, Henrik, 287, 291, 337
Inge, W. R., 331, 354
Isaak of Syria, Saint, 148, 300
Isaiah, 114, 132, 180, 468
Israel of Koznitz, Rabbi, 147
Israel of Rizhyn, Rabbi, 37

Jalalu D-Din Rumi, 88
James, 141, 142, 249
James, Henry, 79
James, William, 144, 211
Jeffries, Richard, 75, 79, 124, 148, 220, 379, 393, 429
Jeremiah, 353
Jerome, Saint, 117
Jewish legends, 69, 113
Job, 199, 374
Johanan, Rabbi, 34
I John, 140, 219
John, Saint, 110, 137, 414
John of Cronstadt, 154
John of the Cross, Saint, 152, 153, 203, 205, 278, 372
Jonah, 33
Joshua b. Levi, Rabbi, 299
Juliana of Norwich, 37, 52

Jung, C. G., 154, 208
Jung, A patient of, 209

Kabir, 203, 427
Kant, 223
Keats, 408
Kierkegaard, Sören, 150, 365

Lavelle, Louis, 329
Law, William, 39, 49, 93, 143, 264, 354, 356, 376
Left News, 185
Leicester Evening Mail, The, 184
Leonardo Da Vinci, 165
Leon, Luis de, 375, 408
Leviticus, 127, 130, 131
Lewis, C. S., 171
Lewis, H. D., 191, 275
Luke, Saint, 99, 107, 134, 135, 137, 236, 272, 353
Luthardt, Christophe Ernst, 373

Macdonald, George, 374, 377
Macgregor, G. H. C., 90
MacLeod, G. F., 88
MacMurray, John, 24, 193, 350, 359
Maha-Bharath, The, 153
Malaval, 374
Manu, The Code of, 364